P9-DCV-947

A Critic's Journey

ALSO BY GEOFFREY HARTMAN

The Unmediated Vision
André Malraux
Wordsworth's Poetry
Beyond Formalism
Akiba's Children (poetry)
The Fate of Reading
Criticism in the Wilderness: The Study of Literature Today
Saving the Text
Easy Pieces
The Unremarkable Wordsworth
Minor Prophecies
The Longest Shadow
The Fateful Question of Culture

Principal Editions:

Midrash and Literature, Sanford Budick, co-editor
Bitburg in Moral and Political Perspective
Holocaust Remembrance: The Shapes of Memory
Psychoanalysis and the Question of the Text
New Perspectives on Wordsworth and Coleridge
Shakespeare and the Question of Theory, Patricia Parker, co-editor

A Critic's Journey

Literary Reflections, 1958–1998

Geoffrey Hartman

Yale University Press

New Haven and London

Published with assistance from the Louis Stern Memorial Fund.

Set in Adobe Garamond type by The Composing Room of Michigan, Grand Rapids, Michigan.
Printed in the United States of America.

Library of Congress Cataloging-in-Publication Data

Hartman, Geoffrey H.
A Critic's Journey: literary reflections, 1958–1998.
p. cm.
Includes bibliographical references and index.
ISBN 0-300-08043-3
1. Literature, Modern—History and criticism. I. Title.
PN710.H324 1999
809′.03—dc21 99-12120
CIP

A catalogue record for this book is available from the British Library.

The paper in this book meets the guidelines for permanence and durability of the Committee on Production Guidelines for Book Longevity of the Council on Library Resources.

10 9 8 7 6 5 4 3 2 1

For
Helen Elam and Leslie Brisman

Contents

Speculations

Acknowledgments

I am grateful to Jonathan Brent, editorial director of Yale University Press, for encouraging this publication. It provides an overview of forty years of writing. I intend to devote a separate publication to essays about subjects of Jewish interest. All of the essays printed here, except "Polemical Memoir," have been published, but many are uncollected. The following is a list of books or periodicals in which the essays first appeared (the original titles are given here): "Tea and Totality" and "The Philomela Project," *Minor Prophecies: The Literary Essay in the Culture Wars* (Cambridge: Harvard University Press, 1991); "Understanding Criticism" and "American Poetry: Purification and Danger," *Criticism in the Wilderness: The Study of Literature Today* (New Haven: Yale University Press, 1980); "The Voice of the Shuttle," "Milton's Counterplot," and "False Themes and Gentle Minds," *Beyond Formalism* (New Haven: Yale University Press, 1970); "Literature High and Low: The Case of the Mystery Story," *The Fate of Reading* (Chicago: Chicago University Press, 1975); "Plenty of Nothing: Hitchcock's *North by Northwest*" and "The Interpreter's Freud," *Easy Pieces* (New York: Columbia University Press, 1985); "A Touching

Compulsion," *The Unremarkable Wordsworth* (Minneapolis: University of Minnesota Press, 1987); "Words and Wounds" (abbreviated here), *Saving the Text: Literature / Derrida / Philosophy* (Baltimore: Johns Hopkins University Press, 1981); "The Struggle for the Text," in *Midrash and Literature,* ed. Sanford Budick and Geoffrey Hartman (New Haven: Yale University Press, 1986); "Higher Education in the 1990s," *New Literary History* 24 (1993); "Public Memory and Modern Experience," *Yale Journal of Criticism* 6 (1993); "Art and Consensus in the Era of Progressive Politics," *Yale Review* 80 (1992); "The Reinvention of Hate," *Yale Review* 84 (1996); "Shakespeare and the Ethical Question," *English Literary History* 63 (1996); and "Benjamin in Hope," *Critical Inquiry* 25 (Winter 1999).

This book is dedicated to dear friends and intellectual companions.

Polemical Memoir

I must admit at the outset that I am not much of a polemicist. It seems remarkable to me that many in my profession remember their own ideas, and so well that they can erect them into a personal or collective ideology. No doubt age has given my own thoughts a certain consistency. But in writing this introduction, I feel like a poet who does not know exactly what will emerge, and who has to regain his balance, his very self, because he is in danger of being dispersed by conflicting ideas and crowded impressions. A friend once accused me of foolishly trying to write for eternity, whereas he wrote for his time. He was really defending his aggressive, even hyperbolic style in an epoch that favors the louder voices, or those with sharply honed reiterations that alone have a chance of being heard when media publicity is essential. But what publicity will remain at the end of the day, or the end of days, remains to be seen. Art, said William Blake, will pass a Last Judgment on us all.

I have not been able to find many guides to the value of polemics. There is general agreement, based on recent political experience, that the marketplace of ideas, its bustle and jostle, will produce at least a negative freedom. The term "civil society," moreover, because of the double meaning of "civil," has gained a strong currency, even though civility is rarely what brings ideas to our attention. But precisely because there is so much hype, counterpunching is a necessity, and so the polemical scene becomes more heated, in response to its internal combustion.

Are the tigers of wrath better than the horses of instruction? When Blake wrote this "Proverb of Hell," he enjoyed being morally incorrect; and the aphoristic mode encourages such purgative clearings of the air. Even Kant allows himself a "Dare to Know," though his cautious and dense argumentation comes closer to Maurice Blanchot's "Watch over absent meaning." Perhaps Gaston Bachelard, the philosopher of science who became a literary interpreter offering remarkable commentaries on the relation of the imagination to air, fire, earth, and water—but who was also inspired by a fifth element, love of literature—makes the best case, at least in science, for the role of a polemics that is both critical and historical. "The atom," he writes, "is precisely the *sum of criticisms* to which its first imaging was submitted. A coherent knowledge is not the product of architectonic reason but of polemical reason. . . . Intuitions are very useful: they serve by dint of being destroyed. . . . The schema of the atom proposed by Bohr a quarter of a century ago [Bachelard's *La philosophie du non,* from which I quote, was first published in 1940] has, in this sense, provided a useful image: nothing of it remains. . . . But these negations ["ces *non*"], coordinated in a happy manner, truly constitute contemporary microphysics." Or, as Bachelard also says, with a flair that anticipates his literary studies: "A single dialecticized axiom suffices to make all nature sing."[1]

Such comments relate polemics to the role that reason, in the form of reasoning, plays in literary criticism. Perhaps the variorum of interpretations that accompanies a durable work of art could be "coordinated" in the happy way Bachelard suggests. But up to now the result has been to confuse historically minded critics. They wonder whether all these commentators are talking about the same object, the same text. Bachelard thinks that, in science, the dialectical and polemical habit not only deconstructs the original scheme or image, by incorporating it into new schemes or even making it disappear, but also builds what he calls a *surobjet* around which all these negations turn. Yet science, according to him, is not simply a function of reason; rather, science instructs reason, which must obey its method. This much is transferable to literary studies, then: whatever polemics we engage in, they do not have the right, as Bachelard puts it, "to augment the immediate experience; they must seek, on the contrary, to be in equilibrium with the most richly structured experience. . . . What is *immediate* must yield to what is *constructed*."[2]

If literary criticism, as Oscar Wilde said, is the only civilized form of autobiography, I should continue in this vein. But I owe the reader something more direct. In autobiographical self-reflection, as distinguished from science, the subject of the narrative aspires to know himself, that is, to communicate a self-awareness that is the ground or residue of a lifetime; and this assumes a persistent identity between the immediacy of "I am" and the peregrinations—the ongoing constructions—of "I think."

"For who himself beginning knew?" Such is Raphael's admonition to Adam in *Paradise Lost.* The very genre of autobiography tempts us to invent a clear, even traumatic (therefore fallible) point of origin, instead of considering that we may have drifted into our identity, or that we continue to reconstruct it. Yet that I had a grandfather who wrote a thesis examining the midrashic literature on the Book of Ruth and who taught religion for the Philantropin in Frankfurt—though I never knew him except as a photo and a legend, given that he died when I was a year old—and that at the age of nine I was forced to leave my home country, Germany, as well as my family, demand some mention in view of my later development.

In England (my place of refuge) I acquired an appetite for knowledge very early, especially a love of words. That passion for words never abated. Until my late teens some emptiness made me devour grammar books as well as word lists; and no pleasures seemed as intense as (1) rugby on the English playing fields, (2) bicycling in the countryside, (3) learning new words, (4) speaking in blank verse, and (4) Latin progress in reading the *Aeneid.*

Close to sixteen at the end of the war, I left England to join my mother, who had emigrated in December 1938 (a month after Kristallnacht) to the United States; and there, during my undergraduate years at Queens College in New York, I would get up at dawn for an extra hour of language study, as if, in the morning freshness, Spanish, Greek, and Italian depended on me alone. They now lurk dusty, reproachful, and generally unused in a corner of my mind. A superb teacher, Konrad Gries (we should name our teachers, especially when they do not achieve the fame of publication) made every stage of Greek an acquisition of delight, and before the year was out his handful of students began to read Homer.

It seemed inevitable that I should choose comparative literature as a major—helped by the fact that Queens College, founded only in 1939, proved hospitable to émigré scholars. Together with exceptional teachers of English, and the personal encouragement of a professor of German we called the Red Dean because of his leftist sympathies, and who suffered in the paranoid time of the Cold War for his views, my education was satisfying though not all-consuming. Somehow I did not get to understand the notion of "secondary literature" and spent all my spare hours reading poetry and novels, writing (bad) poems, founding a new student newspaper (and resigning from it when it became politicized), earning money by tutoring Latin, and assisting in social projects sponsored by the Jewish campus organization Hillel.

In the fall of 1949 I entered Yale as a graduate student. Three distinguished teachers of comparative literature were émigrés: in addition to René Wellek, who had come from Prague via England, there was Henri Peyre from France via Egypt, and Erich Auerbach from Germany via Istanbul. Auerbach was Jewish, though that did not define his intellectual character in any obvious way. He had served in the First World War and was totally assimilated into German and European culture. His influence (at least on me) came more through a certain demeanor than through any methodical or evangelical effort to communicate his vast yet aesthetically centered erudition. He once told me the story of a violinist forced to leave Germany and wishing to take up his profession in America. Alas, his violin no longer emitted the same "tone" in the new country. (Leo Spitzer too, teaching at Johns Hopkins, felt, Henri Peyre reported, *echolos,* without a responsive audience.) Auerbach's teaching method was to read a text aloud, then to venture a few remarks—more like hints than instructions. Those who took pains to follow them up found themselves deep in stylistics, an extraordinary field in its linguistic and sociological range, treating the vernaculars as they evolved from their Latin *souche* toward literary status. Auerbach's ambition, he once said, was to make medieval Latin in its metamorphosis to the Romance literatures as familiar to us as modern letters. His last book, which began to do that, was unfinished when he died prematurely in his early sixties of a heart ailment connected with a wound suffered in the Great War.[3]

Though I had read *Mimesis* (1946) as a graduate student, Auerbach's influence increased during my first year of teaching at Yale. At his request we met almost every week to discuss John Donne, then at the height of his academic reputation. Auerbach wanted to understand metaphysical poetry; needless to say, I learned more from those sessions (accompanied by a ritual cup of tea laced with rum) than he did. What I had always admired was the elegance of his prose, long sentences that never lost their focus and conjured up from a writer's stylistic features his embeddedness in social reality. There was no clutter of documentation—except when semantically necessary as in the famous "Figura" essay—and no ideological preening. (Though his background was Jewish and secular, Auerbach's knowledge of the Church Fathers enabled him to restate the historical pertinence of the figural symbolism, basic to Christian interpretive thought after Saint Paul, that was still the inspiration for Dante's epic.) I encouraged Meridian Press, an early publisher of paperbacks, to gather and issue several key essays, including "Figura" and "La cour et la ville."

What influenced me specifically was, as I have said, his personal style, but this had two aspects. It confirmed the possibility of going beyond formalism, beyond the schoolmasterly close reading practiced by the New Critics. In Auerbach the analysis of Shakespeare or Schiller, of Petronius or Balzac or Woolf, was probative without becoming preacherly, and expansive without ever losing sight of the text. I wanted to achieve the same degree of analytic persuasiveness with lyric poetry. The second aspect of Auerbach's influence is more difficult to describe. In one of his courses I discovered the sixteenth-century poet Maurice Scève and wrote a minutely stylistic study of some of Scève's mystical love poems. Auerbach was pleased, but he allowed himself to remark that to understand Scève I needed more experience of life. Despite his specialized knowledge, then, he was less a professor than a worldly humanist, and close to the seventeenth-century ideal of the *honnête homme* about which he wrote so well, an ideal that presupposed unostentatious learning and conversation. Yet he remained suspicious, at the same time, of any belletristic streak. His best-known essay, the first chapter of *Mimesis,* which juxtaposes the biblical account of Abraham's sacrifice of Isaac and the recognition scene from the *Odyssey* describing the old nurse's reaction to her master's homecoming, left him dubious. Did the contrast not work too beautifully? Had his Homer (but this is my speculation) been simplified by the German classicists' view of the Grecian spirit as noble equanimity? He told me he had considered removing the chapter, and it was only the outcry of "the ladies" that made him retain it.

Wellek's great virtue was to set an example through his scholarship: an omnivorous reader of unbelievable erudition, he refused to relinquish a discriminating view of the development of literary criticism in the nationalist era. Yet I don't recall a single political remark he may have uttered in the classroom. We did not see much of him outside the weekly seminar: his work on the *History of Modern Criticism* was all-consuming, and his graduate classes consisted of reading aloud chapters from that history-in-progress or from the dry yet exciting, because so sure of itself, so definitive, *Theory of Literature.* (At the Indiana School of Letters, two years later, I took a course with Austin Warren, co-author of some chapters from the *Theory of Literature,* a totally different person, deeply, tremblingly religious, always searching for spiritual certainty. He left halfway through the school session, perhaps because of a nervous disorder, though his voice, except for an unusual vibrato, was always controlled.) To return to Wellek, my term papers often had a word scribbled in the margins which I deciphered as "Hegel," and this started me on a lifelong, frustrating yet enjoyable reading of the *Phenomenology.*

I had entered graduate school totally ignorant of both secondary literature and philosophy (with the exception of Martin Buber's popular *I and Thou,* a smattering of Whitehead, and Susanne Langer's *Philosophy in a New Key*); the shock I received from Wellek's courses, with their stenographic and exact reference to almost exclusively secondary materials, was enormous. I woke from my dogmatic dreams of a direct contact with and understanding of art, although I never gave that up entirely. My worst moment came when I submitted four chapters of my dissertation in March 1953. The chapters were on Wordsworth, Hopkins, Rilke, and Valéry: I had proposed to write "inductively" about them in a thesis, later published as *The Unmediated Vision.* Wellek returned my chapters with: "Very good—but where is the thesis?" So, in a month, I added an explicit thesis, received the degree, and, having revised the dissertation for publication by Yale University Press during the summer, reported for induction into the Army in September 1953, just as the Korean War formally ended in an armistice.

What made comparative literature distinctive at Yale during its early years was not a doctrinaire program but a certain "formation" that marked cosmopolitan yet very different scholars. Precisely because we had passed through a terrible war—I believe that in my graduate class almost all comparatists were either veterans or refugees—it seemed necessary to affirm the wealth and worth of a literary inheritance that had brought such a wonderful harvest of modernist works, even as it had not prevented political disaster. It never entered my head to blame that culture in any way. I was glad it was there, as if it too had escaped mortal danger. I am sure the personalities of teachers like Auerbach, Wellek, and Henri Peyre influenced me in this: Henri Peyre, who claimed he came out of the womb talking, was perhaps the most tolerant and eloquent (and atheistic) of the three, truly undogmatic and immensely encouraging not only to me personally but, I think, to most of his students. I could never, instinctively or because of my training, believe that art should conform to role:

like Shakespeare's Ariel, if it serves, it is in the hope of being free again. Art is its own excuse, and useless arguments must always be made for its usefulness.

I began teaching at Yale in 1955, after two funny and futile years of Army service, in which no one seemed to know what to do with a private who had a Ph.D., except to call him Dr. Private. Those years, however, saved me from becoming too professionalized: having the leisure to read whatever I wanted—despite the military's tendency to waste the recruit's time on chicken shit and mock maneuvers—was an exceptional boon. Assigned to Germany, I became for a few months the driver and interpreter for a lieutenant colonel, who was amused to have a Yale graduate at his beck and call—and who himself had almost nothing to do. "Hartman," he jovially said, throwing some charts at me, "reorganize the battalion." I thought of giving literature classes in an Army prison, but one visit to it made me see the incongruity. This was also the time when, to counter my Army surroundings, though I was inspired by the charm of Heidelberg, I used my furloughs to travel to many places in Europe, including Sicily, and began to write poetry in all seriousness. It was an intense period in which what seemed like wasted days reproached me continually, and when I felt that not to be thinking, feeling, writing was sinful.

At Yale I had to start all over again, since I knew relatively little English literature, and indeed learned most of it through teaching it. I was not particularly impressed by the undergraduates there in the 1950s; but the company of those who started teaching at the same time, especially Harold Bloom and Thomas Greene, and the satisfaction of teaching—the act itself, without a conscious pedagogy, without ulterior motives—kept me in the discipline, though I made escapist moves toward law school and the Jewish Theological Seminary. Secular modes of interpretation did not satisfy me entirely; and despite the fact that I had received no formal Jewish education, I read what I could (that is, in translation) in the Talmud, Maimonides, and Yehuda Halevi. More in search of a lost mode of reading than of my roots, I also spent the fall of 1958 teaching the English Romantics at the Hebrew University in Jerusalem, sitting in on Nehama Leibowitz's midrash course (as if something would penetrate despite my totally inadequate Hebrew), and later, when Judah Goldin came to Yale, benefited from his midrash classes.

My relation to texts remained as direct as in my first book, so it did not matter much what I was assigned to teach. Harold Bloom, already sophisticated and polemical, and at that time strongly impressed by Northrop Frye, helped me to think about English Romantics other than Wordsworth and the modern

European writers I was familiar with. (I had a particular affection for French literature, and in 1960 my small book on André Malraux was published.) Bloom shared my admiration for Buber's *I and Thou,* from which he drew an interpretive model important not only to his first publication, *Shelley's Mythmaking,* but to the spirit of direct address that has infused all his criticism.

My focus on Wordsworth, resulting in the book of 1964, was motivated by that poet's strong, archaic sense of place, which often reminded me of the Hebrew Bible. Using what I thought was a phenomenological method, I traced his obsession with certain "spots," the way it developed into a teleological and individuating consciousness of nature, a nature that seemed to designate him as its poet. In time this became a "consciousness of consciousness," portending the imagination's independence from nature, and its temptation to seek a separate reality. In Wordsworth this complex intuition also responded to the deracinating changes brought about by the French revolutionary wars and the rapid advance of England's industrialization. His mission as nature poet resisted this ecological disturbance in the relation between the mind and its rural habitat.

Yet any concern with theory remained secondary. Even when I returned to Yale permanently, after stints between 1960 and 1967 at Chicago, Iowa, Cornell, and Zurich, theory meant for me primarily a level of intensity, a way to closer reading, an analytic style, if you wish. In the unusual period of the 1970s, when Paul de Man, Hillis Miller, Shoshana Felman, and Jacques Derrida were added as colleagues and the Yale student body had become much more brilliant as well as diversified, the excitement of interpreting both literary and philosophical texts was palpable, and my knowledge of Continental sources brought me close to what was happening. I had an admiring relation to Freud as an intrepid interpreter, a difficult and ambivalent relation to Heidegger, especially his extraordinary language of exegesis when focused on such poets as Hölderlin and Trakl, and an exploratory, uncertain relation to Walter Benjamim and Claude Lévi-Strauss. It was during that time that *The Fate of Reading* (1975), *Criticism in the Wilderness* (1980), *Saving the Text* (1981), and *Easy Pieces* (1985) were published.

I never could see deconstruction as a doctrine, however, or more than a way of expanding the range and depth of reading—Paul de Man would have said a way of overcoming the resistance to reading. He noted that most essays revealed a pattern: each new critic complains about a previous critic's misreading, but always represents that "as a contingent, never as a constitutive obstacle to literary understanding." The polemics of such critics differ from Bachelard's concept of the progressive negations of science: literary polemics highlight instead a "systematic avoidance of the problem of reading, of the interpretive or hermeneutic moment."

De Man seeks to clarify rather than resolve the instability of interpretive reading. He is close to Bachelard in stressing the negative moment in interpretation, but the momentum of these negatives is not constructive in the sense of forming a *surobjet,* a definitive structural model of the literary. De Man calls the constitutive misreading of both later interpreters and earlier ones, and their mutual blindness to the issue of reading as such, a temporal predicament. For literary modernity, with its emphasis on a preemptive present, and literary history (the canonical sequence that determines the meaning or value of authors), unsettle each other. Critics, by accepting diachronicity, yet proposing their reading as a rupture or new departure, do not seem to realize the ironic pattern they repeat. In claiming to be modern, in enacting the "persistent temptation of literature to fulfill itself in a single moment," they cancel out their own historicity and forget the mortal and contingent status of their words. This contradictory assertion and erasure of historicity is "constitutive of literary consciousness and has to be included in a definition of the specificity of literature."[4]

In *The Unmediated Vision* (1954), I had described a "modern" aspiration to immediacy that was bound to fail. But since the artist draws new mediational structures out of this failure, I emphasized the heroic nature of the quest, rather than irony, bad faith, or aporia. I accepted modernity as a period term and did not recognize its link to a pattern that repeated itself in literary history. Nietzsche's "Use and Misuse of Historical Knowledge," a key text for de Man, had not fully touched me; not until *The Longest Shadow* (1996), essays on the aftermath of the Holocaust, did Nietzsche's analysis of a relativizing and life-oppressing historical knowledge lead me to the unresolvable antithesis between the duty of remembrance and the necessity of active forgetting.

Despite hostile remarks in the media about Yale as the command center of deconstruction, its literature faculty did not swarm with deconstructionists even in the heyday of theory. Yale remained eclectic, with a preponderance of scholars devoted to the New Criticism. Thomas Greene, for example, used close reading to show how crucial the rise of the historical sense was for Renaissance literature—the beginning, really, of our present focus on how to value cultural difference. Yet de Man's insistence on the irreconcilable and indeterminate aspects of literary study, his calm yet devastating critique of New-Critical complacencies, made him charismatic for students. And despite the gap in style and temperament between us, I was of one mind with him in foregrounding the rhetoric of criticism. "Critical texts," he said, "have to be read with the same awareness of ambivalence that is brought to the study of non-critical literary texts"; and, more radically, "The semantics of interpretation have no epistemological consistency and can therefore not be scientific." The encounter between text and commentary produces difference, not closure or a false equilibrium.[5]

Though to reckon by decades is like counting on one's fingers, the 1970s and '80s were extraordinary years for literary criticism. I have kept one document from that time, "The Deconstruction Blues," written by Dwight Eddins in honor of a lecture. I gave at the University of Alabama, Morgan Hall, and of which I quote only the first two stanzas:

Had a dream last night, nearly drove me insane.
Thought I saw Geoffrey Hartman in a giant crane.
Said, "What you doin' with that wreckin' ball?"
He said "I'm deconstructin' old Morgan Hall."

I said "Geoff, you can't do that." He said, "Don't be
Saussure!
I got it right down here in *écriture*
That I'm supposed to give you damn New Critics
hell,
And have your phonemes disconnected by Southern Bell.
CHORUS:
I got them low-down, spin-around deconstruction
blues,
Call Yale every morning, find out the latest
views.
They told me "Read your Derrida, DeMan, DaBloom
an' all them groovy books;
Stay away from fancy women, fancy liquor, and
Cleanth Brooks!"

The rest is equally lively, but I spare the reader.

For the first time, it seemed, after Heidegger, philosophical minds took the textuality of literature seriously: that was certainly the attractiveness of both Derrida and de Man, quite apart from any specific doctrine. French discourse, not only literary, but also anthropological and psychoanalytic, invaded an Anglo-America that had only recently managed to concentrate on the literary in literature. Very soon feminism and the new historicism, as if bursting into a vacuum, or with all the excitement of a demystification, destroyed the methodical purification of focus barely achieved by the Russian and Czech formalists, the New Critics, and, even more radically, by de Man. My book of essays *Beyond Formalism* (1970) had tried to strike a balance by showing how crucial it was to understand the life of forms, to go "through" forms, as William Blake said we look "through" the eye. It was symptomatic that I introduced, at the beginning of this period, a graduate seminar called "Interpretation: Theory and Practice" in which criticism was extended forward, to the news from abroad, but also backward, to the rich, neglected hermeneutics of midrash and patristics.

Indeed, my interest at that time was as much in commentary as in criticism. Commentary was the encompassing genre; its critical, judicial aspect was exercised in the choice of texts to be considered, and in the honesty with which one recorded one's impression—an impression formed by a comparative perspective, more attentive to distinctions than explicit judgments or academic labels. Contemporary criticism, with its narrow, scientific focus on the overobjectified work of art, did not mingle with the text in the manner of the most intriguing ancient commentaries, including Augustine's *Confessions*—or Derrida's *Glas* and *Circumfession* or Norman O. Brown's experiments. The only overt polemics I conducted were to protest—especially in *Criticism in the Wilderness*—T. S. Eliot's reduction of a more generous, Arnoldian concept of the task of criticism. Poetry, Eliot asserted, must carry a self-reflective charge, however corrosive that might prove to the creative spirit; but the obverse did not hold, that criticism could have a creative component. I objected to "any assignment of criticism to a non-creative and dependent function with second-class status in the world of letters." Literary commentary should have its own standing: it was not servile but took its place within literature, rather than remaining on the outside looking in. Perhaps the poet in me refused to bow down to the work of art despite my enjoyment of it: I had to understand it, to equal it in some way. I betrayed a *creative* jealousy (so I tell myself), and yet one that was not mere self-assertion but a specifically intellectual homage. It shocked me, therefore, when Bill Wimsatt, our senior colleague at Yale, a giant in size and mind, published an essay accusing Harold Bloom and myself of "battering the [literary] object."

In the 1970s too, Harold Bloom formulated his own version of literary history as a personal and agonistic process. He advanced beyond the dizzy antinomianism he had honored in William Blake, having grown doubtful about that poet's attempt to correct Milton's and even the Bible's version. Yet Bloom retained an interest—initiated by Blake and strengthened by Hans Jonas and Gershom Scholem—in gnosticism's belief that nature was deceptive and the god of nature only a demiurge. It shifted the emphasis in the study of the Romantics from nature to imagination, or seriously complicated their relation. It also led to a revised understanding of tradition, which now revealed darker tones.

This was the time of our closest cooperation; and I felt like a midwife to the parturitions that resulted in *The Anxiety of Influence* (1973). Bloom's "revisionary ratios" emerged one after the other, sextuplets in all. His typology of these ratios described the attempt of "strong" poets to deceive themselves into originality, to survive the shadow cast by greatness: the shadow of Milton on Blake, of Wordsworth, Blake, and Shelley on Yeats and Stevens. Misreading became as central a subject as in de Man, but it was understood as a necessary rhetorical strategy by which the later poet made psychological and creative room for himself. A deep skepticism about the claim of poetic originality combined, in this virtuoso revealer of intertextual echoes, with an equally deep conviction about the existence of original genius.

Eventually the Hebrew Bible, or a core Bloom identified as the Book of J (*J* for "Yahwist"), was held not only to eclipse the rest of the Bible but to expose the secondariness of the New Testament. Shakespeare was the other great original, who so transcended his own debts that they became insignificant sources. At the very time I was exploring midrash as a multi-vocal form of commentary neglected by the history of criticism, Bloom turned to the Kabbala for a paradigm of orthodox trespass: of originality's agon, its breaking of the vessels, its struggle with what Scholem once called "the strict light of the canonical." And though Bloom participated in the Yale nonmanifesto *Deconstruction and Criticism* (1979), he increasingly ignored French and Continental gurus, looking homeward to the *genius loci,* to Emerson and American poetry. By the force and number of his publications, he shook up the lingering orthodoxy of Eliot's emphasis on impersonality in art as in criticism. Meanwhile, the School of Criticism and Theory, founded in the 1970s by Murray Krieger, debated and disseminated this ongoing renewal of interpretive energies—a tide that lifted all ships.

I had always, naively, considered Paul de Man as a refugee scholar; and while witty and sociable, and not averse to gossip, he did not have the habit of talking about himself. I once asked him what he had published before 1953, the date of the first essay of his I knew. His reply was, "Nothing but journalism." De Man had invited me in 1965 to leave Iowa and help found the Graduate Program in Comparative Literature at Cornell; at Yale, too, we worked closely together and organized "Literature Z," a course in "Reading and Rhetorical Structure" for a new literature major—established around 1970 to satisfy undergraduates who wished to break out of the framework of national literature departments and to have more popular culture in the curriculum. On one occasion, when I had started our joint course with three lectures on poetry, de Man followed with texts of Locke, Kant, and Marx, and he handled the transition by remarking: "Professor Hartman has given you beauty, now you will get de trut" (his way of pronouncingd "the truth"). (In my last class I had talked about "Beauty is Truth, Truth Beauty," from Keats's "Ode on a Grecian Urn.") One of the junior faculty assisting us was upset by de Man's remark, which she felt was condescending; I thought it was funny, if habitually ironic. Reproached by her, he came to me and asked whether I was offended. There was no lack of courtesy in him, despite the uncompromising nature of his literary analyses; and it pained me greatly, as it did my colleagues, to find out a few years after his death about his early journalism, during the Nazi occupation, for the Belgian newspaper *Le Soir,* especially one distinctly antisemitic article.

Since then, other shocks have followed: revelations about the background in the Waffen-SS of Hans-Robert Jauss, certainly the most innovative scholar of the Romance languages in Germany, who had invited me to lecture at the new University of Konstanz shortly after its founding. There I also taught a summer semester at his and Wolfgang Iser's urging in 1978. The revelations are still coming about other scholars, not only in literature but also in history and the humanities generally.[6] Though Jauss had had an exemplary career after the war and always insisted that he did not know about the fate of the Jews on the Eastern front (where he had fought), in a conversation I said we could not remain friends, though I still would talk and exchange thoughts as a colleague in the joint enterprise of renewing literary studies.

There are those who wish to see continuities between de Man's early journalism or Jauss's Nazi past and their mature scholarly work; these continuities may be reactive and oppositional, however. Each thinker deserves more than partisan defense or denunciation. Though many statements in de Man's later writings echo differently in the mind when read against the disclosed biographical background, I cannot discern a deliberately masked connection, a use of theory to occult virulent or nihilistic ideas. Yet the puzzle remains why de Man, for all his intelligence, could not invent an occasion to talk about those early writings. (Dominick LaCapra once suggested that he would have become somewhat of a hero had he edited them himself.) I agree with Leo Spitzer, who wrote to a younger colleague in Germany shortly after the war: "Surely you cannot believe in earnest that working collectively with Baal did not eat into the human substance."[7]

Basically, I have remained an essayist, experimenting with styles of criticism, enjoying learning for its own sake, though aware in particular how superficially the Romantic movement was being taught, and seeking to reestablish the field as a crucial body of works and a link between the Enlightenment and modernism. At the same time, I came to view period terms as too limiting and began an unfinished project to compose a literary history worthy of the great writers who are supposedly its subject. With my center firmly in Romantic poetry, I traced its complex revival of an older, undying tradition of Romance: oneiric, visionary, vernacular, sporadically supernatural—attuned, that is, to ideas of an animate, sympathetic cosmos, in which humankind was at once kingpin and outcast. The Romantic Enlightenment, though characterized by apocalyptic fears and fancies, refused (sometimes with counterrevolutionary results) to break "the link of nature" and cultivated the sympathetic imagination in an era where belief in a sympathetic cosmos was becoming a superstition. *The Fateful Question of Culture* (1997), in which I tried to encompass and critique an increasingly out-of-control idea of culture, focused on a rational fear: that a spiritual need for embodiment, for an organic personal or collective existence, demanding the total devotion of soul and body, led more to violence than to love.

Yet the evidence I used remained literary: the relation of poem to poem. I took for granted the priority of literature over philosophy, at least over philosophic thought of the academic kind, not that of the Plato said by Shelley to be a poet. As for the issue of social and political history in relation to literature, I found no methodical solution. I considered literature an "unmediated" activity, except for its perennial themes and institutionalized forms. For a time, however, I tried to get my theoretical bearings through philosophy, especially the works of Husserl and Hegel, and was soon enmeshed in the question of how something so densely intertextual as literature achieved a semblance of immediacy.

In 1911 Husserl had published a programmatic essay, "Philosophy as a Rigorous System of Knowledge." He emphasized the radicalism (his word) that philosophy had to practice to be worthy of the name. Nothing given can just be accepted, nothing received or traditional may be counted as a starting point.

No great names should dazzle us. "For the philosopher who is truly without prejudices it is all the same whether an affirmation stems from Kant or Aquinas, from Darwin or Aristotle, from Helmholtz or Paracelsus." Philosophy as knowledge of what is radical must also be radical in its procedures and may not rest until it has won through to its own absolutely clear beginning. Reading such clarion sentences, and fired by words I have since learned to distrust—"absolute," "clarity," "clear beginning"—I was deeply affected by Husserl. I recall struggling—in vain, I then believed—with his *Ideen.* On reperusal, however, of my first book, *The Unmediated Vision,* it could be seen as attempting a *Wesensschau* of the modern literary experience, including its rejection of tradition as a necessary starting point. Despite the inadequacies of the period term "modern," I proposed a theory extracted from certain great poets, starting with Wordsworth. The modern writer, I claimed, "either does not acknowledge or does not know a mediator for his orphic journey. He passes through experience by means of the unmediated vision. Nature, the body, and human consciousness—that is the only text."

These were the concluding sentences of the book. The role of mediator—as well as the role of overcoming the curse of mediacy—was implicitly placed on the poet. (When I read R. W. B. Lewis's *American Adam,* I felt an immediate bond; and between 1960 and 1965 I tried to take on poetry reviewing for the *Kenyon Review* and the *Partisan Review,* testing my direct and naive understanding not only on poets of some reputation, such as Marianne Moore, Robert Lowell, Randall Jarrell, and Robert Graves, but also on poets previously unknown to me, among them Allen Grossman, Frederic Seidel, Gregory Corso, Robert Bly, James Wright, A. R. Ammons, Adrienne Rich, Jean Garrigue, Denise Levertov, and Gwendolyn Brooks.) There were other attempts to value new beginnings. The relational, intuitive certainty of "this river: I am," a modified *cogito* I ascribed to Wordsworth, was derived from Buber's concept of relation in *I and Thou,* even if its absoluteness went back to what Husserl released in me. Original response, as Robert Frost called it, meant everything to me; this included my reaction to commentary, which I read for its daring, eccentric orbiting of the text and for its integrity as prose.

Though impressed by Hegel as well as Husserl, I was looking for a definitive starting point, an "in the Beginning" that would be grounded as well as elaborated by acts of the poetic consciousness. I was charting a realm I would increasingly characterize as dialectical or mediated, without giving up the idea of unmediated *points de repère*—the equivalent of Wordsworth's "spots of time," which at once vitalized his consciousness and bound it to the memory of particular places. I got as close as possible to that poet's material imagination (so Bachelard would have called it), but less its economic determinants than the way both senses and mind engaged with the more permanent, elemental phenomena of rural life. Wordsworth anticipates a new vein of poetry, in which imagination is not transfigurative, or inventive of strange symbols: we continue to recognize in his landscape-visions a common, even commonplace, world of sights and sounds. There is a dialectic of the senses, initiated by the dominance of the eye, by scopic desire; and the poet came to believe that Nature was an agency pitting other senses against the eye and resolving—developmentally and providentially—sensory fixations. Here too, then, in the very play of the senses, mediation entered.

Wordsworth's Poetry went beyond the contending categories of "Nature" and "imagination" to show this dialectic in detail. A traumatic or too immediate experience (a never entirely localized origin, theophanic, though not literally represented as such) became a source of strength and renovation through the "dark workmanship" of a hypostatized Nature. (Many later essays, collected in *The Unremarkable Wordsworth,* continued these explorations.) It is not entirely true, then, when I say theory did not attract me. Most theorizing certainly didn't; but the exertion of mind, precision of observation, and power of generalization in philosophers like Husserl led me to approach a theory linking poetical figures with structures of consciousness. The spot syndrome in Wordsworth (his search for an *omphalos* or mythical navel of the earth) could function like a symbol without ever becoming symbolic. "The flight from these charged places of discourse or imagination," I wrote in a retrospect on my book, "through doublings, circlings, the generation of personae, metaphorical transference, and syntactical distribution . . . suggests a vital schizophrenia or decentering expressive of so much in personal growth. It is like moving away from parental or idolatrous fixation toward the cultivation of a love that is more than pointedly sexual, or like the overcoming of eye concepts that block sense experience."[8]

Husserl declared, a few years before his death, commenting on a crisis that had intensified: "Philosophy as a system of knowledge, as serious, strict, even apodictic knowledge, that dream is finished." Yet dreams are never finished. Perhaps he meant that he saw in Nazi Germany the distorted reality of his dream of discipline. The break-through mentality incited by a fear of Western decadence—the central subject of Thomas Mann's *Dr. Faustus*—had become the Nazi *Aufbruch* toward a militaristic and brazen culture of barbarity.

Significantly, Michel Foucault's rhetorical self-presentation in his inaugural lecture at the Collège de France in 1970, *The Order of Discourse,* is intensely wary of claiming to be an inaugural act. "In the discourse I must present today, and those which I am obliged to hold in this place, for years perhaps, I would have preferred to slip in surreptitiously." And, "Rather than holding forth [*prendre la parole*], I would have liked to have been enveloped by speech, and carried well beyond every possible beginning."

Since the 1980s three further issues have preoccupied me. The first is a variant of "opening the canon": supporting Jewish studies in the curriculum as well as broadening the basis of interpretation by an understanding of the exegetical imagination. The notion of "validity in interpretation" seems to me logically exciting, yet constipated from the point of view of an older, theological tradition of commentary. That never relied on a strict adequation, a restricted economy of text and extracted meaning, but broke the mirror—or vessel—of Scripture, releasing sparks of remarkable verbal energy or reconstituting the shards into nonorganic, kaleidoscopic wholes. Foucault's remark cited earlier reflects a theory in which speech is larger than the ego and its integrative powers—an impersonality theory very different from Anglo-American orthodoxy, and in touch with the intellectual milieu of, among others, Derrida, Deleuze, Lacan, Blanchot, and Levinas.

A second issue focuses on the notion of the aesthetic, and especially aesthetic education. In many books today the fatality of ideology shows itself in a contempt associated with the adjective "aesthetic," which bears the brunt of the failure of culture and the educated class: of their impotence in Germany and Continental Europe in the face of the antisemitism and xenophobia that preceded genocide. In some quarters "aesthetic" has become a dirty word rather than one describing the system of the arts generally, or a collective body of media that share a special quality. It is especially sad that, because of Heidegger's political compromises, his small tractate "The Origin of the Work of Art" has gradually dropped out of sight. In it he not only counters Hegel's challenge in the *Lectures on Aesthetics* that art is no longer the highest form in which truth achieves embodiment—being, in that respect, a thing of the past, transcended by philosophy—but also carefully restores and builds on the original sense of *aistheton* as expressing an "unmediated encounter with things, of what happens," a meaning, therefore, not to be attained by conceptual assault.

The problem is aggravated by Walter Benjamin's critique of fascism as an "aestheticizing of politics." Benjamin's formula is often overinterpreted: it points primarily to the seductive, dynamic visuality of Nazi spectacles of pomp and power. (Ernst Bloch surmised that had the liberal bourgeoisie managed to create spectacles equally attractive, equally unifying, Nazism could not have taken hold.) The *Rausch,* or exaltation, incited by Nazism's Nordic nonsense but converted into disciplined, live displays manipulating masses of people, affected speech as well. For there was also a generic misuse of words that subordinated their critical-reflective aspects to a decisionist and stereotyping rhetoric. This development—anticipated by Georges Sorel's *Reflections on Violence,* his Machiavellian remarks on the need of the populace for ideas and myths embodied in simple, powerful images—should have led to an intensified study of literary language as the most ascetic, critical, and commonplace basis of art. In that spirit, the literary, or the linguistic in the literary, is a counter-propaganda, deconstructing totalizing pretensions and showing that the whole is vaguer than its parts. This kind of scrutiny, however, makes art, with its parts pulling in different directions, seem more fragmented, so that the force of the work as a whole remains—conceptually—unresolved. At the same time, every dubious movement toward unification or consent, however necessary as magic glue or myth, is exposed more clearly. Literary criticism has its own form of antimonumentalism.

Many scholars in my generation have become disenchanted with the present character of literary criticism. The rise of cultural studies has been accompanied by a certain divisiveness, caused less by an increase in self-reflection than by assertive theories or ideologies. Perhaps the period of devotion to art that followed the war of 1939 to 1945, in which we felt no need to justify *le sacré du poète,* was naive and, in America, too neglectful of sociology. But now the disciplinary line between social study and the study of art has practically disappeared. Auerbach's magnanimous vision of the "dialectical forces" that made European civilization, enriched by the very difference between nations, possible as the precursor of a communal life on this planet seems to have dissolved into both polemical strife and actual war.

To this must be added that universities, especially in the United States, are weakening in their will to teach and transmit Western culture. A large contingent of teachers, and empirical evidence from the type of courses most in demand, suggest that we are experiencing a marked change in attitude. The change is recent, and often linked to the new demographics of the university: the result of the attempt to make it truly democratic in its admissions and hiring policy, a process which began in the 1960s.

I am not prepared to argue that the disincentive for learning about Western culture is a necessary consequence of this demographic upheaval. There *is* more awareness now of the link between culture and politics, but this recognition could also sound a warning against using the accident of birth as a cultural claim to gain particular political ends rather than to enhance communal life in a technological and specialized society. Despite outward appearances, our situation in the university is not radically different from that noted by Walter Benjamin in a remarkable essay of 1915 denouncing the falsification of the creative spirit as it turns toward careerism.[9] The equivalent today, *our* careerism, is a divisive form of cultural politics.

A third, challenging issue is how extreme experiences can be presented in the classroom without being deadened by an anaesthetizing, defensive scholarship—and, obversely, without sacrificing the formal element in art. The limits of realism, the effect of the Holocaust on culture, the relation of words and wounds (the psychological complexity of communication), and the possibility of a specifically literary knowledge related to trauma are the topics now closest to me. As a founder and the project director, since 1981, of Yale's Video Archive for Holocaust Testimonies, I give a good part of my time to an audiovisual genre that raises questions about memory, pedagogy, and cultural transmission.

The issues I have mentioned are not subject matters alone; they indicate a need for us to reconsider our teaching practice, as well as to understand better why the study of art and the humanities is necessary. The handling of the distance between present and past, the passion we often feel to witness as well as to rouse the critical faculties, this personal equation, which differs from teacher to teacher and cannot be methodized, must nevertheless be conveyed, consciously or unconsciously, to those who will themselves become teachers. In that light it is necessary to reflect on extreme experiences and to consider such words as the following, written by a fifteen-year-old boy who acted as a covert chronicler in the Vilna ghetto:

> I got a taste of the historian's task. I sit at the table and ask questions and record the greatest sufferings with cold objectivity. I write, I probe into details, and I do not realize at all that I am probing into wounds, and the one who answers me—indifferent to it: two sons Monday, the husband Thursday. . . . And this horror, this tragedy is formulated by me in three words, coldly and dryly. I become absorbed in thought, and the words stare out of the paper crimson with blood.[10]

The wary reader may find more dogma in this collection of essays than is obvious to its author. But the pleasure of the text has always been connected in my work to the pressure of the text. This pressure does not come from concepts so much as from a writing that still carries within it the resistance of the phenomenality of sensory experience to concepts. The luminosity of visual and the music of auditory perceptions, their vibration in the memory as unappropriated images and lyrical transitions, keep me a reader of poetry, or of the residually poetic in the most austere prose. Though my readings stay close to the words of the text, I have tried to respect this freer if evanescent dimension by avoiding a minute or imprisoning kind of literary analysis, one that never allows you to be excursive or exorbitant. Yet I cannot claim to have the courage of an Emerson, who could "entertain the supposition of [literature's] entire disappearance."

My mind, neither transcendentalist nor philosophical, stops far short of that. It is always asking itself: Why are there texts? Why do we need the mediation of art, not only to record otherwise fugitive thoughts but as a contemplative necessity? In what way is literature a "construction" essential to life, and what part is played by its tapping of anarchic or apocalyptic energies? Gershom Scholem, in his famous letter to Franz Rosenzweig on the revival of the Hebrew language, claims that its recreation as a modern, secularized construct was fraught with danger. The "apocalyptic thorn," as he puts it, cannot be removed from words so ancient and charged as those of the Bible. But what he says about modernized Hebrew applies to some extent to all inherited, canonical speech. "Almost all of us live in this speech on top of a volcano, blind to it and feeling secure." The literary critic removes that blindness. A sense of the power of naming revives, and something of the awe and autonomy of the gift of words.

NOTES

1. Gaston Bachelard, *La philosophie du non: Essai d'une philosophie du nouvel esprit scientifique* (Paris: Presses Universitaires de France, 1973), 139–40.
2. Bachelard, *La philosophie du non,* 144. My translation.
3. For a sensitive account of Auerbach's dismissal by the Nazi bureaucracy and his immediate postwar career, in the context of an ideological critique of the humanities, see Karlheinz Barck, "Flucht in die Tradition: Erfahrungshintergründe Erich Auerbachs zwischen Exil und Emigration," *Deutsche Vierteljahrsschrift für Kulturwissenschaft und Geistesgeschichte,* Sonderheft 1994, ed. Aleida Assmann and Anselm Haverkamp, 47–61.
4. See Paul de Man, "Literary History and Literary Modernity," *Blindness and Insight: Essays in the Rhetoric of Contemporary Criticism* (New York: Oxford University Press, 1971). Also the second edition (Minneapolis: Minnesota University Press, 1983), where de Man describes a "double pattern of juxtaposed aberration" (281) and the "double movement of revelation and recoil" in critics who cannot reconcile "the analytical rigor of the exegetic procedure" with "the [absent] epistemological authority of the ensuing results" (289). On the character of polemics and critique overall, in philosophy, and

perhaps the humanities generally, see also some painful reflections of Karl Jaspers in the "Heidegger" chapter (not inserted until after Heidegger's death) of his philosophical autobiography. Karl Jaspers, *Philosophische Autobiographie,* Erweiterte Neuausgabe (Munich: Piper, 1977), 106–11. Jaspers admits to evading a significant confrontation with Heidegger from 1918 to 1933, after which Heidegger's Nazism made it impossible, and they did not meet any more.

5. De Man, *Blindness and Insight,* 104–111.
6. See, especially, O. G. Oexle, "Zweierlei Kultur: Zur Erinnerungskultur deutscher Geisteswissenschaftler nach 1945," *Rechtshistorisches Journal* (Frankfurt: Loewenkalu Gesellschaft, 1997): 16:358–91); also, for an examination of the role of the historians, Georg G. Iggers, "The German Historians and the Burden of the Nazi Past," *Dimensions* 12 (1998): 21–29.
7. "Sie können nicht ernsthaft glauben, daß die Zusammenarbeit mit Baal die Substanz des Menschen nicht anfresse." Cited by Oexle, "Zweierlei Kultur," 383.
8. "Retrospect 1971," in *Wordsworth's Poetry, 1787–1814* (New Haven: Yale University Press, 1971), xvii.
9. "Jene Verfälschung des Schöpfergeistes in Berufsgeist." See "Das Leben der Studenten" (1915). *Illuminationen: Ausgewählte Schriften* (Frankfurt: Suhrkamp, 1961), 9–21.
10. Yitskhok Rudashevski, *The Diary of the Vilna Ghetto,* trans. Percy Matenko (Israel: Beit Lohamei Haghetaot, 1973), 73.

Theory

Tea and Totality

In almost every order of discourse there has been a call at one time or another for a higher seriousness. We are asked to pursue "some graver subject" or a more exacting style. The call may comc, as in Milton or Keats, from within the poet's sense of a vocation spurred on by exemplary forebears: the reputed career of Virgil, for example, who left the oaten pipe of pastoral and playful song for the pursuit of didactic verse in his farmer's manual *The Georgics,* which is climaxed in turn by the trumpets stern of his epic *Aeneid,* which deals with a warrior become culture-bearer. This call for a higher style or a graver subject has also burdened philosophy. However diverse their modes, in Husserl, Heidegger, and Wittgenstein the ideal of rigor besets what with a phrase from Spenser's proem to the *Faerie Queene* we may term their "afflicted style."

It is not otherwise in literary criticism. Grave it certainly is, and didactic, so that the formalist or playful thinker who does not justify his enterprise by appealing to theory or science is not considered worthwhile. The real terror we have experienced, and are still experiencing, produces a pressure on our purposes that is itself not unterroristic. "A theory of culture," George Steiner writes in *Bluebeard's Castle,* "an analysis of our present circumstances, which do not have at their pivot a consideration of the modes of terror that brought on the death, through war, starvation, and deliberate massacre, of some seventy million human beings in Europe and Russia, between the start of the first World War and the end of the second, seems to me irresponsible."[1]

Steiner is right in refusing to neglect a haunting and intractable catastrophe. But as we read his appeal from a book that asks with anguish why European high culture could not stem Nazi barbarism, we wonder how far even a relevant "theory" would take us. It would remain an interpretation; it would raise the further question of how interpretations acquire the force to change anything. The sincere thinker, moreover, need not be the effective one: men and women of conscience may unwittingly trivialize a subject by becoming obsessed with it. At a time when the air is as full of strident sounds as it was once of fairy folk, the question of what kind of seriousness our discipline may claim, or what sort of style might best convey it, is more troublesome than ever. The purpose of literary commentary cannot be simply amplifying the clichés of our predicament.

Some question of style has always existed. Literature, we are told, should please or move as well as teach. Rhetoric has forensic and religious roots, however cognitively developed. Our culture depends on formalized arts of verbal exchange, which have their rules and limits, as in an adversarial court system and a parliamentary mode of debate; and they determine what is evidence rather than what is truth. They may even put obstacles in the way of those who think they know the truth, for we do not live with each other in an unmediated relation but in a strongly rhetoricized world where verbal and stylistic choices must constantly be made.

Yet just as logic tries to escape or purify rhetoric, so literary criticism too has tried to control words or else recall them to their direct, most referential function. It may seem strange to admit that the literary critic is often no friendlier to imaginative literature than the logician. In this self-deputized censor, the critic, there is love-hate rather than friendship; and recently this passionate engagement has tended to sort itself out in a schizoid way. The drift toward the extreme in modern art is so strong that it is not, on the whole, resisted. The resistance comes when a critic breaches the ramparts of decorum and modifies the language of literary criticism itself.

For that language has remained as unpretentious as possible. Critics, after all, should be critical, and fend off inflated rhetoric, faked authority, and indigest foreignness. Suspicious of their love for literature, they are even more suspicious of the literary element in themselves. They are sober people who shield themselves from contamination by the hygiene of their practice. Their tone is nicely aggressive and their nasty conservatism is great fun after the fact—however pernicious and parochial it may have been in its own time.

How many know of Stuart Sherman's attack on H. L. Mencken in a book called *Americans?* His essay is entitled "Mr. Mencken, the *Jeune Fille* and the New Spirit in Letters"; and the *jeune fille* clearly plays the same role for Sherman as the young corruptible student does for Denis Donoghue, who worries about creative critics inciting their disciples to dithyrambs instead of dissertations. Here is one of Sherman's sallies:

> The *jeune fille* . . . feels within herself . . . an exhilarating chaos, a fluent welter . . . She revels in the English paradoxes and mountebanks, the Scandinavian misanthropes, the German egomaniacs, and, above all, in the later Russian novelists, crazy with war, taxes, anarchy, vodka, and German philosophy . . . Lured by a primitive instinct to the sound of animals roving, she ventures a curious foot in the fringes of the Dreiserian wilderness vast and drear; and barbaric impulses in her blood answer the wail of the forest . . . Imagine a thousand *jeunes filles* thus wistful, and you have the conditions ready for the advent of a new critic. At this point enters at a hard gallop, spattered with mud, H. L. Mencken high in oath . . . He leaps from the saddle with sabre flashing, stables his horse in the church, shoots the priest, hangs the professors, exiles the Academy, burns the library and the university, and, amid the smoking ashes, erects a new school of criticism on modern German principles.[2]

Sherman has some reason to be apprehensive of the Germanizing spirit in literary studies: unfortunately even his name sounds as if a German were pronouncing "German." He wanted to save America from the Saxon in Anglo-Saxon.[3] What a paradox that the jeune fille would not prefer the delicacy of the French tradition which has named her type to the Carlylian coarseness of Mencken. Sherman intends the jeune fille to read Sainte-Beuve rather than Nietzsche, though he concludes that Mencken's style, "hard, pointed, forcible, cocksure," might substitute for a stiff freshman course in rhetoric and remove the softer forms of "slush" and "pish-posh" from her mind.

It is clearly not only Mencken's macho manners (Sherman's are nothing to boast of) which cause the offense. As today, there is a struggle going on to define the American spirit in its true independence. There is, further, a struggle over what democracy means in education. Finally, there is a near-physical disgust at German philosophizing as an idiom that could infect our entire verbal constitution. How would Sherman react, now that even philosophers in the Romance languages have succumbed to the Germanizing style? Sartre, Lévi-Strauss, Lacan, Foucault, Derrida, Kristeva, Althusser—where may delicacy and true aesthetic feeling be found?

I have been dealing with prejudices about style rather than with particular philosophical issues. Critics in the Anglo-American tradition are arbiters of taste, not developers of ideas. Their type of judiciousness is almost always linked to a strong sense for the vernacular—more precisely, to the idealization of the vernacular as an organic medium, a language of nature that communicates ideas without the noise or elaboration of extraverted theory. To argue too much about what is deeply English or American means that one has to acknowledge the outside; and being inside—an insider—is what counts. Perhaps this assumption of inwardness can be laid to every nationalism. Acculturated, one secretes one's culture. Yet unself-consciousness or antiself-consciousness, however attractive it may be, is surely a limitation rather than an expansion of the critical spirit. In the Anglophile tradition, the critical spirit, as it approaches Mencken's gallop, is suspected of being a modern form of enthusiasm as dangerous as the dogmatic spirit it displaced.

This suspicion of the critical spirit reaches an English high in the most influential of modern arbiters: T. S. Eliot. Such pronouncements, especially, as "From Poe to Valéry" and *Notes Towards the Definition of Culture* are urbane exercises to limit criticism in the name of culture. It is symptomatic that the epigraph on the title page of *Notes* is taken from the *OED* and reads: "DEFINITION: 1. The setting of bounds; limitation (rare)—1483." This conservative scrutiny of words, which communicates itself even to strong epigones like Trilling (just as Heidegger's etymological virtuosity turns up in Derrida), causes Eliot to say that rescuing the word *culture* is "the extreme of my ambition."

I come then to the extreme of *my* ambition. It is to understand what happened to English criticism in the period of roughly 1920 to 1950, when a "teatotaling" style developed in academic circles despite so many marvelous and often idiosyncratic talents, from Eliot himself to Richards, Empson, Leavis, and (in America) Trilling.

Now, what happened is that, in a sense, nothing happened. An order of discourse strove hard to remain a discourse of order. The happening was all on the side of art and literature; and the courage of the critic lay in acknowledging the newness or forwardness of modernist experiments. Compared to his own *Waste Land,* Eliot's essays are prissy. Compared to the novels of Lawrence, Leavis's revaluations are cultic gestures, precise elliptical movements charged with significance for the one who has truly read. Criticism is asked to exhibit an ideal decorum, to show that despite the stress of class antagonism, national disunity, and fragmentation, concepts of order are still possible.

In adopting this demeanor, English commentators followed an ingrained tradition. They took no solace from the notion of a science or a theory of literature: that was the Continental way, leading from Dilthey to Lukács, and then increasingly to reflections inspired by Marxism and structuralism. The English classical writer, even when the stakes were high, wished to please rather than teach, and to remind rather than instruct. This critical tradition, keeping its distance from sacred but also from learned commentary, sought to purify the reader's taste and the national language, and so addressed itself to peers or friends—in short, to a class of equally cultured people.

The highest recommendation of such criticism was the artfulness of its accommodation. Richards' *Philosophy of Rhetoric* is as careful of its audience as Ruskin's *Sesame and Lilies.* It is not philosophy as Lukács, Adorno, Heidegger, or Benjamin practiced it, who can leave ordinary language behind or beat it into surprising shapes. I emphasize these writers in German not because they had no choice but precisely because they did have a choice: namely, German classical prose as it culminated in Goethe, and still provided Freud with a style that made his science accessible.

The friendship style (as I tend to name this accommodated and classical prose) has political as well as sentimental ramifications. Writers in the later eighteenth century can talk of a "republic of letters," and Keats of a "freemasonry of spirits." Indeed, in Matthew Arnold the idea of culture moves to oppose the idea of class: culture, he said, exists to do away with classes. Even if the audience addressed in the friendship style may be as provisional and uncertain as Addison and Steele's was when they published *The Spectator,* the guiding fiction is that all the members of this society correspond on equal footing. They are "lettered"; and in terms of style there is an attempt to erase from their demeanor the "patronage style," that is, a vacillation between exaggerated modesty and extreme gravity, between presenting oneself as "all too mean" and all too manic. The friendship style cancels the disparity between the social class of the writer and his transcendent subject matter or ambition.[4]

Criticism, then, treads lightly: its prose can be savage, but only when affronted by pedantry or the self-inflated nonsense of other writers. From the time of the neoclassical movement in seventeenth-century France, it was a form of good conversation, a discourse among equals. This speak-easy quality still joins the *Spectator* to the *New York Review of Books,* which is notorious for employing Anglos. Only in Germany, and then after Hegel—when an attempt is made to separate the *Geisteswissenschaften* ("moral" or "human" sciences) from the natural sciences—is literary criticism burdened by ideas of *Bildung* and *Aufbau,* as if it had at once to anticipate and survive "absolute spirit." (So Dilthey's Berlin Academy lectures of 1905–1910, coinciding with Lukács's literary prentice years, were entitled "Der Aufbau der geschichtlichen Welt in den Geisteswissenschaften" [The construction of the historical world in the human sciences]. Yet even after the First World War, when Lukács published his *Theory of the Novel* (1920), then *History and Class Consciousness* (1923)—works whose emphasis on "totality" may be said to have inaugurated the philosophical type of criticism that was to dominate France as well as Germany—even in that postwar decade the radical editor A. R. Orage (*The New Age*) would caution Herbert Read in words that reflect the decorum of Anglo-French criticism, whose pattern-book was Sainte-Beuve's *Causeries.* "Not articles," Orage advises Read, "but causeries." "Beware of the valueless business that insists on *essay* in place of causerie. 'Everything divine runs on light feet.'"[5]

If we take the position, itself a literary one, that how we say something is as important as what we say, then the contrast that developed between English and continental types of discourse should not be disregarded. There is no need to insist that one style must be used for every situation; and there may well be a mingling of tones, sometimes uneasy, in the best critics. But the contrast between "tea" and "totality" is too striking to be evaded by mere habits of tolerance.

Let me recapitulate my argument so far. The great virtue of the English, Basil de Selincourt said in the 1920s, is their unconsciousness. And Goethe remarked of Byron: "All Englishmen are as such devoid of inwardness [*eigentliche Reflexion*]; distraction and party spirit do not allow them to achieve a quiet development. But they are imposing as a practical people."[6] I do not quote these statements to malign a critical tradition but to point out a paradox in it that should make us wary of its practical emphasis. So deliberate an unconsciousness tends to quiet the real unconscious. It does so, Goethe suggests, by diverting the mind from spiritual to practical matters. And when we think of the contemporary situation in the United States, who will cast the first stone? Talent is taking refuge in business schools, law schools, and computer science; and *eigentliche Reflexion,* even when it appears, as in certain types of philosophic criticism, is denounced as navel-gazing or mandarinism.

The dominance of review essay and expository article reflects in a general way the self-delimitation of practical criticism in America and England.

Though these forms of commentary serve primary texts, they now claim to teach rather than preach. And to teach as unself-consciously as possible. "Culture is the one thing that we cannot deliberately aim at," Eliot remarks in his *Notes* on culture. The intrusion of large questions involving religion or philosophy puts the exegete at risk, not because such questions are unimportant but because they are so very important. The practical is defined as the teachable rather than as "lived religion" (Eliot) or the *Umwelt* of "birth-death-existence-decision-communication with others." Paul Ricoeur, author of this rather Germanic phrase, associates "preaching" with such a "totality," as it informs every effort to articulate what we know. Preaching, he emphasizes, invades all good teaching; and teaching that claims to be method rather than discourse—that claims to be a purely objective mode of questioning or communication—has not understood anything about theory, or the domain of preunderstanding.[7]

My own purpose is more modest than to rethink the relation of teaching and preaching, although it seems obvious enough that great preaching did not reject ordinary language but, through the mode of parable, for example, or Swift's "attacking play" (C. J. Rawson), produced a strange intersection of ordinary and extraordinary conversation. My purpose is to reconstruct historically the provenance and character of the classical style in criticism, which has now become the teatotaling style. With a book like Denis Donoghue's *Ferocious Alphabets* we are, in terms of argument, not far from Maugham's summing up of the tradition he embodies. "To like good prose is an affair of good manners. It is, unlike verse, a civil art." To understand why alternate and challenging styles have developed in the last half-century, one must first value an older prose that was at once classic and journalistic.

I begin by stating the obvious: a battle of styles as well as books broke out in the seventeenth century, from which came the clarified expository and journalistic medium we relish today. The Royal Society in England as well as the French Academy played an important role in the spread of this purified style. In America it gradually took hold against the "fantastic school" represented by such forceful theological writers as Cotton Mather. Mather intended to humble the understanding, to make it aware of its "imbecility" by a contagious parody of impotent speculative maneuvers adorned with puns and quibbles. In Mather it is sometimes hard to tell whether his display of learning and parascientific knowledge is a genuine attempt to "solve the phenomena" by elevating the mind toward the wonders and riddles of the universe (that "totality" which mere tea-drinkers can never taste) or whether it is not a subversive manifestation of fallible wit in even the most splendid of bookworms. Whatever the truth, Mather knew his style was questionable, and in his handbook for the ministry, the *Manuductio* published in 1726, he defends himself as follows:

> There has been a great deal of ado about a STYLE; So much that I must offer you my Sentiments upon it. There is a *Way of Writing* wherein the author endeavours, that the Reader may have *something to the Purpose* in every Paragraph. There is not only a *Vigour* sensible in every *Sentence* but the Paragraph is embellished with *Profitable References*, even to something beyond what is *directly spoken* . . . The Writer pretends not unto *Reading*, yet he could not have writ as he does if he had not *Read* very much in his Time; and his Composures are not only a *Cloth of Gold*, but also stuck with as many *Jewels*, as the Gown of a Russian Embassador. This *Way of Writing* has been decried by many, and is at this Day more than ever so . . . But, however *Fashion* and *Humour* may prevail, they must not think that the Club at their *Coffee-House* is, *All the World* . . . After all, Every Man will have his own Style, which will distinguish him as much as his *Gate* [gait].

It was indeed the coffeehouses mentioned by Mather that played a certain role in producing the new, chastened prose; and except for the exigencies of alliteration, I might have entitled this essay "Coffee and Totality." In the sober yet convivial atmosphere of the coffeehouses, news and gossip were exchanged, and the literati conversed on equal footing. As Socrates brought philosophy down from the heavens into the marketplace, so Addison and Steele insinuated it into these bourgeois places of leisure, less exclusive than clubs yet probably as effective for transacting business in a casual setting. I am no sociologist, however, and do not want to ascribe too much to either tea or coffee. In the pleasant spirit of generalization adapted from the English sphere, one might say it was in these sociable places that "theories" were tested, that the conversational habit became the opium of the intellectual and a lucid, unpedantic form of prose developed. It is in this era too that the English tradition modified both the scientific and the French demand for a univocal and universal language by appealing to the mingled force of a middle or epistolary style—more exactly, by appealing to the symbiosis, rather than the clash, of learned and vernacular traditions, a symbiosis that had previously characterized English poetry, even if the results were as different as Spenser and Shakespeare. The mingled style develops into the ideal of unaffected conversation, in which something is held in reserve and solicits reader or listener. It intends to provoke a reply rather than to dazzle, and it subordinates ingeniousness to the *ingenium* of natural wit. Such an ideal naturalizes rather than banishes Latinity, and it seeks an equivalent in English to the philosophic ease of Plato's Greek. "It is straight from

Plato's lips, as if in natural conversation," Pater will write, "that the language came in which the mind has ever since been discoursing with itself, in that inward dialogue which is the 'active principle" of the dialectic method" (*Plato and Platonism,* 1896).[8]

The triumph of modern English, though not quite yet of modern American, is anticipated by this ideal of criticism as an extended conversation, civilizing difficult ideas without falling back into gossip or opinionatedness. That criticism as a causerie may have had its origin in French circles of the seventeenth century, that it was formalized and even patented by Sainte-Beuve (so much so that Proust, closer to Pater, wrote an *Against Sainte-Beuve*), does not make it less attractive to the British. It is true that many intermediary developments should be taken into account, such as the nervy style of Hazlitt, and that even in recent times the grip of the causerie has not gone unchallenged. Many writers between 1920 and 1950 try to make criticism more professional. They feel its dandyish or donnish character, and they signal a return to the vernacularist movement in Puritan England, which intended to "ratifie and settle" English as the national language. "It is more facil," George Snell wrote in 1649, "by the eie of reason, to see through the *Medium,* and light of the English tongue; then by the more obscure light of anie forreign language . . . to learn unknown arts and terms."[9] Yet both in journalism and in the university the following basic features of genteel criticism kept their hold.

It should be neither utilitarian as in business nor abstract as in pure science nor highly specialized as in scholarship. These types of discourse are allowed in only when dressed down, reduced to a witty gentility first attributed to the "honest man" (*honnête homme*) in seventeenth-century French culture—a person, that is, whose rank or profession could not be discerned when he talked in polite society. When a cultured person writes or converses, you cannot tell his profession or background, because, as La Rochefoucauld said, "il ne se pîque de rien." Or, to quote from the definition of the *honnête homme* given by the *Dictionary* of the French Academy, his demeanor is that of "un galant homme, homme de bonne conversation, de bonne compagnie," that is, "a courteous man—a good conversationalist, interesting to be with."

Certainly an appealing ideal, for today we are even less able to talk in a nonspecialized manner. The art of conversation has not improved. But if it has not, perhaps the older ideal was the wrong way of democratizing discourse or limiting pedantry and snobbery. Without the conversational style (still practiced in Oxbridge tutorials) our situation might be worse; yet it must be said that those who at present uphold the art of criticism as conversation too often stifle intellectual exchange. Conversational decorum has become a defensive mystique for which "dialectic" and even "dialogue" (in Plato's or Gadamer's or Bakhtin's strong sense) are threatening words.

In Pater the conversational ideal is the last refuge of a neoclassical decorum striving to maintain the mask of a unified sensibility. Yet it is merely a mask. Pater holds on to the beautiful soul, the *schöne Seele.* It is time to try something else.

What might that be? It is hardly surprising that English studies should resist the influx of a French *discours* heavily indebted to post-Hegelian German philosophy. Tea and totality don't mix. Something should eventually grow from within the English tradition, even if the pressure comes from without. Richards and Empson certainly made a beginning; and criticism did become more principled, more aware of the complex structure of assigning meaning and making a literary judgment. But the problem of style remained, that is, of communicating in colloquial form the theory or methodology developed. Today George Steiner and Frank Kermode are among the few successful translators of technical or speculative ideas into an idiom familiar to the university don brought up "before the flood." Yet it might be said that they are superb reviewers rather than originative thinkers: their vocation is the Arnoldian diffusion of ideas and not a radical revision or extension of knowledge.

We seem to have reached an impasse. What alternatives are there to the conversational style if we grant its necessity as a *pedagogical* rather than *social* matter? This shift of perspective, however slight, indicates that such a style is useful rather than ideal, and no more "natural" than other kinds. We know, moreover, that pedagogical tools can become merely tools: "instrumental reason," as the Frankfurt School calls it, may affect language by homogenizing it. The critic who uses the conversational style because of its propriety may actually be doing a disservice to language. However difficult Blackmur, Burke, Heidegger, or Derrida may be, there is less entropy in them than in those who translate, with the best intentions, hazardous ideas or expressions into ordinary speech.

We have accepted difficulty in art, but in criticism there is still a wish to "solve the phenomena." The irony and intricacy of art were fully described, not resolved, by the New Criticism; nevertheless, a sort of pedagogical illusion arose that codified the language of explication and exempted it from the very analysis it so carefully applied to art. It is not surprising, therefore, to find that Paul de Man's *Blindness and Insight* (1971) is subtitled "Essays in the Rhetoric of Contemporary Criticism." In the aggressively modern thinkers he takes up, de Man is concerned to show traces of a "Hellenic" ideal of embodiment that continued to privilege categories of presence and plenitude.[10] What was passed over, according to de Man, was the "temporal labyrinth of interpretation" with its purely negative kind of totality (Sartre had coined the phrase *totalité détotalise*). But now, some twenty years later—these de Man essays were written in the 1960s—the situation has changed. It is no longer a pseudoclassical notion of *paideia* that needs scrutiny but a para-Marxist and utopian notion of pedagogy.

I mean by that a "dream of communication" that looks not only toward the transparence of the text or the undistorted transmission of messages from sender (writer) to receiver (reader) but also toward a social system that is supposed to create that language-possibility instead of merely enforcing it. Yet everything we have learned from politics or pragmatics has put the dream of communication in doubt. It is an ever-receding horizon like Hegel's state, where subject and substance, real and rational, concrete and universal, coincide. That end-state remains a *topos noetos,* a heaven in the form of a horizon, a glimpse of totality that converts every end into a means and so proves to be the moving principle it sought to arrest. Every style (stile) is also a Gate, to pun with Mather; but a style is at once open and closed.

Developments in criticism since about 1920 show that language can be analyzed more closely than was deemed possible, but not purified by prescriptions arising from the analysis. The intimate alliance of writing with "difference" we find in Derrida, and such typical assertions that "language is the *rupture* with totality itself . . . Primarily the caesura makes meaning emerge," are symptomatic of a cautious attitude toward both theory and the dream of communication. "The theory of the Text," Barthes has said, "can coincide only with a practise of writing." We are now as aware of our language condition as of the condition of our language.

Derrida is important also because he exposes the privilege accorded to voice in the form of the conversational style as it aspires to Pater's "inward dialogue." Derrida's deconstruction of course does not target a specific historical style but the dream of communication which that style, as the proprium of all styles, underwrites. The columns of *Glas* are cut by the arbitrary "justification" of the margins and the edginess of pages that interrupt, like a caesura, the words. *Glas* becomes a stylish reprisal against style—that word whose *y grecque* was hellenized into it during the Renaissance. Derrida rescues style from its confusion with Greek *stulos,* column, and so recovers its link both with stiletto, a pointed weapon, and *stiglus* or *stigma,* which emphasizes cutting, pointing, branding.

Style is in fact short for *vertere stilum,* or turning the incising stylus to its blunt side, which was used to erase the impression made on waxed tablets; writing stylishly is thus to erase what is written and write over it.[11] The term "verse" takes up the other half of that phrase, as in Wordsworth's "the turnings intricate of verse"—although the metaphor accrues overtones of the turning earth, the turning of the plow, and so forth. Style is what cannot stand still.

I want to add a few remarks on a philosopher's recent attempt to introduce the conversational style once more. This attempt is a valiant throw-back to the Age of Hume, when the conversationalists had won out, at least in prose. Yet philosophy remained under the imperative of not entirely forsaking the quest for a universal and immutable discourse. It honored the conversational mode for its virtues of social accommodation. It was philosophy for the salon. But subversively so, if we recall that it led to such strange conversation as *La philosophie dans le boudoir,* which put nature out of countenance. The contemporary post-Wittgensteinian attempt to revive the conversational ethos and to use it as a critique of foundationalist perspectives in philosophy is that of Richard Rorty.

Rorty's *Philosophy and the Mirror of Nature* (1978) examines three modern thinkers who have had an immense influence on both professional and non-professional philosophers. The careers of Wittgenstein, Heidegger, and Dewey are taken to be exemplary. Each began with a project to make philosophy "foundational," that is, to discover a basis for distinguishing truth from falsity, science from speculation, and verifiable representation from mere appearance. Each of the three breaks free of this project (labeled as "epistemological" and "Kantian") so that their work becomes therapeutic rather than constructive, or, as Rorty also likes to say, "edifying" (in the secular sense of the adjective, which conveys the German idea of *Bildung*) rather than systematic. Indeed they warn us against the very temptations acceded to in their earlier, scientific phase.

Rorty ends with a section entitled "Philosophy in the Conversation of Mankind," alluding to Michael Oakeshott's well-known "The Voice of Poetry in the Conversation of Mankind," published in *Rationalism and Politics* (1975). Rorty latches onto the idea of "conversation," which suggests an alternative to the rigorous terminology and analytic pretensions of epistemological inquiry. Contemporary issues in philosophy, he writes, are "events in a certain stage of conversation—a conversation which once knew nothing of these issues and may know nothing of them again." And he distinguishes between treating philosophy as a "voice in a conversation," on the one hand, and treating it "as a subject, a *Fach,* a field of professional inquiry," on the other. This denial of a special field to philosophers has an attractive Emersonian ring and of course brings Plato back as our most edifying thinker. Yet Rorty stops short of exalting even Plato, mainly because "the conversation Plato began has been enlarged by more voices than Plato would have dreamed possible."

This conclusion is surprisingly close to what recent literary critics have wished for. They take back from philosophy what is their own; they are tired of being treated as camp followers of this or that movement in philosophy. When the privilege accorded to science spills over into philosophy, literary culture is considered a dilution of ideas originated by stronger heads, a crude and subjective application of those ideas. Literary critics are then deemed parasitic not only vis-à-vis creative poem or novel but also vis-à-vis exact philosophy. Their very attempt to think independently, intensely, theoretically, is denounced—often by other literary critics. They are said to be big with the "arrogance of theory" and accused of emulating a discipline that should be kept out of the fair fields of literary study. "Whereas a generation ago," we read in an issue of *Novel,* "fine American literary journals would devote complete issues to a Hardy, Yeats, Faulkner, or G. M. Hopkins, current journals devote whole issues to French professors." The complainant goes on to charge that it was Northrop Frye's insistence on criticism as a systematic subject that allowed the "pod-people, so many of them dropouts from technical philosophy, or linguistics, or the half-science of sociology, into the fair fields of Anglo-American literary study."

However comforting it is to have a philosopher like Rorty on one's side, and to have him appreciate the recognitive as well as cognitive function of words, a hard question must be put. Can Rorty's position do more than redress the balance between philosophy and literary studies by demystifying the scientistic streak in modern thought? Can it disclose also something substantive in literary study itself, as the distance between philosophical discourse and literary commentary is lessened by viewing both as "conversation"?

The word "conversation" is a metaphor. It slides over the question of style. Should we really name something conversation when it is written? There is "dialogue" of course; but Rorty does not wish his concept to be dependent on a formal or stylized exchange between persons. Perhaps he would say that all writing is internalized conversation, a select polyphony of voices. The problem is not adequately treated from a literary point of view, nor entirely from a philosophical point of view. Is Rorty arguing that thinking is possible in idiomatic language without special terms or neologisms? Or is he saying that noncolloquial language also, even when it seems harsh and abstract, as so often in Kant and Husserl—in all such Teuton-Titans—is figurative or inventive despite itself? Does he not in fact circle around two claims: that technical terms (which diverge from so-called ordinary language) are necessary for rigorous thinking; but also that ordinary language—vernacular, conversational—is more inventive or figurative than the language of abstruse, systematic thought?

To these challenges there may not be a resolution. What is important is the recognition aroused in us by contemporary philosophers like Rorty and Stanley Cavell that no order of discourse or institutional way of writing has a monopoly on either rigor or invention. Philosophy remains a "conversation" with unexpected turns that cannot all be predicted, though they can later be integrated by subtle adjustments or shifts in the way we think.

At the very moment that Rorty seeks to deliver philosophy from pretentiousness (both metaphysical and epistemological), literary study is seeking to deliver itself from the ideal he propagates: *conversation.*

In fact, the gentility of literary dons and the avoidance of theory are on the increase, because science has invaded literary studies too, and the older ideal is becoming, in reaction, more defensive. Many otherwise intelligent critics turn into bulldogs of understatement as they try to preserve an elegance, however moldy, and a casualness, however false. Even the best British critics succumb. In Christopher Ricks at times, a word-chopping, ordinary-language type of analysis is directed against all who attempt theory, as if the big words were naughty words we had to be shamed out of, and as if any inventive, elaborated schematism were a sin against the English sentence.

What is appealing about Rorty's position is how little difference there is between him and Pater in *Plato and Platonism* (1893). Pater did not wish to distinguish sharply between dialogue and dialectic; the same holds today for Hans-Georg Gadamer (an "edifying" rather than a "systematic" philosopher, according to Rorty). Yet however attractive this Hellenic ideal may be, the results have often been dismaying. An Anglicized version of Greek *paideia* (tutorials pretending to be dialogue) has now become an unthinking attack on theory and is in danger of returning literary study to a supercilious kind of lexical inquisition that undoes everything we have learned from the large-hearted stylistics of a Leo Spitzer, an Erich Auerbach, and others.

Yet it is also clear that to take back from philosophy what is ours cannot mean to propose a method that applies specific philosophical ideas to literature. What does Heidegger really tell us about William Carlos Williams, or Paul Ricoeur about Yeats? Or Derrida about Melville? Such mixing it up may have its uses. We write by assimilating what we read: we could therefore read philosophy as a sister art; and philosophy in turn could consider literature as something better than time out for conversation. "Literature" here should be understood to include essays, and also larger scholarly structures in context: Spitzer in the context of German philology and the making of dictionaries, Auerbach in the context of Marxism and socioeconomic philosophies, Frye in that of anthropology and the ecumenical unifying of all fables, Empson in that of English, abdicating its political supremacy as a culture yet asserting itself as a "moral science" by constructing a new language-centered ethos.

As we pursue this institutional analysis, the thorny issue of whether we need an abnormal or special terminology (a metalanguage) becomes moot. Either we shall give up the idea that there is *one* correct way of talking about literature (in a terminology that is logical rather than literary), or we shall realize that all commentary is as much metacommentary (Fredric Jameson's term) as metacommentary or theory remains context-bound commentary. The real issue that will come forward is how skeptical we should be about *cultural translation*. Can the affairs of one culture (so dependent on a different text-milieu and not only on a different language) be understood by thinkers situated in another culture, even when the latter is a relative? (It may be easier to understand a culture when the distance is great enough to prevent easy rapprochement, or what translators call "false friends.") A creative skepticism about the crossover from culture to culture seems to me the right attitude. We need a "negative capability" that does not deny speculative criticism but engages with the highly mediated status of cultural and verbal facts. The basic question then is about the nature of understanding, and what sort of responsive style might articulate this understanding. Is a conversation between cultures possible? Or is such a conversation, as between persons, always mixed with imposition? Though we talk about "dialogue" and "keeping lines of communication open," it is hard to think of a conversation that is not forcefully interspersed with moments of appropriation and expropriation. The rules of language, the cunning of reasonableness, the sheer display of intellect or personality enter an unpredictable equation. The perfect English style, Orage said, will charm by its power; yet power and charm are precisely what the resistant thinker would like to keep separate.

NOTES

1. George Steiner, *In Bluebeard's Castle: Some Notes Towards the Redefinition of Culture* (New Haven: Yale University Press, 1971), p. 30
2. Stuart P. Sherman, *Americans* (Port Washington, N.Y.: Kennikut, 1922), pp. 4–5.
3. "'Where shall *we fressen?*' says Mr. Mencken. 'At the Loyal Independent Order of the

United Hiberno-German-Anti-English-Americans,' says Mr. Hackett. 'All the New Critics will be there.' "

4. Yet C. J. Rawson shows how precarious the "friendship style" was. Swift, he says, "repudiates that intimacy between author and reader which Sterne and Richardson celebrate," even as he calls for " 'a Parity and strict correspondence of Idea's between Reader and the Author.' " He fears that familiarity may breed contempt or lead to garrulous self-revelations. "Swift, as much as Sterne, is reaching out to the reader, and the alienation I spoke of does not in fact eliminate intimacy, though it destroys 'friendship.' There is something in Swift's relation with his reader that can be described approximately in terms of the edgy intimacy of a personal quarrel that does not quite come out in the open . . . It is attacking play." See *Gulliver and the Gentle Reader: Studies in Swift and Our Time* (London: Routledge & Kegan Paul, 1973), chap. 1. For a recent effort to depict the relation between reader and writer as—potentially, and not always easily—a friendship, see Wayne Booth, *The Company We Keep: An Ethics of Fiction* (Los Angeles: University of California Press, 1988). Also, for an important analysis of the primacy of conversation as a hermeneutic *and* religious model ("There is no intellectual, cultural, political, or religious tradition of interpretation that does not ultimately live by the quality of its conversation"), see David Tracy, *Plurality and Ambiguity: Hermeneutics, Religion, Hope* (San Francisco: Harper and Row, 1989). Tracy's book also considers modern and postmodern theories and forces that *interrupt* conversation.
5. I am told by Wallace Martin, who has excerpted Orage's remarks on style in *Orage as Critic* (London: Routledge & Kegan Paul, 1974), that when this comment was made, *The New Age* was in financial trouble and Orage needed chatty reportage from Read to increase the popular appeal of a weekly devoted to serious literary and political discussion. Orage's remarks, therefore, are more symptomatic of English taste than of Orage. Yet though Orage dreamed of a "fearless English prose," "written in the vernacular with all its strength and directness," he always qualified that: "but with grace added unto it." His statement, similarly, that in a "pure style," the writer's "idiosyncracies, his class, his education, his reading should all be kept out of sight" also betrays the decorum of the *honnête homme*. Yet compared with what was going on in the *Times Literary Supplement*—"the deadliest mouse in the world of journalism," according to Orage—he was indeed a lively presence. When the *TLS* opined, "The English Plato is still to be," Orage countered with: "I shall withdraw Plato from the position of model, in which I put him. Plato, it is evident, is likely to be abused; without intending it, his mood, translated into English, appears to be compatible only with luxurious ease; he is read by modern Epicureans. And I shall put in Plato's place Demosthenes, the model of Swift, the greatest English writer the world has yet seen" (*Orage as Critic*, pp. 194–196).
6. In a Victorian reaction against the German study of language, which had placed Sanskrit alongside Greek and Latin and suggested their Indo-European origin, one English scholar declared: "Englishmen are too practical to study a language very philosophically." Quoted by Linda Dowling, "Victorian Oxford and the Science of Language," *PMLA* 97 (1982): 165.
7. If Ricoeur is right, we would have to rethink the emancipation of the university from seminary and divinity school. "To preach," he has written, "is not to capitulate before

the believable and the unbelievable of modern man, but to struggle with the presuppositions of this culture, in order to restore this *interval of interrogation* in which the question can have meaning." And, "All that reestablishes the question of humanity taken as a whole, as a totality, has a value of preunderstanding for preaching." Marxism and religion (and, to a degree, psychoanalysis) are for Ricoeur, as they were for Benjamin, the giant forms to be confronted, not in order to be reconciled but to discover "a reading of the great forces which regulate our economic life, our political life, and our cultural life" ("The Language of Faith" (1973), in *The Philosophy of Paul Ricoeur,* ed. Charles E. Reagan and David Stewart [Boston: Beacon, 1978]). On the issue of totality see also Geoffrey H. Hartman, "The New Wilderness: Critics as Connoisseurs of Chaos" in *Innovation/Renovation,* ed. Ihab Hassan and Sally Hassan (Madison: University of Wisconsin Press, 1983), now in *Easy Pieces* (New York: Columbia University Press, 1985).

8. "It is two thousand and hundreds of years since, that the theory was proposed that thought is conversation with oneself," Eliot writes similarly in his essay of 1931 on Charles Whibley, which contains important reflections on the conversational style. Of Eliot himself, Blackmur remarked that "his method has been conversational, for he begs off both the talent and the bent for abstract thought." Henry Fielding's "Essay on Conversation," like Swift's "Hints Towards an Essay on Conversation," summarizes toward the midpoint of the eighteenth century the blend of moral, social, and aesthetic motives that go into this ideal. Fielding writes that "the pleasure of conversation must arise from the discourse being on subjects levelled to the capacity of the whole company; from being on such in which every person is equally interested; from everyone's being admitted to his share in the discourse; and lastly, from carefully avoiding all noise, violence, and impetuosity." Erich Auerbach illustrates vividly the rise of this ideal in seventeenth-century France (though there are of course adumbrations in Italian circles of the sixteenth century) through an examination of the phrases "le public" and "la cour et la ville." Hume remarks in "Of Civil Liberty" that "in common life, [the French] have, in a great measure, perfected that art, the most useful and agreeable of any, *l'Art de Vivre,* the art of society and conversation." In the same essay Swift is identified as the first British writer of "polite prose."
9. George Snell is quoted in R. F. Jones, *The Triumph of the English Language* (Stanford, Calif: Stanford University Press, 1953), p. 229. The conversational style never took in the United States, at least not as fixed by eighteenth-century English usage (epistolary rather than spoken and barely concealing its artfulness). There is most of the time a deliberate swerving from elegance, producing the effect of an undertow of colloquialism, or of some kind of slang (real or imaginary). See the form of Blackmur's comment on Eliot, note 8, or the assimilative and proverbial style of Kenneth Burke.
10. De Man is thinking of Hellenism as interpreted in the Winckelmann-Schiller-Hegel tradition, which still reaches into Pater's thought (see the essay on Winckelmann in *Studies in the Renaissance*). He does not oppose Hebraism to Hellenism but suggests, with Hölderlin and Heidegger, a more radical "Greek" attitude, which he refuses to confine within a historicist or periodizing frame. Yet the religious shadows cast by this sort of inquiry cannot be avoided. American criticism, on the whole, is "incarnationist," as de Man recognizes; and it often associates this bias with Christian doctrine. Similarly,

then, contemporary anti- or nonincarnationist views would move toward the pole of Hebraism, whether or not influenced by canonical texts from that sphere. Consult, e.g., Maurice Blanchot's "Être Juif" in *L'Entretien infini* (Paris: Gallimard, 1969) or "L'Interruption" in *L'Amitié* (Paris: Gallimard, 1971); and generally Edmond Jabès, who can aver, "Writing is a revolutionary act, a scrupulously Jewish act, for it consists in taking up the pen in that place where God withdrew Himself from his words; it consists indefinitely in pursuing a utopian work in the manner of God who was the Totality of the Text of which nothing subsists." The withdrawal alluded to is a kabbalistic notation also important for Harold Bloom. The English poet Traherne opposes "an easy Stile drawn from a native vein" to "*Zamzummin* words."

11. The etymology is well known. See F. L. Lucas's fine book *Style* (London: Cassell, 1955), pp. 15–16, which quotes the *OED.*

Understanding Criticism

What difference does reading make? Is it perhaps, like traveling, a fool's paradise? "We owe to our first journeys," writes Emerson, "the discovery that place is nothing. At home I dream that at Naples, at Rome, I can be intoxicated with beauty, and lose my sadness. I pack my trunk, embrace my friends, embark on the sea, and at last wake up in Naples, and there beside me is the stern Fact, the sad Self, unrelenting, identical, that I fled from. I seek the Vatican, and the palaces. I affect to be intoxicated with sights and suggestions, but I am not intoxicated. My giant goes with me wherever I go."

Emerson is urging us to self-reliance; yet the more we read him, the more *he* is the giant, seductive or overwhelming, who stands in the way of a liberation he commends. There is no getting around him: we must think him through, allow him to invade our prose.

The difference that reading makes is, most generally, writing. The thinking through, the "working through" (the metaphor of work applied to psychic process being Freudian, yet appropriate in this context) is hard to imagine without writing. Certain poets, like

Mallarmé, even seek a type of writing that would end reading as tourism or as merely a reflection on a prior and exotic fact.

The division of literary activity into writers and readers, though it may appear to be commonsensical, is neither fortunate nor absolute. It is crass to think of two specialties, one called reading and one writing, and then to view criticism as a particularly specialized type of reading which uses writing as an "incidental" aid. Lately, therefore, forms of critical commentary have emerged that challenge the dichotomy of reading and writing. Besides the involutions of Nabokov's *Pale Fire* (1962) and the essays of Borges, there are such experiments as Norman O. Brown's *Closing Time* (1973), Harold Bloom's *Anxiety of Influence* (1973), Maurice Blanchot's *Le pas au-delà* (1973), Jacques Derrida's *Glas* (1974), and Roland Barthes's *Lover's Discourse* (1977). They are literary texts in their own right as well as commentary. They belong to the realm of "letters" rather than to purely "critical" writing, and they make us realize that we have narrowed the concept of literature.

Even when its form is less spectacular, such criticism puts a demand on the reader that may cause perplexity and resentment. For it does not see itself as subordinated in any simple way to the books on which it comments. It can be pedagogic, of course, but it is free *not* to be so. It is aware that in philosophy there is less of a distinction between primary and secondary literature: ask a philosopher what he does and he will answer "philosophy." It could be argued, in the same spirit, that what a literary critic does is literature.

Yet the reader-critic's claim to parity is continually chastened by the fact that we remain addicted to reading, to traveling through those "realms of gold" in the hope of being instructed and surprised. Our supposed self-reliance is undermined by a famous Miltonic axiom, Satan's boast to the angels in *Paradise Lost* (4.830): "Not to know mee argues yourselves unknown." That is the seductive boast of every book. We are tempted to enter an unknown or forbidden realm.

The spectacle of the critic's mind disoriented, bewildered, caught in some "wild surmise" about the text and struggling to adjust—is not that one of the interests critical writing has for us? In more casual acts of reading, this bewilderment can be muted, for there is always the hint of a resolution further on, or an enticement to enter for its own sake the author's world. However, in *containing* this bewilderment, formal critical commentary is not very different from fiction itself. Fiction also carries within it a hermeneutic perplexity: there is shifting of focus, or a changeable perspective, or a Jamesian effort to discern the "felt meaning." It is not Dr. Johnson alone who has his trouble with *King Lear:* on reading the exchange between Lear and a Gloucester whose eyes have been put out—

LEAR. Your eyes are in a heavy case, your purse in a light; yet you see how this world goes.
GLOUCESTER. I see it feelingly.

—we can only echo Gloucester's own words in accepting so appalling a mixture of pathos and pun.

The critic, then, is one who makes us formally aware of the bewildering character of fiction. Books are our second Fall, the reenactment of a seduction that is also a coming to knowledge. The innermost hope they inspire may be the one Heinrich von Kleist expressed: only by eating a second time of the tree of knowledge will we regain paradise.

Consider, in this light, Yeats's "Leda and the Swan."

A sudden blow: the great wings beating still
Above the staggering girl, her thighs caressed
By the dark webs, her nape caught in his bill,
He holds her helpless breast upon his breast.

How can those terrified vague fingers push
The feathered glory from her loosening thighs?
And how can body, laid in that white rush,
But feel the strange heart beating where it lies?

A shudder in the loins engenders there
The broken wall, the burning roof and tower
And Agamemnon dead.—
Being so caught up,
So mastered by the brute blood of the air,
Did she put on his knowledge with his power
Before the indifferent beak could let her drop?

It comes like a voice from nowhere, catching us too offguard. "A sudden blow: the great wings beating still . . . ." Where got Yeats that truth? Part of the magic to be resisted is the poet's imperious assumption of a visionary mode, as if it were self-justifying. His exotic and erotic subject matter displaces the question of authority. For Yeats may be a voyeur rather than a visionary: we do not know where he is standing or how ancient his eyes are, or if they glitter. Though we grant him, provisionally, the authority of his poem, we note that his empathy runs parallel to Leda's and focuses on the unspoken promise of an initiatory or "strange" knowledge—in fact, on the first temptation Genesis spells out: "Ye shall be as gods, knowing good and evil." Leda, surprised by the swan-god, cannot but "feel the strange heart beating where it lies."

So fiction imposes on us, by a subtle or blatant seduction. We are always surprised or running to catch up or wishing to be more fully in its coils. This may explain why the detective novel, with its mock catharsis of false leads and inconclusive speculations, is a favorite of intellectual readers. Literary commentary is comparable to the detective novel: confronted by a bewildering text, it acts out a solution, trying various defenses, various interpretations, then pretending it has come to an authoritative stance—when in truth it has simply purged itself of complexities never fully mastered.

Seduction, then, in fiction or life, seems to contain the promise of mastery or, paradoxically, of joining oneself to an overwhelming intent even at the cost of being subdued. In more innocent language seduction is called persuasion; and rhetoric, or the art of persuasion, has always been criticized by competing arts, such as logic and dialectic, which assert a higher truth without being less vulnerable to the charge of seeking a powerful epiphany, an all-clarifying solution. Rhetoric, in any case, is to language what science is to the language of nature—a technique that can be mastered, perhaps for the purpose of further mastery. Yet it is also true that the verbal acuities of poetry or fiction challenge the rhetoric they use, as in the subtle, questioning progress of Yeats's poem. Rhetoric is the will doing the work of imagination, Yeats said.

At first we feel mainly the poet's rhetoric, his power in depicting an action that has power as its very subject. An episode that spans centuries is condensed in the representational space of a sonnet. The mimetic faculty is stirred by rhythmic effects (the additional beat in "great wings beating still," the caesural pause between "terrified" and "vague"), while inner bonding through repetition and alliteration ("beating . . . beating," "*He* *h*olds *h*er *h*elpless . . . ") tightens Yeats's verse as if to prevent *its* rupture. The energy of the event seems to produce its own enargeia, as rhetoricians call the picturing potential of words. The eyes are led along an axis that is sharper than ordinary sight: does "there" in "A shudder in the loins engenders there" refer to the place of vision as well as conception, to what is right *there* before the poet's eyes? He sees into the loins as into the heart. "Wisdom begins in images," Yeats remarked; rhetorical skill, the formal magic that re-creates Leda, has made an image come alive.

Yet rhetoric in the service of mimesis, rhetoric as imaging power, is far from being *imitative* in the sense of reflecting a preexistent reality. Mimesis becomes poesis, imitation becomes making, by giving form and pressure to a presumed reality, to "Leda." The traditional theme, by being repeated, is endowed with a past that may never have been present. Leda is not even named within the poem; and the strongest images in the poem are not images at all but periphrases, like "feathered glory" and "brute blood of the air." These non-naming figures have the structure of riddles as well as of descriptions. Even the images in lines 10–12, stark metonymies, are a periphrastic riddle or charade for "The Destruction of Troy."

The last of these non-naming figures, "brute blood of the air," may be the most intriguing. Viewed in itself, detached from the representational frame of Yeats's lyric, it conveys a sense of internal generation, almost self-generation—something engendered from what is barely seen or grasped, that does not recall natural process so much as supernatural agency, not formation but transformation. It evokes the immanence of the visible in the invisible, an absence that can turn into a devastating presence. We are again projected beyond natural sight: air, as in omens, thickens, becomes concrete, theriomorphic, auguring; and to air there corresponds the airy womb of imagination, which also thickens here into an ominous historical projection, a catastrophe-creation of which Leda is but the legendary medium.

Less an image, then, than a phantasm is represented. More precisely: is it an image, or is it a phantasm? By phantasm I mean an image with hallucinatory effect: "out of nothing it came" (see Yeats's "Fragments"). It cannot be explained or grounded by the coordinates of ordinary perception, by stable space-time categories. Does the poem revive a classic myth whose psychic truth is being honored ("to ground mythology in the earth" is one of Yeats's programmatic statements) or does it express a phantasm which that myth holds fast and stabilizes, so that mind can be mind and question it? Second quatrain and last tercet are questioning in form: one function of this form is to hold and elaborate what is happening.

I don't think I exaggerate the image/phantasm indeterminacy. Until we come to the one proper name, Agamemnon, we are kept in the aura of an action whose reference is not fixed. Though a famous legend is presupposed, the poem effects a displacement from "Leda" and "Troy" to a non-proper, that is, unlocalized event that cannot be given a name or one name. The situating reference to "Agamemnon," the locking up of the action into the known if legendary context, is just that, a locking up; it does not resolve the indeterminacy; we continue to feel the imaginary within the reference myth, something that exceeds the latter like a riddle its solution, or periphrasis and metaphor the undisplaced word. As "Agamemnon" hovers between sonant matter and meaning, so the myth between phantasm and legend-laden image.

We cannot, in short, neglect the airy pretension of a poem that fills the vacancy of prehistory with a paradigmatic primal scene. What space or time are we in? Is the poet standing in his own mind? Or in the third heaven of a domestic séance? Is what he communicates a vision or the variant of a traditional theme or his re-creation of a particular painting on that theme? Is he stationing a phantasm or framing something that even if it is an image is so nuclear in lines 10–12 that it could be detached from the poem and seen as Greek epigram or sybilline utterance?

These questions add up to a *hermeneutic perplexity.* Yeats's rhetorical skill has led us beyond or beneath firm knowledge, and we become unsure of the poem's real frame of reference. Who is (the) "Being so caught up"? Correlatively, we become unsure of the poet's authority: is he seer or subjective thinker or superstitious crank? It may be, of course, that it is we who think *against* the poem, who wonder why we were willing to suspend our disbelief and to accept this fiction. We could then follow our own suspensive or "negative" thinking, make it part of the subject matter. But in any significant act of reading, there must be (1) a text that steals our consent, and (2) a question about the text's value at a very basic level: Are we in the presence of a forged or an authentic experience?

There is an alternative to this last question, but it leads to a further uncertainty. For to raise the question of authenticity could be to mistake the mode-of-being of poetry—to make a category mistake about it—by seeing poetry as potentially a revelation, a disclosure of previously unapprehended truth. Should not the very concept of fiction, and of the poet as image-maker, avert that perspective with the help precisely of a poet like Yeats, who is a maker of images and has no further claim? But what are images, then, and fictive images in particular?

Philosophy from Husserl to Bachelard and Merleau-Ponty, and theoretically oriented reflection on art from I. A. Richards and John Dewey to Wolfgang Iser and Murray Krieger, have worked closely with the assumption that aesthetic experience is related to perception (or perceptibility, *Anschauung,* the sighting of insight); further, that this relation is what is expressed by the centrality the word "image" has won. The "image" is the point where the received and the productive meet. Our ideational response to the work of art tends to analyze itself in terms that favor the image. Even without seeking to explain this turn of events, we would find it hard to give up the by now historical liaison between image and formal values in art or between image and any model poetics—despite the counterthrust of semiotic theory and deconstructionist meditation. Perceptibility—that all things can be made as perceptible as the eye suggests—may itself be the great *classic* phantasm, the Mediterranean fantasy, continued even by Romantic or Modernist artists who are aware that the image is also a resonance, a musical as well as visual phenomenon:

> Ces nymphes, je les veux perpétuer.
> Si clair
> Leur incarnat léger . . . [1]

What images are, then, is a question that involves the make-up of our minds, or at least of our terms, our very language.

I have suggested that the image of Yeats's poem serves to stabilize a phantasm or to frame a fantasy. It is tempting to guess at an equation: the more image, the more fantasy. The phantasmic material is brought into a discourse it keeps motivating and unsettling. I have not identified, however, the phantasm or the fantasy; to do so would be to intrude a frame of reference of my own. I am not unwilling as critic or interpreter to do this: to suggest, for example, that the swan-god fantasy potentiates feelings of touch that at once stimulate and unrealize the eyes. A taboo may be breached that involves the relation we have to our own body-image, or the way we organize its capacities into a hierarchy of senses, higher and lower, animal, human, divine. Ordinarily I would have no choice but to develop the poem in this manner. All the more so if the taking-by-surprise so affectively rendered here is not simply a man's version of a woman's presumed desire for "divine rape" but goes behind that doubtful cliché to the question of how ideas of sight exceed sight and elicit monsters or masques. For

1. Mallarmé, "L'après-midi d'un faune." We have no word corresponding to "image" that would express the ideational surge of internal *sound* or *speech.* I sometimes use "soundshape" (Elizabeth Sewell) or "image of voice" (Horace's periphrasis for echo); and "resonance" can be called on to modify "reflection." Poetics has barely begun to struggle with this issue, to take back its own from music, and to bring "clarity" into conjunction with "indeterminacy" via a more sensitive, more poetically centered, theory of meaning. George Steiner sees this challenge in historical terms: he has remarkable comments on the surfacing of inner speech between the seventeenth century and the present. Mallarmé's poetry, he suggests, or the subtle density of diction in his period, still managed to keep the "membrane between inner and outer speech" intact, while allowing the chiaroscuro of self-colloquy to filter through. That membrane is then pierced by psychoanalysis and other soundings. See "A Remark on Language and Psychoanalysis" and "The Distribution of Discourse" in *On Difficulty and Other Essays.*

the moment, however, I want to turn from a particular poem and explore critical thinking generally.

Critical thinking respects heterogeneity. Like good scholarship it keeps in mind the peculiarity of strangeness of what is studied. By "keeping in mind" I mean it does not make art stranger or less strange than it is. But what is *strange* about art? The word may point to the phantasm in the image. It may also point to historical otherness, to assumptions or conventions we have difficulty appreciating. Are we, however, talking about the strange or the other, or both? Strangeness involves a sense that the strange is really the familiar, estranged; otherness (alterity) precludes any assumption about this matter, or it demands of understanding an extraordinary, even self-altering, effort. Something more than empathy; something that carries empathy beyond itself to the point where, as Rimbaud declared, "I is an other."

In biblical hermeneutics there was often a conflict between regarding Scripture as *analogical,* or written in the language of men, accommodated to human understanding, and regarding it as *anagogical,* or taking the mind out of itself, inspiring it until it appeared "beside itself." The question is whether we must insist on the one or the other: on the resolvable strangeness or the unresolvable otherness. Could we not say there must be a willingness to receive figurative language? To receive is not to accept; between these, as between active and passive, critical thinking takes place, makes its place. We cannot solve, a priori, the issue of strange *or* other; we can only deal with it in the mode of "resonance" that writing is. We rewrite the figure, in commentary or fiction, we elaborate it in a revisionary way.

That writing is a calculus that jealously broods on strange figures, on imaginative otherness, has been made clear by poets and artists rather than by the critics. The latter are scared to do anything except convert as quickly as possible the imaginative into a mode of the ordinary—where the ordinary can be the historically unfamiliar familiarized. But a poem like "Leda and the Swan" is not, or not only, a virtuoso staging of ancient myth, a re-presentation that gives it verisimilitude. Yeats sustains or fulfills a figure: myth is used to disclose the shape of history, and history (as we shall see) the truth of myth. Between Yeats's version and the received myth a *typological* relation forms itself. Even though the figures can be given their ancient names (Agamemnon, and so on) they stand in a complex *contemporaneity* to the poet.

This remains true even when the question of time is not raised as dramatically as in "Leda and the Swan." Where there is imaginative impact, and where that impact is worked out in art, a hermeneutic patience appears that can circumvent the desire for advent—or event—but cannot ignore it. In Yeats that patience is a contrary state of soul achieved despite the apocalyptic pressure of an era—his own time—with which he identifies. To abide or not abide one's time, that is the question. Wordsworth too is under pressure, but the way he broods on "a sudden blow" is quite different. However disparate the experiences depicted in "Leda and the Swan" and "I Wandered Lonely as a Cloud," they deal with strong and sudden images. Wordsworth's poem is well known, but I quote it for convenience.

I wandered lonely as a cloud
That floats on high o'er vales and hills,
When all at once I saw a crowd,
A host, of golden daffodils;
Beside the lake, beneath the trees,
Fluttering and dancing in the breeze.

Continuous as the stars that shine
And twinkle on the milky way,
They stretched in never-ending line
Along the margin of a bay:
Ten thousand saw I at a glance,
Tossing their heads in sprightly dance.

The waves beside them danced; but they
Out-did the sparkling waves in glee:
A poet could not but be gay,
In such a jocund company:
I gazed—and gazed—but little thought
What wealth the show to me had brought:

For oft, when on my couch I lie
In vacant or in pensive mood,
They flash upon that inward eye
Which is the bliss of solitude;
And then my heart with pleasure fills,
And dances with the daffodils.

Why did Wordsworth refuse to classify "I Wandered Lonely as a Cloud," with its picture of daffodils seen "all at once," as a "Poem of the Imagination"? Because, he said, the impact of the daffodils on his "ocular spectrum" had been too strong. His lyric moves in two directions, therefore: it respects the near-hallucinatory effect of daffodils that flash even on his inner eye long after they were seen (this reintroduces the coordinate of time), and it shows the receptive mind trying to regain the initiative, to be imaginative vis-à-vis a psychedelic image.

An instinctive phenomenologist, Wordsworth analyzed the insidious role of accident or surprise in stimulating the imagination. The problem as he saw it, was one of separating essential from contingent in such incidents, and to arrive at a view of imagination that would deliver it from novelty or sensationalism—from the accusation that it depended on these quasi-literary drugs, on the need for an induced strangeness. Taken by surprise, the mind might react with superstitious fantasies, or learn to forestall them with trivialized ideas of the supernatural, like the personified spirits in the inane and gaudy poetry around the poet, or the frantic marvels of the gothic novel. The true strangeness of nature should be honored, as childhood had seeded it; images and sounds had their own life, their own agency, even if their impact on the mind derived also from the mind. For Wordsworth insisted that the "images" were not all on the side of nature; mind always blended with nature, even when the imagination was involuntarily aroused; but this curious balance or harmony of image and idea—this "indeterminacy" in the act of imaginative perception—was precarious because the image tended to become a phantasm and so overbalance mind.

The pressure on mind or imagination, then, came from supernatural fantasies. Yet these did not work in a vacuum. Wordsworth was one of the first to talk of sensory shock in relation to the Industrial Revolution: the crowding into cities of people and experiences, the explosion of "news" in the Napoleonic era, that kind of daily assault on the senses. The natural rhythms, he felt, were faltering, eroding; life in rural nature was becoming a memory, and it could not buffer consciousness as before. The health of the pressured mind depended, therefore, on preventing an alliance of supernatural fantasies with political fears and the siege of daily events. New images had to be liberated from within, or old ones cleansed and renewed; and we can watch this happening in another typical poem, "Resolution and Independence," where there is also a sudden appearance: an old leech-gatherer (leeches were used for medicinal blood letting) surprises the poet in a desolate region on the border between England and Scotland. Though the scene is totally realistic, and there is ultimately no question that the old man is of flesh and blood (even if meagerly, almost skeletally so), the poet's mind under the pressure of the strange becomes strange to itself, and the line between imagination and reality begins to waver. The image is also the phantasm. To be surprised by daffodils or by the apparition of this Ancient of Days is curiously similar: behind the startlement lurks a potential phantasm. Strange fits of passion had he known.

These fits are not innocent, even if associated by Wordsworth with "wise passiveness." They are marks of the reception of otherness, but they are equally signs of an exhausting mental struggle ending in a nearly vacant or inert state of being. Wordsworth's complacency is, at times, not far from Dr. Johnson's classicism: "Wonder is novelty impinging on ignorance." There is nothing new under the sun, and the principle of uniformity consolidates this disenchantment in the name of Nature or Reason. Or the struggle ends in too thorough an enchantment, an escape from the vacillation that enthusiasm brings. Sunk too deep or mounted too high, the soul finds its permanent support within, as in mysticism, psychosis, or the continuous allegory of gnostic fantasy. From so absent-minded a mode of being one can expect at most "a flash of mild surprise."

Let me return a moment to Wordsworth's "Resolution and Independence." It depicts as significant a temptation as "Leda and the Swan." Is this old leech-gatherer, met by chance, a decrepit vagabond, or is he an omen, a more-than-natural intimation of a more-than-natural way of sustaining one's life? May he be a kind of phantom: image and *image of voice* working so strangely on the poet that he loses his bearing and sees heaven in a leech-gatherer and infinity in a handful of leeches?

We are certainly close to something crazy in this poem, as Wordsworth's laughter, at the end, suggests: "I could have laughed myself to scorn to find / In that decrepit man so firm a mind." Wordsworth interprets his laughter morally and invents an exit—a Chaucerian "sentence"—to a perplexity which really has no end. The situation is intrinsically a hermeneutic one and focuses on Wordsworth's awareness of his quirky imagination, one that acts up with transformative zeal. The poet's choice lies, essentially, between a preemptive gnosticism that sees not only a tale but an allegory in everything, and so must dull the sharpness of accidents, even of life in time itself; and a religious mania that exults in accidents and in the cathectic power of imagination to view them as magnalia rather than trivia. A third choice is the one actually made, but it is coincident with *timing:* the poem's rhythm, a resonant writing-thinking, a revisionary elaboration that does not end or begin, except formally.

The strangeness of fiction, then, does not issue from its objective character, so that when that object-quality is carefully honored by explication the fiction is understood. On the contrary, objectification may be a way of neutralizing the experience, by boxing it, labeling it *A Vision,* and so forgetting the question of, for example, where Yeats is speaking from, and by what authority. It credits the rhetorical character of the enterprise too much or accepts the figurative language too readily. Hermeneutics is bypassed.

Hermeneutics has always inquired into the scandal of figurative language, when that was extraordinary or transgressive. Maimonides devotes an entire book to explaining the anthropomorphisms in the Hebrew Bible. Christ's language is often a stumbling block, and even today some of his parables appear harsh or obscure. The older hermeneutics, however, tended to be incorporative or reconciling, like Donne's "spider love that transubstantiates all." The Bible and Greek culture, a faith and a philosophy, differing reports of a significant event (as in the case of the Gospels or contradictory traditions), even legends whose colorful features seemed to mask a basic structure: these might be brought into harmony with each other and become fables of identity. German idealism in its major phase, particularly the "identity philosophy" of Schelling, extended this reconciling perspective over the entire sphere of human knowledge, secular and sacred.

Criticism, however, a newer kind of hermeneutics, "affirms" the power of negative thinking.[2] How to define negative thinking, without converting it into a positivistic and dogmatic instrument, is of course very problematic. Not only a philosophy like that of Hegel, whose dialectic is a mode of negative thinking, struggles with this question: Keats's "negative capability" and Wallace Stevens's wish to ablute or withhold the name of the sun—to see it "in the difficulty of what it is to be"—are instances of a parallel concern.

Criticism as a kind of hermeneutics is disconcerting; like logic, but without the latter's motive of absolute internal consistency, it reveals contradictions and

2. For one influential view of negative thinking, see Herbert Marcuse, especially *Reason and Revolution* (1941) and "Note on Dialectic," prefaced to the 1960 reissue. Also, Theodor Adorno, equally dependent on but less appreciative of Hegel, whose *Negative Dialectic* (1966) rejects any thinking about history that results in more than an "ever-new Mene Tekel, residing in the smallest things, in debris hewn by decay itself." Hegel's most famous statement on negative thinking is in the preface to *Phenomenology of Spirit,* which speaks of "the seriousness, the suffering, the patience and the labor of the Negative." The presence of Sartre as writer and philosopher was, until recently, the dominant one in England and America: his dialectic too can be characterized as counteraffirmative and, while remaining deeply engaged with Hegel, is used to purge false totalizations from art and history. The Anglo-American tradition approaches "understanding" from the obverse side of "belief" or "provisional assent": see, for example, Eliot's essay on Dante (1929), or such recent statements as Wayne Booth's *Modern Dogma and the Rhetoric of Assent.*

equivocations, and so makes fiction interpretable by making it less readable. The fluency of the reader is affected by a kind of stutter: the critic's response becomes deliberately hesitant. It is as if we could not tell in advance where a writer's rhetoric might undermine itself or where the reader might be trapped into perplexity. For the older hermeneutics the choice was clear: Yeats's supernaturalism would be blasphemous, competitive with a dominant faith, and so beneath interpretation; or it would be harmonized with that faith and absorbed. The heterogeneity of poem or original text by no means disappears in the older hermeneutics, but it appears only by way of the daring interpretation that is startling and even liberating in its very drive for harmony. Everyone knows the many marvelous acts of exegesis that try to launder the Song of Songs, that see it as a pious poem.

Modern critical exegesis faces a different situation. It must both suspend its disbelief in the scandalous figure and refuse to accept this figure as mere machinery, as only "poetic." It is not sufficient to resolve this dilemma by claiming that no one really takes Yeats's supernatural theme in a literal way. There it is, after all. How are we to think of it? Do we try to resolve "Leda and the Swan" into an "allegory" or a "symbol" or even a "philosophy of symbols"? But that would simply defer the entire question of how this visionary kind of writing can survive: perhaps *the* question when it comes to understanding poetry.

Some might say, at this point, that the survival of visionary or extravagant fictional modes—of nonrealism in fiction—is a matter for time to decide in conjunction with literature as an institution. But this is to forget how often the visionary strain is kindled by scholarship itself: by revivals that include the more learned critics. These "extraliterary" forces are part of the institution of literature. The recovery of pagan forms of rhetoric and myth in the Renaissance, the revival of Celtic and Northern mythology in the eighteenth and nineteenth centuries, the more recent explosion of interest in the matter of Araby and Polynesia, even the continuing presence of Classical themes and figures—these are unthinkable without the devoted, worried, ingenious researches and reconstructions of a host of scholars and critics.

The commentary has entered the text, Sainte-Beuve remarked of Ballanche, whose *Orphée,* a prose epic, was an imaginative rehearsal of Vico's philological speculations on Roman law and literature. Philology is made flesh and provides a new art form as well as a new science. It is hard to conceive of Joyce's later work without Vico. It is hard, also, to consider twentieth-century modernism without recognizing the importance of the Cambridge Anthropologists (Frazer,

Harrison, Murray, etc.), who inaugurated a new revival of the Classics on a broader—an Orientalist and anthropological—base. Nietzsche too started as classicist and philologist. Picasso tells us that the old Musée de l'Homme in Paris (Trocadéro), its collection of masks and fetishes, played a crucial role in his own development and so in that of modern painting and sculpture. As if reading were inevitably a journeying east—and often a resistance to that drift—the Leda phantasm or similar "dark italics" (Wallace Stevens) have underwritten all significant movements of our time, both in art and philology. Leda—or Sheba, Edda, Roma, Gradiva, Orienda—is also part of the hoard of scholarship.

Understanding Art and Understanding Criticism are, even historically considered, cognate activities. Yet while poets and novelists often borrow from each other and seem to communicate across national lines, critics and scholars find it much harder to do the same. The Yeats scholar may skirmish with the Wordsworth scholar, but only the rankest amateur will venture a triangulation of these major writers with Hölderlin. The survival of "supernatural song"—or the difficulty of interpreting visionary trends and their modern persistence—has been central to German hermeneutic scholarship, yet in the Anglo-American domain it all continues to be explained by the term "secularization," which is not reflected on (as in Max Weber) but accepted as an explanatory concept. Nothing is involved save an admirable technical achievement, a calm transfer of properties from one area (the supernatural) to another (the natural).

There is, of course, some truth to this honoring of technique. Technique is a modern and demystified form of magic. In Yeats, as in Goethe, art itself is the magic: it naturalizes mystery by creating so clear an image of it. Yeats's poem grounds an exotic mythology in common psychic experience: the seduction of strangeness and our childish yet persistent interest in the instant of conception. Both types of experience, of course, haunt us because they master or determine us. An active imagination must strike back, repeatedly, at this passivity. The swan-god's supernatural nature encourages in us thoughts of *our* natural supernature.

Yet only the former, supernatural nature, is evident in "Leda and the Swan." While the god is both swan and god, Leda remains Leda. Her humanity is problematized, not redeemed or exalted. Though the assault of the divine on human consciousness is less disturbing here than in other lyrics by Yeats—the bewilderment is Leda's rather than explicitly the poet's—the scene Yeats now projects, now meditates on, builds up masterfully a contrast between mastery and mystery, divine power and human knowledge. "Did she [Leda] put on his knowledge with his power . . . ?"

Through this question Yeats tries to imagine Leda as a person rather than as a medium (persona) through which the god acts. The question implies a further question: if Leda, knowing what the god knows, seeing what the god sees, still has a face, how do we envisage it? Is it gay, mad, or transfigured: Does it "see" in the ordinary sense of the word? The idea insinuated is the insufferable one of a human being having to foresee all that consequence. The sudden blow entails an "elision of the richly human middle term" (Thomas Whitaker), a divine disregard cruelly apparent in the first tercet:

A shudder in the loins engenders there
The broken wall, the burning roof and tower
And Agamemnon dead.

The ultimate indeterminacy, then, centers on this face that cannot be imagined. Face or mask, human or inhuman stare: the indistinctness cannot be resolved, and it is roused by no more than an intonation, a questioning and quasi-musical statement. "Agamemnon," similarly, is more and less than a name. It is a sound-shape with a curious hum and a recursive inner structure. The *m*'s and *n*'s bunch together, so that "Agamemnon dead" is the climactic "And" writ large. The consequence leaves the cause behind, for who could bear that visionary knowledge, that AND? Only a nonperson, a god, or a woman metamorphosed into divine impassibility. Or . . . the poet, who has here, in this very poem, become impersonal and painted himself out of the picture.

Is the poet, then, the last of Leda's brood, the last of these births that are also vastations? The depersonalization of Leda is brought into contact with a poetics of impersonality. The poet *is* present, but as part of this myth, even as an unnamed, unacknowledged deity. Yeats's final question, to which no answer can be given, is undecidable only as it brings us close to the unthinkable. If Leda did put on the god's knowledge, what then? We begin to understand the reserve of that question, and that Yeats wants us to intuit the psychic reality of crazies like Cassandra, or mythic figures vastated by seeing too much and who are mad, divine, or both. A myth of origins is made to yield a clue to the origins of myth.

I have used "Leda and the Swan" as a fable for the hermeneutic situation. Yeats's lyric is, in genre, a prophecy after the event (*ex eventu*) and re-creates the psychic milieu from which such myths of annunciation come. This psychic grounding is interesting, but it intensifies rather than resolves the problem. A discontinuity remains between natural and supernatural, between the mortal psyche and elated states of mind. In a famous notebook passage (13 June 1852), Emerson talks of "Miss B—, a mantua-maker in Concord, [who] became a 'Medium,' and gave up her old trade for this new one; and is to charge a pistareen a spasm, and nine dollars for a fit. This is the Rat-revelation, the gospel that comes by taps in the wall, and thumps in the table-drawer." In *A Vision,* Yeats inserts "Leda and the Swan" into a section given the byline of "Capri"; but "Capri" could also have been "Naples" or "Cuma" or other sibylline places. The impersonality theory that T. S. Eliot and the New Critics furthered (it has links also to Henry James), though less magical or mystical, is no less a form of mystery management.

A critic aware of the survival in art of the *language* of mystery and myth is in a case exactly parallel to Yeats's. What offends cultural standards may still attract us because of its imaginative daring and peculiar organization. Like an observer of alien rites, the critic is often caught between acknowledging the consistency or attractive horror of what he sees and rejecting it in the name of his own enlightened customs. The split may tear him apart, even at a distance.[3] And if, like Kurtz in Conrad's *Heart of Darkness,* or the spy at Bacchic orgies, the critic then immerses himself in the destructive element, he still creates, as it were, the writer who has gone in search of him. The critic is always a survivor or someone who comes late. So the *character* or *role* of being a critic is implicated in this conflict between mastery and mystery, or rhetoric and hermeneutic hesitation.

The theological writings of the young Hegel are instructive in this regard. Hegel wishes to understand the triumph of Christianity over paganism without vulgar apologetics, without denying the integrity of previous life forms or even their present intelligibility. He shows "critical" respect for that which once was and which cannot be entirely superseded. To understand Christianity in its concrete historical life, alien or archaic religious forms must be recalled by the dialectical consciousness of the critic who sees them as stages in the march of reason toward an absolute form. "The heathen too had intellects," Hegel writes. "In everything great, beautiful, noble and free they are so far our superiors that we can hardly make them our examples but must rather look up to them as a different species at whose achievements we can only marvel." A religion, he continues, "particularly an imaginative religion, cannot be torn from the heart,

3. Cf. Clifford Geertz, "Found in Translation: On the Social History of the Moral Imagination," *Georgia Review* 31; and Ludwig Wittgenstein, "Remarks on Frazer's 'Golden Bough,'" *Human World* 3. See also Richard H. Bell, "Understanding the Fire-Festivals: Wittgenstein and Theories of Religion," *Religious Studies* 14 (1978): 113–24.

especially from the whole life and heart of a people, by cold syllogisms constructed in the study." The supersession of paganism by Christianity, therefore, can only be explained by a process far more inward, specific, and dialectical than the model of Providence offered by Christian apologists.

For Hegel the very mobility of human consciousness at once uncovers and resolves contradictions in the forms of life it continues to institute. If there is Providence, it must be understood as the totalizing process we call history, and which the philosopher reads as he runes. The pattern of the gothic novel of Hegel's time, which introduced a strange or uncanny event gradually resolved into the familiar and rational (Kleist's *Marquise of O—* endows this *surnaturel expliqué* with its finest psychological shading), is modified in the direction of modern social anthropology. The strange is construed rather than explained; hermeneutic hesitation leads to a more positive awareness of otherness; and if a teleological rationalism wins the day, that day is as long as history itself and includes mysteries denser and more detailed than are found in the Nine Nights of Blake's *Vala.*

It would be foolish not to claim Hegel as a hermeneutic thinker just because the patience of the negative moment in his system is structural and the ruins of time are always transcended by an eagle-eyed dialectic. Though Hegel remains a master builder, he recalls a capacity we feared was lost: the power of the mind to keep interpreting despite evidences of death, to build on and by means of negation. As this "questionable shape" he confronts Jacques Derrida: "What remains today, for us, here and now, of a Hegel?" Composed of explicit or inner quotations, of verbal debris, *Glas* (whose opening sentence I have just quoted) labors in Hegel's shadow to remove his absoluteness and create a negative or deeply critical work of *philosophic* art.

This philosophic work of art was, of course, an aspiration of German Romantic thinkers. Friedrich Schlegel's *Athenaeum* fragments foresee a synthesizing criticism that would combine art and philosophy. Whether the desired work would be more like art or more like philosophy was an intriguing question never quite answered. Nor is it answered at the present time. Even should Plato's curse be lifted, and poetry be admitted once more into the Republic, "can philosophy become literature and still know itself?"[4]

What is required is a work of power in which philosophy recognizes poetry. Yet a happy ending, as in a comedy of reconciliations, cannot be assured. The recognition scene may lead to tragic or uncertain vistas. After so long a separa-

4. I quote the ending of Stanley Cavell's *Claim of Reason.*

tion, there may not be a shared language anymore. Heidegger fears that, yet he tries to recover a simulacrum of the original, unified language. And literary studies that compare, for instance, Hegel's *Phenomenology* to a Bildungsroman or to the elaborate passage work of a gothic tale, one that never quite purges from its enlightened scheme a dark and daemonic idea, are important not because they colonize philosophy or subject it to the claims of literature but because they raise the question of whether that philosophical work of art is possible even as a heuristic idea.

But the philosophic work of art can also be understood from the side of art. In that spirit I want to conclude: to show how effectively Kleist's *Marquise of O—* rouses the reader from the dogmatic dream that everything can be resolved. Kleist makes us into charmed and bewildered readers who feel that hermeneutic hesitation is the essential quality of philosophical art.

Despite its formal resolution (closure) Kleist's novella unsettles, and keeps unsettled, the relation of the human imagination to the sphere in which it moves. The story begins with a startling solecism. A highborn widow announces in the local newspapers that she is with child and asks the father to come forward that she may marry him. The story then gives the background to this scandalous act and tells how a father is found. Yet we cannot be sure that this "foundling" is the father. Not to accept him as that would mean, however, to abandon the search for "natural" truth and entertain one of two positions: that there is a supernatural cause for the marquise's "unconscious conception," or that a positive identification of the father is less important than his acceptance of that role, demanded by the institution of marriage. A natural relation may prove to be fictional or self-covenanted.

Kleist's story leaves us in this bind, which is perhaps the only thing that ties it, and us, together. He suggests that natural bonding in human life is so fragile that, even when it is strengthened by an etiquette he so beautifully renders, only the violence (war, rape, haste, scandal) breaking that bond is memorable, or else the bind—perplexity of mind—itself.

Now, in Hegel also the riddle of historical existence involves a rift between man and nature. Man leaves the path of natural being, betrays his bond, and continually projects his own self-alienation. This riddle is intensified rather than explained by the Hegelian dialectic, which binds all the violent repetitions we call history together. What is strange in Hegel's story is not so much the "dark" past in relation to the "enlightened" present, but the repeated—if dialectically repeated—link between self-alienation and self-realization. "Man's life is thought," Yeats wrote in "Meru"; he cannot cease "Ravening, raging, and uprooting that he may come / Into the desolation of reality." The violence of the spirit vis-à-vis the natural world (Yeats's philosophy of history is explicitly centered on it, as in *A Vision*'s "Dove or Swan," which is preceded by "Leda and the Swan") is modified only by a laborious and patient mode of negativity—something like philosophical analysis, or a hermeneutic hesitation that construes rather than explains spirituality.

There is a rift, then, between the human imagination and the natural or social sphere, one which no supernatural thought, no violence of spirit, can repair. Spirituality, in fact, in its very violence—even the violence of its drive for harmony and reconciliation—is simply a supreme form of the negative. *The Marquise of O—* is full of this violence of spirit, but it meets us initially as a form of writing: as the scandal of advertising, a magnificent, subversive act of womanly abasement with (in that society) the force of graffiti. When she advertises for a husband, the marquise is no less spiritual, no less *protestant,* than when she insisted on her immaculate state. But now she calls for the demon lover to appear, to take on human form, and so to deny the possibility of an immaculate or purely ideal conception. What is negated by the story is also sublated, to use Hegel's terms: the force of a woman's voice, or of the child's voice in the woman, the voice of someone who gives up without giving up a deeply imagined possibility.

The critical spirit, to conclude, does not automatically place itself on the side of reason, enlightenment, or demystification. Since the Enlightenment, in fact, it has sought to develop a style of discourse of its own which could respect the difference, perhaps discontinuity, between "ordinary" and "extraordinary" language. In England, the problem of "poetic diction" which arose after Milton—whether that kind of diction contains, residually, an archaic but still important understanding of religious mystery or is a mystery only in the sense of "craft"—is a symptom of the general problem of diction, in criticism as well as in poetry. The temptation for criticism to become a type of science, with its own axioms and formal principles, would have been even stronger if this division in language (often simplified into one that opposes prose to poetry) had not continued to challenge the systematizers in several ways. (1) Can literature heal the division in language; or is it as divisive as it is reconciling? (2) Is a comprehensive theory of verbal artifacts, comprising prose and poetry, ordinary and extraordinary language, possible? (3) What should the verbal style of the critic be: how "ordinary," how "prosaic"?

One thing we have learned: whatever style of critical inquiry may be evolving today, criticism cannot be identified as a branch of science or as a branch of fiction. Science is strongest when it pursues a fixed paradigm or point of reference, however subtly modified, however self-transformed. Fiction is strongest as para-prophetic discourse, as prophecy after the event—an event constituted or reconstituted by it, and haunted by the idea of traumatic causation ("A sudden blow," "A shudder in the loins"). But contemporary criticism aims at a hermeneutics of indeterminacy. It proposes a type of analysis that has renounced the ambition to master or demystify its subject (text, psyche) by technocratic, predictive, or authoritarian formulas.

This criticism without a name cannot be called a movement. It is too widespread, miscellaneous, and without a program. Its only program is a revaluation of criticism itself: holding open the possibility that philosophy and the study of art can join forces once more, that a "philosophical criticism" might evolve leading to the mutual recognition of these separated institutions. A corpus of works with some commonality of purpose is already in evidence, but it would be a mistake to identify what is happening with tendencies surfacing in the last twenty or thirty years. My examples from Yeats, Wordsworth, Hegel, and Kleist are meant to point to a longer-range view in which the problem of how to understand visionary or archaic figuration—perhaps figuration as such—draws criticism constantly back into the sphere of hermeneutics through the persistence of the Ancient Classics and Scripture: a language of myth and mystery that has not grown old and continues to be explosive, in art as in politics.

The Philomela Project

For most people literary criticism is something of a mystery. They hear of the latest turbulence in those skies: for example, that deconstruction is shaking things up and has been claimed by a faction in the law schools or an eccentric group of architects. Or a new battle of the books makes it into the *New York Times Magazine,* after conferences at Yale and Princeton on the "canon" and a big curriculum fight at Stanford. What it adds up to is not easy to explain.

Critics face, on the one hand, a simple, down-to-earth task: books must be reviewed, courses must be taught. At a time when shelves are filling up, when more and more subjects are competing for prestige and attention, decisions have to be made not only about what to study, but about what every educated person, irrespective of profession or specialization, should know. Can we prescribe a "core" list that might contain, at least talismanically, what should be read by all? Are there books that could be shared by everyone—when even the Bible today is no longer the passion or obligation of every person?

On the other hand, the issues debated by literary critics are far from down-to-earth, because they involve not particular books but *how to read them.* The point is made that it was less the Bible as such, or the classics as such, that inspired or oppressed, than a certain kind of reading, an enforced mode of interpretation sanctioned by a religious, cultural, or political elite. This elite not only chose the books to be read but limited the way they could be understood. Once we shift emphasis from books to the mode of their interpretation, we cross into an uncertain and disputatious country.

Interpretation is notoriously unstable. Its history is full of swerves and reversals. Reading different critics, we sometimes can hardly believe they are dealing with the same book. Yet the distinction between a canon of books and modes of reading is not absolute. New books have the power to change habits of reading; they not only follow but create methods of study. Our idea of artistic greatness and the English language itself have been influenced by Shakespeare. Obversely, a hermeneutic discovery like Freud's can stimulate a new type of representation: psychoanalysis gradually changes the way we depict character, motivate what goes on—and even what we dream, or record as dream. Alfred Hitchcock's movie *Psycho* can serve as a popular emblem of that change. That there is an interaction between reading and representation simply increases the difficulty of identifying the one reading list everyone should consult.

Not that literary criticism—the formal study of books *and* methods of interpretation—brings order out of chaos. Criticism is often part of the problem rather than the solution. Indeed, skeptics say that whatever the pretension of critics who promote new readings or renew older ones, those critics remain in the service of a dominant ideology, even if as uncomplicated as consumerism. From this perspective, literary criticism is not an independent science or field of study but a by-product of the culture—a surplus verbal and cerebral energy that leaks from the art of the period and has to be blotted like excess ink.

A more flattering view is that literary study, as it reviews and sometimes creates methods of reading, enters the cultural scene as an authoritative voice rather than as a dubious by-product. Books, films, and painting require an interpretive field of force to sustain themselves, and then to become traditionary: to survive beyond a "generation," "decade," "movement." Art does not have its axis of influence only in itself; a certain type of reading may have contributed to its formation, and certain habits of interpretation facilitate its reception. Culture depends on this interaction of "primary" text (Scripture or artifact) and "secondary" text (the work of reading that edits, interprets, mediates).

In the last hundred years there has been an accelerated shift from art to sophisticated theories of art, sometimes even abetted by the artists themselves.

Mallarmé's poetics are couched in a prose as subtle as the diction of his poems. At once self-advertisements and adventures, his pronouncements have their own curious and inwrought integrity. Authors begin to market their very nonconformity. They recapture what they feel was alienated from them by theorists and critics. The aesthetic imperative of a Mallarmé, a Proust, a Rilke, a Stevens, or a Borges acknowledges that a prosaic world, a tide of opinion and theory, is threatening to overwhelm or dilute art. These writers seek to preempt or transform that world by their own highly self-conscious practice.

The astute critic does not automatically take the side of art against the tide of conversation, gossip, or commentary elevated into theory. The reason is twofold. First, the fetishized artwork may be as damaging to cultural life as an overelaborated criticism. Second, for culture to be participatory, artworks must circulate, by passing from private houses to public museums, and being widely thought about, talked about. There may be a greatness in *not* being monumental but in disappearing into the stream of life, the stream of language. I don't quite believe that myself. The real harm, I think, is done not by monumentalism, or haunting ideas of greatness, but by a hierarchical prejudice which holds that creativeness can be achieved only in certain genres, to which other genres are subordinate. In theocracies or totalitarian regimes, both art and criticism serve; in the epoch often called modernism, criticism serves art. A dichotomy reestablishes itself in modernism, with great art idolized despite or perhaps because of the skepticism of the age.

I have been identified with a position that urges a "creative criticism," but that position does not entail a confusion of art and critical essay, or a reversal of values. Rather, it says that we cannot restrict the locus of creativity. A critical essay, a legal opinion, an interpretation of Scripture, a biography can be as inspiring and nurturing as poem, novel, or painting. The prejudice that separates the creative from the interpretive reacts to the fear that the creative element in culture is being swamped by institutional or commercial forces. The wildest paradox in this is that criticism, though considered by many to be on the side of institutionalization, in fact allies itself quite often with the new or the popular. Both criticism and innovation are outsiders, and usually a wave of art, sophisticated or demotic, breaks in together with upstart critical ideas.

Yet can that anxiety about the atrophy of creative genius be dispelled? Some such fear runs deep in every age. Today it fixes on criticism, because that really is a force to contend with. A culture of criticism is developing, one that inspires as well as depresses, one that breaks down media and genres in favor of "discourses." Yet our problem is not, I think, hypercriticism or commercialism, or even the burden of the past in the form of institutionalized Western classics. It is a strange inertia in our progressive thinking.

The heroes of a previous generation—modernists like Flaubert, Proust, Mann, Henry James, Joyce, Virginia Woolf, Yeats, Lorca—fostered an art-ideology. They attacked bourgeois values rather than the concept of Great Book or Masterpiece. The artwork becomes, if anything, more of a sacrificial idol. Have we really jettisoned the modernist art-ideology? Doesn't it keep sticking to us, even in this "postmodern" era?

The problem I discern is the spread of that diluted modernist ideology to every text used as a wedge to "open the canon." Though postmodernism seems to assert the opposite by deprivileging the acknowledged work of art, it may simply be privileging the yet-unacknowledged work. The very notion of criticism is threatened by a proliferation of "significant" or "representative" works, not just by a proliferation of theories. Critical judgment, which had been austere and exclusive—in theory, if not always in fact—is asked to be compensatory and restitutive. The vitality, but also the confusion, of literary studies reflects this double burden: multiplying theories of reading, multiplying works that claim a share of greatness.

To question, as I have done, the prejudice that keeps criticism out of the literary system does not help either the canonizers (the art-ideologists) or the decanonizers. It presents, rather, a conundrum, and challenges an inside-outside or hierarchical way of thinking. Criticism has its own strength; even commentary, as French anthropologist Dan Sperber points out, does not disappear into the Code or Scripture it interprets but must itself be interpreted. A salient example of this is the Jewish oral law, the Talmud, and adjacent compilations called Midrash. They cannot be reduced to a purely exegetical function. They extend or reenvision the original, the "primary" text.

Midrash has always been exemplary for me. I am intrigued by its liberty and autonomy as well as by its strict adherence to proof texts. My interest did not start in the 1980s; I tried to develop a secular parallel in earlier essays. *Beyond Formalism* allowed itself the remark:

> Great exegetes . . . have always, at some point, swerved from the literal sense of the text. This text, like the world, was a prison for Rabbinic, Patristic, or Neoplatonic interpreters, yet by their hermeneutic act the prison opened into a palace and the extremes of man's dependence and of his capacity for vision came simultaneously into view. I feel the poverty of our textual imaginations compared to theirs. The very idea of interpretation seems to have shrunk.[1]

Anthropologists, more skilled in the devious relation of Code (which can be a corpus of stories) to interpretation, especially in oral cultures, may have some sympathy with what I am saying.

I do not argue that there has been no advance, but with advance comes loss or disregard. We live among restitutions, yet the rabbinic mode of reading (or religious exegesis generally) is still disregarded by most secular critics. My plea is not for Midrash as such but for an enrichment or even reconstruction of the literary-critical field. If there is a symbiosis between a discipline and what it seeks to recover, it might be said that criticism today is engaged in a project of *self-restitution:* that Midrash is more important for criticism than literary perspectives are for Midrash. By including Midrash or older types of exegesis, criticism would exercise its power to revalue an alienated practice and enlarge itself at the same time.

As we look across the entire expanse of literary history, we find many moments of revaluation and recovery. The greatest of these may have been the Renaissance. Despite the fact that Europe remained Christian, it brought back a repressed heritage: the pagan classics. By an artistic amalgamation we are still trying to fathom, religiously alien forms blossomed again, fusing with a Christian content. A Jewish medieval tradition, similarly, is only now being retrieved for the nonorthodox world. We have something to learn from a religious culture in which the creative energies went almost totally into commentary and the same basic method of reading was used for law (halakhah) and lore (aggadah). But while a lost masterpiece, once recovered, is like an *objet trouvé,* a neglected tradition requires decades of research and absorption. In an era of restitution, Midrash still needs finding: as a cultural achievement, as a work of the social imagination, and as a distinctive mode of reading.

What is all this talk about Midrash? You're supposed to be a deconstructionist! Well, there was life before, there is life after, Derrida.

The foolishness of labeling aside (about which deconstruction has things to say), the problem facing us is that this age of restitution is also an age of resentment. There is no end to the demand for "identity," as something available to groups or individuals, yet denied them by the social order. The new emphasis on identity is like a rash left by movements that have rigorously questioned it in philosophy, fiction, and social thought. We seem to be passing from exquisite scruples about the "question of the subject" to a credal insistence on the "subject position." To confess "where one is coming from" is no longer a modesty topos but a required affirmation.

Something about this flight to identity is utopian or visionary. In Blake's words,

> All Human forms identified, even Tree Metal Earth and Stone, all
> Human forms identified, living going forth and returning wearied,
> Into the Planetary lives of Years Months Days and Hours, reposing
> And then Awakening into his Bosom in the Life of Immortality.[2]

Restitutive criticism has absorbed this type of liberation theology. Its secular career began with historicism's "resurrection of the past." The massive research inspired by historicism showed how little we knew of other cultures and how much in our own had been marginalized and suppressed. When Herder (only somewhat older than Blake) characterized the neglected poetry of ancient peoples as "voices," the metaphor was just: it indicated an oral source that was effaced by print culture, and it pointed to something that *cried out* to be heard.

Yet this Philomela project (the restoration of voice to inarticulate people) has had a strange result. Retrieval of the past produced a conspicuous increase in feelings of guilt about culture as such. This guilt operates both at the level of intellectual consciousness, as we become aware of how much overhead (Nietzsche called it culture-debt) we must carry along, and at the level of moral consciousness, because history is no longer seen as the story of liberty, of progressive emancipation, but rather of denial, censorship, repression. What can be said for a civilization that exploits its poor, prosecutes bloody wars, and invents genocide? The philosophy of history—the attempt to find a meaningful, progressive pattern in the passing of time—is a dying discipline because a quickened sense of social justice does not allow us to forget realities discounted by previous generations. History, it appears, was always written from the perspective of the conquerors. ("What were the conquerors but the great butchers of mankind?" Locke observed.) Contemporary historical research has become, especially in literary circles, a sort of protest against history: the use of the past to incriminate both past and present.

Walter Benjamin saw that the Renaissance model of restitution was flawed: it merely joined Roman triumphalism to Christianity. Though we are moved by the sheer magnificence of the monuments this combination produced, Benjamin was correct in charging that such achievements may be tainted by barbarity. Are they not built on the blood and sweat of anonymous masses, on victims whose history is ignored? The New Historicism wishes to recover that history (primarily the story of everyday life), and so restore the "material base" of art. It too, however, faces the problem that the material base has largely vanished, and that the process of restitution, of righting wrongs, seems endless.

The task remains visionary or utopian, insofar as a voice must be given to the anonymous, even if there is no voice. "The plaintiff becomes a victim," Jean-François Lyotard writes in *The Differend,* "when no presentation is possible of the wrong he or she says he or she has suffered." We can retrieve, for instance, only a portion of women's experience; the rest has disappeared, or lost its gender-specific aspect.[3] The archives yield something, in the form of letters, unpublished efforts, and legal depositions. Great epics, novels, or dramas also yield something, when imbued with the vernacular zest of a Dante, a Rabelais, a Cervantes, a Shakespeare, or their modern successors. Yet historians or critics must often construct a legal fiction—invent, that is, a persona for absent presences.

What, finally, of deconstruction in relation to this protest movement and its visionary program? Though deconstruction seems negative rather than affirmative in its posture—compared to a curricular politics that *represents* minority interests against the canon—it did set in motion a close questioning of concepts of privilege. Nourished by sources in philosophy and semiotics, it dismantled such essentialist values as origin (genealogy), intent (original intent), and identity (nature), by a study of the temporal aspect of human existence (how our truths remain contingent, how we are never present or transparent to ourselves), and a method of reading that showed an unresolvable doubleness in language. The drive of language toward unmediated expression or sheer transparency of thought could make words superconductive. (Think of merging telepathy and telecommunications, or of a universal sign-system to overcome the babel of tongues.) But there is also the historical and analytic fact that every language is a system of differences, one that defers even while it anticipates meaning—"Success in Circuit lies" (Emily Dickinson). In deconstruction the emphasis on difference rather than identity is not essentialized. The challenge becomes how to support Third World writing, say, or the "minor" literatures, without counteridentifying them so strongly that we reinstate once again the contested notion of privilege, as well as essentialist, and at worst racial, slogans that have bedeviled an era of catastrophic nationalism.

There is of course an antirestitutive bias to deconstruction, both in its concept of dissemination ("that which does not return to the father") and in its claim that voice-metaphors, as in this essay, are intellectually suspect. One supporter of the movement, after hearing me, complained that my emphasis on the Philomela project, although socially valid, undermined itself because, for deconstruction, the problem is "too much voice." Derrida, especially, insists that our thinking has been vitiated by equating voice and presence, an equation that reinforces a metaphysics of presence and leads to disastrously false, even apocalyptic, expectations. "Too much voice" means that we are swayed by rhetoric, that we respond to it literally rather than critically, that we allow ourselves to be not only moved, but moved to action, by the mimetic and promissory thrust of language. We neglect the semiotic aspect of words, which is more perceptible in writing, when writing is not considered as simply a pallid transcription of voice, or a script that points to a reality whose sensuous presence must be restored.

I find this critique of mimetic representation an important *spiritual* move akin to the antitheatrical prejudice that restrains, usually within the context of the major religions, the attempt to achieve a quasi-Dionysian identification with the divine, here and now. Deconstruction's methodical suspicions of the privileging of voice may also have been influenced by fascist uses of radio and film to restore a lost and unifying word. Still more relevant overall is Benjamin's understanding of what follows from the fact that our capacity for mimesis has progressed radically in a technological era. That the mechanical powers of reproducing simulacra are at the point where everything can be re-presented (where presence can be achieved through representation) degrades, according to Benjamin, the unique, in situ "aura" of the valued object. Benjamin saw that the "aura" was commodifiable, and that fascism (or for that matter communism, in its own way) could appropriate it through technological means. The sacred or epiphanic notion of embodiment suffers, as absence and presence become less absolute and enter a dialectical process leading to their indistinction. It becomes harder to discriminate between false and true representations, and this added burden on our powers of discernment, this incentive to distrust and suspicion, can intensify a reactive desire for charismatic closure, and so the movement of a metaphysics of presence into the political process. It is not restitution that is attacked by deconstruction but the use of restitutive pathos, of a politics of desire once associated with messianic religion and now responsible for political theologies.

The problematics of restitution are never simple. Let me turn to a movie, Wim Wenders's *Wings of Desire.* It enacts a pastoral version of the mimetic dilemma I have described. Wenders is never naive about place or its phantom relation to presence: *Paris, Texas* is a classic on the theme. The quest for emplacement or embodiment that he portrays in *Wings of Desire* is necessitated by Germany's guilty relation to a past it has destroyed no less than twice: through the war, which abolished monuments and sites (the setting of the film is Berlin); and through a repression of memory, which obliged Adorno to ask as late as 1959: "What does it mean to come to terms with the past?" The Germans—but they are only the extreme case for Wenders—must learn to experience their past without evasion, and this the film translates as *to experience for the first time.* This "first time" is a purely mythical event. To exemplify it, Wenders appropriates the theme of the angel who falls (falls in love) because he envies mortals their fully sentient being. He renounces angelhood (hearing and seeing everything without being heard or seen) in order to enjoy the earthly pleasures of a finite body.

Despite this brilliant joining of historical and mimetic issues, the movie does not rejuvenate what it touches on. It collapses under the inner quotations it recycles: the weight of culture—the reproducible culture of film—militates against the allegory of a repristinated nature, a "first time" tasting of the fruit of mortal experience. For the viewer, ironically, there is more abstractness, more stereotyping in the colorful reality and pantomimic legerdemain of the circus which is the object of the angels' envy than in the monochromatic and voyeuristic existence to which the heavenly homunculi are doomed before the film switches to color. The object of the angels' desire remains obscure, and the reduction of the world to the love-clichés of one man and one woman, with which the film ends, indicates a retreat from words that is more forgetful of realities than the reality-loss the film addresses.

Perhaps only one thing is certain after such movements as deconstruction and the Frankfurt School ("Critical Theory"). Essentialism is instrumentalism in disguise; and instrumentalized reading has been the norm. Yes, we hunger to engage literature, morally and politically; we want to escape Lukács's contempt for the Western intellectual's "permanent carnival of fetishized interiority." But this cannot be achieved by turning up the volume of moralistic pronouncements through affirmations—or denunciations—which act as the equivalent of loyalty tests. Today the entire landscape of moral philosophy is in motion, shaken by events that hardly seem related to questions of language yet are not separable from an inveterate pattern of verbal abuse that has come to light.

There are signs that the challenge to create a new moral criticism is being taken up. The impact of John Rawls's *Theory of Justice* and the way contemporary thinkers are engaging issues of literature in relation to moral philosophy are among those signs. Let me single out Charles Taylor's *Sources of the Self: The Making of the Modern Identity*.[4] It holds that we are living beyond our moral means because we pretend that contemporary life has overcome theism (or religious worldviews, however vague), Romantic expressiveness (or some belief in an organic connection with Nature), and similar "sources." More, we actively deny them. This "stripped-down secular outlook" is not the product of an irrational denial but is based on experience and prudence. "We tend in our culture to stifle the spirit—after the terrible experience of Millenarist destruction in our century." Spirit has acquired a bad name. There are other causes too, in addition to this prudent reaction to the knowledge that "the highest spiritual aspirations must lead to annihilation or destruction"—obvious causes such as partisan narrowness and less obvious ones such as the creed of naturalism. Yet Taylor refuses to let his diagnosis limit our moral and philosophical options. To accept spiritual impoverishment—to be ashamed of one's explicit religious and spiritual motives—is simply a countermutilation, and so an evasion of the dilemma.

What makes Taylor of particular interest in the context of this discussion is that his book provides not only a richer moral phenomenology but also an attempt to redress the situation. He seeks to *restitute* the denied sources—resources—of the self. Modern analytic philosophy has been propositional in its approach, seeking a stripped-down truth; Taylor puts analysis in reverse gear to recover by his account of intellectual history (Hegelian in its confident sweep) the problematics of invalidating a quest for the good because that too has led to suffering. We may bridle at his effort to narrate history once more, after so many thinkers, analytic or anti-Hegelian, have deflated that tendency, and we may regret his resuscitation of the concept of a "modern identity," however critical he is of its anemic texture. But his challenge to rethink issues in moral and not just political terms, and to reconsider a superficially transcended past, demands consideration.

Restitutive criticism requires serious debate. It is something old rather than new, and still a sharp turn on society's path toward the recognition of collective as well as individual rights and talents. The classic analysis of recognition in a situation of social inequality is by Hegel: a famous section of his *Phenomenology of Spirit* traces the aroused consciousness of master and bondsman, as they grow aware of their interdependence. Recognition is the key, rather than restitution, though restitution is often the acknowledgment of an achieved recognition. The end is not righting wrongs as such (there may be several rights in conflict), nor a reversal (which serves a retributive rather than restitutive end), but a new, spiritually as well as politically effective, respect.

Turning back from political philosophy to literature, it is important to recall the recent emergence of oral history. Popular traditions challenge as well as inspire high culture; they question the confusion of art with ideas of order by revealing the heterogenous and often folkloric elements of canonized books like Homer and the Bible. Literature grows from traditions rather than tradition, as the ballad collectors knew; and insofar as it helps honor such sources, literary criticism is restitutive. The Philomela project, giving a voice to the voiceless, a name to the anonymous, merges at the literary horizon of history with another myth: Orpheus compelling Acheron to yield and restore a lost object of desire. That Eurydice is twice-lost suggests, however, that the magic of art is limited to the recovery of the story rather than of the object itself.

NOTES

1. Geoffrey H. Hartman, *Beyond Formalism* (New Haven: Yale University Press, 1970), p. xiii.
2. William Blake, *Jerusalem,* last plate.
3. We do have considerable information about the political and intellectual influence of women when they belong to or rise into *le grand monde,* as in eighteenth-century France. Their conversation is recorded by the men who passed through their salons or observed them at court or in the *coulisses,* yet their own correspondence too is significant. "The relique of woman's grace, the letter, is her conversation itself," Edmond and Jules de Goncourt comment in *La femme au dix-huitième siècle,* 3d ed. (Paris: Firmin Didot Frères, 1887), chap. 11. Sometimes even an extraordinary poetic achievement, like that of Mexico's Sor Juana, may need rescue because of our parochialism, not only sexism. Octavio Paz calls his book on her a restitution: the historian combines in Paz with the imaginative writer to remove a falsification of her life's work, to restore her to herself and our century. See Octavio Paz, *Sor Juana: or, The Traps of Faith,* trans. Margaret Sayers Peden (Cambridge, Mass.: Harvard University Press, 1988). An unusual effort to reach into the life of women who belong to the illiterate or lower classes is that of Natalie Zemon Davis, *Fiction in the Archives: Pardon Tales and Their Tellers in Sixteenth-Century France* (Stanford, Calif.: Stanford University Press, 1987), esp. chap. 3, "Bloodshed and the Woman's Voice."
4. Charles Taylor, *Sources of the Self: The Making of the Modern Identity* (Cambridge: Harvard University Press, 1989). In France, Emmanuel Levinas's ethical philosophy—on a phenomenological base—has gradually been recognized.

The Voice of the Shuttle

Aristotle, in the *Poetics* (16.4), records a striking phrase from a play by Sophocles, since lost, on the theme of Tereus and Philomela. Tereus, having raped Philomela, cut out her tongue to prevent discovery. But she weaves a telltale account of her violation into a tapestry (or robe) which Sophocles calls "the voice of the shuttle." If metaphors as well as plots or myths could be archetypal, I would nominate Sophocles' voice of the shuttle for that distinction.

What gives these words power to speak to us even without the play? No doubt the story of Tereus and Philomela has a universally affecting element: the double violation, the alliance of craft (cunning) and craft (art), and what the metaphor specifically refers to: that truth will out, that human consciousness will triumph. The phrase would not be effective without the story, yet its focus is so sharp that a few words seem to yield not simply the structure of one story but that of all stories insofar as they are telltales. Aristotle, in fact, mentions Sophocles' kenning during his discussion of how recognition scenes are brought about; and it is interesting that other examples cited by him share the characteristic of seeming to exist prior to the plays that embody them, as if they were riddles or gnomic words imposed by tradition and challenging an adequate setting. Take, for example, "So I too must die at the altar like my sister" (Orestes); or "I came to find my son, and I lose my own life" (Tydeus); Or, again, "Here we are doomed to die; for here we were cast forth" (Phineidae, *Poetics* 16.6). These phrases, overheard, bring about a recognition. Like the voice of the shuttle they have little meaning without a story that sets them. Yet once a story is found, their suggestiveness is not absorbed but rather potentiated. And this, perhaps, is what *archetype* means: a part greater than the whole of which it is a part, a text that demands a context yet is not reducible to it.

Can a rhetorical analysis of this phrase clarify its power? "Voice" stands for the pictorial legend of the tapestry by a metonymic substitution of effect for cause. We say similarly, if less dramatically, that a book "speaks" to us. "Shuttle" stands for the weaver's instrument by the synecdochal substitution of part for whole, but it also contains a metonymy which names the productive cause instead of the product. Thus we have, in the first term (voice), a substitution of effect for cause, and in the second (shuttle), of cause for effect. By this double metonymy the distance between cause and effect in an ordinary chain of events is significantly increased, and the termini of this chain are overspecified at the expense of intermediate points (figure 1). What this etiologic distancing means is not clear from the expression taken out of context. You and I, who know the story, appreciate the cause winning through, and Philomela's "voice" being restored; but by itself the phrase simply disturbs our sense of causality and guides us, if it guides us at all, to a hint of supernatural rather than human agency. (The inanimate speaks out, as blood cries out from the earth in Genesis 4.)

A rhetorical analysis, therefore, brings us quickly to a limit. But we learn certain things from it. The power of the phrase lies in its elision of middle terms and overspecification of end terms. This could bear on two features every theory of poetic language seeks to explain: "aesthetic distance," which usually favors the cool, reflective, nonrepresentational virtues; and "iconicity," which usually abets the concrete, motor, representational ones. These features, however, are no more dissociable than are periphrasis and pointedness in Sophocles' figure. We find ourselves in the presence of an antinomy which is restated rather than solved by calling art a concrete universal. The tension of this figure from Sophocles is like the tension of poetics.

I make this large claim in purely heuristic spirit. There is something cross-eyed about the figure and something cross-eyed about every explanatory poetics. "It must be visible or invisible," says Wallace Stevens in *Notes Toward a*

Supreme Fiction, "Invisible or visible or both / . . . An abstraction blooded, as a man by thought." Now while Nature, according to an old saying, loves mixtures ("la nature aime les entrecroisements"), science does not. I must therefore steer an ambiguous course between nature and science and sketch for you a playful poetics: one that asserts nothing directly about logic, ontology, or linguistic science yet brings together the smallest literary patterns with the largest, the analysis of single metaphors or verses with the comprehensive kind of anatomy practiced by Aristotle in the *Poetics.* So far all we have learned is that figures of speech may be characterized by overspecified ends and indeterminate middles, that this structure may explain the shifting relations of concrete and abstract in poetics, and that (I add this now) the very elision or subsuming of middle terms allows, if it does not actually compel, interpretation. I mean that the strength of the end terms depends on our seeing the elided members of the chain (in this case, the full relation of Tereus and Philomela); the more clearly we see them, the stronger the metaphor which collapses that chain, makes a mental bang, and speeds the mind by freeing it from overelaboration and the toil of consecutiveness. A great verbal figure gives us the second wind of inspiration; it makes us sure, after all, of overtaking the tortoise.

I begin with a line from Milton: "Sonorous metal blowing martial sounds" (*Paradise Lost,* 1.540). A balanced line, with adjective-noun phrases flanking the pivotal verbal phrase. The syntactical sequence (1 2 1 2) is counterpointed, however, by a chiastic pattern of alliteration (1 2 2 1, s m m s). Milton, too, it seems, "aime less entrecroisements." Yet it is very hard to make something significant of such formal patterns, which are not unusual in Milton. Suppose, however, you take the line as complete or self-balanced: an inspired throw of the verbal dice. We may then look at it as generated from a redundant concept, "sonorous sounds," which we recover by collapsing the ends. The verse, from this perspective, is the separating out of "sonorous sounds"; a refusal, by inserting a verbal space between adjective and noun, to let them converge too soon. "Sonorous" is divided from "sounds" and assigned to "metal"; while "metal," as it were, gives up "martial" which is assigned to "sounds" by syntactical transfer. Here metaphor is as much a function of syntax as syntax of metaphor. While the chiastic alliteration, moreover, helps to overcome the redundancy of "sonorous sounds," the syntactical parallelism lightens the secondary redundancy of "martial metal." These two features, previously mentioned, distribute and differentiate the sonic mass like God dividing elemental matter in order to get the sixfold creation.

Compare now Sophocles' metaphor and Milton's line. In Milton the middle terms need not be recovered by interpretation: his line effects its own middle by separating the ends (figure 2). What is created in both is a breach or space—an opening with the sense of freedom implicit in that word—but while in Sophocles this space functions as etiologic distancing, as a suspension of normal causality, in Milton it allows the emergence of words out of sheer sound and is linked to a distancing intrinsic to language, one which differentiates sounds as meaning by a method of "diacritical" (de Saussure) or "binary opposition" (Jakobson).

The idea of space now introduced is not the same as aesthetic distance, nor is the tendency of the Miltonic or Sophoclean figure to collapse into a strong redundancy or tighter than normal idea of causation the same as iconicity. I doubt we can reach these very general concepts except by approximation. But we already glimpse what makes the "tension" of single figures or the literary work as a whole. Take a second, and more ambitious, Miltonic figure. In *Comus,* music is heard "smoothing the Raven doune / Of darkness till it smiled." Here "smoothing" and "smiled" converge slightly, but the real interest lies in the central metaphor, the raven down of darkness. The most likely model of how it originated is to posit a seed-phrase, "the raven of darkness," a simple imaginative concept justified by Virgil's "bird of night" (*Aeneid,* 8.369), and with a tang of redundancy which can be brought out by translating it as "the dark bird of darkness." Some such overlap exists in any metaphor, insofar as it is analogical; and Milton diminishes the redundancy by the syntactical insertion of a second figure which distances "raven" from "darkness." This figure, the "down of darkness," has nothing conceptually redundant in it. A surprising trope, it is linked to one terminus—"darkness"—by alliteration and to the other—"raven"—by imagistic extension.[1] Thus the linear, syntactical insertion of this second metaphor works exactly like the "metal . . . martial" segment which was also linked by consonants. In Milton, syntax differentiates metaphor just as metaphor differentiates something more massive which it continues to express.

The "transformational" poetics here emerging can be clarified by polarization: going, on the other hand, to the microstructures of literature, entities studied by linguists, and on the other hand to the macrostructures studied by all of us. In a phrase like "le monocle de mon oncle" the redundancy of sounds is obvious, yet there is no semantic redundancy. Indeed, the wit of the phrase is

1. The possibility that "down" puns on the adverb ("At every fall [of music] smoothing the Raven doune / Of darkness") increases, if anything, its tmetic force.

that a slight difference in sound (between "monocle" and "mon oncle") releases such vast, if dubious, difference of meaning. It's like a man slipping on a banana peel—cause and effect are totally disproportionate. Technically defined, the difference in sound is a slight distortion of quantity but primarily a matter of what linguists call "boundary" or "juncture"—here typographically indicated by "monocle" dividing into two words, "mon oncle."[2] What metonymy is to the "voice of the shuttle" or syntax to Milton, juncture is to this witty title from Wallace Stevens (figure 2).

Juncture is simply a space, a breathing space: phonetically it has zero value, like a caesura. But precisely because it is such a mini-phenomenon, it dramatizes the differential or, as de Saussure calls it, diacritical relation of sound to meaning. In any crucial arrangement of words, a small change goes a long way, as we learn through slightly mistranslated words in diplomatic messages. Split the atom of sound (and speech is fission) and you detonate an astonishing charge of meaning. With juncture we may have reached an analogue on the level of speech to aesthetic distance in art, especially as it remains linked to that explosive, if harnessed, *enargeia* (picture power) which we sometimes name iconicity.

The importance of zero values like juncture becomes more obvious when we turn to the smallest literary unit, the pun. Artemidorus records in his *Oneirocritica* that when Alexander of Macedon was besieging Tyre, he dreamt he saw a satyr dancing on his shield. By dividing the word into sa-tyros, "Tyre is thing," this became a favorable omen for the siege. Freud, who cites the story and is fascinated by the immense role words play in dreams, gives many examples of what he calls condensation. The image of the satyr, for example, is a visual condensation of a compound phrase (sa-tyre), but when the form of condensation remains verbal, we get punning or portmanteau phrases like Joyce's "mamafesta." Joyce extraverts the fact that language itself has its dream-work which dreams seem only to imitate. This dream work shows itself, before Joyce, in naming rather than nouning, and especially in the resonant appeal of mythic names:

> Abhorred *Styx* the flood of deadly hate,
> Sad *Acheron* of sorrow, black and deep;

2. I am not attempting an exact linguistic analysis: *juncture* is used only as the best available term, and I am aware that "oc" and "onc" contain different phonemes. However, the impression occurs that as "mon" separates from "ocle," the latter compensates by expanding into "oncle." Elizabeth Sewell calls such impressions the "sound-look" of words.

Cocytus, nam'd of lamentation loud
Heard on the rueful stream; fierce *Phlegeton*
Whose waves of torrent fire in flame with rage

(*Paradise Lost,* 2.577–81)

Each of these lines is, as it were, a decontraction of the name.

This leads to the thought that nouns may be demythologized names. We are told that under the Hebrew word *TeHOM* in Genesis 1 (translated "the deep") the divine Babylonian monster *TIAMAT* may be couchant, reduced by the Bible from monster to mere noun. How are the mighty fallen, into syntax! What is true of nouns may be true of language in general. For Emerson language is fossilized metaphors; de Saussure thought that grammatical systems might have originated in anagrammatic distributions of a sacred name; and Shelley asserted "language itself is poetry. . . . Every original language near to its source is itself the chaos of a cyclic poem."

Whatever the truth of these speculations, they share a common feeling. Reading a poem is like walking on silence—on volcanic silence. We feel the historical ground; the buried life of words. Like fallen gods, like visions of the night, words are erectile. A poet can "speak silence" as simply as Chatterton did by opening up words through a mock-archaic spelling: "When joicie peres, and berries of blacke die, / Doe daunce yn ayre, and call the eyne arounde." That "joicie" is Joycean. Joyce's more Freudian understanding of words simply brings literature abreast of language: he dramatizes the language jam in which we are stuck, the intrinsic duplicity, racial mix, and historically accreted character of living speech. "Mamafesta" not only mocks patriarchal imperatives but plays on the structural impurity of language, which mingles, like any doctrine or myth, opposing strains. There is the mother tongue (mama) and the learned, generally latinate layer (manifesto). English is especially prone to this happy impurity, not having suffered, like French or Italian, a decisive neoclassical sublimation of the vernacular. The division of language into sounding words or periphrases (for instance, "the deep backward and abysm of time," a Shakespearean blend of colloquial and learned) and its contraction into those resonant vocables from which, like dream interpreters of old, Milton draws new meanings, are part of one and the same rhythm. It compounds "the imagination's Latin with / The lingua franca et jocundissima" (Wallace Stevens).

It is a far cry, of course, from mystical semantics to modern semiotics. Both, however, respect the function of silence, those zero values of juncture, elision, and decontraction which play so vast yet intangible a role in poetry. It is not mystical to call poetic language the voices of silence. Let us watch Milton creating meaning out of zero values in a famous pun: "O Eve in evil hour." (*Paradise Lost,* 9.1067).

The pun again involves a name, though the latter does not release a new meaning by juncture. Instead, as is characteristic of Milton, it distributes itself in linear fashion by transfer or contamination. To go from "Eve" to "evil" is metaphor on the level of sound. But is the direction of the transfer from "Eve" to "evil," or from "evil" to "Eve"? Milton, it could be argued, does not need the word "Eve," except to spell out a pun that is not particularly good. He adds reader insult to language injury. But the double "Eve-evil" gives us the sense of a third term or matrix, a common root from which both might have sprung. Thus juncture may be involved after all: whatever the matrix malorum is, it contains at this fateful hour both "Eve" and "evil."

This hypothetical matrix is like the redundant concept, "sonorous sounds," which generated a verse-line already studied. The present half-line is also curiously, beautifully redundant. The more we listen to it, the more it becomes one modulated crying diphthong—a breaking or ablauted Oh. . . . The end terms "O" and "hour" stand in the same intensified relation as the chiastic middle terms "Eve" and "evil." It is fanciful, yet true to the sound-shape of the line, to say that "evil" is "Eve" raised a phonetic rather than a grammatical, degree, an impression reinforced by the fact that both "evil" and "hour" are quantities hovering between one syllable and two so that "evil" can be heard as a decontraction of "ill" (figure 2). The semantic energy and affective pitch of the line is again determined by properties that approach zero value (O . . . hour; Eve . . . evil).

From juncture, usually represented by a slash, it is only a step to the grammatical figure of tmesis, best represented by a dash. Tmesis, from the Greek "to divide" (cf. *atom,* "the indivisible"), can be as simple as in Gerard Manley Hopkins's "Brim, in a flash, full." Two words conventionally joined, are disjoined to accommodate an intruded middle (figure 2). The effect is that of interjection, of bursting in, but it gives extra value to the enclitic "full," which otherwise would have been slurred. The end terms are stressed ("in-stressed," Hopkins would say) by their being distanced, crowded away from each other. This is not unlike what happens through metonymy in the voice of the shuttle.

The continuity of juncture and tmesis is best shown by a graded series of examples. The enjambment in

I have
Immortal longings in me

is a hovering kind of juncture and depicts Shakespeare's Cleopatra on the point of crossing a fearful divide. She crosses it, wishfully, by a mere breathing or aspiration. Donne's running speech, his self-persuasive eloquence, tries to leap a similar divide, but the strain is more evident:

> thinke that I
> Am, by being dead, Immortal. . . .

At once nervous and peremptory, this "I Am Immortal" asserts itself in quick sequence against the line-end severance of subject and copula and a tmetic severance within the copula. Severance may seem too strong a word for pauses ("I/Am") or suspensions ("Am . . . Immortal") natural to spoken speech. Tmesis here is not a violent or an artificial device but a more difficult enjambment, a heightened form of juncture which continues to individuate the basic words as they incline toward finality, carried by the proleptic verve of speech. "Severance" is the right term, however, when we look beyond speech to poetry. The qualified haste, the precarious finality of Donne's poetry is also that of religious hope. How to "cross over"—or the dangers of passage—is the central theme:

> In what torn ship soever I embark
> That ship shall be my emblem of thy ark.

"Whatsoever" opens and swallows "torn ship" as the poet severs the grammatical bond to interject his fear. But "embark" also opens to let a saving rhyme, "emb(lem) . . . ark," emerge as the poet converts fear into hope by further prolepsis.

A more complicated form of tmesis distends the syntactical bond almost beyond repair. The normative adjectival space in "a lush-kept plush-capped sloe" is strained to the utmost; in fact, by the internal rhyming of the twofold compound adjective, Hopkins reverses ends and middles, since rhyme is characteristic of line endings. Wishing to restore, in "The Wreck of the Deutschland, our sense of the scriptural "In the beginning was the Word," which he opposes to the understated habit of English speech, Hopkins creates these hysteron-proteron formations (the Word, that is, Christ as the Word, which is always confessed last, should be uttered first by us). We can see another result of this upbeat style in a line which describes the Windhover riding "The rolling underneath him steady air" (figure 2). The intraversion of all these modifiers between the adjective ("rolling") and the noun ("air") parallels the trick of inversion in classical imitators or neoclassical rhymers. The middle of the line is so strong, compared to the conventional ends, that it almost jumps out like the word "Buckle" in the same poem, which, escaping its grammatical tie like a chemical its bond, becomes plosive:

> Brute beauty and valour and act, oh air, pride, plume, here
> Buckle!

"Buckle" (the first word of the second line) is as true a rhyme word as "here" (the last word of the first line) because it at once condenses and detonates the sound pattern of the preceding words with their complex chiastic alliteration. The last becomes the first once more. (Compare the relation of "west" and "Waste" in "Her fond yellow hornlight wound to the west, her wild hollow hoarlight hung to the height / Waste" ["Spelt from Sibyl's Leaves"].)

It is strange that the ultimate form of a zero value like temsis should be a surplus value like rhyme. But tmesis, you will remember, splits a conventionally bonded phrase by means of an assertive middle term, creating stronger poles as well as intruding a strong middle. Now, in rhymed verse the poles regress to a line-end position, becoming *bouts rimés,* while the rest of the verse is inserted between these rhymed ends. We see by this that Milton's rejection of rhyme is related to Hopkins's freeing rhyme from its fixed terminal position and making the last first (in sound-shape, not merely line-place). The end terms of Milton's figures tend, in fact, to be redundant like perfect rhymes; and he uses syntactical tmesis to distance them, to insert phrases that remain bonded to the poles. A Miltonic middle, which separates, for example, "sonorous" and "sounds" or "raven" and "darkness," is a brilliant modification of redundancy, the distribution of an overly rich mental or aural concept.

Thus rhyme is not an isolated phenomenon. Every birth of meaning has, like rhyme, a binary form, since meaning emerges through the opposition of similar-sounding entities. Consider "Humpty-Dumpty": it suggests, like "Eve . . . evil," a unitary word embracing the divided elements, yet nothing can put Humpty-Dumpty together again. Humpty-Dumpty is the portmanteau word that failed, but its fortunate failure reveals the binary form. The hyphen joining Humpty and Dumpty is at once disjunctive and conjunctive; we may interpret it as the generalized tmetic sign which points to the middle between all *bouts rimés.* When a pun or portmanteau word sorts itself out, and similar sounds are put in line-end positions, we get rhyme. Rhyme is but another example of a figure with overspecified ends and an indeterminate middle. Is all poetical or figurative speech of this structure? Is it all a modified punning?

You can define a pun as two meanings competing for the same phonemic space or as one sound bringing forth semantic twins, but, however you look at it, it's a crowded situation. Either there is too much sound for the sense or too much sense for the sound. This aspect we have named the redundancy principle, and it makes poetry radically oblique in terms of sign function. Poetry either says too much—approaches the inexpressible—or too little—approaches the inexpressive. "The voice of the shuttle" could be an inflation of the proper term, an inane periphrasis for tapestry ("fruit of the loom"). It could also be a miraculous condensation so packed with meaning that it skirts the oracular. Poetry will always live under a cloud of suspicion which it discharges by such lightnings.

We don't know, to be honest, what a perfect verbal system is like. But we do know language develops by what Coleridge calls desynonimization and the structuralists call binary opposition. A breathing space, a division within redundancy, appears and makes room for us, for our word. So Tiamat, its mythological fatness, is degraded from name to noun, and from monster to vague mystery. But the artist, like God, broods on the deep noun and makes it pregnant. A new meaning comes forth, a new word, a new world.

You probably feel as impatient with me, and all this talk about zero values, as Bishop Berkeley with Newton's infinitesimals. He called these entities, calculable only by Newton's theory of fluxions, the "ghosts of departed quantities." I now turn from minims to maxims, and to more tangible values.

No critic can refrain from having his say on *Oedipus*. I am tempted to build on it not only a theory of life, like Freud, but a theory about what makes literature vital to life. Freud never brought his theory of "dream-work" together with his theory about Oedipus. Yet it is clear that what he calls "condensation" is crucial to a tragedy which compresses life to coincidence and a smallest possible freedom. For, talking now about plot, mythos, and such maxi-structures, we can say that Oedipus, killing his father and marrying his mother, simply elides individual identity and is allowed no being properly his own. The oracle takes away, from the outset, any chance for self-development. Oedipus is redundant: he is his father, and as his father he is nothing, for he returns to the womb that bore him. His lifeline does not exist.

Except for the illusion that it exists, which the play relentlessly negates. This illusion is important, it is all Oedipus has to develop in. Achilles' career is also limited by a prophecy: short life and glory, or long life and none. But it is not "condensed" like a Greek epigram in which the marriage bed is also the deathbed. Oedipus converges with his fate like an epigram on its point or a tragedy on its recognition scene. The etiologic distancing collapses, the illusion bursts, the supernatural leaves the natural no space. The placenta of illusions has been eaten by the stichomythia.

Human life, like a poetical figure, is an indeterminate middle between overspecified poles always threatening to collapse it. The poles may be birth and death, father and mother, mother and wife, love and judgment, heaven and earth, first things and last things. Art narrates that middle region and charts it like a purgatory, for only if it exists can life exist; only if the imagination presses against the poles are error and life and illusion—all those things which Shelley called "generous superstitions"—possible. The excluded middle is a tragedy also for the imagination.

In human history there are periods of condensation (or concentration, as Matthew Arnold called them) where the religious spirit seems to push man up tight against the poles of existence. Middles become suspect; mediations almost impossible. Things move by polarizing or reversing (peripeteia) or collapsing. "The best lack all conviction, and the worst / Are full of passionate intensity," as Yeats said, seeing the center breaking up. The Reformation was an era of this kind, and it produced, in its purity, a most awesome concentration of human consciousness on a few existentials. The space filled by boughten mercies and mediations is collapsed into a direct, unmediated confrontation of the individual and his God. What does art do in this situation? Does it—can it—save the "ghost of departed mediations"? Is there any authentic way of inserting a middle strong enough to satisfy a now extremist imagination?

Emily Dickinson often begins with death, or a moment near it. Her poems are as laconic as tombstones that speak from the wayside. In the following poem she has come to a way station called Eternity. The poem "condenses" at that point:

> Our journey had advanced—
> Our feet were almost come
> To that odd Fork in Being's Road—
> Eternity—by Term—
>
> Our pace took sudden awe—
> Our feet—reluctant—lead—
> Before—were Cities—but Between—
> The Forest of the Dead—
>
> Retreat—was out of Hope—
> Behind—a Sealed Route—
> Eternity's White Flag—Before—
> And God—at every Gate—

These are strangely detached, inconclusive verses for all their exactitude. We are told that the soul must pass through death ("the forest of the dead") to the city of God. Yet though you cannot reach Eternity except through death, the poet opened by saying that she was near Eternity to start with, while in the last stanza Eternity precedes the soul with a safe-conduct. In this little quest-romance Eternity is always *before* you.

The difficulty may lie in the very idea of Eternity, which cannot be represented by space or time categories. This does not explain, however, why Emily Dickinson is haunted by a conception impossible to depict. The conception, obviously, is a motivating one in terms of the poem. The poet sees to see. Her mode is infinitive. Each stanza infers that one step which is not taken—into epiphany, or visibility. Nothing is at once more and less visible than white: "Eternity's white flag before." There is, to quote Wallace Stevens once more, a "seeing and unseeing in the eye." The god at every gate multiplies an opening through which we do not pass.

It is a poem, therefore, which three times brings us to a limit and three times displaces that limit. Our feet had "almost" come (stanza 1); "The Forest of the Dead" intervenes (stanza 2); the gate god is as concrete as eternity's color (a "colorless all-color") is vague (stanza 3). The limit is also, of course, a limen or threshold; yet the imagination that moves to cross it and see God does no more than see limits. Will God open or block the gate? And is not his very appearance, finally, as gate god, the block? Eternity becomes seeable only at that risk: the poet has advanced, if she has advanced at all, from Terminus to Janus. Her destiny—or is it her choice—seems to be to stay profane: *profanus,* on the threshold of vision.

The space Sophocles wrested from the gods was the very space of human life. That space is illusory, or doomed to collapse as the play focuses on the moment of truth which proves the oracle. In Emily Dickinson, predestination corresponds to the oracle. No wonder "Our pace took sudden awe." That next step, into death, is also, according to the faith of her fathers, a step into destination—into judgment and eternity. Protestantism has shrunk the breathing space between death, judgment, and apocalypse, so that the last things are one thing, and purgatory is no more. Like an oracle, in fact, judgment is already there at birth; death only justifies it or renders it visible. What is life, then, except death's threshold? Since the "ocular proof" comes with death, the life of the mind is centered on that moment, which is any moment. A person should live as if it were the moment preceding judgment. He is always, to quote the absolute opening of another poem, "The man—to die—tomorrow." We anticipate for whom the bell tolls; the time is always zero minus one.

Yet Emily Dickinson's tone is unhurried, as if there were time to puzzle over "that odd Fork in Being's Road." Placing "Eternity" near "term" even shows, in the following line, a bookish wit. The mind remains slightly apart or off-center, like the rhymes; off-center also to the body. The impersonal constructions—"our journey," "our pace," "our feet"—elide the agony of self-consciousness and suggest a speaker positioned above the vehicular body. There is a distance between her and her feet compounded at once of awe and detachment. Her attitude is almost spectatorial.

Can we define that attitude exactly? It is clear that Emily Dickinson's art creates a space. It allows the threshold to exist; it extends the liminal moment. The poet's minutes are our days and hours. If rhymes are there, it is not because they condense, but because verse should be orderly, even in extreme situations. They decondense rather; especially the last and best of them: "God . . . gate." Here off-rhyme moves from line-ending into the midst of the verse. Some will hear in "God . . . gate" the echo of a closing door: she fears she may not be admitted. But it is better to leave it, like the rhyme itself, slightly ajar.

That her feet are toward eternity does not alter, radically, the poet's state of mind. She is carried off, perhaps, but she does not give herself. As the journey takes her along, her poem remains a bourgeois ledger, an extension of Christian watchfulness. To remain what she is steadfastly, unterrified, amounts to an election of self: she will not change utterly. Thus personality is not pushed beyond the human sphere as in Greek tragedy. Behind Philomela—the weaver—looms, like an oracular or archetypal shadow, the figure of fate. Fate too spins. On her shuttle she divides and spins the thread of human existence. But also, perhaps, a sound: is not Sophocles' "the voice of the shuttle" a symbol for oracular utterance? Fate alone could tell all, and Philomela, when her voice is restored through art, participates for a moment in divinity. She triumphs over a terrible doom, yet the recognition she brings about continues a tragic chain of events. Emily Dickinson does not "tell all"; there is no staring recognition in her poetry. Her fate is to stay profane, outside the gates, though in sight of "the promised end."

Interpretation is like a football game. You spot a hole and you go through. But first you may have to induce that opening. The Rabbis used the technical word *patach* ("he opened") for interpretation. Gershom Scholem has shown that the extravagance of the Kabbalah is linked to their opening Scripture to the suffering and concreteness of secular history. Deucalion's interpretation of the "bones of his mother" as the "stones of the earth" was an imaginative wager that saved a race.

We have art, said Nietzsche, so as not to die of the truth. A vital hermeneutics, it limits the sacred or makes room for life in life. The truth unmediated by art is deadly because it is too present, too specific. The truth-seeker is like the child who sees exactly "a hundred and three" sheep in a landscape; the artist like one who knows that what was seen is "about a hundred over there *and* three here," in which "103" is shown to be a hendiadys, or a poetic diction, which overspecifies the ends (as does "finny tribe," or "the voice of the shuttle") yet saves the sense of a middling.

Naming, like counting, is a strong mode of specification. It disambiguates the relation of sign to signified, making the proper term one end and the thing that is meant the other. Two terms complete the act; signification itself is elided, or treated as transparent (figure 3). Naming of this kind does not draw attention to itself. Literary speech does, however; and not by an occult quality (a secret third term), but rather by structures like periphrasis which under- and overspecify at the same time. Poetical figures habitually take away the proper term: "The sun must bear no name." Yet when Stevens adds "gold flourisher," he suggests how creative this decreation is, how his "abstraction" compounds under- and overspecification.[3]

The final hermeneutics art practices on itself. "It is written" or "everything has been said" is the somber oracle that denies the individual talent. In stories there is a period of error or quest, that wonder-wandering which makes them stories and evades an eternally fixed world. In this "wonder and woe" youth becomes *mündig*—is given its proper voice. Old names are cleansed; new tongues flicker. Creative error makes the blue darter hawk (it is blue and it darts) into a "blue dollar hawk," "the outmost sentinel of the wild, immortal camp." Tribal imperatives remain, however: individuality is wrested from the overwhelming presumption that we have a duty in common. Stories begin, therefore, with something that means too much: a corpse (as in *Hamlet* or the latest thriller), an oracle, an archetype, an overdeterminable symbol. Art does not add itself to the world of meanings: it makes room in meaning itself.

It is an axiom of contemporary poetics that a word is not simply a meaning: "A poem should not mean / But be." Confusion sets in, however, as soon as we attempt to define how words are released from their bondage to meaning. The

3. This holds true even when abstraction is attacked. The *New Republic*, wishing to restore the proper term, spells it like it is: A + B + M = Lunacy. The scientific form loses its cool; it is made to collapse into the colloquial, like technical into ordinary language philosophy. An abstract ABC adds up to a Luna—C. One side of the mock equation, by overspecifying the "proper" term, reveals a deceptive underspecification in the other.

alternative to meaning must be within the aura of meaning, even part of its structure: so Kant's "purposiveness without purpose" remains within the aura of teleology. Meaning is everywhere; the problem is that of fullness rather than emptiness, of redundancy and insignificant signification. Things come to us preinterpreted: Stevens asks the sun to shine in a heaven "that has expelled us and our images." Superfetation of meanings in our world is like the proliferation of gods and spirits in the ancient world. "And still the world pursues"—no wonder Mallarmé wished to evoke an "objet tu" by means of an "ombre exprès." There is always something that violates us, deprives our voice, and compels art toward an aesthetics of silence. "Les yeux seuls sont encore capable de pousser un cri," writes Char about his experiences in the Second World War. And Nelly Sachs, alluding to the suffering of her people:

> Wailing Wall Night
> Carved in you are the psalms of silence.

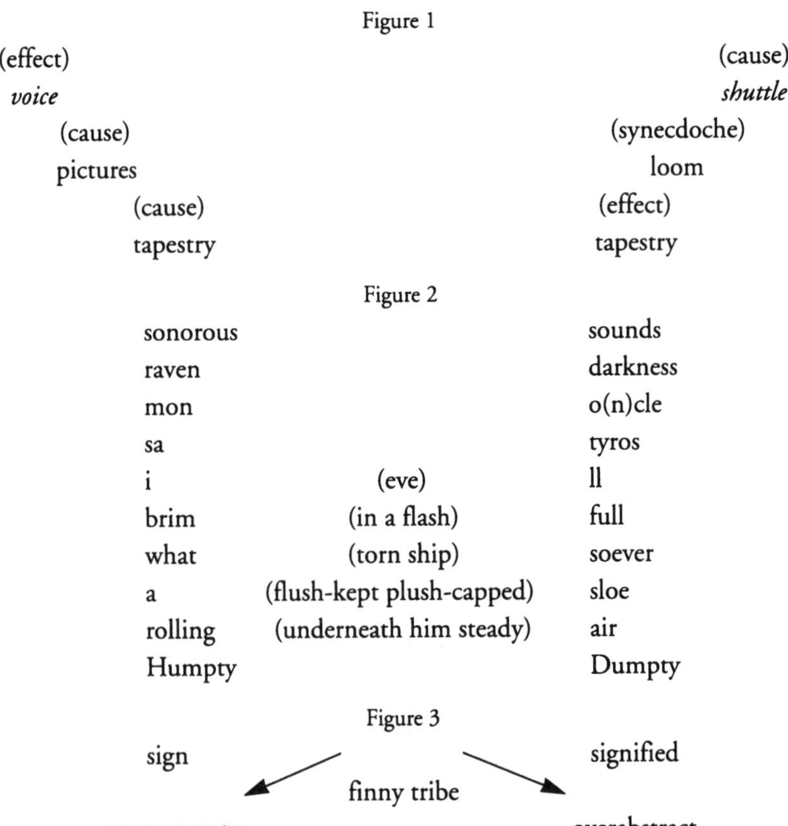

BIBLIOGRAPHICAL NOTE

On "condensation," see Sigmund Freud, *The Interpretation of Dreams* (Vienna, 1900). The satyros story is mentioned on p. 99 of the 1911 edition. On the glamor of grammar, see C. Brooke-Rose, *A Grammar of Metaphor* (New York, 1959); Morton W. Bloomfield, "The Syncategoremic in Poetry: From Semantics to Syntactics," in *To Honor Roman Jakobson* (The Hague, Janua Linguarum Series Major 31, 1967), 1: 309–17; and T. Todorov, "La grammaire du récit," *Langages* 12 (1968): 94–102. A. J. Greimas's remarks on the "syntactical distance" between defined and solving word in crossword puzzles may have implication for poetics through the intermediate notion of periphrasis (*To Honor Roman Jakobson,* 1: 799–815). W. K. Wimsatt, Jr., notes Milton's syntactical "dislocations" in "One Relation of Rhyme to Reason," *The Verbal Icon* (Lexington, Ky., 1954).

Owen Barfield in *Poetic Diction* (London, 1928), pp. 66 ff. and 116 ff., has genial remarks on the making of meaning through abridgment or etymological development. He utilizes Emerson's essay "Language" and Shelley's "Defense of Poetry." De Saussure's notes on words within words and anagrammatic grammar are analyzed by J. Starobinski, *Mercure de France* (février 1964); and in *To Honor Roman Jakobson,* 3: 1906–18. Kenneth Burke's "On Musicality in Verse," *The Philosophy of Literary Form* (Baton Rouge, 1941), studies concealed alliteration in Coleridge and approaches De Saussure. His "A Theory of Terminology," in *Interpretation: The Poetry of Meaning,* ed. R. Hopper and D. L. Miller (New York, 1967), pp. 88 ff., summarizes much of his concern with tautology and graded series. For "Joyce as Philologist," see Richard M. Kain, *Mosaic* 2 (1969): 74–85, and the relevant works of David Hayman and J. S. Atherton. I have previously tried a structuralist analysis in *Hopkins: A Collection of Critical Essays* (Englewood Cliffs, N.J., 1966), pp. 8–9.

In Lewis Carroll's *Through the Looking Glass,* Humpty-Dumpty defines a *portmanteau* phrase as "two meanings packed up into one word." See also Carroll's preface to the 1896 edition of that book. His story "Novelty and Romancement" is based on the misapprehension of "boundary." The ontological role of error in figurative speech is the subject of Walker Percy's "Metaphor as Mistake," *Sewanee Review* 67 (1958): 79–99. I take from him the example of the "Blue Darter Hawk." Sigurd Burkhardt's *Shakespearean Meanings* (Princeton, 1968), esp. chap. 2, discusses the "bondage of meaning" and how poetry breaks the "semantic identity" of words. Cf. Elizabeth Sewell, "The Structure of Poetry (London, 1951), esp. p. 16. The modern "Aesthetics of Silence" is discussed by Susan Sontag in *Styles of Radical Will* (1969). Also, for the basically oblique relations between literary sign and signification, see Maurice Merleau-Ponty, "Le Langage indirect et les voix du silence," in *Signes* (Paris, 1961). On the possibility of a "science de la littérature" based on a linguistic model, see Roland Barthes, *Critique et vérité* (Paris, 1966), pp. 56–63. The Russian Formalists' distinction between the significant (phonemic) and nonsignificant (phonetic) relation of sound to meaning is summarized by V. Erlich, *Russian Formalism,* 2d ed. (New York, 1965), pp. 218 ff.

Of the many areas omitted in this essay, the most important perhaps is that of the sociology of language, or rather "literacy." The work of Kenneth Burke, Roland Barthes, Michel Foucault, George Steiner, and others complements in this field philologists like Karl Vossler, Leo Spitzer, and Erich Auerbach. The notion of an "écart stylistique" is essential to them. Some studies of particular interest: A Van Gennep, "Essai d'une théorie des langues spéciales," *Religion, moeurs et légendes* (Paris, 1909); J. Huizinga, *The Waning of the Middle Ages* (London, 1924); Ernest Jones, "A Linguistic Factor in English Characterology," *Essays in Applied Psycho-Analysis* (London, 1923); Wilhelm von Humboldt, *Schriften zur Sprachphilosophie* (Wissenschaftliche Buchgesellschaft, Darmstadt, 1963).

Cases

The Struggle for the Text

O which one? Is it each one?
—Gerard Manley Hopkins

The question I have put to myself is: How is this text, the Hebrew Bible, different from all other texts? Is there a basis to the distinction between fiction and Scripture? Can we discriminate the two kinds by rhetorical or textual qualities, rather than by external criteria that remain mysterious? To call the Bible a sacred text is to set it apart, to constitute it as such for the reader, but as Auerbach[1] and others have argued, there is something in the text that prompts us toward this, not in order to keep the text's message hidden or enclosed, but on the contrary to make us enter its originative space: the unsaid as well as the said, the unmarked as well as the marked terrain, where the going is complex from both a scholarly and a spiritual point of view.

What complicates the critic's situation is also, of course, that we cannot even begin to move into that territory without certain assumptions: for example, that despite the antiquity of the Bible or our removal in time from it, it has not become estranged beyond repair, or that it was not totally other to begin with (that, divinely inspired or not, it speaks, as the rabbis said, in the language of men), or that it was faithfully transmitted, or that, however accidented it may be, however diversified from book to book as well as within each book, there is something like a unitary perspective, if only as a horizon. Moreover, I cannot claim to possess enough global knowledge of texts that function as Scripture within other cultures to be sure that the qualities of the Hebrew Bible make it unique. My question as to its special character makes sense primarily within a tradition whose poetics have been Hellenic rather than Hebraic, so that the Bible, however influential, has never been entirely naturalized and even today remains a resident alien, at once familiar and unfamiliar.

Jacob's struggle with the angel, in Genesis 32, has become an inexhaustible source for parables and analogies in the Western tradition; in that sense it is not at all strange but rather a familiar guest in the literary and popular mind. The words are all known, and there are very few of them. One of the most uncanny stories in the Bible, it is also one of the sparest, even more so in Hebrew than in English. The core narrative consists of six verses and seventy words in all: to these are added an epilogue in which Jacob names the place of encounter, Peniel, and supplies the etymology "for I have seen God face to face," while the narrator appends what scholars call an etiological frame, which links this event to a dietary taboo.

The economy of presentation is closer to the Classical than to the Shakespearean stage: in the spotlight a man and another man, wrestling, then exchanging three sets of words. But the context remains unlit. Why does the fight begin? We are not told. Its outcome is as mysterious as its onset, though decisive for at least one of the protagonists. On the fringes, of course, are the people in the patriarchal narratives, reduced for this exceptional moment to extras: Esau and the Edomites, Laban and his retainers, the family and flock of Jacob. The Classical stage, after its stichomythia, often relieves and broadens its perspective by the great odes of the chorus. But here, where we might expect a breach in the narrative style, where a song-like elaboration might occur modeled on Genesis 27, Isaac's blessing of Jacob and then of Esau—episodes that anticipate the famous copia of blessings Jacob and Moses bequeath before their death on the B'nei Israel—here the style remains so laconic that one could suspect a decision to truncate, to allow the present moment a minimal telling. Wit, at this juncture, is not the wit of words: there is no rush of rhetoric, no verbal testing as so often in Shakespeare, where the characters parry and thrust and wound by overflowing puns. Wit is a matter of bearing up under, standing under, a directive called the Covenant or Promise or Blessing. It is no accident that the story turns on the manifestation of a name and a blessing: these charged vocatives have ominous as well as nominative value and are to be won rather than willfully seized or expended.

The words, then, stacked so close, with their roots still showing, are, as Auerbach says, *deutungsbedürftig:* demanding interpretation. Their meaning is a sediment that needs settling, almost like the wandering patriarchs themselves. I shall come back to this point; let me stress for the moment that the presence of a redactor, fusing cult legends centered on person and place, is more than an erudite hypothesis. The redactional process, provable or not, is descriptive of a style in which every sentence is a jealously guarded deposit, as if language had to have authority, whatever uncertainties encompassed the reported event or act of naming it. In that sense Jacob's struggle continues within the interpretive communities that receive this story as Scripture. In its determinate indeterminacy, in its authoritative and inscriptive spareness, it reminds one of Herman Melville's impression of Judea: "Stones of Judea. We read a good deal about stones in Scripture. Monuments and memorials are set up of stones; men are stoned to death; the figurative seed falls in stony places. . . . Judea is one accumulation of stones."[2]

Here is, in the King James version, what I call the core story, framed by Gen. 32:1–22 and 33:

> And Jacob was left alone; and there wrestled a man with him until the breaking of the day. And when he saw that he prevailed not against him, he touched the hollow of his thigh; and the hollow of Jacob's thigh was strained, as he wrestled with him. And he said, Let me go, for the day breaketh. And he said, I will not let thee go, except thou bless me. And he said unto him, What is thy name? And he said, Jacob. And he said, Thy name shall be called no more Jacob, but Israel: for thou hast striven with God and with men, and hast prevailed. And Jacob asked him, and said, Tell me, I pray thee, thy name. And he said, Wherefore is it that thou dost ask after my name? And he blessed him there. And Jacob called the name of the place Peniel: for I have seen God face to face, and my life is preserved.

Nothing readies us for this event. Jacob is journeying to Canaan; he reaches Maḥanaim and makes preparations for meeting Esau. Suddenly, at night, this man (*ish*) appears. Was it a dream, perhaps? Maimonides thought so. Jacob, who had a vision at Beth-el, now has a vision at Peni-el. He is always, in his semitic state, in his wanderings, met by angels or divine messengers. Yet there is a difference. The meeting is not only sudden, like a vision or dream—this time what happens can be called a vision only by analogy, because the text is so terse, and says "man" not "angel," and no word about dreaming. Emily Dickinson expresses our feeling when she concludes a poem inspired by the episode,

> And the bewildered Gymnast
> Found he had worsted God.[3]

Such bewilderment is not lessened by the placement of the story, as chapter 32 becomes chapter 33. It is a combat not necessary to the sequence of events. We could omit it and still have a continuous narrative—indeed, a more continuous one. Remember the circumstances in which Jacob finds himself. He is afraid of Esau and wants to appease him. He settles down for the night in the camp (v. 14) and sends before him a vanguard of propitiatory gifts: "two hundred she goats and twenty he goats, two hundred ewes and twenty rams, thirty milch camels," and so forth. A few lines further on we read again: "So these gifts passed over before him; and he himself lodged that night in the camp." Then, as if he were woken by a dream or unsure that enough gifts had been sent before, the text informs us, "he rose up that night, and took his two wives and two handmaidens, and eleven children, and passed over the ford of the Jabbok. He took them, and sent them over the stream, and sent over that which he had" (v. 23). From that somewhat tautological statement, which sounds to me like an attempted coda, we go to the laconic struggle with the "man." But in terms of the narrative we could cross easily to chapter 33, assuming the night has gone by. "Jacob lifted up his eyes, and looked, and behold, Esau came, and with him four hundred men."

Now everything is sequential, logical: this is how Jacob's camp meets that of Esau, and Jacob's cunning preparations work out. The brothers reconcile. Chapter 33, in fact, does not refer to Jacob as Israel but still as Jacob: the struggle by night is clearly an episode that has inserted itself into a funny-fearful story illustrating Jacob's resourcefulness.

So the struggle with the angel is not only a stark, mysterious event, but unnecessary in terms of the unfolding narrative. This narrative exhibits Jacob's character, or his conduct, which is prudent though not exactly courageous. In his wish to appease and flatter Esau, Jacob is almost blasphemous. In words that strangely echo "for I have seen God face to face and my life is preserved," Jacob says to his brother, "If I have found favor in your sight, receive my gift, for indeed I have seen your face as one sees the face of God."

Jacob is not an admirable person, patriarch though he may be. (Gunkel, in *The Legends of Genesis,* laconically entitles one section, "The Patriarchs Not

Saints."[4]) But it is not entirely Jacob's fault, for this is the story of two camps, Maḥanaim (Gen. 32:2–3), two nations, Edom and Israel, from the start—from the very womb of Rebeccah in which Jacob and Esau struggle. There too is a wrestling, and Jacob's name comes from that neonatal fight. "His hand had hold of Esau's heel (*akev*), and they called him Jacob (*Ya'akov*)." You will also recall his tricking Esau out of his birthright and blessing; and his behavior with Laban. "Vayignov Ya'akov Lavan." (31:20). Jacob is a ganef, though I won't claim Laban was much better; Jacob, I am sorry to say, is what he is called in the Bible: a heel.

Let me continue to put together what is well known. The mysterious episode of Jacob's contest is actually what gives him his chance to prove himself. He has struggled with men and prevailed—but at some cost to his father, his brother, and *our* moral sense. No redactorial revision, no appeal to his fated role in a providential drama, can remove the suspicion that he is cunning rather than noble—in short, a trickster. It is true that Abraham and Isaac too can use deceit and subterfuge, but they are less called upon to do so. Did Abraham try to pass off a ram for his child? That is not what the Bible says. Yet about Jacob it is candid; and Jacob too, of course, will be deceived by his children when they break his heart by showing him Joseph's technicolor coat dipped in goat's blood.

How does Jacob prove himself during that night-contest? Think first of the irony of his situation: he prepares to meet the wrath of Esau; he puts his property and even his family in front of him, and whom does he meet, and when? "And Jacob was left alone." As Speiser says, "The carefully calculated never comes off."[5] There is nothing between Jacob and the wrestler, that antagonist from nowhere. Then it turns out the man is not a man, but God himself. Even if he is an angel and not God, no other patriarch, no other biblical character except for Moses has so direct and dangerous an encounter with a divine agent.

Genesis Rabbah makes a startling suggestion when it quotes R. Berekiah. "There is none like God (Deut. 32:26); yet who is like God? Jeshurun, which means Israel the Patriarch. Just as it is written of God, And the Lord alone shall be exalted (Isaiah 2:11), so of Jacob too: And Jacob was left alone (Gen. 32:25)."[6] This is more than eulogy, for the allusion that identifies Jacob and Jeshurun is underwritten by the opening prooftext of the midrash: "There is none like unto God, O Jeshurun." The word *alone* acquires two senses: *only* Jacob, among all men, is noble or straight enough to be compared to God; but also, more radically, the *loneliness* of the human Jacob in this encounter can remind us of the *aloneness* of God. Jacob wrestles with God as God wrestles with Himself.

Through this unmediated encounter, everything shady in Jacob is removed: the blessing he stole he now receives by right; and his name, tainted by his birth and subsequent behavior, is cleared. No longer will he be called Jacob, that is, Heel or Usurper, but Israel, the God-fighter—quite a title, even if the redactor draws back and shows some cunning of his own, claiming it means "You have striven with God [Midrash: Angels] *and with men.*" "As with men" would seem more exact, if it is an anaphoric reference to Jacob's trouble with Laban and Esau. Or should we take "You have striven with God [*elohim*] and with men" as a hendyadis, intending "you have striven with godlike men," or "with a godlike man"? The narrator's gloss tries to settle the meaning of *Yisrael* but only complicates it. In the later Torah Commentary issued by the Union of the American Hebrew Congregations, modern scholarship develops, without alluding to it, Rabbi Berekiah's midrash. *Jeshurun,* another name for Israel the Patriarch, "means noblest and best": the rabbis suspect the name is rooted in the word for "upright" (*yashar*). So Yisrael, we learn from this Commentary, is probably derived from *yashar-el,* the one whom God makes straight, as opposed to *ya-akov-el,* the one whom God makes to limp.[7] Moreover, it has been suggested, the stems *akov* (heel) and *avek* (wrestle) may chime like anagrams. It hardly matters: the eponymic privilege passes to Jacob, whatever the title means. The name change denotes a character change, or the inner sense of Jacob's previous life breaking through. *Anokhi imkha,* God had said to him in the Bethel or house of God vision (Gen. 28:15); there "I am with you" sounded comforting, but here the testing and dangerous side of it is disclosed, as a divinely inflicted bruise replaces a flaw of character.

"It is no sin to limp," Freud writes at the end of *Beyond the Pleasure Principle.*[8] He knows his démarche in this treatise has not been as straightforward, not as logical or scientific as he might wish; and I can only repeat Freud's genial self-defense. For you may wonder what is literary about my reflections so far. Am I not constructing a homily or midrash, and so competing with the rabbinic sages instead of separating out a literary field with its own distinctive boundary?

While Midrash must be viewed as a type of discourse with its own rules and historical development, and while we cannot assume that its only function was exegetical, little is more important today than to remind secular literary studies of the richness and subtlety of those strange rabbinic conversations which have been disdained for so long in favor of more objective and systematized modes of reading. Moreover, for any text to remain alive, it requires the attention and supplementation of commentary. But this sets up a paradox involving the relation of source-text to the concept *literature*. If we accept von Rad's view that the lateness and literariness of the Yahwist (the supposed author-redactor of the combat story) go hand in hand, and that "becoming literature meant in a sense an end for this [biblical] material, which until then had already had a varied history behind it,"[9] then the proper task of midrashic or non-midrashic exegesis is to keep the Bible from becoming literature. Becoming literature might mean a material still capable of development turning into a closed corpus, a once-living but now fossilized deposit. The only virtue I can claim for the literary study of the Bible is, therefore, that while it can hardly be more imaginative than the masters of old, *it can dare to go wrong*. Let me try.

I return to our brief story. I have suggested its extraordinary summation of Jacob's character, its conversion of a cunning person, a sort of Jewish Odysseus, into a consecrated patriarch, touching and touched by God. Yet there are disturbing currents in the episode, which the rabbis picked up but did not always pursue explicitly. Berekiah's remarks on "Jacob was left alone" show what the rabbis could do. For the contemporary reader one perplexing feature is the sudden appearance of that "man." Another is the fact that he wishes to leave before sunrise. Finally, there is the unusual theme of wrestling with and overcoming divinity.

Maimonides, as I reported, thought it must have been a prophetic dream of Jacob's.[10] Rashi, abbreviating various commentators, suggests that the mysterious man was indeed an angel, but of a special sort—Esau's guardian angel. The encounter has a divine but also an unkosher aspect: this may be Esau's protector waylaying Jacob. In this case the surprise would be that Jacob encounters not the flesh-and-blood Esau, for whom he has so carefully prepared, but his demonic double. His being a ghost or demon, moreover, would explain why the man must get away before sunrise, although Rashi will not say more about this peculiarity than that the angel leaves to offer praise at break of day.

Gunkel too senses something strange in a story seemingly unable to make up its mind about the natural-supernatural character of this episode. "Jacob was really a Titan, and consequently we can scarcely avoid seeing a faded out myth."[11] Now Jacob himself, as well as his opponent, is more than human. In Genesis Rabbah we find, to our surprise, that the conversation turns mainly on the nature of angels: whether or not "the Holy One, blessed be He" creates a new company of angels every day, who utter a song before Him and then depart —that is, cease to exist.[12] (This is a thought, by the way, which still haunted Walter Benjamin's imagination, as Scholem has shown.) Do we need this additional distraction, however beautiful, especially since it introduces yet another uncertainty? If, indeed, the angels are new each morning and do not last the rest of the day, what sort of being is this phantom of the night? Rabbi Helbo has an answer. "It was Michael or Gabriel, who are celestial princes; all others are exchanged, but they are not exchanged." In sum, the man may be divine and not divine; he may be a demon and not a demon; while Jacob may be a man or a transformed Titan, a usurper or a heroic challenger who wrests the blessing from God even as he had wrested it, by sleight of hand, from his father.

So far everything I have said merely emphasizes the betwixt-and-between status of Jacob: he is a wanderer; he dwells in the space of Maḥanaim, the double camp on this and the other side of the river; the outcome between him and his brother is not assured; and the combat itself, climaxing in the key phrase "you have striven with elohim and with men," keeps the nature of the opponent undecidable. On what side of the stream Jacob was, what the name of a person is or what it means, whether Peniel or Penuel is the right spelling, and whether Jabbok is or is not a metathesis of a Ya'akov cannot be determined like a clearly marked border.

The same questionable border affects the filiation, in this episode, of folktale and Scripture. Gunkel sees in the combat a faded myth; we may also recall legends in which an evil spirit waylays, through jealousy or malice, a person chosen to be superior to the realm of such spirits. The rabbis' learned discussion about the praising, ephemerid angels may not be a digression after all, but rather a tacit acknowledgment that there is not always peace in the high heavens; that even up there beings exist who are jealous of man, who accuse him the more they praise God. For there is no praise without slander; and the angel who attacks Jacob may be the Satan who accuses Job. It is, fundamentally, Jacob's good name that is in question. What is man, that Thou (God) shouldst magnify him? It is just as well the angels last only until sunrise, for this guarantees our safety: the dawn which means a return of life to us, of the soul to the body, means they cannot carry our night-thoughts before God's throne. They praise Him, then cease to exist.

Nothing said so far, I want to emphasize again, is strictly literary, except for the question of how much legend or folktale Scripture has displaced. But the type or structure of displacement, which interests Roland Barthes, for example, has not been explored. What interests me are the fault lines of a text, the evidence of a narrative sedimentation that has not entirely settled, and the tension that results between producing one authoritative account and respecting traditions characterized by a certain heterogeneity. In Scripture, despite doubled stories and inconsistencies, there is a sometimes laconic, sometimes wordy, but always imperious unity. In Jacob's combat that unifying tension reaches a peculiar pitch. Listen once more to the following sentence:

> And when he saw that he prevailed not against him, he touched the hollow of his thigh, and the hollow of Jacob's thigh was strained, as he wrestled with him. And he said, Let me go.

There is something twisted here, because while it is Jacob who is wounded, it is his antagonist who immediately pleads for release. This fact is sometimes explained by saying that Jacob triumphed despite the wound inflicted on him. But suppose that the text has passed over or modified a difficulty in the received versions. That difficulty would be, as I see it, that it was Jacob who touched the man's thigh and wounded him, but that it seemed impossible—to the narrator—for a divine being to be physically, literally hurt. One tradition or solution, therefore, might be to represent Jacob's antagonist as a "man." Yet the story has little point unless it bestows on Jacob the title Yisrael, and its connotation of a consecrating contact with divinity. It is possible, moreover, that the tradition was handed down in ambiguous form and made more believable or homogeneous by a redactorial process which, however, was careful to leave some traces. To understand the process, all we have to do is omit one word, the name Ya'akov from verse 26. The first "he" could then be Jacob rather than the angel: "And when he saw that he prevailed not against him, he touched the hollow of his thigh, and the hollow of his thigh was strained, as he wrestled with him." It could be Jacob who touched his opponent's thigh and by that blow—a low blow—assured victory for himself. This could be consistent with the Jacob we know, the trickster who gains the blessing by deceit.

It is the privilege of a literary interpreter to revive this uncomfortable perspective, though not in order to slander Jacob. Rather, once again, to reveal the Maḥanaim situation, the doubleness and duplicity out of which Jacob must always emerge. Or simply to respect the hendyadic, even polyphonic nature of all texts, as they strive for a single, authoritative point of view. There are interesting asymmetries and superfluities in so economical a story—the entire story itself, in fact, introduces something baffling on the level of narrative that cannot be smoothed over or harmonized without further redactional or interpretive moves. Without producing incoherence, these baffles raise questions that are at once textual and interpretive. A stronger way of putting it is that the mode of existence of the text and the mode of representation (mimesis) have fused beyond alteration—though not, of course, beyond analysis.

Imagine a section of Genesis beginning, "Call me Israel." However deep, struggling, or myriad-minded the ensuing narrative, we would know ourselves in the presence of fiction, not Scripture. The same holds, of course, for texts more scrabbled than the Bible, texts like Joyce's *Finnegans Wake*. "Shem is as short for Shemus as Jem is joky for Jacob." The problem we face, strangely enough, is not that we cannot define Scripture but that having gradually redefined fiction in the light of Scripture, we now find it hard to distinguish between them. We see both within a global definition of what textuality is; and the same merging occurs as we recover a knowledge of midrash, so that literary criticism and midrashic modes begin to blend into each other. It is no accident that recent theories of intertextuality have devalued the principle of unity as it lodges with some organic or magical mastery attributed to the author of the work. The authority of the author, like that of the biblical redactor or redactors, comes from the way the intertextual situation is handled; and in this authors are close to being redactors, even if they do not acknowledge it. Any text, however seemingly autonomous, is also what Coleridge said truth is: a ventriloquist. Through this text other texts speak. Eliot, when he characterized poetry as a "medium" that digested the most disparate experiences, raised the same issue of the unstable unity of art, or the tensions within it. The New Criticism explored these tensions as the source of aesthetic value and identified them with such formal properties as paradox, irony, ambiguity, and the use of complex or multiple plots. The newer criticism, however, is less concerned with unity and more with the uniformity that comes through too anxious an emphasis on unity. It uses intertextuality as a "technique of suspicion" directed against both the romantic myth of originality and the classicist myth of normative language behavior.

The awareness that all writing is a fusion of heterogeneous stories or types of discourse—that it is layered or even macaronic while seeking the appearance of unity—has been fostered by some of the most important scholarship of recent times. Although there are anthropologists and historians of religion who still aim to find the dominant myth of a particular culture (that of the "High God," for example), many others dispute that there is a myth *an sich* rather than a corpus of stories interacting with a commentary process that continually modifies, updates, and syncretizes what is at hand. Levi-Strauss, while maintaining the concept of a "myth of reference" as the hypothetically stable, synoptic focus of stories called myths, and while trying to extract from them a logic common to all minds, savage or sophisticated, also describes the bricolage that repairs or revises the always faltering mythic narrative. Mikhail Bakhtin discloses a "heteroglossia" within novels that seem spoken or coordinated by a single authorial presence. Clifford Geertz and Jonathan Smith, like good literary exegetes, train our eyes to appreciate the thick tricky texture of native informants as well as distant fables. This more complex understanding came initially through the Higher Criticism of the Bible, which analyzed a unified, authorless narrative into its redacted and blended strands. With the Higher Criticism we are back, of course, to German scholarship of the nineteenth century, which introduced a sort of geologically structured sense of time into the development of Scripture.

I would like to assert that Scripture can be distinguished from fiction by its frictionality: not only its respect for friction, which exists also in literary texts, but its capacity to leave traces—which incite and even demand interpretation of what it has incorporated. Yet the contemporary theories I have described, which derive partly from biblical scholarship, make such a distinction more difficult. There may be more cryptomnesia in fiction than in the Bible. But if there is a major difference, it bears on the fact that the respect which shapes variant stories into a narrative does not—in Scripture—reflect only the aesthetic problem of blending them into a unified whole. It recalls, or should recall, the authority of traditions handed down, each with its truth claim—a respect which makes every word, and not only the characters, "schwer von ihrem Gewordensein," to quote Auerbach: heavy with the fullness of having had to be formed.

Let me conclude by exemplifying this problem of definition in the work of Roland Barthes, whose essay "The Struggle with the Angel" on Genesis 32 is, except for Auerbach's chapter in *Mimesis,* the best modern commentary on a biblical episode. Barthes is not interested in what makes this text Scripture rather than fiction. After Propp and Levi-Strauss he might dispute such a distinction. In his *Morphology of the Folktale* Propp established the structure of that form by analyzing out a finite number of "functions" or type-episodes which every folktale combines.[13] To describe Jacob's combat, Barthes cites type-episodes 15 through 19, including the perilous *passage* from place to place; *combat* between villain and hero; *branding* or *marking* the hero or bestowing on him a special gift; *victory* of the hero; and so forth. Associated episodes such as the difficult crossing of a ford guarded by a hostile spirit also identify Jacob's struggle as having the same structure as a folktale. But this resemblance is not what holds Barthes's attention, and doubtless he could have analyzed a

Homeric sequence in the same structuralist fashion. "What interests me most in this famous passage," he writes, "is not the 'folkloristic' model but the abrasive frictions, the breaks, the discontinuities of readability, the juxtaposition of narrative entities which to some extent run free from an explicit logical articulation. One is dealing here (this at least is for me the savour of reading) with a sort of *metonymic montage:* the themes (Crossing, Struggling, Naming, Alimentary Rite) are *combined,* not 'developed.'" Barthes ends by claiming that this "asyndetic character" or "metonymic logic" of the narrative expresses the unconscious, and he asks for a reading that would lead to the text's "symbolic explosion," its "dissemination, not its truth," so that we would not reduce it to a signified, whether "historical, economic, folkloristic or kerygmatic," but would manage "to hold its *significance* fully open."[14]

Barthes's powerful application of Propp places the folkloric context beyond doubt. Yet one peculiarity of his account must be mentioned. How can he talk of the "asyndetic character of the narrative" when its most obvious syntactical feature is parataxis or syndeton: the linking of every verse segment by the conjunction *va* (and)? Only the last verse differs by substituting a coda-like *al ken* (therefore) and *ki* (because), which are simply heightened conjunctives.

Barthes cannot reply that he is referring to structural juxtapositions, for he has said specifically he is commenting on the "savour of the reading" not the "structural exploitation." In truth, this proclitic and ubiquitous *va* is like the rarer enclitic *yah* or *el,* signifying "God." Barthes cannot value this initial sign tacked on to so much and pointing in a teleological direction, even if God remains hidden most of the time. Von Rad, a theologian, is nearer the mark when he observes that "the divine promise is like a sign before and over all these individual narratives, and within this bracket, so to speak, there is much good and evil."[15]

Barthes, then, is too obviously "deconstructing" a text normally identified as belonging to Scripture and teleological in its orientation. He does not see that the teleological impulse participates in the concatenative power of storyteller or redactor, in that motivating *va,* and in the will to shape by combining. The process of composition here is not exclusively unifying or agglomerative: divergencies are not always resolved. This produces a textual quality which is peculiar enough to be given a separate name, despite structural similarities with saga, folklore, or stories stuck together by what scholars call "contamination."

When Barthes, therefore, asks us to hold the significance of this Bible story "fully open," by stressing an asyndetic and metonymic logic that unsettles the signified and enables the story's "dissemination, not its truth," he leaves out, even structurally, what Auerbach in his *akedah* interpretation stresses so effectively. The truth claim of the Bible, Auerbach says, is so imperious that reality in its sensuous or charming aspect is not dwelt upon; and the spotlight effect, which isolates major persons or happenings, is due to the same anagogical demand that excludes all other places and concerns. Bible stories do not flatter or fascinate like Homer's; they do not give us something artfully rendered; they force readers to become interpreters and to find the presence of what is absent in the fraught background, the densely layered (Auerbach uses the marvelous word *geschichtet*) narrative.

By comparing two passages, the *akedah* from the Bible and a recognition scene from the nineteenth book of the *Odyssey*—passages that do not have the slightest thematic relation—and by refusing to disqualify one in the light of the other or to find the same basic structure in them, Auerbach maintains a gap between Scripture and fiction, if only in the form of Hebraic versus Hellenic. It is possible to object that this gap narrows because of the New Testament, or because of the Hellenic phase that Hebrew learning goes through. It is also possible to plead that the Hellenizing did not really change the Hebraic tradition in the long run. What remains important is that one mind brings together radically divergent modes of representation under the sign of difference. This would not have been possible if both stories did not belong, at some level, to the same culture. This culture is, or was, a reading culture: the curator not only of widely divergent types of literature but also of informed modes of interpretation that encouraged perspectival empathy. Yet by the time Auerbach wrote, a nationalism that had fostered the development of the vernaculars in the Renaissance, and made *Mimesis* possible by reflecting the depth and concreteness of historical life, was imposing a doctrinaire canon and tyrannical unity of expression. As an expatriate victim of German National Socialism, Auerbach was himself a *Maḥanaim* figure, though he did not seek a truer homeland, like Abraham, nor did he venture, like Odysseus, to return to his old place, in the hope it would still know him.

The question of the relation of place to destiny or spiritual strength is given extraordinary resonance by the story of the patriarchs and here by Jacob's combat. I am reminded of Booker T. Washington's remark about another people emerging from slavery. "They must change their names. They must leave the Old Plantation." In the Hebrew Bible this imperative is related to literature from the beginning: these narratives of exodus (starting with the command to Abraham, *lekh lekha,* or "get out"), these episodes fixing place names or proper names by paranomasia to a particular theophany continue to demand an exegete despite various etiological frames intending to make those names less opaque. Each storied reasoning upon names recharges the name: semantic opaqueness is not removed, it is simply surrounded by the possibility that there was an original meaning or a specific and authoritative act of designation. Where did that authority, that performative strength come from? Does *nomen* become *numen,* except through the story inspired by it? Can spirit and place ever coincide except through the extended naming that fiction enables?

The universality of Jacob's combat with the angel lies, finally, in that struggle for a text—for a supreme fiction or authoritative account stripped of inessentials, of all diversions, of everything we might describe as arbitrary, parochial, even aesthetic. It centers on a sparse and doubtful set of words, handed on by an editorial process which in its conflations or accommodations could seem to be the very antithesis of the unmediated encounter it describes. Nicknames like Ya'akov or Yisrael, place names like Peni'el, and other agnominations accumulate as a sacred or a silly burden: they are, we sense, a stock of vocatives (ex-vocatives, perhaps) which the redactors cannot let go but must count and recount, sorting gods and goats into something more than a list, a proprietary catalogue, a hoard of names. The accreted, promissory narrative we call Scripture is composed of tokens that demand the continuous and precarious intervention of successive generations of interpreters, who must keep the words as well as the faith.

NOTES

1. Erich Auerbach, *Mimesis: The Representation of Reality in Western Literature,* trans. Willard R. Trask (New York: Doubleday, 1957).
2. Herman Melville, *Journal of a Visit to Europe and the Levant, October 11, 1856—May 6, 1857,* ed. Howard C. Horsford (Princeton: Princeton University Press, 1955).
3. Emily Dickinson, "A Little East of Jordan," in *Complete Poems,* ed. Thomas H. Johnson (Boston: Little Brown, 1960), no. 59.
4. Hermann Gunkel, *The Legends of Genesis: The Biblical Saga and History,* trans. William Herbert Carruth (New York: Schocken Books, 1970), pp. 113–16.
5. *The Anchor Bible: Genesis,* ed. and trans. Ephraim Avigdor Speiser (Garden City, N.Y.: Doubleday, 1964–1983), p. 256.
6. *Genesis Rabbah,* vol. 1 of *Midrash Rabbah,* ed. Harry Freedman and Maurice Simon (London: Soncino Press, 1961), p. 710. Cf. the remarkable "we do not know who was victorious," p. 712. Berekiah's remarks do more than ennoble Jacob. They make Jacob and his story also reveal something about God: an attribute, or *His* "character." God, after all, is the ultimate author of Scripture, and midrash holds up the mirror to that textual image in order to search out and catch what is knowable about Him.

7. *The Torah: A Modern Commentary,* ed. W. G. Plaut, B. J. Bamberger, and W. Hallo, Union of American Hebrew Congregations (New York, 1981).
8. Sigmund Freud, *Beyond the Pleasure Principle,* in *The Standard Edition of the Complete Psychological Works of Sigmund Freud,* trans. James Strachey (London: Hogarth Press, 1955), vol. 18, p. 64.
9. Gerhard von Rad, *Genesis: A Commentary,* rev. ed. (Philadelphia, 1972), p. 18.
10. Moses ben Maimon (Maimonides), *The Guide of the Perplexed,* 2d ed., trans. Michael Friedlander (New York: Dover Publications, 1956), pt. 2, chap. 43 (in some editions chap. 42).
11. Gunkel, *Legends of Genesis,* p. 120.
12. *Genesis Rabbah,* p. 710.
13. Vladimir I. Propp, *Morphology of the Folktale,* rev. ed., trans. Laurence Scott, ed. Louis A. Wagner (Austin: University of Texas Press, 1968).
14. Roland Barthes, "The Struggle with the Angel," in *Image Music Text,* trans. Stephen Heath (London: Fontana Collins, 1977), pp. 125–41.
15. Von Rad, *Genesis: A Commentary,* p. 268. Von Rad also describes eloquently the stratified nature of this text. He writes: "In this narrative more than in any other of the ancient patriarchal traditions something of the long process of formation to which this material was subjected in history becomes clear. . . . There are scarcely examples in Western literature of this kind of narrative, which combines such spaciousness in content with such stability in form. Many generations have worked on them, as in the case of an old house; much of the content has been adjusted in the course of time, much has again been dropped, but most has remained. . . . Here is a passage where a much older form of our saga is revealed. . . . One might think at first, in view of the hopelessness of the fight, that Jacob has won the upper hand over his antagonist (by a trick of fighting?). This interpretation would best suit the continuation, in v. 26, where the antagonist asks Jacob to let him go and then also the later statement that Jacob had prevailed (v. 28b). This monstrous conception, however, that Jacob nearly defeated the heavenly being, is now concealed by the clear text of v. 25b and v. 32b" (pp. 320–21).

Shakespeare and the Ethical Question

The violent carriage of it
Will clear or end the business: when the oracle
(Thus by Apollo's great divine seal'd up)
Shall the contents discover, something rare
Even then will rush to knowledge. Go: fresh horses!
And gracious be the issue.
—William Shakespeare, *The Winter's Tale*

A joining of East and West, which is the occasion of our meeting in Weimar, whether we understand it as a sacred union or simply a marriage of convenience, prompts me, at the beginning of this talk,[1] to repeat a wishful declaration by Goethe in his *West-Östlicher Divan:*

So der Westen wie der Osten
Geben Reines dir zu kosten.

[So the West like the East
May give you pure things to taste.][2]

As is always the case, one can't stop quoting Goethe. The next two lines run, just as deliciously:

> Lass die Grillen, lass die Schale
> Setze dich zum grossen Mahle.
>
> [Leave aside suspicion and externals:
> Sit down to the festive meal.]

Goethe's invitation can serve as motto for our intellectual feasting during the next few days.

But on these convivial occasions there is often a Banquo's ghost, who disturbs the well-ordered proceedings. "Do not stand upon the order of your going," Lady Macbeth says, waiving protocol primly or sardonically, as the Scottish nobles exit in disarray (3.5.118).[3] Weimar, as *lieu de mémoire,* and this lecture-occasion itself, commemorating both Shakespeare and Goethe, must remind us that we are only a few miles from another memory-place, the Gedenkstätte Buchenwald. How tragic this proximity, how treacherous that a center of barbarity existed at close quarters to a center of culture. A chasm opened up, no, was actively, by every device of cultural propaganda, dug deep, dividing neighbor from neighbor, driving into exile or death those who had shared, with likeminded enthusiasm, a love for Goethe and his concept of *Bildung.*

Can anything now remove the suspicion which has not dwindled in the years since Walter Benjamin articulated it: that every cultural monument might be unmasked as a document of barbarism? That even so high an ideal as Weimar Culture was impotent to stem barbarism? Or that, in the case of Germany, what went under the name of culture wasn't that at all but rather a *Scheinkultur?* Goethe himself already suspected dilettantism and superficiality, but that was over two hundred years ago, near the beginning of Germany's entry into "world literature." Goethe knew that Germany was, in cultural and political affairs, an apprentice: it still had to pass through the full historical appreciation of other peoples, whether Greek or French or English or Persian. He ransacked for his work all the points of the cultural compass; as late as 1827, on sending the Helena episode of *Faust* to the printer, he complained: "We Germans were born yesterday" ("Wir Deutschen sind von gestern").

Leo Löwenthal, to whose memory I dedicate this talk, observed that Goethe's consciousness of the exemplary achievements of the past, and his cosmopolitan willingness to make use of them, was otherwise missing in his time and remains unrealized to this day. He reinterprets "die unbewältigte Vergangenheit" ("the unmastered past") as symptomizing a basic fault which even Goethe's life-long efforts failed to change. This fault, Löwenthal suggests, has been there all along as a formative trait of German bourgeois society. That society "did not master its prehistory but overwhelmed it" ("Sie hat ihre Vorgeschichte nicht bewältigt, sondern überwältigt").[4]

Löwenthal's analysis is also important for the conviction it upholds that history is intelligible: however dispiriting its course in Europe, the Enlightenment's *aude sapere* is not extinguished, and our moral intelligence continues to take history as a text. Goethe can still speak to us, though always as critic, not as accomplice; so Goethe himself, addressing Shakespeare as "my friend" in his youthful and effusive speech of 1771, adds that the English bard shamed as well as liberated him.

In what way is Shakespeare our friend today? Can we learn from him without making him our accomplice and merely riding his words to pursue a specific ideology or ideology-critique? There is a voice in me that replies, Don't worry, Shakespeare looks after himself; he throws off, like Proteus, all constraints. Matthew Arnold's famous sonnet guides us: "Others abide our question. Thou art free."[5] No culture politics can long hold Shakespeare down. It is his greatness that he delights in an Iago as well as an Imogen, that his plays are an unfailing cornucopia. The speech of his characters has an exuberance and authority irreducible to the numerous plots and counterplots that swarm in these highly dramatic plays. It is this purposiveness beyond purpose that made Goethe exclaim: "Natur, Natur! nichts so Natur als Shakespeare's Menschen"; "Seine Pläne sind, nach dem gemeinen Stil zu reden, keine Pläne" ["Nature, Nature! nothing is closer to Nature than Shakespeare's characters"; "His plans are no plans at all, in the common sense of the word"].[6]

The "piedness" which Shakespeare shares "with great creating Nature" (*The Winter's Tale* 4.4.87–88) raises, nevertheless, a question it is hard to shake off. We do not have to worry, as I have said, about appropriating him, since he offers so much and is not diminished by it. Let everyone create a Hamlet of his own, or reconfigure Caliban. But the relation of Shakespeare's art to an ethics, however close his art is to nature, and perhaps because it is so close, remains a haunting issue. Each of us must hope that "something rare . . . will rush to knowledge," as in Apollo's oracle described by *The Winter's Tale:* this "rush," in fact, an impatient search for evidence and sometimes a miraculous disclosure, is part of my subject.

Perhaps I should have called my talk "Shakespeare and the Ethics Question." For ethics can be distinguished from the ethical; and Shakespeare's plays are certainly pervaded by moral concerns, by questions about public and private life, by concerns about justice, goodness, friendship, fidelity, love. He rouses our sympathy for all these positive qualities, even when he shows their defeat. He makes us think, again and again, How should one act in such a world? A "What shall I do?" challenges the actors as agents, "places them at the crossroads of a choice in which they are totally committed; it shows them on the threshold of a decision, asking themselves what is the best course to take."[7] Asked in this dramatistic way, the question opposes the easy complicity with shameful compromise, seductive evil, or suicidal passion. The playwright's magic even aligns occasionally with an actual magic, like Prospero's, to evoke the very process of deliberation, that is, to induce exquisite moments of poetry and romance that make a tragic or star-crossed course of events hesitate, as if capable of reflection. Yet though these plays are moral through and through, we find it impossible to draw from them a consistent system of attitudes that might be called an ethics.

Indeed, in Shakespeare as dramatist the ethical verdict is as riddling as the actions of a concealed God. What are the playwright's beliefs? He is "everywhere and nowhere." How could we judge those rash teenagers, Romeo and Juliet, or willful Lear and equally willful Cordelia, or gullible yet noble Othello?[8] What shall we say of Iago, surrogate dramatist, whose devices we watch with fascination? Or of Richard III wooing Lady Anne at the funeral of the father-in-law he murdered? If Polonius is not true to his own self, why give that sinister or foolish counselor such fine maxims as "To thine own self be true"? It is possible to moralize about the flaws, mistakes, and worse, of these characters; yet they are encompassed by an action so vast, a poetry so memorable, that we are magnetized by the spectacle and view ethical considerations, at least those based on the character-virtues of sincerity or honesty, as a defense of the reader against the *theatrum mundi.* Perhaps, as Lionel Trilling has said, summarizing Hegel on Diderot's *Rameau's Nephew,* "the nature and destiny of man are not ultimately to be described in moral terms," since they are marked by a necessary, compulsively histrionic, and self-alienating drive.[9] Or, to cite Jan Kott's more dualistic (and less dialectical) vision: "In Shakespeare's world there is a contradiction between the order of action [politics] and the moral order. This contradiction is human fate. One cannot get away from it."[10]

There is, at the same time, no aloofness, no indifference, in Shakespeare: he is not a divinity standing *ab extra,* paring his fingernails.[11] If his beliefs remain enigmatic, it may be because of excess of empathy. A sympathetic power of imagination seems to have left his own identity obscure. "It was only by representing others that [Shakespeare] became himself," Hazlitt remarks. Keats penetrates deeper into the enigma, and sets up a paradox: this most natural of writers has no nature of his own. "A Poet," Keats declares in the famous letter to Richard Woodhouse (27 October 1818), thinking of both Shakespeare and himself, "A Poet . . . has no identity—he is continually in for [informing?] some other Body. . . . Not one word I ever utter can be taken for granted as an opinion growing out of my identical nature—how can it, when I have no nature?"[12] (This opinion too, just uttered, cannot be taken for granted as Keats's own). A psyche evermore about to be, pressured by real or fictive others, is marked by an involuntary, passionate self-emptying.

It is not, of course, the biographical void that is the problem—even though Keats admits to moments in which he is "in a very little time an[ni]hilated."[13] Our interest focuses less on what the Bard was like as a person than on the equation between absence of self and presence of otherness: on a "negative capability" linked by Keats to the sympathetic imagination. John Middleton Murry, too, counsels us to "surrender to Shakespeare" and so to shuffle off the "mortal coil of moral judgement." He objects to critics that thrust a "proper self" on the author instead of admitting that "in the world of spirit, absolute identity supervenes on annihilation."[14] In Murry's Christian perspective the "nihil" (annihilation of identity) becomes a precondition for a higher identity.

A. D. Nuttall and Harold Bloom see a "new mimesis" in Shakespeare, one that has changed our conception of character. It allows the *dramatis personae* more self-reflection, more access to conscious and perhaps unconscious process. Hamlet is a "representation so original that conceptually *he contains us,* and has fashioned our psychology of motives ever since."[15] That psychology, however, in Bloom's description, returns us to the old "nihil," now flavored by Freud:

> Like the Hebrew hero confronting Yahweh, Hamlet needs to be everything in himself yet knows the sense in which he is nothing in himself. . . . And what Hamlet first loves is what biblical and Freudian man loves: the image of authority, the dead father. . . . When Hamlet matures, or returns fully to himself, he transcends the love of authority and ceases to love at all, and perhaps he can be said to be dying throughout all of Act V, and not just in the scene of the duel.[16]

This package contains a stunning, de-Christianizing insight. But does it encompass Shakespeare's imaginative wildness? "Perhaps what we should take seriously," writes Ruth Nevo, thinking mainly of the later comedies, but not excluding any of Shakespeare's plays, "is precisely the raw, the odd, the counter-rational in them . . . rather than allowing their improbabilities to become familiar to us."[17] The ethical (or meta-ethical) question I raise includes this exuberant "nihil," affecting fable as well as character.[18]

I see at the level of fable a "rush" or "violent carriage" that, like Shakespeare's Cleopatra, leads to "the very heart of loss" (4.12.29)—though, in the Romances, also to a miraculous recovery from that. I see at the level of character an unresolvable element, the overmotivated hesitation of Hamlet or the "motiveless malignancy" of Iago. In either case, *to ethos,* character, is closely connected with *to pathos,* that is, extreme suffering or exposure, episodes in theatrical form that incorporate the "nihil," whether as a single event, a killing, baiting, or blinding on stage, or as a more continuous exhibition, like that of Lear on the heath.[19]

Before Shakespeare, I will surmise, *to pathos* was linked to the sacred. With Shakespeare, passion or *pathos* in its original sense as a suffering that renders us passive, or tempts our imagination to place agency beyond us (in the stars or the gods, for example), this passion, however extreme, is secularized and transformed.[20] Provocative players on the stage of the world drive toward a maximum of self-exposure (but what are they trying to prove, what doubt are they seeking to dispel?[21]) without any assumption that humanity is in the presence of the sacred.

Religious feelings, of course, sincere or exploited, continue to play a role in this intensely human desire to know and be known, to see and be seen, whatever the cost. Prince Hal, echoing Paul's *Letter to the Ephesians,* soliloquizes that, by consorting with the likes of Falstaff, he "will . . . imitate the sun": the prince must withhold his true self-presence in order to shine the more brightly later, "Redeeming time when men think least I will" (*Henry IV,* Pt. 1, 1.2.195–217). His condescension or disguise aligns itself with a curious mix of Christian and Machiavellian attitudes and evokes the double nature of *kenosis*—a concept I wish to introduce formally at this point.[22]

Kenosis can motivate, on the one hand, a self-occulting delay or moratorium, such as Hamlet's "antic disposition," that slows the coming out or "rush to knowledge"; and, on the other, a "going out of our own nature" akin to love, an empathic, active self-alienation necessary for achieving a higher identity—or a state higher than identity.[23] The ethical question cannot bypass this kenosis, deliberate or driven, so close to Diderot's paradox of the effective actor or to Hamlet's reflection on the players ("What's Hecuba to him . . . ?"). The Cambridge anthropologists recovered the structural relation between sacred orgy and drama, only hinted at by Aristotle; the relation of double-natured kenosis to dramatic persona is equally fundamental, and turns Shakespeare's theater into a *secular revelation*.[24]

No playwright before Shakespeare had displayed such brazen theatricality, speeding up both external and internal developments and staging the most frontal contrasts. The theater, as a place of cynosure, of deliberate exhibitionism and licensed voyeurism, approaches contemporary practices, though the risks Shakespeare took were much greater.[25] The contrast with developments in France is a telling one. Rules of decorum were far stricter in the era of Corneille and Racine; so strict, in fact, that even Voltaire—after his visit to England, where he saw Shakespeare performed—called for some relaxation. Though Voltaire could not approve "the barbaric irregularities" of *Julius Caesar,* "a work composed in a century of ignorance by a man who did not even know Latin," he admired the play and regretted his country's "excessive delicacy," which "obliges us sometimes to put into narrative what we should wish to expose to sight." Violent action in the French theater took place mostly off-stage and had to be conveyed in the form of the *récit;* as Voltaire also wrote, "The English give much more to action than we do, they address themselves rather to the eyes."[26] It is this *address to the eyes* which is remarkable, a fearless scopophilia that brings everything onto the stage, not only carnage and ghosts but thought itself, as it emerges out of the private depths.

Yet what is the relation between showbiz of this kind (I use the modern term advisedly) and the moral sense? Is Shakespeare's stage more than the television of its time, the amoral if thrilling spectacle of a violent society? "We pause stupefied," Taine wrote in his *History of English Literature* (1863), "before these convulsive metaphors, which might have been written by a hand in a night's delirium, which gather a pageful of ideas and pictures in half a sentence, which scorch the eyes they would enlighten."[27] When Edgar says to the blinded Gloucester, "Bless thy sweet eyes, they bleed," what saves our own from being scorched?

A reflection of that kind obliges us to face the nature of our seduction: how this spectacular art, "past the size of dreaming," entices us not only to suspend disbelief but also to defer judgment. So forceful is Shakespeare in this regard that I have no difficulty in understanding that though the ethical question never dies, it is displaced into an exacerbated anti-theatrical prejudice.[28] The taboo that is broken, of decorum or delicacy or whatever we may wish to call our defended eyes, can never be entirely restored after Shakespeare, no matter how many *Lettres sur les spectacles* are issued.

Thus difficulties with what Murry calls Shakespeare's moral "vortex" often present themselves as praise of what is *more than theatrical* in his work. Like Charles Lamb, we think the stage cannot contain Shakespeare's imagination, or that seeing instead of reading limits the poetic effect. This is a very subtle move on the chessboard of our unease. It is also present in Goethe's nuanced, late (1826), and deeply ambivalent "Shakespeare as Poet of the Theater" ("Shakespeare als Theaterdichter").

Shakespeare, he declares, "belongs necessarily in the history of poetry; but his presence in the history of theater is only a coincidence."[29] Goethe acknowledges Shakespeare's gift for making the inner life visible, for turning it inside out, but he then claims that by using theatrical shortcuts, as in the Prologue to *Henry V,* Shakespeare does not visualize adequately; he simply induces the impression, in reader or listener, that the wonderful things he recounts might be pictured.

The key to Goethe's dissatisfaction is found in the maxim "nothing is theatrical that is not symbolic for the eyes" ("nichts ist theatralisch, als was für die Augen zugleich symbolisch ist"), and in his elliptical definition of the symbolic as "an important action that points to a still more important one" ("eine wichtige Handlung, die auf eine noch wichtigere deutet").[30] "Symbolic" means, I suspect, the moral adequacy of visual representation. Only occasionally, according to Goethe, does Shakespeare's theater present symbolic "jewels" of that kind (he instances Harry removing the crown from his slumbering father's head and strutting about with it). Goethe adds that the Elizabethan technique of stagecraft—machinery, scene design—was not as advanced or realistic as Weimar's; what the audience had before it was a scaffolding "where there was little to see, and instead everything was merely allegorical" ("ein Gerüste, wo man wenig sah, wo alles nur bedeutete").[31]

I will come back to Goethe; for the moment let me point out that he finesses a religious or moral scruple by adducing what appears to be an aesthetic criterion. Art, he claims, exhibits at Weimar Shakespearean intensities in a more socially accommodated form. (Goethe's "Confessions of a Beautiful Soul," inserted as the sixth book of *Wilhelm Meister,* stands as Goethe's highest, though "epic," achievement in that accommodating mode.) Weimar was, as Goethe tells us, preparing to stage *Romeo and Juliet;* I now turn to that play and describe its visual-theatrical complex; I then return to Goethe and his understanding of the link between that complex and the ethical question.

In *Romeo and Juliet* the theatrical momentum foreshortens time in order to bring love, as well as love's speech, fully "to men's eyes." One of the sanest writers on the play, E. E. Stoll, considers its love at first sight a dramatic shortcut, one of Shakespeare's many "summary and compendious devices." "There is justification enough," he comments, "for this instantaneous and explosive temperament—[especially] in drama, which has no more than three or four hours at its disposal."[32] *Romeo and Juliet,* as the Chorus announces, is intended to take only two hours. Stoll mentions other instances of time-compression that precipitate and complicate the dramatic action: slander in *Othello* or in the subplot of *Lear,* disguise and mistaken identity in the comedies. "What in all these cases is secured is motivation not for psychology but for story. . . . The presentation of character is poetical rather than psychological and ethical."[33]

Yet this begs the question of what "story" or the "poetical" is. Stoll delights in artifice, in narrative conventions that seem to have appealed to all classes among the Elizabethans. Instead of analyzing the pleasure given by these conventions he denies their implausibility: that was, he claims, diminished by ancient use and made further acceptable by Shakespeare's stagecraft and poetry. But Stoll is wrong about how the stagecraft works. He seems to forget that showing is very different from telling. Shakespeare, by staging these narrative shortcuts, does not soften but rather heightens their unrealism.

Shakespeare's poetry, moreover, has a function considerably more complex than that of providing a source of pleasure to distract us from improbability awhile. A sort of competition, in fact, takes place between poetry and theater, especially in *Romeo and Juliet:* at times it is the poetry that is being staged, or given the sort of display that a leading ballerina receives from her partner. Two different kinds of intensity, of poetry and theater, are distinctly felt.[34] Shakespearean drama, always seeking to replace everything indirect by directly represented action, by addressing the eyes, prolongs what it compresses rather than decompressing it; the poetry functions in a similar way, slowing the "forward progress of the turmoils" by a density of its own, a sort of vertical dimension.[35]

Now there is a puzzle here, similar to that of tragic pleasure. What catharsis, or pleasurable release, does Shakespeare's compression of time achieve, to which, in its own way, the heightened language contributes? We do not, I think, accept what is implausible and unrealistic—especially his representation of time—because it is a convention, suitably accommodated and controlled: *we accept it because it evokes something always about to run out of control, an extreme pressure on mind or heart which brings us close to madness but also to revelation.* Compression of time deprives time of meaning and leaves only "a woman, a man, and a sea of spilt blood."[36] Perhaps it is our fear of those moments, verbal or physical, a fear mingled with desire, that is given release.

By revelation, then, I mean something secular: causing a naked and occulted truth to appear, or disclosing a state of mind—even making the mind itself (including the unconscious) visible. When Hamlet, in a marvelous bit of stage-business, suddenly remarks "My father, methinks I see my father" (1.2.184), how much has his "prophetic soul" intuited, or how much had it previously repressed? Horatio does not immediately take the bait, if it is a bait. He circles warily:

HORATIO. Where, my lord?
HAMLET. In my mind's eye, Horatio.
HORATIO. I saw him once; a was a goodly king.
HAMLET. A was a man! take him for all in all: I shall not look upon his like again.
HORATIO. My lord, I think I saw him yesternight.

(1.2.185–89)

You are made to sense something dangerous, even in the very mention of the event, an uncanny mole of a thing that has to be broached carefully to the listener, or which may not be mentioned at all unless the timing is propitious.

Timing as a quality of speech, of deliberation, is much more subtle in *Hamlet* than in *Romeo and Juliet;* yet both plays have a problematic and pressured relation to it. Whether we stress the two hours of (Elizabethan) representational time or the three days of depicted time, the quality of temporality is strained and matures Romeo and Juliet prematurely. "Almost without knowing, the protagonists in this love-drama develop from childish to tragic," Erich Auerbach remarked. But they do know it, of course; an extraordinary rhetorical intensity or, more exactly, voice-maturity (*Mündigkeit*) accompanies their sudden passage from latency, or playing at love, to full-blown passion.[37] ("Love is mature as soon as born" is Hazlitt's comment.) Shakespeare deploys, through both personae, such fertile wit, such an epidemic of paradox and rapidity of repartee, that one might have thought these characters existed to make the language pregnant, to deliver it from relative shyness into multiple births.

It is indeed the pressure of time on human time, regret for even a moment's infertility, that hurries the play along. Nature itself shames or accuses mankind: every moment or word withheld is *contra naturam.* The Nurse's first words are typical: "Now by my maidenhead at twelve years old . . ." (1.3.2). Old Capulet's beautiful lines about Juliet, asking her suitor Paris to wait,

She hath not seen the change of fourteen years.
Let two more summers wither in their pride
Ere we may think her ripe to be a bride.

(1.2.9–11)

undercut themselves by that figure of "withering pride," which contrasts nature's ready fertility with a too noble infertility. Are we back in the world of Shakespeare's sonnets, and their argument that the noble youth addressed should not waste his essence?[38]

What importunes the lovers may be convention or it may be nature: the demand is there, from whatever source. Nature brooks no delay; Capulet's authority brooks no delay; as for the lovers, nothing delays them except the dilation of rhetoric. If it is impossible to tell narcissism from passion in their love, it is because there is a "force" of secular revelation (Goethe defined Nature as "the open secret") that through the green fuse drives the flower. Hamlet's delay, whose source is obscure, may counterpoint this "rush," this existential and evidential impatience.[39]

When we look, then, at Shakespeare's plays as a whole, we find a double and contrasting rhythm of action, with very little intermediate between fast forward and pause. Yet the intensity of speech remains constant. *Romeo and Juliet* is especially noteworthy for its overflow of poetic feeling, cadenzas that retard a fatal action they illumine. The question, What is discovered or brought to light? cannot be divorced from the flare of an imagery that suggests the opacity of truth *and* an existential haste to make truth visible, a haste that is deeply, if suicidally, satisfying. "I stand on sudden haste" (2.3.93), Romeo remarks at one point; and had not the Friar commented on it, we might not notice this paradox among so many in the play.[40]

Within this haste, as I have said, the one constant is that everything must pass through a language exchange; all merchandise of heart or mind must be traded there; nothing is exempt, allowed to be mute or muted, because of depth or holiness of feeling. Speech of one kind or another forces the issue, tests and tempers the mettle of each emotion, each character. That is not ethical in itself; indeed, it may violate developmental time. Yet within the *pauses* of that pressure, or the pausal structure of poetry itself, its metrical as well as metaphorical qualities, a mutable beauty appears, "messenger of sympathies / That wax and wane in lovers' eyes."[41]

To illustrate in detail how the lovers exchange those sympathies, we need only the famous aubade scene (3.5.1–36), a perfect instance of how the language exchange works, how each lover takes the words of the other into account, maturing a theme or a metaphor. It is in this pause, also, that Juliet is allowed full expression of her desire, and that the man abides it: *repression* comes totally from the outside, from the obscure enmity of the two houses, from untimely blows of fortune, and from the joint pressure of nature and social convention on the man, who must woo, and the woman, who must be matched.

Though all the forces of repression are external, at least one desire impedes *itself,* and its omission from *Romeo and Juliet* gives that play its fresh and exceptional status.[42] For here there is no overt quest for the truth, for definitive evidence or self-knowledge. Except for coy doubts in Juliet, which are more like a dallying that questions love only to affirm its power—"Dost thou love me? I know thou wilt say 'Ay', / And I will take thy word" (2.2.90–91)—except for such short-lived misgivings that quickly become a "luring" of the "tassel-gentle," no stratagems test love, they only facilitate its consummation. The "rush to knowledge" is purely that of ecstasy, not of evidence. But in *Hamlet* the desire for evidential knowledge, a desire which becomes its own impediment, returns with a vengeance.

The difference between the two plays is not absolute, of course. The Shakespearean imperative to *show* everything is now trained inward and finds a baffled accomplice in the character of Hamlet. His soliloquies remove a blind or muteness from thought; the flux and reflux of consciousness give visible audition to a region of human experience—ambivalence, vacillation, self-questioning—which we do not see at all in *Romeo and Juliet.* Scopophilia and epistemophilia merge. Even more remarkably, the soliloquies in *Hamlet* affect the rhythm of the action by a sort of decelerando, a musical pausing, whereas in *Romeo and Juliet* reversals of fate and bullets of wit come so fast and furious that there is no place to hide, to recollect. What retardation there is enters the service of an exuberant rhetoric, an expansion of the moment of speech that has little bearing on the speed of events. So the lovers' duet at dawn dilates the moment but does not delay the sun, and Romeo's speeches when he is alone are like inserted arias.

In Shakespeare's more lyrical and memorable pauses, such as Macbeth's instant elegy on his wife, "She should have died hereafter" (5.5.17), the "fearful date," as Romeo calls it, is deferred, if only by the wishful reflection that time might have altered its course to allow a timely word.[43] The incredible speed of repartee common to all of the characters, the overflowing wit, however quibbling, is not so much an infection of the time as it is a response to the pressure of time itself: a response that counters, even while it takes the imprint of, time's fatal chariot. A play like *The Winter's Tale* starts as a "violent carriage" or miscarriage; after which it becomes, with the exception of Polixenes' outburst (parallel to that of Leontes), a pausal pastoral, moving toward rebirth and the redeeming of time past.[44]

The pressure of time is often associated with the pressure of a particular time, of an age that makes its demands on the writer. It is part of our confusion about ethics that we cannot relate these two dimensions of time in Shakespeare's work. The first is so powerful that it seems to have absorbed the second: the literary ethics, politics, or whatever we call the writer's *topical* response to his age is not really available to us. We glimpse it as in a glass darkly, and may be tempted to reconstruct it. But what moves us is the opposite of shadowy: Shakespeare's revelatory and expressive and totally unreticent projection of the most basic as well as terrible aspects of human life.

Yet we can tell something about a later age through the way Shakespeare is received. The impact of Shakespeare on Goethe was, in 1771, almost that of a new creation ("fast eine neue Schöpfung").[45] Could German culture be created or recreated in this original, "Shakespearean" manner? What concerned Goethe was how such a genial and magical act might come about: how the inertial history that separated Germany and Shakespeare by two centuries might be overcome. He undertook to remedy Germany's cultural belatedness and achieve a living poetry through a *translatio studii*—necessarily more learned and mediated than Shakespeare's, though of comparable scope. A German literary Renaissance was in the offing.[46]

But how could he repair the split between popular and high culture, or between a barbaric nationalism and a pedantic classicism? Herder described that cultural schizophrenia again and again. "With us, everything grows a priori." The absence of a national tradition, he added, offered the artist merely a primitive "stock of fairy tales, superstitions, songs, raw language"; yet without the benefit of this "Grundsuppe" a refined classical literature would prove an airy bubble. "If we are not a people, then we have no public, no nation, no language and poetry that is ours, that lives and develops in us. . . . Our classical literature is a bird of paradise, O so colorful, neat and high-flying, and—has never set foot on German soil." More ominously, Herder expressed a resentment of Germany's status in Europe, similar to that echoed in the "Aufbruch" of 1933. "We miserable Germans are fated never to be ourselves, but always the legislators or servants of foreign nations, masters of their destiny yet their bartered, bleeding, exploited slaves."[47]

Löwenthal is right: it is time as history that weighs on Goethe, a cultural (as well as political) history that Germany, not a nation-state till the late nineteenth century, had missed or ignored. All of Goethe's work is a historical drama in that sense. Rejecting allegory in favor of a symbolic method said to be derived from Nature itself, Goethe holds that what is known is also, ultimately, what is visible: the one cannot be in excess of the other. The symbolic method creates that adequacy by penetrating—as gradually as a plant unfolds—to the visible idea of each thing. There is an attempt, as Wordsworth says of his own project, to resolve "into one great faculty / Of being, bodily eye and spiritual need," so that our conversation with Nature becomes limitless.[48] In Goethe's case, however, given German cultural belatedness rather than English embarrassment of tradition, art's recuperative patience must have a transfigurative effect, like that of Nature itself when it draws life from decay. Art functions as "almost a new creation" by turning an inorganic heritage into an organic and viable national culture.[49] Yet Goethe, to achieve this end, turns away from Shakespeare and toward a representational mode that culminates in the "epic theater" of *Faust* Part Two.

What Goethe does with the idea of Hamlet in *Wilhelm Meister* is characteristic of his method and can illustrate his wish to go beyond Shakespeare's "address to the eyes." Hamlet, as Wilhelm explains him in book 3, has a family resemblance to the beautiful soul (*schöne Seele*), whose "confession" is inserted in book 6. There the beautiful soul is typified by a woman who has every social chance yet gives up society through an unexplained though not irrational withdrawal from human relationships. Her growing spirituality is represented by Goethe less as a weakness than as a near-daemonic kind of strength, one that turns character into fate. We are made to suspect, as in Wilhelm's psychological profile of Hamlet, "a great deed imposed on a soul, which is not up to it" ("eine grosse Tat auf eine Seele gelegt, die der Tat nicht gewachsen ist").[50] Except that, in Goethe's depiction, the exact nature of the deed remains a secret and seems to coincide with the soul in its individual and naked subjectivity. Eventually, at the horizon or climax of its withdrawal, the beautiful soul seeks its justification (or audience) only from God.[51]

But the voice of Goethe's narrator, so procedural and calm, invests inwardness with a regard for representability (*Anschaulichkeit*) very different from what Shakespeare strives for. The eloquent men and women that tread the great O of Shakespeare's stage are never so transparent, never so "knowable," either to themselves or to the viewer. That is why the motion of their thought toward self-discovery is so powerful: it wishes, against all odds, to make their innermost being—its ambitions, passions, fears—visible.

Hamlet's soliloquies do not express a flight from worldly visibility, such as we find in the confession of Goethe's anonymous, pietistic, upper-class woman. They are carried by a momentum that strives for a maximum of theatrical and profane disclosure. Though there is in Hamlet "that within which passeth show" (1.2.85)—we recall Mallarmé's remarkable characterization of the prince as "le seigneur latent qui ne peut devenir"—his struggle for self-knowledge coincides with that for self-manifestation. Hamlet has been deprived of his debut, of coming out as king; his uncle has made a ghost of him too. A wound has been inflicted not only on the individual psyche but also on a principle of order, of ritual emergence.

Ultimately, then, Goethe's "epic" turn differs radically from Shakespeare's theatrical mission, though Goethe, by insisting on the Bard's poetical rather than theatrical genius, tries to minimize the difference. Unlike Goethe, Shakespeare is not always a friend to mankind; he may even evince an anti-Pelagian streak. Who has howled against humanity more stridently than Timon of Athens or King Lear? "I am *Misanthropos,* and hate mankind" (*Timon of Athens,* 4.3.54). We are often exposed to a hostile ranting that astonishes and sickens at the same time. Desdemona's patient being stands no chance in Shakespeare's sterner *société du spectacle:* Othello fortifies himself for her murder with "It is the cause, it is the cause, my soul" (5.2.1), which is the mutter of every criminal with pretentions. Any evidence will do: let it be found, let it put out the eyes with "ocular proof," and negate what little negative capability soldiers have. We can scarcely believe Othello's blindness, or that of Lear; yet each one in his search for absolute proof (whether of fidelity or infidelity) uncovers more of the earthly sphere of ear and eye, "condemning shadows quite," like Cleopatra in her quest for an Antony, who is "nature's piece 'gainst fancy" (5.2.100–101). We honor this desire that things be made clear on earth rather than in heaven, even as we *see* the tragic consequences. Thus a verbal will drives everything through comic confusion or tragic impasse toward an impossible clarification, like that suggested by Anne in *Richard III,* who asserts that the dead man's wounds, in the presence of the murderer, "Ope their congeal'd mouths and bleed afresh" (1.2.56).

"Zur rechten Zeit," Mignon sings in *Wilhelm Meister,*

 vertreibt der Sonne Lauf
Die Finstre Nacht, und sie muss sich erhellen,
Der harte Fels schliesst seinen Busen auf.

[At the right time
The sun's course dispels the sinister night

Which must become luminous;
The hard rock unlocks its bosom.][52]

Softly but intensely, such songs express the transfigurative moment in which ideal visibility returns, and all cognitive dissonance, as between thought and world, desire and world, is purged. There is no "right time" in Shakespeare's plays, when things can innocently or untraumatically disclose themselves. Disclosure is trauma. The time is always out of joint, and the demand put on truth as the daughter of time is unceasing and pathological. Mignon's verses suggest a sympathetic transformation of the hard rock into a motherly, receptive, even erotic presence; and Shakespeare does allow such moments in his Romances. But always an antithetical pressure brings a dark truth to light, *whatever the consequences.*

In brief, we often stand toward the enigma of "Shakespeare" as do his characters toward the world. The demand put by such dramatic personalities on the world, and on each other, has something testing and violent in it: as if, just as the new science of Francis Bacon "questioned" (tortured) nature to make it reveal its secrets, so here humanity were "questioning" itself. Anything, love or political ambition or "a straw," can be the pretext for this excess of demand.[53] The human condition, staged as theater, rouses daring sympathies with whatever impels mankind to be the agent, rather than patient, of so spectacular a revel. Yet however sympathetic an audience may be, the passivity intrinsic to spectactorship can never be entirely removed.

In conclusion I recall the issue raised by Augustine in the Alypius episode of his *Confessions* (6.8). Alypius "fixed his eye" on the bloody sport of the Roman circus and became intoxicated with that spectacle. Given such vulnerability, how much should be addressed to the eyes? Obversely, can the stage respect inwardness or privacy or an ethos based on a nonhistrionic, nonrevelatory kenosis—on latency, asceticism, or any unhypocritical masking of self and power—especially when wordly pressures force the issue; when, for example, Henry Prince of Wales and Henry Hotspur must vie for dominance like enemy brothers?

I have to acknowledge the empirical truth of Jan Kott's observation that the contemporary theater-goer is not particularly upset by the conspicuous display of wordly power and cruelty:

> He views the struggle for power and the mutual slaughter of the characters far more calmly than did many generations of spectators and critics in the nineteenth century.

> More calmly, or, at any rate, more rationally. . . . The violent deaths of the principal characters are now regarded rather as an historical necessity, or as something altogether natural. . . . When *Titus Andronicus* received a production like that of Peter Brook, today's audiences were ready to applaud the general slaughter in Act Five no less enthusiastically than Elizabethan coppersmiths, tailors, butchers and soldiers had done.[54]

Terrence des Pres adds that a shift in the means of representation (a shift beyond theater) has changed the way we perceive the world. Intolerable conditions may always have existed; the decisive factor is that through photography's "technological extension of consciousness," through that kind of evidentiality, "we cannot not know"—which is how Henry James defined "the real."[55]

If this is modern fate, the question becomes what we can hope for, morally speaking. Among our minima moralia might be that the plea of innocence on account of ignorance—of our not having known—is finally removed. It is no longer possible to assert that only rumor or hearsay reached us: today every act of violence, political or domestic, is served up on the screen. Sightsay has replaced hearsay. The world is our circus; and the "rush to knowledge" is hindered only by excess of knowledge, by a rush of information or disinformation. But what if sympathy, pressured this way, succumbs to a sensory and psychic numbing, as the clownish sexton does in the famous graveyard scene from *Hamlet?*[56]

Remedies are hard to imagine, our eyes being so cold. Yet an attempt was made by Sigurd Burckhardt, connoisseur of both Shakespeare and German literature. He sought to reverse, by the unlikely medium of literary-critical reflection, the strange spectatorial enthusiasm described by Kott. A poem, he claimed, especially a dramatic poem, "is an act, not just a report"; it reinstates the performative dimension of words.[57] Let us define, he continued, tragedy as a *killing poem;* let us see the playwright, quite literally, as the killer, the one who devises the deadly plot and so must take responsibility for it. This might revive our sense of participation and blow the aestheticizing cover of both artist and spectator.

It is an extreme solution and suggests the depth of the ethical dilemma. It is also faintly absurd: the fine art of murder is practiced in the most popular and stylized of genres, the detective novel. Burckhardt's scruple would soon repress what escapes repression in and through art. To put it another way: Burckhardt knows that the very spaciousness of literature depends on its *not* being literal; indeed, on loosening the referential bond between word and meaning, or fixed role and meaning. A purgative irony or playfulness, which is the mark and wisdom of Shakespeare's clown-figures, turns words into "rascals." Words rebel against their bond and promote that active forgetfulness ("aktive Vergesslichkeit") which Nietzsche saw as unavoidable, if madness was to be avoided by the thinking person.

Yet Burckhardt won't give up a "love of the Word in its absolute integrity," one that makes him priest as well as fool.[58] "Words are grown so false" says Feste, that self-confessed "corrupter of words" in *Twelfth Night,* "I am loath to prove reason with them" (3.1.36–37). Can we, as literary critics, defeat their defeat?

NOTES

1. This essay was given at Weimar in April 1993 as the first *Rede zum Shakespeare-Tag* celebrating the reunion of the two German Shakespeare Societies which had split into Eastern and Western groups in 1962. The version in German (the language in which it was originally delivered) can be found in Geoffrey H. Hartman, "Poesie und Einfühlungskraft: Shakespeare und die ethische Frage," *Deutsche Shakespeare Gesellschaft Jahrbuch, 1994,* ed. Werner Habicht and Günther Kotz (Bochum: Verlag Ferdinand Kamp, 1994).
2. Johann Wolfgang Goethe, *West-Östlicher Divan,* ed. Hans-J. Weitz (Frankfurt: Insel Verlag, 1979), 279.
3. *The Riverside Shakespeare,* ed. G. Blakemore Evans (Boston: Houghton Mifflin, 1974). All Shakespeare quotations are from this edition and will be cited parenthetically in the text by act, scene and line.
4. Leo Löwenthal, *Goethe und die falsche Subjectivität* (Festrede zu Goethes 150. Todestag in der Frankfurter Pauluskirche am 22. Marz 1982) [Brochure] (Darmstadt: Technische Hochschule, n.d.).
5. Matthew Arnold, *Matthew Arnold,* ed. Miriam Allot and Robert H. Super (Oxford: Oxford Univ. Press, 1982), 8.
6. Goethe, "Zum Shakespeare-Tag," in *Goethes Werke* 12 (Munich: C. H. Beck, 1982), 226.
7. See the selections from Jean-Pierre Vernant and Mary Whitlock Blundell in *Essays on Aristotle's Poetics,* ed. Amélie O. Rorty (Princeton: Princeton Univ. Press, 1992).
8. My edition of Hazlitt's lectures on Shakespeare has a note on the character of Romeo and Juliet. "Shakespeare was portraying the manners of a more southern people than ourselves, where women arrive at womanhood early, and where, especially in high families, it would scarcely have been etiquette for the lover and his mistress to see much of each other prior to the nuptials."
9. Lionel Trilling, *Sincerity and Authenticity* (Cambridge: Harvard Univ. Press, 1972), 33. His entire chapter on "The Honest Soul and the Disintegrated Consciousness" is remarkable.
10. Jan Kott, *Shakespeare Our Contemporary* (London: Methuen, 1967), 15.
11. Coleridge, in fact, explains the English dramatist's extraordinary, nonclassical unity by the theory of inward or organic form. "The harmony that strikes us in the wildest landscapes," he writes, comes from the fact that all its parts, all its phenomena "from

verging autumn to returning spring," are "effected, as it were, by a single energy *ab intra* in each component part." Shakespeare and Nature, he finds, are the same, which was also Goethe's claim.

12. John Keats, *The Letters of John Keats,* ed. Hyder Edward Rollins, 2 vols. (Cambridge: Harvard Univ. Press, 1958), 1: 387.
13. Keats, *Letters,* 1: 387.
14. John Middleton Murry, *Shakespeare* (London: Jonathan Cape, 1936), ch. 1, "Everything and Nothing." Murry, then, is actually closer to Blake than to Keats. Charactered self, in Keats, is not viewed as a reaction-formation to an annihilating experience, though the latter persists in what Keats named "negative capability."
15. Harold Bloom, *Ruin the Sacred Truths: Poetry and Belief from the Bible to the Present* (Cambridge: Harvard Univ. Press, 1989), ch. 3; A. D. Nuttall, *A New Mimesis: Shakespeare and the Representation of Reality* (New York: Methuen, 1983). Cf. Hazlitt on *Hamlet,* in *Characters of Shakespeare's Plays:* "We hardly know how to criticize [this tragedy] any more than we should know how to describe our faces." Even more to the point is Owen Barfield: "There is a very real sense, humiliating as it may seem, in which what we generally venture to call *our* feelings are really Shakespeare's 'meaning.'" *Poetic Diction: A Study in Meaning* (1928; rpt. London: Faber and Faber, 1952), 137.
16. Bloom, *Ruin the Sacred Truths,* 61–62. Bloom sees Hamlet's character as one that changes under the pressure of his own thoughts (that is capable of self-revision or self-fashioning) and stresses what Nuttall calls Shakespeare's "cognitive mimesis" (*A New Mimesis,* 166–67).
17. Ruth Nevo, *Shakespeare's Other Language* (New York: Methuen, 1987), ch. 1, "Beyond Genre."
18. Does Shakespeare, in representing an ideal of tragic heroism, also represent a "reality"? Nuttall, *A New Mimesis,* is persuasive that protagonists like Brutus and Othello embody aspects of an ideal that can be identified as belonging to a "shame culture," presumably then in the process of evolving. But the concept of such a culture, expressed for Shakespeare's age by stoicism, remains a grid or *verum factum* (Vico). It may have been as unreal, if rhetorically and ethically enticing, as the more patently fabulous features of Shakespeare's plays.
19. Or the Passion of Prometheus or Christ: "Behold what I a god suffer at the hand of the gods!" (from Aeschylus's *Prometheus*). For *to pathos,* see Aristotle's *Theory of Poetics and Fine Art,* ed. and trans. S. H. Butcher, 4th ed. (New York: Dover, 1951), 11.6 and 14.4. Pathos, in Aristotle, is one of three plot elements needed to produce pity and fear; the others are reversal and recognition.
20. There is an interesting short history of *pathē* in Amélie Rorty, "Aristotle on the Metaphysical Status of *Pathē,*" *Review of Metaphysics* 38 (1984): 521–46.
21. It is here that my reflections join those of Stanley Cavell, which focus on human finitude and its tragic nonacceptance: on a certainty and a knowledge which are avoided, or converted into doubt, into a motivating, driving uncertainty. See, for example, pt. 4 of *The Claim of Reason* (New York: Oxford Univ. Press, 1979).
22. Christ's kenosis (in the Paulinian concept) is a self-sacrificial emptying of his divinity, a humbling assumption of mortality. A link between kenosis, myth, and drama in the

ancient Near East is documented in Theodor H. Gaster, *Thespis* (New York: Schuman, 1950). Immensely suggestive, it presents kenosis as an "occlusion of personality" through rites of mortification and mourning preparatory to a "plerosis" or jubilant merging with a corporate personality, related to seasonal ceremonies of invigoration. This sort of mimesis (close to *participation mystique*), which reenacts through a dramatic ritual the passage from a state of suspended animation to renewal, has what Gaster names a "topocosmic" function, merging the human community of a particular place ("Denmark," "England") with the spirit that sustains the cosmos as a whole. This "old" mimesis, based on the interplay of kenosis and plerosis, still has to be explored in relation to both Shakespeare's sympathetic imagination and his poetic language. Whether Socratic irony should be viewed as a "pedagogical" type of kenosis would be an interesting question.

23. I allude to Shelley's famous definition linking love and morals in "A Defense of Poetry," *Shelley's Poetry and Prose,* ed. Donald Reiman and Sharon Powers (New York: Norton, 1977).
24. The analyses, in the wake of James Frazer, of Jane Harrison and Gilbert Murray, and somewhat later Gertrude Levy.
25. See, for instance, Annabel Patterson, *Censorship and Interpretation: The Conditions of Writing and Reading in Early Modern England* (Madison: Univ. of Wisconsin Press, 1984).
26. Voltaire, "Preface to *Brutus*" (1731), in *Shakespeare in Europe,* ed. Oswald LeWinter (London: Penguin, 1970), 29–41.
27. Hippolyte A. Taine, *History of English Literature,* 4 vols. (New York: Frederick Ungar, 1965), 2: 71.
28. Everyone writing about this subject is indebted to Jonas Barish, *The Antitheatrical Prejudice* (Berkeley: Univ. of California Press, 1981). For an important analysis of spectatorship, or what is involved in visualization on the basis of dramatic performance, see David Marshall, "Exchanging Visions: Reading *A Midsummer Night's Dream,*" *ELH* 49 (1982), 543–75.
29. "So gehört Shakespeare notwendig in die Geschichte der Poesie; in der Geschichte des Theaters tritt er nur zufällig auf." Goethe, "Shakespeare und Kein Ende," in *Goethes Werke* 12, 295.
30. Goethe, "Shakespeare und Kein Ende," 296–97. Cf. Goethe's conversations with Eckermann, 26 July 1826, *Sämtliche Werke* 12 (Munich: Carl Hanser Verlag, 1986), 161–68.
31. Goethe, "Shakespeare und Kein Ende," 298. The former director of Weimar's theater goes so far as to opine that were Shakespeare's plays put on in a literal translation and without adaptation they would disappear from the German stage in a very short time.
32. E. E. Stoll, *Shakespeare's Young Lovers* (New York: Oxford Univ. Press, 1937), lecture 1, p. 12. All my quotations come from this lecture.
33. Stoll, *Shakespeare's Young Lovers,* 18.
34. Both Shakespeare's dramatic and his poetic form may have a revisionary relation to the clotted verse typified by Aeneas' tale about "The rugged Pyrrhus," the *récit* from Marlowe's *Dido, Queen of Carthage,* recalled in Act 2.2 of *Hamlet* and close to the style of the sonnet spoken by the Chorus, that sets the scene for *Romeo and Juliet.* Poetry and drama are doublets, a hendiadys developing out of a heavier verse narrative.

35. The quotation is a term used by the Donatan tradition. See J. V. Cunningham, *Woe or Wonder: The Emotional Effect of Shakespearean Tragedy* (Denver: Alan Swallow, 1964), and Ruth Nevo, *Transformations in Shakespeare* (New York: Methuen, 1980).
36. Kott, *Shakespeare Our Contemporary*, 37. The reference is to *Richard III.*
37. I don't mean that they are language-poor before their smitten state; but love allows them to manifest to the full their "passion." For Erich Auerbach, see *Mimesis* (1946; trans. Princeton: Princeton Univ. Press, 1953), ch. 13.
38. Capulet's wife has no qualms whatsoever when she points out that at Verona younger girls than Juliet are mothers, indeed that she was a mother by Juliet's age. Her daughter is given "this night" to look upon and seek to love Paris, while the Nurse, Nature's own dame, if not pimp, cheers her on: "Go girl, seek happy nights to happy days" (1.3.68).
39. Patricia Parker has shown how Shakespeare condenses the terms "delay," "dilate," and "delate" (accuse) into a pun, whereby rhetorical, legal, and temporal perspectives are made to intersect. See "Shakespeare and Rhetoric: 'dilation' and 'delation' in *Othello,*" in *Shakespeare and the Question of Theory*, ed. Patricia Parker and Geoffrey Hartman (New York: Methuen, 1985).
40. Another telling instance is Old Montague's doubting the "truth" of his son's secretive behavior. Romeo's turning day into night and vice versa (a further dislocation of time) is described as an escape from nature's sunlight into narcissism:

    he, his own affection's counselor,
    Is to himself—I will not say how true—
    But to himself so secret and so close,
    So far from sounding and discovery,
    As is the bud bit with an envious worm
    Ere he can spread his sweet leaves to the air
    Or dedicate his beauty to the sun.

    (1.1.145–51)

    The image is motivated by Romeo's strange melancholy, perhaps the parallel to green sickness in young girls; but its very brilliance shifts interest from the dramatic action to a questionable yet poetically attractive inwardness.
41. See Shelley's "Hymn to Intellectual Beauty," in *Shelley's Poetry and Prose* (note 23), 94. Also its precursors, Spenser's "Fowre Hymnes." David Marshall, in "Exchanging Visions" (note 28), suggests also a sight-exchange with empathic-moral implications: so Helena to Hermia, in *A Midsummer Night's Dream,* "O, teach me how you look" (1.1.192). I continue to hear in that the desire for an absolute disclosure.
42. So innocent and traditional a figure as dawn's "envious streaks" (3.5.7) discovers the antipathy of sun, stars, the environing cosmos. Nothing is neutral, or mere cosmic furniture: the quarrels, passions, jealousies of this lower world are also found in the empyrean. This very fact, however, makes that higher, myth-eaten realm redundant, reduces it to an amplifying device for the human drama we are given to see. Fulfillment in love or death is the only reality; in other plays empire, succession, revenge, and restitution join these irrepressible desires, while the impediments to fulfillment become more variegated.

43. The textual crux in *Julius Caesar* 4.3.180–94, where Brutus receives (a second time?) news of his wife's death, and which is discussed by Nuttall (*A New Mimesis,* 111) in terms of Shakespeare's understanding of the stoic mentality, is compared to this moment in *Macbeth,* a word that failed doubly: even the reflective pause in which Brutus might have worded his regret for the untimely news is not granted. A formula, however motivated by stoic philosophy, substitutes. Nuttall views stoicism as a heroic "shame culture," recreated in Shakespeare's Roman plays with extraordinary insight; but Shakespeare's "cognitive" mimesis does not have to exclude the possibility of emotional failure. (See Nuttall's own remarks on what it means for us to belong to a later and different culture, 186.) I mention this here because of what I say about our own, perhaps even colder, spectatorial culture in the last section.
44. Hamlet's "The funeral bak'd meats / Did coldly furnish forth the marriage tables" (1.2.180–81), commenting on the obscene speed of his mother's marriage, has in its thematic and verbal compression a dark affinity to "Thou met'st with things dying, I with things new born" in *The Winter's Tale* (3.3.112–13), which by that point has become a miraculous machine to make such a statement possible. The pauses, though conspiring with "golden-tongued Romance," remain an integral part of "the bittersweet of this Shakespearean fruit" (Keats).
45. Goethe, "Zum Shakespeare-Tag," 226.
46. Herder's concern in the 1770s ran strictly parallel: he envied other nations their ancient, vernacular songs, and held up Shakespeare as the poet who had refused to let them and their spirit die, who had somehow linked a native poetry with high culture. This had, in effect, produced a *translatio studii,* but not in Germany. "From older times we have no living poetry at all, from which our newer art might have sprouted on the stem of the nation." ("Aus älteren Zeiten haben wir also durchaus keine lebende Dichterei, auf der unsre neuere Dichtkunst wie Sprosse auf dem Stamm der Nation gewachsen wäre.") "Über Ossian und die Lieder Alter Völker," *Von deutscher Art und Kunst* (1773).
47. Herder, "Über Ossian." "Bei uns wächst alles a priori, unsre Dichtkunst und klassische Bildung ist vom Himmel geregnet"; "doch bleibt's immer und ewig, dass, wenn wir kein Volk haben, wir kein Publicum, keine Nation, keine Sprache und Dichtkunst haben, die unser sei, die in uns lebe und wirke. . . . Unsre klassische Literatur ist Paradiesvogel, so bunt, so artig, ganz Flug, ganz Höhe und—ohne Fuss auf die deutsche Erde"; "Wir armen Deutschen sind von jeher bestimmt gewesen, nie unser zu bleiben: immer die Gesetzgeber und Diener fremder Nationen, ihre Schicksalsentscheider und ihre verkauften, blutenden, ausgesogenen Sklaven."
48. From MS. drafts and fragments, 1798–1804. See William Wordsworth, *The Prelude 1799, 1805, 1850,* ed. J. Wordsworth, M. H. Abrams, and S. Gill (New York: Norton, 1979).
49. "He penetrated to the visible idea [*Anschauen*]," Goethe writes in 1802 of the classical translator and poet Johann Heinrich Voss: "he made what was distant present and grasped, happily, the childlike meaning with which the first cultured nations, with limited imagination, represented their great dwelling-place, the earth. . . . Then, attentive to the progress of the human mind, which does not cease to observe, to reason, to poeticize, his inquiring spirit allowed the perfected representation of the structure of earth and cosmos and its inhabitants, which we moderns possess, to gradually emerge

and grow out of its first seeds. . . . He knew how to value what was characteristic in each century, each people, each poet, and transmitted older writings with the practiced hand of the master, and so well that foreign nations in the future will have to estimate very highly the German language as mediator between ancient and modern times" (my translation).

50. Goethe, *Wilhelm Meisters Lehrjahre,* in *Goethes Werke* 7 (Munich: C. H. Beck, 1982), 306.
51. Whether or not this was intended by Goethe's conception of the "eternal feminine," the unnamed woman who is typified as the beautiful soul, and who draws *herself* upward, becomes in our eyes an early form of unconscious protest against the condition of women, rather than a warning against the Protestant extreme of religious quietism. In this exemplary role she is stronger than Rousseau's Julie and reminds us of Heinrich von Kleist's *Marquise von O—*, while anticipating Alissa's heart-breaking withdrawal from earthly love in André Gide's *La porte étroite.*
52. Goethe, *Wilhelm Meisters Lehrjahre,* 357.
53. Often mimicked vaingloriously in comic exchanges between servants or side-kicks. "*Sampson.* I strike quickly, being moved. / *Gregory.* But thou are not quickly moved to strike" (*Romeo and Juliet,* 1.1.5–6).
54. Kott, *Shakespeare Our Contemporary,* 5.
55. Terrence des Pres, *Praises & Dispraises: Politics and Poetry, the 20th Century* (New York: Viking Penguin, 1988), "Prolog." Des Pres acknowledges Walter Benjamin and Charles Simic.
56. There is surely something too accepting in Kott's realism (*Shakespeare Our Contemporary*), in his approval of the gusto of the groundlings. Postmodern apatheia may be a "Roman" virtue; more likely it signals once more a failure of sympathy.
57. Sigurd Burckhardt, *Shakespearean Meanings* (Princeton: Princeton Univ. Press, 1968), especially ch. 1, "How Not to Murder Caesar," and ch. 2, "The Poet as Fool and Priest: A Discourse on Method."
58. Burckhardt, *Shakespearean Meanings.*

Milton's Counterplot

Milton's description of the building of Pandemonium ends with a reference to the architect, Mammon, also known to the ancient world as Mulciber:

>   and how he fell
> From Heav'n, they fabl'd, thrown by angry *Jove*
> Sheer o'er the Crystal Battlements: from Morn
> To Noon he fell, from Noon to dewy Eve,
> A Summer's day; and with the setting Sun
> Dropt from the Zenith like a falling Star,
> On *Lemnos* th'Ægæan Isle.
>
> (*Paradise Lost,* 1.740–46)

These verses stand out from a brilliant text as still more brilliant or emerge from that text, which repeats on several levels the theme of quick or erring or mock activity, marked by a strange mood of calm, as if the narrative's burning wheel had suddenly disclosed a jeweled bearing. Their subject is a fall, and it has been suggested that Milton's imagination was caught by the anticipation in the Mulciber story of a myth which stands at the center of his epic. Why the "caught" imagination should respond with a pastoral image, evoking a fall gradual and cool like the dying of a summer's day and the sudden, no less aesthetically distant, dropping down of the star, is not explained. One recalls, without difficulty, similar moments of relief or distancing, especially in the cosmic fret of the first books: the comparison of angel forms lying entranced on the inflamed sea with autumnal leaves on Vallombrosa's shady brooks; or the simile of springtime bees and of the dreaming peasant at the end of Book 1; or the applause following Mammon's speech in Book 2, likened to the lulling if hoarse cadence of winds after a storm; or even the appearance to Satan of the world, when he has crossed Chaos and arrives with torn tackle in full view of this golden-chained star of smallest magnitude.

The evident purpose of the Mulciber story is to help prick inflated Pandemonium and, together with the lines that follow, to emphasize that Mammon's building is as shaky as its architect. This fits in well with the plot of the first two books, a description of the satanic host's effort to build on hell. But the verses on Mulciber also disclose, through their almost decorative character, a second plot, simultaneously expressed with the first, which may be called the counterplot. Its hidden presence is responsible for the contrapuntal effects of the inserted fable.

The reader will not fail to recognize in Milton's account of the progress of Mulciber's fall the parody of a biblical rhythm: "And the evening and the morning were the (first) day." The thought of creation is present to Milton, somehow associated with this fall. Moreover, the picture of angry Jove blends with and gives way to that of *crystal* battlements and the imperturbability of the summer's day through which the angel drops:

from Morn
To Noon he fell, from Noon to dewy Eve,
A Summer's day:

while in the last part of his descent an image of splendor and effortlessness outshines that of anger or ignominy:

and with the setting Sun
Dropt from the Zenith like a falling Star.

In context, of course, this depiction is condemned as mere fabling, and there is nothing splendid or aloof in the way Milton retells the story:

thus they relate,
Erring; for he with his rebellious rout

Fell long before; nor aught avail'd him now
To have built in Heav'n high Tow'rs; nor did he scape
By all his Engines, but was headlong sent
With his industrious crew to build in hell.

(1.746–51)

Yet for a moment, while moving in the charmed land of pagan fable, away from the more literal truth in which he seeks supremacy over all fable, Milton reveals the overwhelming if not autonomous drive of his imagination. Mulciber draws to himself a rhythm reminiscent of the account of the world's creation, and his story suggests both God and the creation undisturbed ("Crystal Battlements . . . dewy Eve") by a fall which is said to occur later than the creation yet actually preceded it. Here, surely, is a primary instance of Milton's automatically involving the idea of creation with that of the Fall. But further, and more fundamental, is the feeling of the text that God's anger is not anger at all but calm prescience, which sees that no fall will ultimately disturb the creation, whether Mulciber's fabled or Satan's real or Adam's universal fall.

Milton's feeling for this divine imperturbability, for God's omnipotent knowledge that the creation will outlive death and sin, when expressed in such an indirect manner, may be characterized as the counterplot. For it does not often work on the reader as an independent theme or subplot but lodges in the vital parts of the overt action, emerging from it like good from evil. The root feeling (if *feeling* is the proper word) for imperturbable providence radiates from many levels of the text. It has been given numerous interpretations in the history of criticism, the best perhaps, though impressionistic, by Coleridge: "Milton is the deity of prescience: he stands *ab extra* and drives a fiery chariot and four, making the horses feel the iron curb which holds them in." Satan's fixed mind and high disdain are perverted reflectors of this same cold passion, but doomed to perish in the restlessness of hell and its compulsive gospel of the community of damnation. So deep-working is this spirit of the "glassy, cool, translucent wave," already invoked in *Comus,* that other poets find it hard to resist it and, like Wordsworth, seek to attain similar virtuosity in expressing "central peace, subsisting at the heart / Of endless agitation." Milton's control is such that, even in the first dramatic account of Satan's expulsion, he makes the steady flame of God's act predominate over the theme of effort, anger, and vengefulness: in the following verses "Ethereal Sky" corresponds to the "Crystal Battlements" of Mulciber's fall, and the image of a projectile powerfully but steadily thrust forth (evoked in part by the immediate duplication of stress, letter, and rhythmic patterns) re-creates the imperturbability of that other, summer space:

> Him the Almighty Power
> Hurl'd headlong flaming from th'Ethereal Sky
> With hideous ruin and combustion down
> To bottomless perdition, there to dwell
> In Adamantine Chains and penal Fire . . .
>
> (1.44–48)

One of the major means of realizing the counterplot is the simile. Throughout *Paradise Lost,* and eminently in the first two books, Milton has to bring the terrible sublime home to the reader's imagination. It would appear that he can only do this by analogy. Yet Milton rarely uses straight analogy, in which the observer and observed remain, relative to each other, on the same plane. Indeed, his finest effects employ magnifying and diminishing similes. Satan's shield, for example, is described as hanging on his shoulder like the moon, viewed through Galileo's telescope from Fiesole or in Valdarno (1.284–91). The rich, elaborate pattern of such similes has been often noted and variously explained. Certain details, however, may be reconsidered.

The similes, first of all, not only magnify or diminish the doings in hell but invariably put them at a distance. Just as the Tuscan artist sees the moon through his telescope, so the artist of *Paradise Lost* shows hell at considerable remove, through a medium which, while it clarifies, also intervenes between reader and object. Milton varies points of view, shifting in space and time so skillfully that our sense of the reality of hell, of its power vis-à-vis man or God, never remains secure. Spirits, we know, can assume any shape they please; and Milton, like Spenser, uses this imaginative axiom to destroy the idea of the simple location of good and evil in the spiritual combat. But despite the insecurity, the abyss momentarily glimpsed under simple events, Milton's main effort in the first books is to make us believe in Satan as a real and terrible agent, yet never as an irresistible power. No doubt at all of Satan's influence: his success is writ large in religious history, which may also be one reason for the epic enumeration of demonic names and place names in Book 1. Nevertheless, even as we are closest to Satan, presented with the hottest view of hell's present and future appeal, all suggestion of irresistible influence must be expunged if Milton's two means of divine justification—man's free will and God's foreknowledge of the creation's triumph—are to win consent.

These two dominant concepts, expressed through the counter-plot, shed a calm and often cold radiance over all of *Paradise Lost,* issuing equally from the heart of faith and the center of self-determination. The similes must persuade us that man was and is "sufficient to have stood, though free to fall" (3.99): that his reason and will, however fiercely tempted and besieged, stand on a pinnacle as firm and precarious as that on which the Christ of *Paradise Regained* (4.541 ff.) suffers his last, greatest, archetypal temptation. They must show the persistence, in the depth of danger, passion, or evil, of imperturbable reason, of a power working ab extra.

This the similes accomplish in several ways. They are, for example, marked by an emphasis on place names. It is the *Tuscan* artist who views the moon (Satan's shield) from the top of *Fiesole* or in *Valdarno* through his optic glass, while he searches for new Lands, Rivers, Mountains on the spotty globe. Do not the place names serve to anchor this observer and set him off from the vastness and vagueness of hell, its unnamed and restless geography, as well as from his attempt to leave the earth and rise by science above the lunar world? A recital of names is, of course, not reassuring of itself: no comfort accrues in hearing Moloch associated with *Rabba, Argob, Basan, Arnon,* or sinful Solomon with *Hinnom, Tophet, Gehenna* (1.397–405). The point is that these places were once neutral, innocent of bloody or holy associations; it is man who has made them what they are, made the proper name a fearful or a hopeful sign (11.836–39). Will *Valdarno* and *Fiesole* become such bywords as *Tophet* and *Gehenna?* At the moment they are still hieroglyphs, words whose ultimate meaning is in the balance. They suggest the inviolate shelter of the created world rather than the incursions of a demonic world. Yet we sense that, if Galileo uses the shelter and Ark of this world to dream of other worlds, paying optical rites to the moon, Fiesole, Valdarno, even Vallombrosa may yield to the tug of a demonic interpretation and soon become a part of hell's unprotected marl.

Though the figure of the outside observer is striking in Milton's evocation of Galileo, it becomes more subtly patent in a simile a few lines further on which tells how the angel forms lay entranced on hell's inflamed sea,

> Thick as Autumnal Leaves that strow the Brooks
> In *Vallombrosa,* where th'Etrurian shades
> High overarch't imbow'r; or scatter'd sedge
> Afloat, when with fierce winds *Orion* arm'd
> Hath vext the Red-Sea Coast, whose waves o'erthrew
> *Busiris* and his *Memphian* Chivalry,
> While with perfidious hatred they pursu'd
> The sojourners of *Goshen,* who beheld

From the safe shore thir floating Carcasses
And broken Chariot Wheels . . .

(1.302–11)

A finer modulation of aesthetic distance can hardly be found: we start at the point of maximum contrast, with the angels prostrate on the lake, in a region "vaulted with fire" (298), viewed as leaves fallen seasonally on a sheltered brook vaulted by shade; go next to the image of seaweed scattered by storm; and finally, without break of focus, see the Israelites watching "from the safe shore" the floating bodies and parts of their pursuers. And, as in music, where one theme fades, another emerges to take its place; while the image of calm and natural death changes to that of violent and supernatural destruction, the figure of the observer ab extra becomes explicit, substituting for the original glimpse of inviolable peace.

Could the counterplot be clearer? A simile intended to sharpen our view of the innumerable stunned host of hell, just before it is roused by Satan, at the same time sharpens our sense of the imperturbable order of the creation, of the coming storm, and of the survival of man through providence and his safe-shored will. Satan, standing clear of the rout, prepares to vex his lesions to new evil:

on the Beach
Of that inflamed Sea, he stood and call'd
His Legions, Angel Forms, who lay intrans't
Thick as Autumnal Leaves . . .

but the scenes the poet himself calls up mimic hell's defeat before Satan's voice is fully heard, and whatever sought to destroy the calm of autumnal leaves lies lifeless as scattered sedge. The continuity of the similes hinges on the middle image of Orion, which sketches both Satan's power to rouse the fallen host and God's power to scatter and destroy it. In this plot counterplot, the hand of Satan is not ultimately distinguishable from the will of God.

A further instance, more complex still, is found at the end of Book 1. Milton compares the host gathered in the gates of Pandemonium to bees in springtime (1.768 ff). The wonder of this incongruity has been preserved by many explanations. It is clearly a simile which, like others we have adduced, diminishes hell while it magnifies creation. The bees are fruitful, and their existence in the teeth of Satan drowns out the sonorous hiss of hell. Their "straw-built Citadel" will survive "bossy" Pandemonium. As Dr. Johnson kicking the stone kicks all excessive idealism, so Milton's bees rub their balm against all excessive demonism. But the irony may not end there. Are the devils not those bees who bring food out of the eater, sweetness out of the strong (Judg. 14: 5–14)?

It may also be more than a coincidence that the most famous in this genre of similes describes the bustle of the Carthaginians as seen by storm-exiled Aeneas (*Aeneid,* 1.430–40). Enveloped in a cloud by his divine mother, Aeneas looks down from the top of a hill onto a people busily building their city like a swarm of bees at summer's return and is forced to cry: "O fortunati, quorum iam moenia surgunt [Oh fortunate people, whose walls are already rising]!" Then Virgil, as if to dispel any impression of despair, adds: "mirabile dictu!" Aeneas walks among the Carthaginians made invisible by divine gift.

Here the counterplot thickens, and we behold one of Milton's amazing transpositions of classical texts. Aeneas strives to found Rome, which will outlast Carthage. The bees building in Vergil's text intimate a spirit of creativity seasonally renewed and independent of the particular civilization; the bees in Milton's text represent the same privilege and promise. Aeneas wrapped in the cloud is the observer ab extra, the person on the shore, and his impatient cry is of one who desires to build a civilization beyond decay, perhaps even beyond the wrath of the gods. An emergent, as yet invisible figure in Milton's text shares the hero's cry: he has seen Mammon and his troop build Pandemonium, Satan's band swarm triumphant about their citadel. Despite this, can the walls of creation outlive Satan as Rome did the ancient world?

All this would be putative or extrinsic if based solely on the simile of the bees. For this simile, like the middle image of Orion vexing the Red Sea, is indeterminate in its implications, a kind of visual pivot in a series of images which act in sequence and once more reveal the counterplot. The indetermminacy of this simile is comparable to Milton's previously mentioned use of proper nouns and his overall stylistic use of the pivot, by means of which images and words are made to refer both backward and forward, giving the verse period unusual balance and flexibility. The series in question begins with the trooping to Pandemonium, and we now give the entire modulation, which moves through several similes:

all access was throng'd, the Gates
And Porches wide, but chief the spacious Hall
(Though like a cover'd field, where Champions bold
Wont ride in arm'd, and at the Soldan's chair
Defi'd the best of *Paynim* chivalry
To mortal combat or career with Lance)
Thick swarm'd, both on the ground and in the air,

Brusht with the hiss of rustling wings. As Bees
In spring time, when the Sun with *Taurus* rides,
Pour forth thir populous youth about the Hive
In clusters; they among fresh dews and flowers
Fly to and fro, or on the smoothed Plank,
The suburb of thir Straw-build Citadel,
New rubb'd with Balm, expatiate and confer
Thir State affairs. So thick the aery crowd
Swarm'd and were strait'n'd; till the Signal giv'n,
Behold a wonder! they but now who seem'd
In bigness to surpass Earth's Giant Sons
Now less than smallest Dwarfs, in narrow room
Throng numberless, like that Pigmean Race
Beyond the *Indian* Mount, or Faery Elves,
Whose midnight Revels, by a Forest side
Or Fountain some belated Peasant sees,
Or dreams he sees, while over-head the Moon
Sits Arbitress, and nearer to the Earth
Wheels her pale course, they on thir mirth and dance
Intent, with jocund Music charm his ear;
At once with joy and fear his heart rebounds.

(1.761–88)

The very images which marshal the legions of hell to our view reveal simultaneously that the issue of Satan's triumph or defeat, his real or mock power, is in the hand of a secret arbiter, whether God and divine prescience or man and free will. In the first simile the observer ab extra is the Soldan who, as a type of Satan, over-shadows the outcome of the combat between pagan and Christian warriors in the "cover'd field." The second simile is indeterminate in tenor, except that it diminishes the satanic thousands, blending them and their warlike intents with a picture of natural, peaceful creativity, Sun and Taurus presiding in place of the Soldan. "Behold a wonder!" echoes the *mirabile dictu* of Virgil's story and prepares the coming of a divine observer. The mighty host is seen to shrink to the size of Pigmies (the third simile), and we know that these—the "small infantry," as Milton had called them with a pun reflecting the double perspective of the first books—can be overshadowed by Cranes (1.575–76). The verse period then carries us still further from the main action as the diminished devils are also compared to Faery Elves glimpsed at their midnight revels by some belated Peasant. From the presence and pomp of hell we have slowly slipped into a pastoral.

Yet does not this static moment hide an inner combat more real than that for which hell is preparing? It is midnight, the pivot between day and day, and in the Peasant's mind a similar point of balance seems to obtain. He is not fully certain of the significance or even reality of the Fairy ring. Like Aeneas in Hades, who glimpses the shade of Dido (*Aeneid,* 6.450–55), he "sees, Or dreams he sees" something barely distinguishable from the pallid dark, obscure as the new moon through clouds. What an intensity of calm is here, reflecting a mind balanced on the critical pivot, as a point of stillness is reached at greatest remove from the threats and reverberations of hell! But even as the man stands uncertain, the image of the moon overhead becomes intense: it has sat there all the time as arbiter, now wheels closer to the earth, and the Peasant's heart rebounds with a secret intuition bringing at once joy and fear.

The moon, clearly, is a last transformation of the image of the observer ab extra—Soldan, Sun and Taurus, Peasant. What was a type of Satan overshadowing the outcome of the real or spiritual combat is converted into a presentiment of the individual's naïve and autonomous power of discrimination, his free reason, secretly linked with a superior influence, such as the moon overhead. The figure of the firmly placed observer culminates in that of the secret arbiter. Yet this moon is not an unambiguous symbol of the secret arbiter. A feeling of the moon's uncertain, changeable nature—incorruptible yet spotty, waxing and waning (1.284–91; 2.659–66; see also "mooned horns," 4.978, quoted below)—is subtly present. It reflects this series of images in which the poet constantly suggests, destroys and recreates the idea of an imperturbably transcendent discrimination. The moon that "sits Arbitress" seems to complete the counterplot, but is only the imperfect sign of a figure not revealed till Book 4. Thus the whole cycle of to and fro, big and small, Pigmies or Elves, seeing or dreaming, far and near, joy and fear—this uneasy flux of couplets, alternatives, and reversals—is continued when we learn, in the final lines of Book 1, that far within Pandemonium, perhaps as far from consciousness as hell is from the thoughts of the Peasant or demonic power from the jocund if intent music of the fairy revelers, Satan and the greatest of his Lords sit in their own, unreduced dimensions.

We meet the Peasant once more in *Paradise Lost,* in a simile which seems to want to outdo the apparent incongruity of all others. At the end of Book 4, Gabriel and his files confront Satan, apprehended squatting in Paradise, a toad at the ear of Eve. A heroically contemptuous exchange follows, and Satan's taunts finally so incense the Angel Squadron that they

Turn'd fiery red, sharp'ning in mooned horns
Thir Phalanx, and began to hem him round
With ported Spears, as thick as when a field
Of *Ceres* ripe for harvest waving bends
Her bearded Grove of ears, which way the wind
Sways them; the careful Plowman doubting stands
Lest on the threshing floor his hopeful sheaves
Prove chaff. On th'other side *Satan* alarm'd
Collecting all his might dilated stood,
Like *Teneriff* or *Atlas* unremov'd:
His stature reacht the Sky, and on his crest
Sat horror Plum'd; nor wanted in his grasp
What seem'd both Spear and Shield: now dreadful deeds
Might have ensu'd, nor only Paradise
In this commotion, but the Starry Cope
Of Heav'n perhaps, or all the Elements
At least had gone to rack, disturb'd and torn
With violence of this conflict, had not soon
Th'Eternal to prevent such horrid fray
Hung forth in Heav'n his golden Scales, yet seen
Betwixt *Astrea* and the *Scorpion* sign,
Wherein all things created first he weigh'd,
The pendulous round Earth with balanc'd Air
In counterpoise, now ponders all events,
Battles and Realms . . .

(4.978–1002)

The question of Satan's power does not appear to be academic, at least not at first. The simile which, on previous occasions, pretended to illustrate hell's greatness but actually diminished hell and magnified the creation, is used here just as effectively against heaven. Milton, by dilating Satan, and distancing the spears of the angel phalanx as ears ready for reaping, creates the impression of a balance of power between heaven and hell. Yet the image which remains in control is neither of Satan nor of the Angels but of the wheatfield, first as its bearded ears bend with the wind, then as contemplated by the Plowman. Here the counterplot achieves its most consummate form. *Paradise Lost* was written not for the sake of heaven or hell but for the sake of the creation. What is all the fuss about if not to preserve the "self-balanc't" earth? The center around which and to which all actions turn is whether man can stand though free to fall, whether man and the world can survive their autonomy. The issue may not therefore be determined on the supernatural level by the direct clash of heaven and hell but only by these two arbiters: man's free will and God's foreknowledge. The ripe grain sways in the wind; so does the mind which has tended it. Between ripeness and ripeness gathered falls the wind, the threshing floor, the labor of ancient *ears,* the question of the relation of God's will to man's will. The ears appear to be at the mercy of the wind; what about the thoughts, the "hopeful sheaves" of the Plowman? The fate of the world lies between Gabriel and Satan, but also between the wind and the ripe ears and between man and his thoughts. Finally God, supreme arbiter, overbalances the balance with the same pair of golden scales (suspended yet between Virgin and Scorpion) in which the balanced earth weighed at its first creation.

False Themes and Gentle Minds

The writers of the Enlightenment want fiction and reason to kiss. They are inexhaustible on the subject. "Buskin'd bards henceforth shall wisely rage," Thomas Tickell announces, foreseeing a new Augustan age.[1] "The radiant æra dawns," writes Akenside, when the long separation of imagination and science shall be overcome, and wisdom shall once more "imbrace the smiling family of arts."[2] The anonymous French author of *Poésies philosophiques* (1758) admonishes the new school of poets to invent "believable marvels": "Sans marcher appuyé du mensonge et des fables / Venez nous étaler des merveilles croïables." Another explains more curiously his desire for chaster fictions. "Women of today," he writes, "are so sated with fine phrases that there is no way of succeeding with them except to appeal to their reason."[3] The enthusiasm for reason—and reasoning—is so great that Crébillon fils, in *Le Sopha* (1740), a degraded and libertine version of the metamorphosis myth, puts his hero-narrator in jeopardy of

1. Thomas Tickell, *On the Prospect of Peace* (1712, dated 1713).
2. Mark Akenside, *The Pleasures of Imagination,* 1st ed. (1741), Bk. 2.
3. A. Berquin, "Discours sur la Romance," in *Romances* (1776).

having his head cut off should he be tempted to *reflect upon* rather than simply *tell* his story. "By my faith," says the Sultan, "I swear I shall kill the next man who dares to reflect in my presence." Even with this threat, the novel ends on a defeated note. How difficult it is to tell a good, rousing story in an Age of Reason. "Ah Grandmother," sighs the Sultan, thinking of Scheherazade, "that's not the way you used to tell stories!"

It does not prove easy to give up the sophisticated superstitions by which literature has always amused, shocked, or instructed. Writers become intensely conscious of the primitive nature of these beliefs but also ingenious in accommodating them to rationality. In William Collins's *Ode on the Popular Superstitions of the Highlands of Scotland,*[4] the problem is honestly and movingly set forth. Collins feels that he must forbear those great local myths which now live only in the far north and which he encourages his friend Home to keep up:

> Nor need'st thou blush, that such false themes engage
> Thy gentle mind, of fairer stores possest;
> For not alone they touch the village breast,
> But fill'd in elder time th'historic page.
> There SHAKESPEARE's self, with ev'ry garland crown'd,
> In musing hour, his wayward sisters found,
> And with their terrors drest the magic scene.

This dichotomy of "gentle mind" and "false themes" (where "false themes" means the materials of romance, popular or classical in origin) remains the starting point of the great majority of writers between the late Renaissance and Romanticism.

The story I wish to tell is how that dichotomy is faced and perhaps overcome. Many, of course, accepted the alienation of the literary mind from the "exploded beings" (the phrase is Dr. Johnson's) of folklore or mythology. They know too well that great literature was magic and that reason could only flee from it, as from an enchanter. But others dared to think that literature might become a rational enchantment. They toyed with forbidden fire (with the "Eastern tale," the gothic romance, the sublime ode) and called up the ghosts they wished to subdue. In this they followed the example of the great poets of the Renaissance, who had at once revived and purified romance tradition. I begin, therefore, with Milton, the last about whom Collins could have said, as

4. Written in 1749; published in 1788 in the *Transactions* of the Royal Society of Edinburgh.

of Tasso: his "undoubting mind / Believed the magic wonders which he sung."[5]

Milton is already belated; and it is his problematic rather than naïve relation to Romance which makes him significant. He somehow transcends the very dichotomy of "gentle mind" and "false theme" which appears early in his poetry. Thus he dismisses as a false surmise his vision of nature spirits lamenting for Lycidas without renouncing that machinery of spirits, that multiplication of persons and gods, which is the clearest feature of romantic art—romantic in the largest sense of the word. He accepts a principle of plenitude which belongs to the Romance imagination rather than to an epoch in Lovejoyan history and which sets all action within a conspiracy of spirits. The world is made new or strange by opening into another world: an overhead—or underground—of mediations, of direct, picturable relations between spirit-persons. In such a world the human actor is only one kind of being, and his mind—or whatever else makes him the king-piece—is the target of a host of contrary intelligences.

Keats, thinking about the Enlightenment (the "grand march of intellect"), said that in Milton's day the English were only just emancipated from superstition. It is true: Milton's consciousness is always ambushed by pagan or Christian or poetical myths. He is important for Collins and the Romantics because he shows the enlightened mind still emerging, and even constructing itself, out of its involvement with Romance. He marks the beginning of modern Romanticism, of a romantic struggle with Romance; and it is as a stage in the growth of the English poetic mind that I now want to present his poetry's earliest magic, the *Allegro-Penseroso* sequence.

You know how each poem opens, with a ritual exordium banning the undesired mood. In the first poem melancholy is dismissed; the second poem, like a recantation, hails melancholy and banishes joy. Milton, it has been argued, wished merely to picture the right kind of joy and a purified melancholy. Yet the dramatic aspect of each poem is the stylistic breach as the speaker turns from anathema to invitation. It is like going from an older world creaking with morality plays and heavy emblems to a brave new world in which man is the master of his mood, and his spirit-machinery correspondingly fluent. The poet seems as interested in purifying an older style as in purging a humor. The poems are Milton's notes toward a gentler fiction.

5. William Collins, *Ode on the Popular Superstitions,* xii.

If mythology old-style showed the mind at the mercy of humors or stars or heavy abstractions, these personifications of easy virtue, which constitute a mythology new-style, reflect a freer attitude of the mind toward the fictions it entertains. The change from

Hence loathed Melancholy
   Of *Cerberus,* and blackest midnight born,
In *Stygian* Cave forlorn
   'Mongst horrid shapes, and shreiks, and sights unholy

to

Come pensive Nun, devout and pure,
Sober, stedfast, and demure

recapitulates the entire Renaissance movement toward a *dolce stil nuovo.* It recalls the great change in attitude toward the ancient superstitions, which in the century preceding Milton allowed that freer use of Romance associated with (among others) Ariosto and Spenser.

In Milton's double feature it is not the character contrast of the two personae (melancholy and mirth) which is important, but this newer and emancipated kind of myth-making. Milton uses no less than three sorts of mythical persons: established divinities (Venus, Mab, Aurora); personified abstractions (Melancholy, Tragedy, Mirth); and spirits of place (the "Mountain Nymph, sweet Liberty"). He does not encourage us to discriminate between these kindred spirits; in fact, by mixing them with a fine promiscuity, he produces the sense of a middle region in which everything is numinous or semidivine. This in no respect demythologizes his poetry but suggests that we live in easy rather than fearful, and daily rather than extraordinary, intercourse with an ambient spirit world. We walk in a feather-dense atmosphere among "the unseen Genius of the Wood," strange music, "dewey-feathered sleep," and the phantasms of our own imagination. It is an atmosphere that works against sharp moral or ontological distinctions; when the merry person is said to view

Such sights as youthfull Poets dream
On Summer eeves by haunted stream

there is delicate ambiguity, because the sights could be public performances ("mask, and antique Pageantry"), dream thoughts, or a real vision. And when Shakespeare is called "fancy's child," the cliché has power, in this context, to suggest once more an intermingling of gods and humans—a numinous half-essence bathes every feature of these landscapes.

What is the reason for this promiscuous and light-hearted divinization? Milton has created a new and sweeter style, but also one that is peculiarly English. Most of his early poetry moves programmatically beyond the erudite pastoralism of the Italians and toward the fresher pastures of an English lyricism. Yet in *L'Allegro* and *Il Penseroso* Milton does more than state his program. He seems to have found the right kind of spirit, or spirits, for English landscape. He has taken the exotic machinery of the classical gods and the ponderous abstractions of moral allegory and treated them all as, basically, local spirits. In Britain they must be temperate like the British, so that extremes of mirth and melancholy, and even of divinity itself, are exorcized. The genius loci suits the religio loci: Milton's romantic machinery is grounded in the reasonableness of a specific national temperament.

That this reasonableness, this pride in a via media, may be a national myth does not concern us: although it will concern Blake, who rejects Milton's compromise and engages in a radical confrontation of the poetic genius with the English genius. Milton himself takes the issue to a higher level in *Paradise Lost,* where the old and sublimer mode of myth-making is reasserted. From that postbellum height, *L'Allegro* and *Il Penseroso* appear like exercises in the minor mode of pastoral romance. Even as only that—as an accommodation of Romance to the English mind—they remain a significant attempt to allow this kind of fiction to survive an increasingly enlightened climate.

That *L'Allegro* and *Il Penseroso* are a special type of romance appears as soon as we go from the nature of the personifications to that of the persona or presiding consciousness. Who is the speaker here if not a magus, dismissing some spirits and invoking others? If we do not have an actual romance, at least we have a romancer: the poems are thoroughly ritualistic, with their exordium, invocation, and ceremonial tone. But the imperatives ("Tow'red Cities please us then," "There let *Hymen* oft appear") are really optatives, while the tone is lightened by Milton's easy, peripatetic rhythm. His style of address intimates a new power of self-determination vis-à-vis the spiritual environment in which we live and move and have our being. Though that environment remains demonic, the magus is clearly in control: the most formal sign of control is, in fact, the conceit governing his invitations, which reverses the oldest religious formula known to us, the *do ut des*—I give, so that you give. In *L'Allegro* and *Il Penseroso* the poet is not petitioning but propositioning his goddess: you give me these pleasures, and I will be yours. He lays down his conditions and enjoys them in advance. It is his pleasure or option to do these things, to be merry or melancholy—a pleasure of the human imagination.

Thus psyche emerges from the spooky larvae of masques and moralities like a free-ranging butterfly. Though still in contact with a world of spirits, it is no longer coerced or compelled. The spiritual drama is, as always in Milton, seduction rather than compulsion. The poet begins to invite his soul and opens the way to an authentic nature poetry. A similar development takes place on the Continent with Théophile de Viau and Saint-Amant, imitators of the lighter Pléiade strain, who may have influenced Marvell. Their nature poems are little romances, adventures of the liberated and—as the case may be—libertine spirit.

Our mention of psyche may be more than a figure of speech. According to traditional speculation on genius or ingenium, each person was accompanied by two genii, a good and a bad, a protector and a deceiver. These are important figures in many morality plays and still appear in Marlowe's *Faustus.* Could Milton have changed this feature of popular demonology into his humors or states of mind, which are competing spiritual options? If so, he has adjusted an axiom of demonic religion to a more temperate zone and brought us an essential step closer to the modern idea of genius. By tempering the genii's astral nature, he has made them into attendants of the creative mind.[6]

With Milton the spirit of Romance begins to simplify itself. It becomes the creative spirit and frees itself from the great mass of medieval and postmedieval romances in the same way as the Spirit of Protestantism frees itself from the formalism of temples. *L'Allegro* and *Il Penseroso* are not romances but romantic monologues. They show a mind moving from one position to another and projecting an image of its freedom against a darker, demonic ground. Poetry, like religion, purifies that ground: it cannot leave it. The newborn allegoric persons retain, therefore, something of the character of demonic agents even while being transformed into pleasures of the imagination. Indeed, the poems' rigidly stylized form reminds us that the imaginative man must join some god's party: the either/or situation remains; he cannot but assume a persona. Personification is still derived from the persona instead of the latter being freely inferred, as it is in modern poetry, from the projection of living thoughts.

If Romance is an eternal rather than archaic portion of the human mind, and poetry its purification, then every poem will be an act of resistance, of negative creation—a flight from one enchantment into another. The farewell to the impure gods becomes part of a nativity ode welcoming the new god. New

6. E. Panofsky's study of Dürer's *Melencolia I* has pointed to one source of the modern idea of Genius in the Renaissance concept of "generous melancholy." See Klibansky, Panofsky, and Saxl, *Saturn and Melancholy* (New York, 1964), chap. 2, and also pp. 228 ff. on *Il Penseroso.*

personifications are born from old in *L'Allegro* and *Il Penseroso;* and *Lycidas* purges the genii loci of Italian pastoral only to hail a new "genius of the shore." This romantic purification of Romance is endless; it is the true and unceasing spiritual combat. At the conclusion of the first book of *Paradise Lost,* Milton transforms the satanic thousands into fairies of Albion. Their moony music charms the ear of a belated peasant. It is, surely, a similar conversion of the demons which helps to animate the landscapes of *L'Allegro* and *Il Penseroso.* The haunted ground of Romance is aestheticized; the gods become diminutive, picturesque, charming—in a word, neo-classical. But is this change perhaps a Mephistophelian deceit, a modern seduction? The gentle mind thinks it is free of demons, but they sit "far within / And in their own dimensions like themselves" (*Paradise Lost,* 1.792–93).

It is as if Milton had foreseen the triumph and trivialization of the descriptive-allegorical style. *L'Allegro* and *Il Penseroso* become the pattern for eighteenth-century topographical fancies, with their personification mania. His nature-spirits are summoned at the will of every would-be magus. Romance loses its shadow, its genuine darkness: nothing remains of the drama of liberation whereby ingenium is born from genius, psyche from persona, and the spirit of poetry from the grave clothes of Romance. By the end of the eighteenth century, poets must begin once more where Milton began, though fortified by his example. They must "in the romantic element immerse" and not be deceived by the neoclassical psyche flitting with faded innocence through gaudy landscapes. Keat's imitation of Milton leads from those superficial bowers to the face of Moneta, dark (like Melancholy's) with excessive bright, from pleasures of the imagination to the burdens of a prophetic spirit. This is the path inaugurated by Collins, who uses the formula of *L'Allegro* and *Il Penseroso* to invite a creative Fear—stronger even in Shakespeare than in Milton—back to his breast:

O Thou whose Spirit most possest
The sacred Seat of *Shakespear's* Breast!
. . . .
Teach me but once like Him to feel:
His Cypress Wreath my Meed decree,
And I, *O Fear,* will dwell with *Thee!*

The theories accompanying the revival of Romance in the second half of the eighteenth century have often been studied. Van Tieghem's chapter on "La Notion de la vraie poésie" in *Le Préromantisme* contains in suggestive outline what needs to be known. But a fine essay by Emil Staiger on that strange confectioner of supernatural ballads, the German poet Bürger, takes us beyond theory to the inner development of romantic poetry.[7]

Gottfried August Bürger was a witting cause of the ballad revival in Germany and an unwitting influence on Wordsworth and Coleridge. His ballads, first collected in 1778, sent pleasurable shudders through the sophisticated literary circles of Europe. Their influence reached England in the 1790s: Scott became a ballad writer because of him, and Anna Seward describes how people petitioned her to read them Bürger's most famous work, the *Lenore:* "There was scarce a morning in which a knot of eight or ten did not flock to my apartments, to be poetically frightened: Mr. Erskine, Mr. Wilberforce—everything that was everything, and everything that was nothing, flocked to Leonora. . . . Its terrible graces grapple minds and tastes of every complexion."[8] Bürger is like the country boy in the fairy tale who finally taught the princess to have goose-pimples by putting a frog in her bed. Yet, like almost every poet of the period, his first treatment of supernatural themes was jocose. Staiger shows that what began as a literary flirtation led suddenly to genuine "terrific" ballads. The sorcerer's apprentice is overpowered by spirits he had evoked playfully.

What interests us here is Bürger's literary situation and its difference from that of the English poets. Collins and later writers of the Age of Sensibility were also making mouths at the invisible event. When Gray, Percy, Mallet, Mason, Macpherson, and Blake were not redoing old romances, they inflated the neoclassical "godkins and goddesslings" as giant epiphanic forms—pop art addressing a spiritualistic society. They could risk this because they knew the Enlightenment had gone too far for the old superstitions really to come back. Collin's visionary cry

Ah *Fear!* Ah frantic *Fear!*
I see, I see Thee near

invokes an emotion which is truly frantic: it wants to get at the poet, who wishes to be got at, but a historical fatality—the gentle mind, polite society—keeps them apart.

7. Emil Staiger, "Zu Bürgers 'Lenore,' vom literarischen Spiel zum Bekenntnis," *Stilwandel* (Zurich, 1963).

8. *Letters of Anna Seward, Written Between the Years* 1784 *and* 1807, 6 vols. (Edinburgh, 1811), 4:231. The letter is from the year 1796, in which five separate translations of *Lenore* were published. See Alois Brandl, "Lenore in England" in Erich Schmidt, *Charakteristiken* (Berlin, 1902), pp. 235–38; also F. W. Stokoe, *German Influence in the English Romantic Period* (Cambridge, 1926).

Now, Bürger's situation is both more hopeful and more difficult. German poetry had had no golden age, no Renaissance. Hence there was no one between the poet and Romance tradition—no one, like Milton, to guide his steps, but also no one to demonstrate the difficulty and belatedness of such an enterprise. Where are *our* Chaucer, Spenser, Shakespeare, and Milton, Herder asks in an essay of 1777, which commends Bürger.[9] English Renaissance poetry, according to Herder, was reared on the old songs and romances which originally belonged just as much to German poetry, because of a common Nordic heritage and because the spirit of Romance is everywhere the same: "In allen Ländern Europas hat der Rittergeist nur ein Wörterbuch." But this heritage not having been mediated by poets like Shakespeare and Milton, the German writer of that time has no living tradition of older poetry through which he might renew himself and grow as if on the very stem of national life. With us Germans, laments Harder, everything is supposed to grow a priori ("Bei uns wächst alles a priori").

Thus Bürger must somehow raise the Romance tradition by his own arts. What he knows of that tradition is limited: mainly popular songs and superstitions, copied (so he claims) from songs picked up in city or village streets at evening, in the awareness that the poems of Homer, Ariosto, Spenser, and Ossian were also once "ballads, romances, and folksongs."[10] He is like a Faust who does not need the devil because the *Erdgeist* has agreed to be his guiding spirit.

Among the most famous of Bürger's ballads is *The Wild Huntsman (Der wilde Jäger)*. It depicts the rising blood-lust of a Sunday morning's hunt, and its tempo is wild from the start:

Der Wild- und Rheingraf stiess ins Horn:
"Hallo, Hallo, zu Fuss und Ross!"
Sein Hengst erhob sich wiehernd vorn;
Laut rasselnd stürzt ihm nach der Tross;
Laut klifft' und klafft' es, frei vom Koppel,
Durch Korn und Dorn, durch Heid und Stoppel.

9. "Von Ähnlichkeit der Mittlern Englischen und Deutschen Dichtkunst" (*Deutsches Museum*). How fast things were moving toward a recovery of the Romance heritage is evidenced by the fact that Goethe's *Urfaust* dates from 1775 and Wieland's *Oberon* ("the first long romantic poem of modern Europe," says W. W. Beyer in his *Enchanted Forest*) was published in 1780.

10. "Aus Daniel Wunderlichs Buch" (*Deutsches Museum*, 1776). Bürger probably knew something of Percy's *Reliques*, although he did not study them till 1777. See Staiger, *Stilwandel*, p. 90; and Erich Schmidt, *Charakteristiken*, pp. 93–94.

This breakneck pace augments: two horsemen enter to accompany the earl; the right-hand one counsels him to respect the Sabbath and turn back, the left-hand rider spurs him on. The hunter overrides every objection; the pack rampages on, over a poor farmer's property, over the very bodies of a cowherd and his cattle; finally the earl pursues the beast into a hermit's sanctuary, violating it and blaspheming God. All at once—the transition takes place within one stanza—the clamor of the chase is gone, everything is vanished except the earl, and a deathly silence reigns. He blows his horn, it makes no sound; he halloos, no sound; he cracks his whip, no sound. He spurs his courser: it is rooted in the ground, stock-still. The silence is that of the grave; into it comes, from above, a voice of thunder condemning the hunter to be, until the Last Judgment, the prey of an eternal and hellish hunt.

The poem is totally steeped in myth and superstition: there is the motif of the blasphemy immediately answered (call the devil, and so on); that of the ride ending in the grave, perhaps indebted to the Nordic myth of Odin, who rides in the sky with his troop of dead souls; and, above all, the theme of the hunter lured by his prey beyond nature into visionary experience.[11] Bürger wants to pack as much Romance as possible into each poem, as if to make up for Germany's lost time. He even classifies the ballad as a lyric kind of epic, not so much to stress that it must tell a story as to emphasize its ambition. The ballad is an epic in brief, a romance in brief. It sums up a life, a destiny, a whole ancient culture.

Yet behind these ballads is a pressure not explained by this ambition, which shows itself in their precipitous, "Würfe und Sprünge," the speed of action ("gesagt, getan"), the heroes' reckless *amor fati,* and everything else that tends to minimize the reflective moment. Here there is no shadow between the conception and the act, or even between this life and afterlife. No sooner has the earl blasphemed than he reaps the punishment for his blasphemy; and Lenore's bitter yet innocent death wish is rewarded in the same gross way. The mind is not given enough natural time in which to reflect.

Indeed, time in Bürger is intrinsically demonic. Although the supernatural erupts only at the climax of the action, it is there from the outset. One cannot speak of development: the earl is a hunted man from the first lines, a fated part

11. The theme of the spectral horseman is most vivid, of course, in *Lenore:* on the folkloric (popular) as distinct from the mythic (learned) basis, see Scott, *Ballads and Lyrical Pieces* (1806), introductory note to his translation of Bürger's poem. On the hunter lured into visionary experience, cf. Malory's *Morte Darthur,* 1. 19–20; and D. C. Allen, *Image and Meaning* (Baltimore, 1960), pp. 99–101.

of horse and pack and spurring sound; and the fearful symmetry whereby hunter and hunted are reversed in the second part appears like a natural rather than supernatural consequence. The first open hint of the supernatural is, of course, the appearance of the right and left horsemen, whose intrusion is so easy because in a sense they have been there all along. They are clearly the good and evil genii; and we see how externally, even superficially, the theme of reflection is introduced. There is only token retardation: the action consists of incidents arranged in climactic order with time moving irreversibly to the point of retribution. Having reached that point, the nature of time does not change: the hunter has simply run into himself. After a moment of absolute silence, which is like entering the looking glass, the reversed image appears and time continues its avenging course. There is no reflection and no true temporality: only this eschatological self-encounter.

Thus Bürger's ballads are ghostly in the deepest sense. But are they Romantic? Are they not gothic—or, if you will, gothic romances? They belong to the world of that *Totentanz* explicitly evoked in *Lenore* and not absent from the mad and macabre ride of the earl. Death marries the bride, Death leads the hunt. This is not the world of the romances, not chivalry, and not *Rittergeist.*[12] There is little of genial disgressiveness, courtesy, or natural magic. Instead, the classical unities of action, time, and place become the straight and narrow road leading to a single, surreal, pietistic confrontation. The space for reflection is tighter than in Poe's *Pit and the Pendulum* and more stingily inauthentic than in Kafka. Bürger did create a new visionary form, but at a certain cost. The false theme triumphs at the expense of falsifying the mind, which has become a mere reflector of compulsions and spectator of fatalities.

To turn from *The Wild Huntsman* to Wordsworth's *Hartleap Well* (1800) is to know the rights of the mind—the pleasures and pains of ordinary consciousness—fully restored. No ballad could be more parallel, and more opposed. The first lines strike the keynote of difference:

> The Knight had ridden down from Wensley Moor
> With the slow motion of a summer's cloud.

We begin with the chase almost over; that dramatic accumulation of incident, so essential to Bürger's pace, is at once subordinated to what Wordsworth

12. In Chaucer's *Pardoner's Tale,* where Death leads the hunt for Death, the Christian elements blend with, rather than overpower, such figures from Romance as the Old Man whose mode of being contrasts so movingly with the unreflecting action of the rioters.

named character, but which is more like a consistent weather of the mind.[13] His first image therefore describes a mood as well as a motion and places both into encompassing nature. The stanzas that follow explicitly defuse Bürger's climax by incorporating it in the features of a natural scene:

> But, though Sir Walter like a falcon flies,
> There is a doleful silence in the air
>
> But horse and man are vanished, one and all;
> Such race, I think, was never run before.
>
> Where is the throng, the tumult of the race?
> The bugles that so joyfully were blown?
> This chase it looks not like an earthly chase:
> Sir Walter and the Hart are left alone.

The silence means only that Sir Walter has outdistanced his helpers; there is nothing supernatural in it. Yet it does lead to an unearthly moment of solitude and reflection. There is something mysterious in the staying power of the stricken animal and in the knight's joy, which overflows in a vow to commemorate the hunt. His joy, even so, may be consonant with a chivalric ethos, while the strength of dying creatures is proverbial. A naturalistic perspective is maintained. What hidden significance there may be must await the second part of the ballad, which is purely reflective.

This part introduces no new incidents. The poet, speaking in his own person and not as a naïve bard à la Bürger, reveals that the story just told was learned from a shepherd he met on the way from Hawes to Richmond while pondering in a desolate spot marked by ruins. The natural and the contemplative frame of the story come together as he and the shepherd exchange views in the very spot where Sir Walter was left alone with the Hart. If part one is action, part two is reflection; yet part one was already reflective in mood. Hunter, shepherd, poet: all are contemplatives.

Their contemplations, however, are of a deeply primitive kind. They center on a feeling of epiphany, of revelation associated with a particular place: here a revelation of nature as a sentient and powerful being. Sir Walter erects his pleasure-house on a spot where a natural power verging on the supernatural was manifested. The peasant thinks the spot is cursed, because nature sympathized

13. Some remarks by Wordsworth on "character" versus "incidents" can be found in a letter to Coleridge on Bürger (Wordsworth read him in Germany during the winter of 1798–99). See *The Collected Letters of S. T. Coleridge,* ed. E. L. Griggs, 4 vols. (Oxford, 1956, 1959), 1 (1956): 565–66.

with the agony of the beast. The poet also thinks its death was mourned by "sympathy divine," by "The Being, that is in the clouds and air, / That is in the green leaves among the groves," but he refuses to go beyond what nature itself suggests, beyond the simple, imaginative feeling of desolation. He rejects the idea that there is a blood curse. Thus the poem is really a little progress of the imagination, which leads from one type of animism to another: from the martial type of the knight, to the pastoral type of the shepherd, and finally to that of the poet. And in this progress from primitive to sophisticated kinds of vision, poetic reflection is the refining principle: it keeps nature within nature and resists supernatural fancies.

Wordsworth's animism, his consciousness of a consciousness in nature, is the last noble superstition of a demythologized mind. All nature-spirits are dissolved by him except the spirit of Nature. His poetry quietly revives the figure of *Natura plangens,* one of the great visionary personae of both pastoral and cosmological poetry.[14] This link of Wordsworth's Nature to the Goddess Natura makes the formal moral of *Hartleap Well* almost indistinguishable from that of Bürger's poem: the one turns on "the sorrow of the meanest thing that feels," the other on "das Ach und Weh der Kreatur."[15] But while Bürger's demoniacal horseman parodies the chivalric spirit (the *Rittergeist*), Wordsworth accepts chivalry as a false yet imaginative and redeemable way of life. In Wordsworth the new and milder morality grows organically from the old: there is no apocalyptic or revolutionary change, just due process of time and nature.

Now this kind of continuity is the very pattern, according to Herder, of the English poetic mind, which builds on popular sources and so revitalizes them. By giving the ballad precedence over his more personal reflections and allowing the characters of knight and shepherd their own being, Wordsworth exemplifies a peculiarly English relation of new to old. The internal structure of his poem reflects a historical principle of canon formation. Even when, as in *The White Doe of Rylstone,* he begins with personal speculation rather than with an impersonally narrated ballad, the essential structure remains that of the reflective encirclement and progressive purification of symbols from Romance.

There are, in the Romantic period, many variations on this structure. The emergence of the gentle out of the haunted mind is not always so gradual and assured. Coleridge's *Ancient Mariner,* a "Dutch attempt at German sublimity,"

14. E. R. Curtius, *European Literature and the Latin Middle Ages* (London, 1953), chap. 6, "The Goddess Natura."

15. Cf. also Coleridge's *Ancient Mariner,* with its obliquer use of the hunt theme, but overt moral: "He prayeth best who loveth best / All things both great and small."

as Southey called it, follows the Bürgerian model. Yet it has, in addition, something of the meander of Romance and of that strange interplay of dream vision and actual vision found in Malory or Spenser. It is clear that Milton is not the only master for the English mind. But he is among those who assured the survival of Romance by the very quality of his resistance to it.

Wordsworth's Touching Compulsion

In recent years psychoanalytically oriented criticism has become increasingly harder to do. Yet more and more people are doing it.

The reason interest has grown lies perhaps in the heightened difficulty of the venture. As the psychoanalytic study of art has become problematic, it has also become more worthwhile. Today no one can line up writers or their books according to clinical categories or an applied science model. Nor are we intrigued by how many sexual images lie behind the screen of words.

What, then, can psychoanalysis tell us about literature? Even if we overcome methodological and moral scruples, it is not at all clear that the light thrown on the literary text by psychoanalytic investigation does more than make a darkness visible. By darkness I do not mean only the "excrementitious" base which the work of art seems to refine into a curious and complex structure. In the "riddle of the sphincter," as Kenneth Burke calls it, the riddle interests us more than the sphincter. We all in a sense build on hell; and it is not merely a literary problem to what use, clinically or humanly, that knowledge may be put.

The *other* darkness is that of the elusive psyche, or the supposed subject of psychoanalytic investigation. The closer we get to that subject the less of a subject it is: the ego, personal center, *sujet* or signified, dissolves into a field of forces and is depicted by unstable diagrams, "with cycles and epicycles scribbled o'er."

The very language of psychoanalysis has become heavily aggregative, as traces of older models retard sentences laboring toward yet another revision. There comes a point when the question arises about what the subject of psychoanalysis may be. Is it still the psyche? Or how can we distinguish the psyche from 1) the involution of those sentences, more particularly of the Freudian corpus of texts which keeps revising itself, and 2) the involution of Freud's original *Project for a Scientific Psychology,* with its coil of neurological and topographical complexities? The speculation that the psyche is "like" a text corresponds to a state of affairs in which the psyche is burdened by texts explanatory of what the psyche is like.

Perhaps we have entered a period of constitutive doubt vis-à-vis speculative psychoanalysis. That there is need for a therapy along psychoanalytic lines I myself do not question. But the shape and rationale of that therapy keep shifting, and to the point where the presumptive *authority* which medical science cannot give up without becoming another ex-theology is in danger of being lost.

I offer the following pages as an attempt to lessen our dependence on the applied science model of psychoanalytic inquiry. Yet they could not have been written without Freud's exemplary formalizations that encompass such basic experiences as imagining, wishing, sensing, writing, and mourning. Since my treatment of these issues arises as much from art as from Freud's science of mind, it may be best to call it *psychoesthetic* rather than *psychoanalytic.*

I

> Think, we had mothers . . .
> —William Shakespeare, *Troilus and Cressida,* V, v

The created world, according to Blake, was a divine act of mercy to keep us from falling, endlessly, into a void. Even Satan's fall, in *Paradise Lost,* is bottomed—by Hell. Blake's imaginative axiom does not intend so much to honor nature as to indicate its limited providential function. But how do we understand this void, or voiding, of which the familiar world is the "lower" limit?

On reading Wordsworth's "Prospectus" to the 1814 *Excursion,* especially the lines,

Jehovah—with his thunder, and the choir
Of shouting Angels, and the empyreal thrones—
I pass them unalarmed . . .

Blake complained that it gave him a bowel complaint that almost killed him. Henry Crabb Robinson reports, "I had the pleasure of reading to Blake in my best style (& you know I am vain on that point & think I read W[ordsworth]'s poems peculiarly well) the Ode on Immortality. I never witnessed greater delight in any listener & in general Blake loves the poems. What appears to have disturbed his mind, on the other hand, is the preface to the Excursion. He told me six months ago that it caused him a bowel complaint which nearly killed him." Blake has a figurative way of expressing himself which the bourgeois observer (a Crabb Robinson, for example) might take too literally. Perhaps Wordsworth's exaltation of Nature in the Prospectus, and his vaunted "passing by" of the visionary realms, did literally make Blake sick. Or perhaps the comment is Blake's way of saying "Shit!"

Blake's reaction to another bard, Klopstock, was not dissimilar: "If Blake could do this when he rose up from shite / What might he not do if he sat down to write?" The imagery of purging (not necessarily anal purging) is very strong in Blake's poetry. Sometimes indeed one has the impression Blake wants to purge or void nature altogether. How different this seems to be from Wordsworth's honoring and reinforcing of "earth's materials." The "Prospectus" that so upset Blake goes on to declare:

. . . Paradise, and groves
Elysian, Fortunate Fields—like those of old
Sought in the Atlantic Main—why should they be
A history only of departed things,
Or a mere fiction of what never was?
For the discerning intellect of Man,
When wedded to this goodly universe
In love and holy passion, shall find these
A simple produce of the common day.

Yet there is something strange, too, about Wordsworth's relation to Nature. He tells us that when young he had to touch things to convince himself they were there. "I used to brood over the stories of Enoch and Elijah, and almost to persuade myself that, whatever might become of others, I should be translated in something of the same way to heaven. With a feeling congenial to this, I was often unable to think of external things as having external existence, and I communed with all that I saw as something not apart from, but inherent in, my own immaterial nature. Many times while going to school have I grasped a wall or tree to recall myself from this abyss of idealism to the reality" (Fenwick note to "Intimations of Immortality").

The difference between Wordsworth and Blake is not absolute, then. Nature, touched, also kept Wordsworth from falling into a void. What the poet calls "brooding" seems to have made his sight less real: if seeing is believing, here touching is believing. It is interesting that Wordsworth describes our earthly progress, our sensuous and psychic development, as moving subtly from a *drinking touch* to a *drinking via the eyes:*

> . . . blest the Babe,
> Nursed in his Mothers' arms, who sinks to sleep
> Rocked on his Mother's breast; who with his soul
> Drinks in the feelings of his Mother's eye!
> For him, in one dear Presence, there exists
> A virtue which irradiates and exalts
> Objects through widest intercourse of sense.[1]

This passage anticipates a central argument of the entire *Prelude:* our ability to make a transition from the first (and lost) love object to object love. There is a tendency, as in contemporary American psychoanalysis, to understand object relations as love relationships taken in their broadest sense. Yet *The Prelude* is mainly, of course, about the hazards of that broadening. Loss of an earlier relation, or of the primary love object (the mother, "heaven"), is not easily compensated. When Wordsworth was eight years old, his mother died, and he was consciously troubled by the very "Nature" that comforted him:

> . . . now a trouble came into my mind
> From unknown causes. I was left alone
> Seeking the visible world, nor knowing why,
> The props of my affections were removed,
> And yet the building stood, as if sustained
> By its own spirit!
>
> (*Prelude* II, 276–81)

How are we to interpret this? On the surface it states a perplexity. The mother dies, the world remains, and as an object of quest or desire. Why should the fact perplex Wordsworth who has just argued in the "blest babe" passage that the mother's function is to effect precisely this bonding: "along his infant veins are interfused / The gravitation and the filial bond / Of nature that connect him to the world" (*Prelude* II, 234–36)? You may say that the child did not know what the adult knows; that the child's ignorant wonder is what is expressed by the poet in a movement of sympathetic recollection. The child is astonished and troubled, not the mature poet. The child has to face the fact of survival, and particularly the evidence of a "spirit" independent of mother and child—to which the grown man can give the name of Nature.

But is the child's wonder so simple an emotion? Or is it not the "trouble" itself? Wordsworth's phrasing is difficult; yet clearly the child knows the mother has died, so that the "unknown causes" must refer either to the spirit in Nature now manifest or to a psychic, if blind, reaction to that event. The mature poet seems to know two things rather than one, and the exclamation point suggests that his knowledge does not lessen the original emotion. He knows why the world survives the mother as an object of affection, and what made the child's astonishment a "trouble." The first kind of knowledge harmonizes with Freud's understanding of how the lost object becomes by internalization a constitutive part of the self that has lost it—how it helps to build the identity of the person or, as Richard Onorato has argued in Wordsworth's case, even the very notion of *poet* as a human type. But the second kind of knowledge is regressive rather than progressive and qualifies Wordsworth's optimistic theory about the growth of the mind. The troubled astonishment of the child may have expressed a defeated expectation, even perhaps a frustrated death wish. Nature should not have survived! The reality-bond of motherly affection, being dissolved, should have meant the collapse of everything! Potentially there is here as deep an ambivalence as in Blake about Nature as a substitute love-object.

We are now in a better position to understand the young poet's touching compulsion. It is incited by a ghostliness in nature deriving from two related sources. (I omit his fascinating reference to brooding on visionary stories from the Bible.) The fixated or literally animistic mind feels that if nature remains alive when what gave it life (the mother) is dead, then the mother is not dead but invisibly contained in nature. On the other hand, if the mother *is* dead, then the affective presence of nature is but a phantom reality that must dissolve just like the illusion it has replaced—the illusion of a permanent *Dasein* (the mother's). Wordsworth's touching, then, is a kind of reality testing: it wants to undo the spell, or make contact with the "one dear Presence" in hiding.[2]

Let me try, somewhat quickly and aggressively, to generalize. Is not artistic representation (understood as a re-presencing) a similar kind of touching, or reality testing? There is, first of all, something inevitably regressive, animistic, or overcompensatory about all modes of mimetic representation; and if there were no other justification for critics, we would need them to free the work of art from the potentially regressive understanding it elicits.

Second, art restores the sense of touch, for the artist at least. This is clearest in arts that involve more tactility than the passage of pen over paper. "When I draw I have a feeling of tactile communication as if every line and stroke palpitated under my hand and through this process only I learn to understand the essence of the model, in taking it into myself." Ernst Kris records this remark of a patient in his *Psychoanalytic Explorations in Art,* but of course it raises other issues too: those of sexual or libidinal feedings, and of incorporation. It serves to suggest that music, poetry, painting, even writing, involve touch through material composition or related psychic impressions. We "touch back" to move forward.

Last, the reality testing of art verges on reality challenging: the desire not to be mastered by, but rather to master, that phantom presence. Art is craftiness as well as craft. Its maneuvering of words or feelings can be as complex as that attributed to the ego in Anna Freud's *Ego and Its Mechanisms of Defense*—a veritable war-game manual. For the act of writing is deeply associated with feelings of trespass, theft, forgery, self-exposure. These are not merely private to the artist, and extricated by depth psychology; they are, as recurrent theme and subject, matters of public record. Our great myths display confidence men or thieves: cunning liars like Odysseus, amorous gangsters like Don Juan, Robin Hoods like Satan or Prometheus.

By means of representation the artist steals something from God (or Nature) or steals it back; and so it is almost inevitable that the representation, *qua* substitute object, will invest itself as an autonomous, if alienated, source of value. "To counterfeit is death," we read on old American paper money. The game of art may run that risk: its reality testing wants reality to manifest itself, or let its mock be.

II

> An esperance so obstinately strong
> That doth invert th' attest of eyes and ears.
> —*Troilus and Cressida,* V, v

Art's restorative *touch* must be acknowledged, yet we should not forget the role of *sight.* It is the eyes which, naturally ghostly, suggest the possibility of "action at a distance." Yet they are unable to accept this negative touching and so are always questioning themselves. Though ears too are ghostly, sight, contrasted with hearing, seems to need more purification: always as full as it is empty ("O dark, dark, dark, amid the blaze of noon")[3] it must be purged of mere images, of the dead weight of *visibilia,* or "questionable shapes" possessing uncanny affectivity.

Wordsworth's "I Wandered Lonely as a Cloud" moves with grace in this area of dreamy traumatism where sights or sounds "halt" the poet with "a gentle shock of mild surprise" (*Prelude* V, 382). One hardly feels the voracity of the poet's visual desire because it is so finely, gradually revealed through his casual encounter with the "golden daffodils." Yet what we are given here, and in many other poems, is a strange moment of bliss, a mild seizure or ecstasy that betrays the internal pressure—one that climaxes when the poet's "vacant" or "pensive" mood "fills" with the image of the daffodils. When Wordsworth writes: "I gazed—and gazed—but little thought / What wealth the show to me had brought," our ear may be justified in adding "I grazed—and grazed." Touch, or materiality, returns to the phantom of sight. The ear develops the image in its own way.

Wordsworth, of course, often singles out the ear as an "organ of vision," or a sense both intensely pure and deeply in touch with earthliness:

> . . . I would walk alone,
> Under the quiet stars, and at that time
> Have felt whate'er there is of power in sound
> To breathe an elevated mood, by form
> Or image unprofaned; and I would stand,
> If the night blackened with a coming storm,
> Beneath some rock, listening to notes that are
> The ghostly language of the ancient earth,
> Or make their dim abode in distant winds.
> Thence did I drink the visionary power.
>
> (*Prelude* II, 302–11)

Where other poets might have invoked a heavenly music, he evokes a music of the earthly sphere.

The dialectic of the senses in Wordsworth is psychagogic and can be analyzed even if we are not sure where it leads. Interestingly enough, he rarely makes use of synaesthesia: his typical intensities are those in which he is "now all eye and now / All ear" (*Prelude* XII, 93–100 and XIV, 38ff.). The senses counteract the tyranny of the eye *and* themselves (*Prelude* XII, 127-39). An intrapsychic sensory process is said to free the poet from quasi-epiphanic fixations, from overinvested ideas or images. Nature functions here like Plato's dialectic (*Republic,* Jowett, trans., 523ff.) and encourages a *via negativa.*

Such natural transcendence remains, however, quite problematic. Indeed, it generally perplexes rather than purifies eye and ear. We get a feeling more of impasse than of facilitation. When the limits of perceptibility are reached, through that process of

> . . . obstinate questionings
> Of sense and outward things,
> Fallings from us, vanishings;
> Blank misgivings of a Creature
> Moving about in worlds not realized
>
> ("Intimations of Immortality")

—when the light of sense goes out, and intimations of the death or the blankness of nature arise, there is a resistance, a counter-obstinacy. The line leading to vision or methodical hallucination is not crossed. Hence a poetry that fixes so constantly, retentively, on bare markers, totems or natural steles—"But there's a Tree, of many, one, / A single Field which I have looked upon" ("Intimations Ode").

Such markers, which still seem to point to what has departed, are strangely individuated. The "single" tree is not a prophetic and lamentable prop (a Dodonian oak) that has survived the stage set of more visionary epochs: it is part of an earth-writing, an undecyphered geography or geometry. One may call these markers boundary images or omphaloi (navel-points of the cosmos), a term Mircea Eliade adapts from Homer, and they link poetic to geometric absoluteness:

> On poetry and geometric truth,
> And their high privilege of lasting life,
> From all internal injury exempt,
> I mused.
>
> (*Prelude* V, 65-68)

Geometry/Geomatry: mother nature, or the mother-in-nature, is the guardian of something invulnerable, which is either the mother-child relation itself or an ideal of psychic development.

Yet every child is "untimely ripped from the womb," according to Freud's understanding of human prematurity. Later too, there are no timely separations. The wound of birth, that primary separation from nature, is but the prelude to a psychic development subject to related wounds or traumas. Things always happen untimely, prematurely—Matthew, at seventy-two, still sings "witty rimes / About the crazy old church-clock / And the bewildered chimes" ("The Fountain," *Lyrical Ballads* of 1800). The wound supposedly overcome by the strangely consorted disciplines of poetry and geometry lies in the very necessity of growing up, of maturation.

Let me return a moment to the dialectic of the senses and specify the role it plays in psychic development. How do ears counteract eyes? There is, for example, a "gravitation" (*Prelude* II, 243) induced by music, or by periods of silence. It makes the sights of nature—when too still, and thus seemingly dead—rotate, or sink down into the mind (*Prelude* II, 169–74). These pauses, as in "The Boy of Winander" episode, may be untimely, yet that seems to allow something to penetrate so "far" into the mind that it is lodged as deeply as the dead mother, the "one dear Presence" in hiding:

> . . . in that silence while he hung
> Listening, a gentle shock of mild surprise
> Has carried far into his heart the voice
> Of mountain torrents; or the visible scene
> Would enter unawares into his mind,
> With all it solemn imagery, its rocks,
> Its woods, and that uncertain heaven, received
> Into the bosom of the steady lake.
>
> (*Prelude* V, 381–88)

The embosoming effect is unmistakable. Hearing seems to mediate touch.

In other poets too the ears can be a "trembling" medium that restores touch to visible things by picking up vibrations:

> I caught this morning morning's minion, king-
> dom of daylight's dauphin, dapple-dawn-drawn Falcon, in his riding
> Of the rolling level underneath him steady air, and striding
> High there . . .

In this eye-catching bird-catching, the sense of distance is qualified by the contagious touch of the elliptical metaphor ("I caught"). It renders both a far-striking image and the attempted grasping of it by the poet's appetitive eye. The air has waves.[4]

Yet here we approach the notion of what always defeats as well as exalts art. Eyeing is to become a kind of touching, but touching only augments the desire for ocular proof. Glittering eyes turn therefore into glittering hands. Like those of Midas, they compulsively gild everything—make it accountable, touchable, money for sight. Art's attempt to "materialize" or "fix" a "presence" betrays paradoxically an "idealizing ("eye-dealizing") motive that ends in fixation. Whether it is Othello assaying Desdemona or the believer searching for evidence of the Divine—this quest for ocular proof culminates in desolation rather than consolation: in a deepened awareness of loss. What Freud named *Schau-Lust* (scopophilia) verges on *Schau-Verlust* because of (1) what the eyes actually discover (say, what Troilus sees in Shakespeare's *Troilus and Cressida* V, iii–v), and (2) what they can never discover, since there is no complete compensation for the first love object. Indeed, the very idea of a "first" love may be a fiction to anchor and so limit our sense of betrayal. We blame a particular experience or person rather than life itself. It is better, as Kierkegaard suggests in the "Prelude" to *Fear and Trembling,* to blacken the mother's breast. If we overcome that first "death," as Dylan Thomas writes, "there is no other."

III

> My negation hath no taste of madness.
> —*Troilus and Cressida* V, v

Homer sings the wrath of Achilles. But what is inspiring about that teen-age tantrum? The hero who accepts no substitutes challenges more than the ethos of compromise and accommodation that preserves the social order. He challenges life—nature—itself, with its supposedly progressive sacrifice of love objects. To have a divine mother, as Achilles does, is hazardous: for how can you lose her? Achilles has no human fears. His wrath is not a human but a divine tantrum.

Art displays an anger, a *furor poeticus,* similar to that of Achilles. But its anger includes itself, for art remains as ambivalent about its own status as about the comfort or complicity of all compensatory substitutions. In its cunning protest against life, art now sets nature against art, now art against nature.

Consider once more those apparent opposites, Wordsworth and Blake. Wordsworth tends to sacrifice art to nature, because the latter, as the first love-substitute, is the basis of all further sublimation in growing up. Blake, however, wishes to sacrifice nature, precisely because it exacts the "sacrifice" of substitution. His rage against the "Religion of Nature" and its artificial code is clearly against something that diminishes our imaginative energies and fosters instead an unreal or compensatory god-symbolism.

Yet there may be a resentment of nature even in Wordsworth. He says, in

"Tintern Abbey," that nature never betrayed the heart that loved her; but that is already a betrayed person speaking. Nature is second best, a substitute heaven; and the object of Wordsworth's nature poems is not nature but the "one dear Presence," lost yet perhaps recoverable—like Eurydice. His moving beyond the eye (toward touch) is therefore tantamount to making nature disappear: collapsing it into the cache he is seeking. And often, rather than be deceived again—by "mother" Nature this time—he cultivates an ideal blindness not unlike that of the abstract sciences. He brings together, as in *Prelude* V, 65ff., poetry and geometric truth. They identify the *precious* as the *constant* object and anticipate a psyche "from all internal injury exempt."

No wonder, then, that a "quiet" or "listening" eye determines the kind of poetry Wordsworth writes. His stately but static figures barely differentiate themselves from their landscape. It is hard to *see* them: insofar as they move, it is in a blind or hypnotic trance as if they too did not need sight, theirs or ours. They are so stripped, so elemental, that little remains of them except the constancy of blind faith. At times, therefore, Wordsworth's poetry almost transcends representation, and thus reality testing. It gives up not only the eyes but also touch—tangible words. It seems to exist then without the material density of poetic texture—without imagistic or narrative detail. The presence it continues to evoke becomes "untouchable"; and the impossibility of being wounded through eye or ear adds to this untouchableness and intensifies human invulnerability, as in the famous short lyric:

A slumber did my spirit seal;
I had no human fears;
She seemed a thing that could not feel
The touch of earthly years.

No motion has she now, no force;
She neither hears nor sees;
Rolled round in earth's diurnal course,
With rocks, and stones, and trees.

Sudden death does not wound either the loved person or the lover. The relation of the ecstatic consciousness (first stanza) to the mortal consciousness (second stanza) is more like image to afterimage than illusion to the shock of disillusion. Each of the stanzas shows a spirit sealed up and something that remains untouchable. The loved person, called a "thing" by proleptic or intensely understated phrasing, passes from life to death as if in fulfillment of the immutability attributed to her. There is no melancholy fit or cry of surprise: an image of "gravitation" elides the grave and suggests that poetry is a work of mourning that lies "too deep for tears." Mourning becomes Wordsworth.

IV

> Your passion draws ears hither.
> —*Troilus and Cressida,* V, v

If what Wordsworth represents in his poetry is an absence, does not the term "representation" become questionable? The beloved is never present in the Lucy poems except as the absent one. The hypothesis, moreover, that the absence is the mother's cannot be verified. The psychic role of the lost mother could be, as I have said, a fiction to ground a sense of betrayal arising with consciousness, or self-consciousness. It is, in any case, the interpreter's hypothesis, since Wordsworth nowhere explicitly makes the connection.

A related difficulty is that the loss of the mother need not determine the feeling of loss. When the mother is around, there may still be a sense that she is absent, that she is not the real mother. Freud discussed this feeling, common to many children, under the concept of Family Romance. The father, moreover, is not excluded from being the subject of the romance. For all we know, the absent mother may be a screen for a sense that the father is absent—that *his* nurturance is lacking or inadequate. It is unlikely that the interpreter can come to a firm conclusion on the nature of the felt absence.

What, then, is the value of psychoesthetic inquiries? Perhaps that they lead us to this indeterminacy. They make us less sure, less dogmatic, about the referent of art, and without denying a mimetic principle, they show the distance between mimetic and symbolic representation. Instead of taking as our starting point a presence that is lost, and viewing representation as a re-presencing of what is lost, we might alternatively begin with absence. As conscious beings, we are always at a distance from the origin. Yet to begin with absence is still an epochal or grounding maneuver. It may also be a contemporary and formalistic memento mori acknowledging unsentimentally that what individuates us is at once ineffable *and* mortal. The stronger our consciousness of individuality, the stronger our sense of the betrayal that might befall it. Only the individual can be "betrayed" by death, mutability, or the awareness of not being individual enough: in short, reproducible. Hence a temptation to reground the individual on nothing; more precisely, on his power continually to negate nothing. A quest for the Story of Nothing arises.

Wordsworth's role in this Story of Nothing is clear. Despite *expressions* that intimate a striving for absolute knowledge ("Praise to the End," "How shall I trace the history, where seek / The origin . . . ?"), he *depicts* the lost object not literally but symbolically, that is, as a limiting or boundary term without which the mind might lose itself in the hallucinating void of visionary images. Wordsworth does not make absence present in the manner of gothic, ghostly, or surrealist fantasies, or animated spectres. The absent one remains absent in his representations. What is depicted is, as it were, the legacy of this absence, which he circumscribes with periphrastic inventions that have the strength of a breaking wave: "And something evermore about to be" (*Prelude* VI, 608); "the soul, / Remembering how she felt, but what she felt / Remembering not, retains an obscure sense / Of possible sublimity, whereto / With growing faculties she doth aspire / With faculties still growing, feeling still / That whatsoever point they gain, they yet / Have something to pursue" (*Prelude* II, 315–22). This kind of periphrasis is not indebted to school rhetoric or precious diction. It does not assume there is a proper term that could be expressed yet is avoided. Rather, the gerundive evokes something "to be continued" and borders on the infinitive. Things remembered or imagined are viewed as absent not because they are lost (though they may be), but because their "trace" is difficult to substantialize as a noun or a name.

So in poetry we often sense a word under the words. This *paragrammatic doubling*,[5] which may induce a *doubting* of the literal or referential meaning, can be compared to what happens when the boundary between living and dead becomes uncertain in the mind of the mourner. The poet feels that what is lost is in language, perhaps even a lost language; under the words are ghostlier words, half-perceived figures or fragments that seem to be at once part of the lost object and more living that what is present.

The ideal of psychic health deems it better, of course, to declare the absent one as dead—absolutely lost to present experience. It asks the mourner to separate from the dead through public rituals of a well-defined and terminal kind. Mourning may last seven or thirty days: specific words of lament or consolation are enjoined. The dead person is laid to rest in language and in time, and the living find that they can and must continue as the living. But some situations are less determinable. When Wordsworth opens "Tintern Abbey" with "Five years have past; five summers with the length / Of five long winters! and again I hear . . . ," the drawn-out words express a mind that remains "in somewhat of a sad perplexity," a mind that tries to locate in time what is lost, but cannot do so with therapeutic precision. Or to adduce a more dramatic instance: Margaret's husband in "The Ruined Cottage" is absent rather than dead and leaves her in a mental state uncomfortably close to that of believers who know Christ is absent, not dead, and await his return. In the passion of Margaret the period of mourning extends itself until it is coterminous with time. Christ, of course, is not a "lost object" (like Margaret's husband or Wordsworth's parents) but an object of faith—the evidence of things not seen. Yet Wordsworth generally hovers between one passion and the other: his Christianity, such as it is, is not a congealed myth but keeps growing out of a secular understanding.

"The sounding cataract haunted me like a passion" is part of this understanding. And it reminds us of something evaded in the present essay: that laying the absent one to rest means silencing a voice as well as an image. The memorial poetry Wordsworth writes ("and again I hear . . .") at once expresses and represses a "ghostly language." The identity of this language remains uncertain: Is it the mother's voice that, like Derwent's (*Prelude* I, 269 ff.), flowed along the child's dreams, or the lost sublime of Miltonic and biblical figuration ("I used to brood over the stories of Enoch and Elijah")? Biblical and balladic harmonize uneasily in Wordsworth's lyric experiments: both seem like the inland murmur of ancient tongues. Veritable ghost-meanings thus undermine the simple words he uses. "Strange fits of passion have I known"—how do we interpret "fits" and "passion"? Could the line mean, "I have been subject to the fitful (hallucinatory) hearing of an affecting voice"? Is the cry, "If Lucy should be dead!" which he voices only at the end of the poem, heard internally from the beginning? In "A slumber did my spirit seal," voice is completely internalized: there is no cry-ing.

"Sei allem Abschied voran," Rilke declares in one of his sonnets to Orpheus: "Outpace all separation." So Wordsworth's "fit" is also a quasi-heroic "feat" which fails to outrun an infinite misgiving. Even the most present gift of Nature—Lucy or the beloved in the prime of love—is subject to this misgiving: "Blank misgivings of a Creature / Moving about in worlds unrealized." A remark in Wordsworth's "Essay on Epitaphs" can serve to conclude my analysis; it reminds us of Wordsworth as a schoolboy grasping wall or tree to save himself from intimations of unreality: "I confess, with me the conviction is absolute, that if the impression and sense of death were not thus counterbalanced [by internal evidences of love and immortality anterior to memory], such a hollowness would pervade the whole system of things, such a want of correspondence and consistency, a disproportion so astounding betwixt means and ends, that there could be no motions of the life of love; and infinitely less could we have any wish to be remembered after we had passed away from a world in which each man had moved about like a shadow." In Wordsworth's poetry, mourning and memory converge as an infinite task, a "work."

NOTES

1. *Prelude* II, 234–40. All references to *The Prelude* are to the version of 1850. On "intercourse of touch" see also *Prelude* II, 265–68.
2. On the concept of reality testing, see Freud, "Negation" (1925) in *The Complete Psychological Works* (Standard Edition), 19, 235–39, and the further references indicated there. Freud's "Verneinung" includes both negation as a *judgment* ("She is not there" or "It's not my mother") and negation as *denial* (the refusal to accept the reality principle, or "Nature" as Wordsworth mythifies it). See also Freud's "Metaphysical Supplement to the Theory of Dreams" (1916) and J. Laplanche and J. B. Pontalis, *The Language of Psychoanalysis,* sv. "reality-testing."
3. Milton, *Samson Agonistes,* line 80; and cf. my *Unmediated Vision* (New York, 1966), 127ff. My remark on ears as less ghostly than eyes has to be modified by an analysis that would examine the link between poetry and "hearing voices" (see section IV of this essay). The visual stationing achieved in fiction or dreams may already be a way of giving voices that cannot be purged a "local habitation and a name." Despite Wordsworth's explicit statements, it may be the tyranny of the ghostly ear which poetry or nature seeks to counteract.
4. On the relation of visual desire to scientific construction, including geometry, and to the theory of light waves, and perhaps imaginative logic generally, there are a large number of texts, from Valéry's early essay on Leonardo da Vinci to Jacques Lacan's studies on "speculation." In Wordsworth there is considerable ambivalence, of course, concerning the "geometric" habit of mind. See especially *Prelude* II, 203ff.
5. Cf. Ferdinand de Saussure's concept of the anagram developed in the notebooks presented by Jean Starobinski, *Les mots sous les mots* (Paris, 1970). The remarks I adjoin on mourning are influenced, of course, by Freud's essay "Mourning and Melancholia" (1917).

Purification and Danger in American Poetry

a reply to Greek and Latin
  with the bare hands . . .
  —W. C. Williams, *Paterson*

Art is a radical critique of representation, and as such is bound to compete with theology and other, ritual or clinical, modes of purification. "The pure products of America / go crazy," William Carlos Williams wrote; and it is necessary to admit from the outset that the word "pure" has many meanings, some ambiguous, some downright deceptive. Though my theme is purity, and more specifically language purification in American poetry, one could easily write on "Seven Types of Purity." Empson's *Seven Types of Ambiguity* was, in fact, a response to doctrines of "pure poetry" around him.[1] Our new, hypo-

1. In America Kenneth Burke is sensitive throughout his writings to the "pure poetry" movement, and interesting polemical analyses can be found in R. P. Warren's "Pure and Impure Poetry" (1942), reprinted in *Selected Essays;* and Frederick Pottle's *The Idiom of Poetry* (1941), chap. 5. George Moore's *Anthology of Pure Poetry* had been published in 1924; in his introduction Moore contrasts

thetical book would start by explaining purity in the strictly rhetorical sense: *sermo purus, Latinitas, katharotes, kathara lexis, Ellenismos.* I am not as learned as I pretend: this comes right out of the magisterial compendium on literary rhetoric by Heinrich Lausberg. It allows me to make the point that a first definition of purity would already involve historical notions: of Latinity and Hellenism, of classical norms in opposition to Oriental or so-called barbaric features of style.

When the vulgar languages, the national vernaculars, developed their own literature, they were surrounded by classicist censors and snobs. The native product was often denounced as foreign, incult, Asiatic. Voltaire found many of Shakespeare's and Dante's expressions "barbarous." The decorum of the diction itself was taken to be the meaning. It is a nice irony that in our own time Leavis and Eliot attacked Milton's grand style for the obverse reason: their claim was that Milton, unlike Shakespeare, violated the spirit of the vernacular. How complicated and fertile in its tensions this battle over style could become is suggested by the fact that those suspicious of native developments were often fostering a different kind of rejuvenation, a renaissance of the Classics. Contaminated antiquity was to be purified by being reborn in its pristine *vetustas* and *majestas;* this aim of the Renaissance Humanists compared with the birth of a modern, vernacular literature. The break with Latin as an idealized father tongue, an Adamic yet a learned language, was so traumatic because it came at the very time the mother tongue was being cultivated.

Dante, for example, promoted his native dialect not only in the *Commedia* but also in two prose tracts, the *De vulgari eloquentia* and *The Banquet.* The first was written in Latin; and both spoke with a cleft tongue in favor of Latin and the vernaculars. Two centuries later, Du Bellay's treatise on the enrichment of French was one of the important Renaissance apologies aiding the rise of the national vernaculars as sophisticated media, but it was not uncritical. There was a recognized need to chasten the vernaculars, to purge them of national or local

---

didactic verse or thought with "Greek" innocency of vision, claiming also that "Shakespeare never soiled his songs with thought." This antididactic strain in definitions of purity goes over into New Critical precepts, and it is strongly influenced by Flaubert, Mallarmé, Gide, and the French Symbolists generally. See the extracts bearing on "purification" in Ellmann and Feidelson's *Modern Tradition.* This perspective, however, leads back to Hegel's (later, Pater's) understanding of Hellenic "purity" in art, and to Schiller's famous essay *Naive and Reflective Art* (1795–96).

idiosyncrasy and to make them as elegant as Latin. Against their greening was set a weeding and a pruning: a Latinity to emerge from within.

What I want to emphasize is twofold. It was a poet, Malherbe, who proclaimed, "I will always defend the purity of the French tongue," and it was a poet, Mallarmé, who set out once again to "purify the language of the tribe." Purity is not a scholarly imposition. It is intrinsic to the care of the language we now speak. A "lingua franca et jocundissima" is always being challenged by some ideal of purification: by the very Latin Stevens here uses against itself, or scientific standards of correctness, or "debabelization" (C. K. Ogden's word) through an artificially engendered language, a "Universal Character." Moreover, the issue of poetic diction—an *English* version of the *French* concern for purity—is not a one-sided but a rich and baffling subject. (Owen Barfield's *Poetic Diction* and Donald Davie's *Purity of Diction in English Verse* are still exemplary books in this area.) Good poetic diction is felt to be a language within language that purifies it, restoring original power; bad poetic diction is felt to be artificial rather than natural, a deadening if ornamental set of words and rules. Literary history shows, however, how impossible it is to uphold this distinction between repressive artifice and natural virtue, between conceptions of language that stress an original purity and strength and those that impose an immaculate "classical" or "Aryan" ideal.

Any call for purification or repristination is dangerous. For it is always purity having to come to terms with impurity that drives crazy. The situation is familiar; and whatever the motive for purity, language and religion are its major battlegrounds. The language of religion especially; but also the religion of language itself, language as a quasireligious object when a new vernacular is developing. And American poetry, still striving to break with Anglophile burdens in the 1920s, and more puritanical than it knew, was making the vernacular into a religion.[2]

There is a Nyakyusa saying: "The dead, if not separated from the living, bring madness on them." Ritual helps this separation, according to Mary Douglas in her fascinating book, *Purity and Danger.* Literature is ritual in this sense. William Carlos Williams, writing in the 1920s, after the charnel house of the First World War, in which the dead had risen to claim the living, pro-

2. For American reflections on purity of style before the twentieth century, see *The Native Muse: Theories of American Literature,* vol. 1, ed. Richard Ruland (New York: E. P. Dutton), esp. pp. 32–33, 76–77, and 182–83.

claimed that America had to separate itself from "a civilization of fatigued spirits," from the defiling if urbane and polished plagiarisms of European culture.[3] Williams can justify even Henry Ford in this light. "My God, it is too disgusting," he writes, thinking of Ford (who said "History is bunk") as the solution. And he adds: "Great men of America! O very great men of America please lend me a penny so I won't have to go to the opera."

He means to "*Lohengrin* in Italian SUNG AT MANHATTAN"—that is, to this artificial international culture, this elitist hybrid art totally alien to native America. Instead of supporting opera, let the commercial industrial complex support real works, and pay the artist a tithe to create the new culture, or as he says satirically, to "capitalize Barnum." The circus metaphor catches something; for the culture that would emerge had plenty of trained animals and clowns (T.V. before T.V.) yet lacked the good old animal guides, Blake's "Animal Forms of Wisdom."

For the moment we are still in Williams' grain, looking for a penny to escape the "Traditionalists of Plagiarism," who perpetuate their dead culture through the star-spangled absurdity of multinational opera. (In Germany, through the genius of Brecht, a Threepenny Opera does develop.) But are we not also, already, with Allen Ginsberg—thirty years, a generation later? A Ginsberg who is equally broke, though trying to "make contemporarily real an old style of lyric machinery," "W. C. Fields on my left and Jehovah on my right," crying "howly, howly, howly," ready to abandon the false India of America for a true one more holy in its stink:

America, I've given you all and now I'm nothing.
America two dollars and twentyseven cents January 17, 1956.
I can't stand my own mind. . . .
Asia is rising against me,
I haven't got a chinaman's chance.
I'd better consider my national resources. . . .
American how can I write a holy litany in your silly mood?
I will continue like Henry Ford my strophes are as individual
as his automobiles more so they're all different sexes.

("America")

3. I quote from the following sources: *Spring and All* (1923), *The Great American Novel* (1923), and "Marianne Moore" (1925). The text used is that presented in *Imaginations,* ed. Webster Schott.

Where am *I* going, you wonder. It is my purpose to convey a sense of the impasse that came with the Spring Cleaning that Williams undertook in *Spring and All,* and other works of language purification. The impasse was not unproductive: it patented an American type of sublimity. Since then we have not gotten tired of hearing about the American Sublime; its capaciousness, spaciousness, greatness, newness; its readiness to take on experience and remain sublime. Despite ecological and economic disasters that mock these ideals and bust their adherents, the goldrush of every latest poem recycles the agony, redeems the dirt.

Is the pattern, then, so very different from the familiar one of the old European codgers, of William Butler Yeats, for instance, who embraced the "desolation of reality" after the circus animals, his illusions and histrionic attitudes, had gone? At the very time Williams is thinking of capitalizing Barnum, Marianne Moore is "translating" Old World "Animal Forms of Wisdom" in her own way. Her splendor too is Menagerie. Compulsively we wash our hands of the old culture, of its *opera* (in the sense of masterworks as well as the baleful Wagnerian instance); we denounce it for being sublime junk, an artificial resuscitation of decadent art; we ritually strengthen ourselves for a rejectionist type of verse close to improvisation and prose poetry, but it never refines itself into actual gold. Dirt and paydirt become one. That puristic turning away from opera, why does it produce so much soap opera? Warmed-over Whitman, confessional poetry? Or why, at best, only golden projects, elaborate scales, played on bluesy piano or jazzed-up guitar, all prelude it seems, as we wait for the human story to commence?

Stevens is one of these preludists, a sublime improviser; he too is purging Europe from America, but enjoying and exploiting the thought that it can't be done. The purification, if it is to be, must be more radical than cultural concepts imply. No ideas but in things, was one of Williams's slogans. The idea is that things are cleaner than ideas; and Stevens replies: "How clean the sun when seen in its idea, / Washed in the remotest cleanliness of a heaven / That has expelled us and our images." Where would that cleaning, purging, expelling, end? The paradoxes are many. Williams realizes that the affected words are not purer than before. "I touch the words and they baffle me. I turn them over in my mind and look at them but they mean little that is clean." The dirt of Europe may have been removed, but now the words are plastered with muck out of the cities. When he does write an exemplary poem, antithetical to his prose, with its involuntary waves still tiding after Whitman ("We have only mass movements like a sea"), when he gives us

So much depends
upon

a red wheel
barrow

glazed with rain
water

beside the white
chickens

it is marked less by purity than by neatness and composure.

I slow down to look more closely at this well-known poem. It is a sequence of pauses filled by words. It is as if language had only nonnatural sentences, and Williams were seeking a natural sentence: properly rhythmed, punctuated, by the mind pressing against what it perceives. Yet the caesuras here are too sharply, too keenly placed to be only rhythmic pauses. They are deliberate cuts—as deliberate as cutting in the movies or surgery—and place things "beside" each other, avoiding plot or temporal climax. The cutting edge of the caesuras, moreover, here turned inward, suggests an outward-turned force that excludes or could exclude all but its own presence. There is meaning, there is an object focused on, but there is also something cleaner than both: the very edge of the pen/knife that cuts or delineates these lines. "A word is a word most," Williams wrote, "when it is separated out by science, treated with acid to remove the smudges, washed, dried and placed right side up on a clean surface. . . . It may be used not to smear it again with thinking (the attachments of thought) but in such a way that it will remain scrupulously itself, clean perfect, unnicked, beside other words in parade. There must be edges."

The cleanness, however, of Williams' phrasing depends so much on what is edged out that we become more interested in what is not there than in what is. The red wheelbarrow moves us into the forgetfulness of pure perception, but also suggests someone can't stand his own mind; it is as functional a carrier of the cultural surplus or whatever nonpluses clean thinking as Ford's slick cars and other vehicular gadgets made in America. A wheel is a wheel, however glossy, however intricate: the earth itself is a wheel we forget. Gilded chariots or red wheelbarrows are equally soothers of memory, antimnemonic like a pastoral nature that hides its motives. The strength of *pure* poetry resides, then, like all poetry, in the impure elements it cuts out, elides, covers up, negates, represses

. . . depends on: and the strength of *impure* poetry in the very idea of purity that makes it go—and go like—crazy.

I am as susceptible as anyone to the dream of a clean-perfect language: one that no longer mixes images and meanings, desire and memory; that cuts off, leanly, the attachments of thought; that does not contaminate life with dead matter, or the new and the old. I would like Williams's wheel to be my will, and to carry me beyond mere instrumentality: I'd like to think of it as at the navel or omphalos of a spontaneously constituted place of affection, not barren like the backyards of hospitals, even if relieved by that red and white. I'd like those contagious colors, in fact, to carry me by unconscious metaphor beyond the suggestion of disease into a world where "it seems sufficient / to see and hear whatever coming and going is, / losing the self to the victory / of stones and trees" (A. R. Ammons, "Gravelly Run"). Even here, of course, one cannot lose the self entirely: a certain glaze meets one's gaze, "air's glass / jail seals each thing in its entity." Yet in such a prison one could live happily enough as god's spy or transparent eyeball. No Hegel or Heidegger there to turn a wheelbarrow into a philosophic tool. Best of all, I'd like that wheel to depend, to swing low, and carry me "up" and "on," and make me forget what I am now doing, namely, playing with words that do not stand on themselves but rest on other words. That red wheel, that red barrow, archaic mound of adamic or decomposing flesh, that wheelbarrow left there to cart manure, culture, cadaver, whatever: I want it to compost spiritually, to become words forgotten by words, as nature by nature when Ammons writes: "the sunlight has never / heard of trees." *There* is purity: in that "Nothing that is not there and the nothing that is" (Stevens, "The Snow Man"). "Gravelly Run" ends on the run, as it were, and frosty, as befits a self-purifying landscape, or verses that recall the link of nature poetry to epitaph: "stranger, / hoist your burdens, get on down the road."

> exposing his gifted quite empty hands
>
> (Geoffrey Hill, "In Piam Memoriam")

American poetry, then, like that of older vernacular traditions, is enmeshed in the paradoxes of purifying its words, of constituting itself as a Palladium in the city of words. This relativizing conclusion is unsatisfying, however; it says nothing about why poets have become absolute for poetic purity, martyrs to the art like Mallarmé or Dickinson. I want to discuss the latter of these near contemporaries by looking closely at two lyrics written about three years apart. Read in sequence, their quest for purity appears in a revealing and frightening way. We glimpse, as in the early Williams, and originally in Wordsworth, the link between nature poetry and language purification; between questions of representation and purity of diction; and we understand that nature enters not as the pretext for sublime self-projections but as a privative and admonitory force. The language of nature replaces the dead language of classical or poetic diction; but the language of nature proves to be as monumental as what it replaced. It is a voice speaking from landscape as from a grave; a modern classical idiom in the making; a hieratic vernacular inscription. The burden hoisted by the stranger, or the promise to be kept, includes this purification of the vernacular.

Here is the earlier of the lyrics (783):[4]

The Birds begun at Four o'clock—
Their period for Dawn—
A Music numerous as space—
But neighboring as Noon—

I could not count their Force—
Their Voices did expend
As Brook by Brook bestows itself
To multiply the Pond.

Their Witnesses were not—
Except occasional man—
In homely industry arrayed—
To overtake the Morn—

Nor was it for applause—
That I could ascertain—
But independent Ecstasy
Of Deity and Men—

By Six, the Flood had done—
No Tumult there had been
Of Dressing, or Departure—
And yet the Band was gone—

The Sun engrossed the East—
The Day controlled the World—
The Miracle that introduced
Forgotten, as fulfilled.

4. The text of the poems as well as their numbering is taken from *The Poems of Emily Dickinson,* ed. Thomas H. Johnson.

There is a plot. Two events, perhaps three, are coordinated, and form a beginning and an end. At four the bird song starts, at six it has stopped. That the sun has risen is the third event, unless contemporaneous with the second. But this plotlike division of time, and these numbers, four, six, are in stylized opposition to the multiplying "force" or flood of the passing music. There is something uncountable despite the counting, the bookkeeping; and it extends to a sun that arrives on the scene with "engrossing" power.[5]

The temporal sequence, then, is deceptive. "Their period for dawn" already suggests the birds have their own dawn within a scheme of "Independent Ecstasy" (stanza 4): their song, neither sanctifying nor theatrical, neither expressly for God nor for Society, cannot be subordinated to an "end." Nor is it subordinated to sunrise, since it is said to be "neighboring as Noon." The sun is already in the music. When the sun is mentioned in the last stanza, it is depicted as risen: already in place. Its exact position or power in the scheme of things cannot be calculated any more than the "miracle"—the numerous music—that came and went. The presence of Day is a second "miracle" that replaces the first so completely that the first is "Forgotten, as fulfilled."

The relation between "forgotten" and "fulfilled" is the depth-charge of this small poem; but on the surface Dickinson's lyric carries a moral message as clear as its plot. Nature has style, Nature has the right decorum. Its daily miracles are enacted unself-consciously. Joyful and strong they may be, but never self-regarding. The birds "expend" their voices, the sun "engrosses" the world. It is a lavish economy, without inhibition or Puritan restraint. "Engross" may imply an overbearing result, but from intrinsic power rather than from a striving for effect. As a statement about devotional verse, or religious rhetoric, the lyric is impertinent: do we need, it hints, a mode of worship that is pretentious, inmixing self-regard or the wish for applause? Yet Dickinson's lyric is itself not beyond reproach: though it exalts unself-consciousness, its "palpable design" conveys a moral that is witty at best, childish at worst. How *neat* all this is, including her verses! "No Tumult there had been / Of Dressing, or Departure." But neatness is not a major virtue. It is a form of cleanliness in a religion that puts cleanliness next to Godliness.

To purify words about God is Dickinson's apparent aim. She can do more, as we shall see: she can purify God of words. Here she plays an old game, and

5. Dickinson likes to use "counting house" terms: her lexicon, Noah Webster's *American* dictionary of the English language, includes the economic sense of "engross" (s.v. 4 in the first, 1828 edition) as well as "to copy in a large hand" (s.v. 5) and "to take or assume in undue quantities or degrees; as, to engross power" (s.v. 6).

confuses cleanliness with purity. Almost every religion claims to institute the right worship, the right words. Evangelical religion, in particular, is often fanatic about purity of diction. The peculiar and fascinating thing is that in Dickinson's lyrics nature and style are the same, a divine etiquette. Nature teaches art to hide art for the sake of unself-consciousness. What is described here is not Nature, but *a mode of being present* that at once values and cancels the self. If there is "imitation of nature" it focuses on how to rise, that is, come to presence, come into *the* Presence.

That sunrise may be sunset, that "the King / Be witnessed" only "at" death (465) makes no difference to the poet. For the "I" is always in a state of mortification: it is both a witness, a self-hood, and purged from or transmuted by the act of witnessing. "The Absolute removed / The Relative away" (765, written circa 1863); the pun on "Relative" suggests that there may have to be a separation from family as well as from time. What o'clock it is becomes irrelevant, therefore; and when the first-person form is used, it expresses incapacity: "I could not count their Force," "Nor was it for applause / That I could ascertain." The strong, elliptical ending, "Forgotten, as fulfilled" is as close as one comes to an absolute construction: if it relates to anything it must be the eclipsed "I." The apparent referent, of course, is song, "the miracle that introduced"; but that song is really the poet's, whose presence is elided, "Forgotten, as fulfilled."[6]

The more we ponder this lyric, or its pseudoprogression, the more curious it appears. Is the desire to come to or into Presence so strong that it verges on a death wish? Could we read stanza 5 as intimating: May the departure we call death be as orderly! Could we interpret the hiatus between stanzas 5 and 6—no explicit casual connection joins the vanishing of the birds with the risen sun—as a space death has made or could make? With the last stanza something other than common day seems to be evoked. It is as if the daily event we call sunrise had been quietly displaced by divine day. Do we, after all, reach "Degreeless Noon" (287) "Without a Moment's Bell" (286)? Is the natural silence also the preternatural, as the sun's absolute presence obliterates everything else?

6. Sharon Cameron's *Lyric Time: Dickinson and the Limits of Genre* (Baltimore: Johns Hopkins University Press, 1979) has exact remarks on the stanzas as "flashcards" suggesting "the absence of any trace left from a previous moment/picture." See her discussion of "The Birds begun" and "At half past three" on pp. 176–78. She calls "begun" a "strange preterite" (perhaps, I would add, a nominative absolute or pseudo-infinitive, though the 1828 Webster lists *begun* as an alternate preterite form) and points to the complicated grammar of the poem's last line.

Dickinson's ellipses bear study, though they put an interpreter in the uncomfortable position of arguing from silence. This silence becomes typographic in one formal device, baffling, but at least obtrusive. In many poems an idiosyncratic mark—dash, hyphen, or extended point—replaces the period sign and all other punctuation. It can appear at any juncture, to connect or disconnect, generally to do both at once. It is a caesura or *coupure* more cutting than that of Williams. It introduces from the beginning the sense of an ending and both extends and suspends it. The semantic value of this hyphen is zero, but it allows the asyndetic sentences to become an indefinite series of singular and epigrammatic statements. The zero endows them with the value of one, with loneliness or one-liness as in an amazing poem that begins "The Loneliness One dare not sound" (777).

Why does this formal mark, this hyphen with zero meaning, have intraverbal force? Perhaps because it both joins and divides, like a hymen. Perhaps because it is like the line between dates on tombstones. It may be an arbitrary sign or it may be nakedly mimetic. In any case, the decorous proposition that nature is style is radicalized: this elliptical, clipped mark evokes style as nature. That hyphen-hymen persephonates Emily. At every pause, which it institutes, it can remind us of her wish to be a bride of quietness. "Title divine—is mine!" (1072) But her only title may be her epitaphic lyrics, that sum up a life by brief inscriptions, very much like titles. The briefest inscription would be the letters E. D. and a set of hyphenated dates. The hyphen-hymen matters more than the dates, for what is crucial is the moment of juncture: dawning/dying, an unviolent transition from natural to supernatural, like waking into a dream, nature not being put out but "Forgotten, as fulfilled."

We come to Dickinson's later, less readable poem (1084):

At Half past Three, a single Bird
Unto a silent Sky
Propounded but a single term
Of cautious melody.

At Half past Four, Experiment
Had subjugated test
And lo, Her silver Principle
Supplanted all the rest.

At Half past Seven, Element
Nor Implement, be seen—
And Place was where the Presence was
Circumference between.

How dry and bookish, as if a computer had been given a number of words, and instructed to produce a minimal narrative! Only that narrative remains from the earlier version, though more stark, more outlined; the pathos and the moral play are gone. The sun too is gone, and the personal focus of reference. In this emptied landscape, abstractions nest a "single Bird," the remnant of a purification whose motive we are trying to find.

Now, "one stanza, one act" is the formula; and this new, unlavish economy extends to theme. A single term, a single note, rather than a numerous and multiplying music begins the action; then the bird sings freely; then it has ceased. One, two, three.

The time indicators, which periodize the event, terminating its three parts like a stop watch, heighten the contrary force of the poem's last word. That last word is like the first of each stanza, "At Half past. . . ." It marks what lies *between* integers.

The between remains: something not whole, not at one. Yet the drive toward atonement is haltingly continued in this poem, which is paced without auction or augmentation—without pseudoprogression. "Half past" is repeated, and half past is a turning point that does not turn. The first of these poems was written when Dickinson was close to the age of thirty-three; the second, three years later.

Though "between" sticks out, is it a middle or a mediation? Other words too stick out, despite their effort to blend. They resemble each other as terms, even when their meanings are separable. So "Experiment," "Element," "Implement" rhyme obscurely. It is hard, moreover, to hold on to the distinction between "Place" and "Presence." A nonrepresentational quality suffuses everything and counterpoints the temporal markers—we don't even know, for sure, whether morning or evening, sunrise or sunset, is the period, because all mention of light is omitted. We could be listening from the grave.

Not quite: "silver Principle" contains a hint of light breaking. Yet the paradox remains that light breaks what it should illumine. Something, at the end, is not seen that was seen before. The very words become obscure. What *visibilia* do "Element" and "Implement" describe? Does "Element" refer to sky or bird or the music itself? Since "Implement" follows, we assign "Element" to a range of meanings exclusive of "Bird." The technique, if we can so designate it, approaches modern devices that Hart Crane called "as independent of any representational motive as a mathematical equation."[7] The earlier lyric had as

7. See his "Modern Poetry" (1929), published in *The Complete Poems of Hart Crane,* ed. Waldo Frank (New York: Liveright, 1933).

its subject a problematic coming to or into Presence; now it is a coming into absence or indeterminacy.

The only way to resolve the indeterminate meaning of "Element" and "Implement" is to remember the earlier lyric and its conclusion: "Forgotten, as fulfilled." This suggests that "Implement" may have its etymological meaning of *implere,* that which fills, and "Element" could denote either what is filled or the beginning, the first term, in contradistinction to the last. "Neither beginning nor fulfillment is seen" (at the end), is what the stanza says. The meaning of the two poems is comparable.

If so, how do we interpret the later poem's shift toward verbal abstraction and a nonrepresentational method? Hart Crane thought that between Impressionism and Cubism, poetry as well as painting was moving away from religion and toward science. This largish and imprecise speculation does not help much. For the themes of Dickinson's lyric are neither religion nor science. Words as words have moved to the fore, words that are about to be "terms"—fixed, as if by rigor mortis. The clock strikes for them too. If they escape that fixity, that transformation of language into *last words,* it is because they still evoke, in their very abstraction, past meanings, referents at once mathematical, musical, chronometric, experimental, teleological, even typological.[8]

The poem, therefore, never progresses; it is still moving, at the end, toward a "single term." This term is not found in the dictionary: the dictionary, perhaps, is in search of it. At present, or *at* any moment that can be fixed with the mock precision of "Half past," it is merely a cipher, a divine clue. An expected *god-term* (to borrow from Kenneth Burke) supplants all the rest and places what was life and time in a radically displaced position: into a place for which the names Death or Purgatory have been used, though they are not definitive. If we take this "term" seriously, then time may be transformed at any moment: by a

8. *Implere figuram* is the term in theology for the *kairos* moment, when history moves "from shadowy Types to Truth" (Milton). The shadowy types are Old Testament figures or events, the Truth their repetition with fulfillment in the New Testament. This figural or typological perspective was extended to secular history in general: its happenings were similarly conceived as types or emblems for a superseding truth. The pattern of "Forgotten, as fulfilled," since it embraces "Implement" as well as "Element," last and first, suggests a metatypological perspective, an overcoming of typology. Cf. Robert Weisbuch, *Emily Dickinson's Poetry* (Chicago: University of Chicago Press, 1975): "The bird song is a foreshadowing type of the day, and yet we suspect that the introductory 'forgotten' miracle is granted superiority over its fulfillment" (pp. 122, and 193, n. 20). Roland Hagenbüchle's "Dickinson Criticism," *Anglia* 97 (1979): 452–74, may be consulted for others who have dealt with the issues of reference and indeterminacy.

cockcrow that is taps, or a single note that is the trumpet call of the Apocalypse. As you lie down, each bed is a grave. "The Grave preceded me—" (784). As you rise up, a bird is the prelude to revelation. The structure of human life, from this phantomizing perspective, is a chiasmus, a crossing over from nothing to all and vice versa: from life to death, from death to life, absence to presence, and so on. "Love—is anterior to Life— / Posterior—to Death— / Initial of Creation, and / The Exponent of Earth—" (917).

Looking back at both poems, we can spot where that chiasmus rises up and phantomizes as well as founds the terminological work. "And Place was where the Presence was" is two-faced, since it could be an expression for sheer vacancy or sheer plenitude. Place is the absence of a Presence that had been; *or* Place coincides with Presence. The one meaning does not merely coexist with the other as a type of ambiguity: the one meaning is the other, so that both remain occupying, in the same words, the same place. That is the unsettled and interminable state of affairs which "Circumference between" seems to fix forever.

Let me conclude by exploring this cryptic phrase. It is again an "absolute" construction, which we cannot attach to specific meaning or referent. To play a little, we might say that it makes reference circumferential; it so broadens it by abstraction that referentiality itself, or the representational force in words, is simultaneously evoked and revoked. Representation itself is "between" us and Presence. Or representation is the only Presence we have. "Myself—the Term between—" (721).

Whether or not this impasse (founded in the religious sensibility, but removed from institutionalized words that refer us to religion) is the residual meaning, the absoluteness of "Circumference between" is like a shudder, a cold shower perhaps. Faith and Hope, that rely on "the evidence of things not seen," are emergent at this point; yet there is no overt sign of this, and it is hard to imagine what sustenance they could find in such a void. The silent sky has returned, and the landscape is washed out, though we don't know if by radiance or if by darkness. All we can do is explore the impasse by means of those terminating words.

Circumference is a periphery, away from the center, whether the figure thought of is spatial (a circle) or temporal (the earth's circuit around the sun, bringing back the beginning or the whole event just recounted). "Circumference between" could point to earth (life on earth), or the clock itself in its roundness: that repeated watching and waiting which is a religious duty as well as a symptom of alienated labor. "Circumference between" could be that displaced place for which the Christian name is Death or Purgatory, and which intrudes "between" us and God, eternally perhaps. Circumference as that which interposes could be the most abstract cipher of them all, zero, or whatever nonrepresentational figure can hold together, in some imageless image, the juncture of life and death, death and life, self-presence and the divine presence. "I could not see to see—" (465). If we ask what "be seen" at the end, as at the end of this poem, the answer would have to be: nothing, *or* all, *or* their juncture as zero.

The two endings, then, "Forgotten, as fulfilled" and "Circumference between" are simply a hyphen-hymen written out, or last words *not* given to the void. They help us to understand why the poetry Dickinson brings forth is so lean. It would not be wrong to ask how she can be a great poet with so small a voice, so unvaried a pattern, so contained a form of experience. Is her desire for purity perhaps the sign of a sensibility easily exhausted, depleted by smallest things that inflate: "You saturated Sight—" (640)? Whereas, with many poets, criticism has to confront their overt, figurative excess, with such purifiers of language as Emily Dickinson criticism has to confront an elliptical and chaste mode of expression. The danger is not fatty degeneration but lean degeneration: a powerful, appealing anorexia. She herself called it "sumptuous Destitution" (1382). Since this is certainly prompted by her interpretation of Puritan scruples about language-art—"Farewell sweet phrases, lovely metaphors" (George Herbert)—we cannot dismiss the possibility that she so identifies with an ascesis forced upon her, that instead of the milk of hope she substitutes the "White Sustenance— / Despair" (640). Her criticism of Puritan culture, or of the God of the Puritans, would have been to make herself a visible reproach by becoming so invisible, by wasting the substance of poetry with such deliberation and precision, like a saint. Yet not believing in saints or mediations, only her poetry can stand for her: representation, not mediation, is her hope. Her words, always tending toward last words, may be an act of resistance: her literal acceptance of Puritan decorum figures forth the uncompromised life of the words that remain.

> Capacity to terminate
> Is a Specific Grace
>
> (1196)

I am not good at concluding; I would prefer at this point to lose myself in the thought that poetry, like life, goes on, despite this amazing, dangerous quest for purity, manifested in Dickinson's endgame of words. I would prefer to quote

John Ashbery, for example, because he is more relaxed, always convalescing it seems, converting what was oracular and blazing into divine chatter:

> Light falls on your shoulders, as is its way,
> And the process of purification continues happily.
>
> ("Evening in the Country")

The burden of light, in Dickinson, despite her attempt to maintain decorum, seems heavier. Like Mallarmé, she is a crucial poet, a dangerous purifier, the offspring of a greater Apollo. In the German tradition Hölderlin, Rilke, and Celan have a similar relation to a purity more radical than what went under the name of Classicism. These poets are so intense—Shelley is another—they place so great a burden on the shoulders of poetry, that language breaks with itself. Mallarmé said he wanted to take back from music what belonged to poetry; that is one way of describing a break with representation more complete than conventional or classical form allowed. That form is but a second nature, a cleansing and not a purification. A more radical Classicism had to be discovered: that of Dionysos or, according to Nietzsche's interpretation of Wagner, Dionysian music. Theology may inspire but it no longer mediates this break with representation. Poets having expelled the old gods, their images, their phraseology—in short, poetic diction—and, having instituted a more natural diction, the process of purification continues, not so happily, and the purified language proves to be as contaminated as ever. We see that the poetic diction once rejected had extraordinary virtues, including its nonnatural character, its lucid artifice, the "mirror-of-steel uninsistence" (Marianne Moore) by which it made us notice smallest things and ciphered greatest things, and gathered into a few terms, magical, memorable, barely meaningful, the powers of language.

The Case of the Mystery Story

The terms "reversal" (*peripeteia*) and "recognition" (*anagnorisis*) are well known. They name, according to Aristotle, the essential ingredients of complex plots in tragedy. "Reversal" he defines as a change which makes the action veer in a direction different from that expected, and he refers us to the messenger from Corinth who comes to cheer Oedipus and eventually produces the recognition leading to an opposite result. Recognition is often linked to this kind of reversal, and is defined as a change from ignorance to knowledge. "Then once more I must bring what is dark to light," Oedipus says in the prologue of the play—and does exactly that, however unforeseen to him the result. In most detective stories, clearly, there is both a reversal and a recognition, but they are not linked as powerfully as in tragedy. The reversal in detective stories is more like an unmasking; and the recognition that takes place when the mask falls is not prepared for by dramatic irony. It is a belated, almost last-minute affair, subordinating the reader's intelligence to such hero-detectives as Ross Macdonald's Archer, who is no Apollo, but who does roam the California scene with cleansing or catalyzing effect.

I wish, however, to draw attention to a third term, left obscure in the *Poetics.* Aristotle calls it *tò pathos,* "the Suffering," or as Butcher translates it, the "Scene of Suffering." *Tò pathos,* he says—and it is all he says—"is a destructive or painful action, such as death on the stage, bodily agony, wounds and the like."[1]

Aristotle is probably referring to what happens at the conclusion of *Oedipus Rex,* though chiefly offstage: the suicide of Jocasta and self-blinding of Oedipus. Or to the exhibition of the mangled head of Pentheus by his deluded mother, in Euripides' *Bacchae.* He may also be thinking of the premise on which the tragic plot is built, the blood deed from which all consequences flow, and which, though premised rather than shown, is the real point of reference.[2] I wish to suggest that some such "heart of darkness" scene, some such *pathos,* is the relentless center or focus of detective fiction, and that recognition and reversal are merely paths toward it—techniques which seek to evoke it as strongly and visually as possible.

I don't mean that we must have the scene of suffering—the actual murder, mutilation, or whatever—exhibited to us. In *The Chill,* and in Ross Macdonald's novels generally, violence is as offstage as in *Oedipus Rex.* (The real violence, in any case, is perpetrated on the psyche.) But to solve a crime in detective stories means to give it an exact location: to pinpoint not merely the murderer and his motives but also the very place, the room, the ingenious or brutal circumstance. We want not only proof but, like Othello, ocular proof. Crime induces a perverse kind of epiphany: it marks the spot, or curses it, or invests it with enough meaning to separate it from the ordinary space-time continuum. Thus, though a Robbe-Grillet may remove the scene of pathos, our eyes nervously inspect all those graphic details which continue to evoke the detective story's lust for evidence.

The example of Robbe-Grillet—I want to return to it later—suggests that sophisticated art is closer to being an antimystery rather than a mystery. It limits, even while expressing, this passion for ocular proof. Take the medieval carol, "Lully, lulley," and regard how carefully it frames the heart of darkness scene, how with a zooming motion at once tactful and satisfyingly ritual, it approaches a central mystery:

Lully, lulley,
The faucon hath born my mak away.

He bare him up, he bare him down,
He bare him into an orchard brown.

In that orchard there was an halle
Which was hanged with purpill and pall.

And in that hall there was a bed,
It was hanged with gold so red.

And in that bed there lith a knight,
His wounds bleding day and night.

By that bed side kneleth a may,
And she wepeth both night and day.

And by that bed side there stondeth a stone,
Corpus Christi wreten there on.

Here we have a scene of pathos, "death on the stage, bodily agony, wounds and the like," but in the form of picture-and-inscription, a still-life we can contemplate without fear. It is a gentle falcon, even if it be a visionary one, that lifts us in this ballad from the ordinary world into that of romance. This is no bird of prey attracted to battlefield carnage. And though the heart of the romance is dark enough, it is also comforting rather than frightening because interpreted by the inscription. We do not have to overcome an arresting moment of pity or fear, we do not even have to ask, as in the Parsifal legends, "What does this mean?" in order to redeem the strange sight. Its redeeming virtue is made clear to everyone borne away on this ritual trip.

The relation of the ballad to the modern mystery story is a complicated one; and my purpose here is not historical genealogy. The ballad revival had its influence not only on the gothic novel with its mystifications but also on the tension between brevity and elaboration in Melville's *Billy Budd,* the tales of Henry James, and the Gaucho stories of Borges. The modern elliptical ballad as well as the "novel turned tale"[3] qualify the element of mystery in a definably new, even generic way.

Consider Wordsworth's "The Thorn," first published in *Lyrical Ballads* (1798). The movement of this ballad is so slow, the dramatic fact so attenuated, that we begin to sense the possibility of a plotless story. A line of descent could easily be established between pseudonarratives like "The Thorn," which converge obsessively on an ocular center of uncertain interest (has a crime been committed near the thorn, or is the crime an illusion to stimulate crude imaginations?) and lyrical movies like Antonioni's *Blow-Up* or Resnais's *Last Year at Marienbad.* The center they scan is an absence; the darkness they illumine has no heart. There is pathos here but no defined scene of pathos. Instead of a whodunit we get a whodonut, a story with a hole in it.[4]

Wordsworth's poem begins and ends with a thornbush seen by the poet "on the ridge of Quantock Hill, on a stormy day, a thorn which I had often passed in calm and bright weather without noticing it. I said to myself, 'Cannot I by some invention do as much to make this Thorn permanently an impressive object as the storm has made it to my eyes at this moment?'" The narrator's eye, therefore, remains on the thorn, or the thorn (if you wish) in his eye: as always in Wordsworth the path from thing to meaning via an act of imaginative perception (an "invention") is fully, almost painfully respected. Though consciousness moves toward what it fears to find, a scene of ballad sorrow and bloodiness, it never actually presents that beautiful and ominous "still" which the Corpus Christi poem composes for us. The corpse has vanished and will not be found. The strange spot is not approached on the wings of a falcon, nor does it ever become a burning bush. Instead we approach it from within a peculiar consciousness, whose repetitive, quasi-ritual stepping from one object to another, from thorn to pond to hill of moss, as well as spurts of topographical precision—"And to the left, three yards beyond, / You see a little muddy pond"—suggests we are behind the camera-eye of a mad movie maker, or . . . on the way to Robbe-Grillet.

But what exactly are we on the way to? Robbe-Grillet, after hints in Henry James, Gide, Faulkner, and Camus, has killed the scene of pathos. We all know that a corpse implies a story; yet Robbe-Grillet's contention that a story kills, that a story is a corpse, may be news for the novel. In his fiction the statement "He has a past" is equivalent to "He is doomed" or "It is written." So Oedipus, or a Robbe-Grillet hero, is safe as long as he has no past. So the detective in *The Erasers* commits the crime he is sent to solve: he enacts the prefigurative or formalistic force of traditional story-making which insists on its corpse or scene of suffering. If, moreover, we identify that scene of suffering with what Freud calls the primal scene—the "mystery" of lovemaking which the child stumbles on—then we also understand why Robbe-Grillet is opposed to character or plot based on a psychoanalytic model. For him Freudianism is simply another form of mystery religion, one which insists on its myth of depth and hidden scene of passion. Robbe-Grillet formulates therefore, what might be called the modern script-tease, of which Antonioni's *Blow-Up* and *L'Avventura,* Bergman's *A Passion,* and Norman Mailer's *Maidstone,*[5] are disparate examples. What they share is the perplexing absence of *tò pathos:* one definitively visualized scene to which everything else might be referred.

I have brought you, safely I hope, from ancient to modern mystery stories by following the fortunes of the scene of pathos. But one comment should be added concerning this scene, and its structure. Comparing the scene of suffering with Freud's primal scene, we gain a clue to why it is able to motivate entire novels or plays.

It resembles, first of all, a highly condensed, supersemantic event like riddle, oracle, or mime. Now whether or not the power of such scenes is linked to our stumbling as innocents on sexual secrets—on seeing or overhearing that riddling mime[6]—it is clear that life is always in some way too fast for us, that it is a spectacle we can't interpret or a dumb show difficult to word. The detective novel allows us to catch up a little by involving us in the interpretation of a mystery that seems at first to have no direct bearing on our life. We soon realize, of course, that "mystery" means that something is happening too fast to be spotted. We are made to experience a consciousness (like Oedipa's in Thomas Pynchon's *Crying of Lot* 49) always behind and running; vulnerable therefore, perhaps imposed on. But we are also allowed to triumph (unlike Oedipa) over passivity when the detective effects a catharsis or purgation of consciousness, and sweeps away all the false leads planted in the course of the novel.

No wonder the detective's reconstitution of the scene of pathos has something phantasmagoric about it. So quick that it is always "out of sight," the primal scene's existence, real or imagined, can only be mediated by a fabulous structure in which coincidence and convergence play a determining role. Time and space condense in strange ways, like language itself, and produce absurdly packed puns of fate. What is a clue, for instance, but a symbolic or condensed corpse, a living trace or materialized shadow? It shrinks space into place (furniture, and so forth) exactly as a bullet potentially shrinks or sensitizes time. The underdetermined or quasi-invisible becomes, by a reversal, so overdetermined and sharply visible that it is once again hard on the eyes. Bullet, clue, and pun have a comparable phenomenological shape: they are as magical in their power to heighten or oppress imagination as Balzac's "oriental" device of the fatal skin in *La Peau de Chagrin.*

Is it less oriental, magical, or punning when, in a Ross Macdonald story, the same gun is used for killings fifteen years apart or the murders of father and then son take place in the same spot also fifteen years apart (*The Underground Man*)? Or when, as in *The Chill,* a man's "mother" turns out to be his wife? Or when, in Mrs. Radcliffe's *Romance of the Forest,* a marriageable girl happens to be brought to the very castle chamber where her true father was killed while she was still an infant? Recall also the speed with which things move in *Oedipus Rex,* and how a messenger who on entry is simply a UPI runner from Corinth proves to be an essential link in Oedipus' past, part of the chain that preserved him from death and for a second death—the consciousness to befall him. There is nothing more fearfully condensed than the self-image Oedipus is left with: "A man who entered his father's bed, wet with his father's blood."

I am haunted therefore by André Breton's image of "le revolver aux cheveux blancs." There has always been something like this white-haired gun, some magic weapon in the service of superrealism. The movie camera that "shoots" a scene is the latest version of this venerable gadget. Our reality-hunger, our desire to know the worst and the best, is hard to satisfy. In Sophocles' day it was oracular speech that prowled the streets and intensified the consciousness of men. "This day will show your birth *and* will destroy you." Try to imagine how Tiresias' prophecy can come to pass. A lifetime must depend on a moment, or on one traumatic recognition.

Tragedy as an art that makes us remember death is not unlike a memory vestige forcing us back to birth—to the knowledge that a man is born of woman rather than self-born, that he is a dependent and mortal being. We become conscious of human time. The detective story, however, allows *place* to turn the tables on *time* by means of its decisive visual reanimations. The detective's successful pursuit of vestiges turns them into quasi-immortal spores; and while this resuscitation of the past partakes of the uncanny,[7] it also neatly confines the deadly deed or its consequences to a determinate, visualized, field.

This observation brings me to a central if puzzling feature of the popular mystery. Its plot idea tends to be stronger than anything the author can make of it. The *surnaturel* is *expliqué,* and the genie returned to the bottle by a trick. For the mystery story has always been a genre in which appalling facts are made to fit into a rational or realistic pattern. The formula dominating it began to emerge with the first instance of the genre, Horace Walpole's *Castle of Otranto* (1764), which begins when a child who is the heir apparent of a noble house is killed by the enormous helmet of an ancestral statue which buries him alive. After this ghostly opening Walpole's novel moves, like its descendants, from sensation to simplification, from bloody riddle to quasi-solution, embracing as much "machinery" as possible on the way.

The conservative cast of the mystery story is a puzzle. Born in the Enlightenment, it has not much changed. As mechanical and manipulative as ever, it explains the irrational, after exploiting it, by the latest rational system: Macdonald, for instance, likes to invent characters whose lives have Freudian or Oedipal explanations. In *The Underground Man,* the murderer turns out to be a murderess, a possessive mother with an overprotected son. The real underground man is the underground woman. With a sense of family nightmare as vivid as it is in Walpole, the novel advances inward, from the discovery of the corpse to the frozen psyche of the murderess, Mrs. Snow. All the characters are efficiently, even beautifully sketched, but they are somehow too understandable. They seem to owe as much to formula as the plot itself, which moves deviously yet inexorably toward a solution of the mystery.

A good writer, of course, will make us feel the gap between a mystery and its laying to rest. He will always write in a way that resists the expected ending: not simply to keep us guessing (for, as Edmund Wilson remarked, "The secret is nothing at all") but to show us more about life—that is, about the way people die while living. What is uncovered is not death but death-in-life.[8]

Perhaps endings (resolutions) are always weaker than beginnings, and not only in the "explained mystery" kind of detective story. What entropy is involved? Pynchon's *Crying of Lot* 49, more imaginative than Mailer's *Barbary Shore,* and one of the few genuinely comic treatments in America of the detective story formula, suggests an answer. It is not simply a matter of beginnings and endings but of two sorts of repetition, one of which is magical or uncanny, the other deadly to spirit. Magical repetition releases us into the symbol: a meaning that sustains us while we try to thread secondary causes, trivialities, middles-and-muddles—the rich wastings of life in pre-energy-conserving America. As Pynchon's novel unfolds, we are literally wasted by its riches; those cries and sights; that treasure of trash; and to redeem it all only the notion of anamnesis, which reintroduces the idea of a "first" cause, counterbalances the drag:

> *She was meant to remember.* . . . She touched the edge of its voluptuous field, knowing it would be lovely beyond dreams simply to submit to it; that not gravity's pull, laws of ballistics, feral ravening, promised more delight. She tested it, shivering: I am meant to remember. Each clue that comes is *supposed* to have its own clarity, its fine chances for permanence. But then she wondered if the gemlike "clues" were only some kind of compensation. To make up for her having lost the direct, epileptic Word, the cry that might abolish the night.

Oedipa's vision of being trapped in an "excluded middle," that is, having to desire always some first or last event that would resolve life in terms of something or nothing, meaning or meaninglessness, is reenforced, in the novel's last pages, by a haunting blend of metaphors:

> It was like walking among matrices of a great digital computer, the zeros and ones twinned above, hanging like balanced mobiles right and left, ahead, thick, maybe

> endless. Behind the hieroglyphic streets there would either be a transcendent meaning, or only the earth, . . . either an accommodation reached, in some kind of dignity, with the Angel of Death, or only death and the daily, tedious preparations for it.

If Pynchon's novel ends strongly, it is because it doesn't end. "It's time to start," says Genghis Cohen, of the auction, and by a kind of "honest forgery" (a sustained theme in the book) we find ourselves with Oedipa, absurdly, lyrically, at the threshold of yet another initiation.[9] This outwitting of "the direct, epileptic Word" is like purifying the imagination of *tò pathos;* for the ritual "crying" evoked but not rendered at the close of Pynchon's book is simply a version of that "long-distance" call which perhaps began everything.

The detective story structure—strong beginnings and endings, and a deceptively rich, counterfeit, "excludable" middle—resembles almost too much that of symbol or trope.[10] Yet the recent temptation of linguistic theorists to collapse narrative structure into this or that kind of metaphoricity becomes counterproductive if it remains blind to the writer's very struggle to outwit the epileptic Word. Take a less symbolic novel than Pynchon's, one in the European tradition of selfconscious realism. In Alfred Andersch's *Efraim's Book* the narrator generates an entire novel by writing *against* a final disclosure.[11] Efraim keeps interpolating new incidents although he knows the book will trump him in the end. A journalist shuttling between London, Berlin, and Rome, he is moved to write a book whose climax is the embarrassing secret he continually delays telling. Efraim is a post-Auschwitz Jew and uprooted intellectual who broods on the human condition, yet the secret obsessing him is simply that his wife is unfaithful. It is as if Andersch wants to reduce the dilemmas of moral existence in postwar Europe to a humiliating sexual disclosure.

We are not deceived by this deflation any more than by the inflated secret of detective stories. I prefer Andersch's novel, a work of political and artistic intelligence, to most mystery stories, but there is much in it that suggests it is in flight from the detective novel mood—from a "mystery" too great to face. What if Efraim, after Auschwitz, had assumed the role of hero-detective and investigated that crime in order to fix its guilt with moral and visual precision? An impossible project: there is no language for it. Efraim thinks he is writing to delay facing a painful ending, but he is really writing against the terror and intractability of historical events which the mind cannot resolve or integrate. He chooses a substitute secret, the infidelity of his wife, to keep himself writing, and moving into ordinary life. *Efraim's Book* has no formal ending other than the decision of the writer to accept himself: to accept to survive, in spite of Auschwitz and the defiling reality of posthumous existence.

Most popular mysteries are devoted to solving rather than examining a problem. Their reasonings put reason to sleep, abolish darkness by elucidation, and bury the corpse for good. Few detective novels want the readers to exert their intelligence fully, to find gaps in the plot or the reasoning, to worry about the moral question of fixing the blame. They are exorcisms, stories with happy endings that could be classified with comedy because they settle the unsettling. As to the killer, he is often a bogeyman chosen by the "finger" of the writer after it has wavered suspensefully between this and that person for the right number of pages.

There exists, of course, a defense of the mystery story as art, whose principal document is Raymond Chandler's *The Simple Act of Murder.* In his moving last pages about the gritty life of the hero-detective, Chandler claims that mystery stories create a serious fictional world:

> It is not a fragrant world, but it is the world you live in, and certain writers with tough minds and a cool spirit of detachment can make very interesting and even amusing patterns out of it. . . . In everything that can be called art there is a quality of redemption. It may be pure tragedy, if it is high tragedy, and it may be pity and irony, and it may be the raucous laughter of the strong man. But down these mean streets a man must go who is not himself mean, who is neither tarnished nor afraid. . . . He is a common man or he would not go among common people. He has a sense of character, or he would not know his job. He will take no man's money dishonestly and no man's insolence without a due and dispassionate revenge. . . . He talks as the man of his age talks—that is, with rude wit, a lively sense for the grotesque, a disgust for sham, and a contempt for pettiness. The story is this man's adventure in search of hidden truth.

Ross Macdonald has also defended the social and psychological importance of the detective story and described it as rooted "in the popular and literary tradition of the American frontier." Neither writer puts much emphasis on problem solving, on finding out who killed Roger Ackroyd. But as the claims grow for the honesty, morality, and the authentic American qualities of the detective novel, one cannot overlook the ritual persistence of the problem-solving formula.

Only in France has the eye of the private eye been thoroughly questioned. I have mentioned Robbe-Grillet; his collaboration with Resnais on films like *Marienbad* is also significant in this respect. What is missing from *Marienbad,* yet endlessly suggested, is *tò pathos.* Nothing moves us so much as when the image on the screen tries to escape at certain points a voice that would pin it down to one room, one bed, one time, one identity. Yet the screen image cannot be "framed": by remaining a moving picture, it defeats our wish to spot the flagrant act, or to have speech and spectacle coincide. The scene of pathos—call it Hiroshima, Marienbad, or Auschwitz—eludes the mind it haunts.

A danger, of course, is the closeness of all this not only to mobile dreaming but also to erotic fantasy. The inbuilt voyeurism of the camera eye makes love and death interchangeable subjects. It cannot distinguish between these "mysteries" because of the mind's hunger for reality, its restless need to spot, or give the lie to, one more secret. It seeks to arrest the eyes yet is never satisfied with the still or snapshot that reveals all.

After writers like Andersch and Robbe-Grillet, one turns with relief to Ross Macdonald and the naive reality-hunger of American detective fiction. In *The Underground Man,* Macdonald keeps entirely within the problem-solving formula but broadens it by providing a great California fire as the background. This fire is an "ecological crisis" linked more than fortuitously to the cigarillo dropped by Stanley Broadhurst, the murdered son. Stanley belongs to a "generation whose elders had been poisoned, like the pelicans, with a kind of moral DDT that damaged the lives of their young." By combining ecological and moral contamination Macdonald creates a double plot that spreads the crime over the California landscape.

California becomes a kind of "open city" where everyone seems related to everyone else through, ironically, a breakdown in family relations that spawns adolescent gangs and other new groupings. The only personal detail we learn about the detective, Lew Archer, is that his wife has left him, which is what we might expect. Neither cynical nor eccentric, Archer resembles an ombudsman or public defender rather than a tough detective. He doesn't seem to have a private office, often being approached by his clients in public. One might say he doesn't have clients, since anyone can engage his moral sympathy.

He is, then, as Chandler prescribed, a catalyst, not a Casanova, who sees more sharply than others do. It is curious how the detective, as a type, is at the same time an *ingénu* and a man of experience—his reasoning must take evil or criminal motives into account, but through his eyes we enjoy the colors of the familiar world. Like other realistic artists, the good crime writer makes the familiar new, but he can do so only under the pressure of extreme situations. It is as if crime alone could make us see again, or imaginatively enough, to enter someone else's life.

Archer is not better than what he sees but rather a knowing part of it. His observations (acute, overdefined, "Her eyes met me and blurred like cold windows") are those of an isolated, exposed man with a fragmented life. He finds just what he expects, people like himself, reluctantly free or on the run, and others equally lonely but still living within the shrinking embrace of an overprotective family. Yet just because Archer is so mobile and homeless, he can bring estranged people together and evoke, as in *The Underground Man,* a consoling myth of community where there is none.

It is a myth only for the time being, perhaps only for the time of the book. Down these polluted freeways goes a man with undimmed vision, cutting through sentimental fog and fiery smog to speak face to face in motel or squalid rental or suburban ranch with Mr. and Mrs. and Young America! Superb in snapshot portraiture of California life, Macdonald gives us a sense of the wildlife flushed out by the smoke, the way people lean on one another when they fear crime and fire. They are neatly described by Archer, who moves among them as erratically as the fire itself.

This panoramic realism has its advantages. It is outward and visual rather than introspective, and so tends to simplify character and motive. There is a terrible urge—in Raymond Chandler even more than in Ross Macdonald—to make the most of gross visual impressions. Hence Moose Molloy in Chandler's *Farewell, My Lovely,* "a big man but not more than six feet five inches tall and no wider than a beer truck" who "looked about as inconspicuous as a tarantula on a slice of angel food." The images flash all around us like guns, though we can't always tell to what end. Their overall aim is to make the world as deceptively conspicuous as Moose Molloy.

The detective (American style) tortures human nature until it reveals itself. People froth or lose their nerve or crumple up: the divine eye of the private eye fixes them until their bodies incriminate them. What can't be seen can't be judged; and even if what we get to see is a nasty array of protective maneuvers and defense mechanisms, the horror of the visible is clearly preferred to what is unknown or invisible.

There are, of course, differences of style among American mystery story writers. Macdonald's characters, for example, are more credible than Chandler's, because they are more ordinary, or less bizarre. Chandler is often on the verge of surrealism, of tragicomic slapstick: the first meeting between Marlowe and Carmen Sternwood in *The Big Sleep* goes immediately as far as a relation can go, short of complicity. The novels of Chandler and Macdonald have, nevertheless, the same basic flaw: the only person in them whose motives remain somewhat mysterious, or exempt from this relentless reduction to overt and vulnerable gestures, is the detective.

Yet Chandler's Marlowe is not really mysterious. Just as in his world punks are punks, old generals old generals, and the small guys remain small guys killed by small-time methods (liquor spiked with cyanide), so a detective is a detective: "The first time we met I told you I was a detective. Get it through your lovely head. I work at it, lady. I don't play at it."

When Marlowe is asked why he doesn't marry, he answers, "I don't like policemen's wives." To marry Mr. Detective means becoming Mrs. Detective. Nothing here is immune from specialization: you can hire killers or peekers or produce sex or sell friendliness. Identities are roles changed from time to time yet are as physically clear as warts or fingerprints. Your only hope is not being trapped by your *role* into an *identity.* Once you are marked, or the bite is on you, the fun is over. It is, consequently, a clownish world: grotesque, manic, evasive, hilariously sad. Chandleresque is not far from Chaplinesque.

The one apparent superiority of the detective is that although he can be hired, he doesn't care for money (even if he respects its power). We really don't know whether the other characters care for it either, but they are placed in situations where they *must* have it—to make a getaway, for instance—or where it is the visible sign of grace, of their power to dominate and so to survive. What Marlowe says to a beautiful woman who offers him money is puzzlingly accurate: "You don't owe me anything. I'm paid off." Puzzling because it is unclear where his real satisfaction comes from. He seems under no compulsion to dominate others and rarely gets pleasure from taking gambles. What is there in it for him? The money is only expense money. We don't ever learn who is paying off the inner Marlowe or Archer. Their motives are virtually the only things in these stories that are not visible.

We are forced to assume that the detective is in the service of no one—or of a higher power. Perhaps there is an idealism in these tough tales stronger than the idealisms they are out to destroy:

> I sat down on a pink chair and hoped I wouldn't leave a mark on it. I lit a Camel, blew smoke through my nose and looked at a piece of black shiny metal on a stand. It showed a full, smooth curve with a small fold in it and two protuberances on the curve. I stared at it. Marriott saw me staring at it. "An interesting bit," he said negligently. "I picked it up the other day. Asta Dial's *Spirit of Dawn.*" "I thought it was Klopstein's *Two Warts on a Fanny,*" I said.

This is merely a sideshow, but behind other and comparable scenes big questions are being raised: of reality, justice, mercy, and loyalty. When Lew Archer says, "I think it started before Nick was born, and that his part is fairly innocent," he begins to sound theological, especially when he continues, "I can't promise to get him off the hook entirely. But I hope to prove he's a victim, a patsy" (*The Goodbye Look*).

The moral issues, however, are no more genuinely explored than the murders. They too are corpses—or ghosts that haunt us in the face of intractable situations. So in *The Goodbye Look,* a man picks up an eight-year-old boy and makes a pass at him. Boy shoots man. But the man is the boy's estranged father and the seduction was only an act of sentiment and boozy affection. Grim mistakes of this kind belong to folklore or to high tragedy. The detective story, however, forces them into a strict moralistic pattern or, as in Ross Macdonald, into a psychoanalytic parable with complicated yet resolvable turns.

Because man does not live by tragedy alone, and because the crime story could be considered a folk genre, this may seem no condemnation. There is, however, an exploitative element in all this: our eyes ache to read more, to see more, to know that the one just person (the detective) will succeed—yet when all is finished, nothing is rereadable. Instead of a Jamesian reticence that, at best, chastens the detective urge—our urge to know or penetrate intimately another person's world—the crime novel incites it artificially by a continuous, self-canceling series of overstatements, drawing us into one false hypothesis or flashy scene after another.

Thus the trouble with the detective novel is not that it is moral but that it is moralistic; not that it is popular but that it is stylized; not that it lacks realism but that it picks up the latest realism and exploits it. A voracious formalism dooms it to seem unreal, however "real" the world it describes. In fact, as in a B movie, we value less the driving plot than moments of lyricism and grotesquerie that creep into it: moments that detach themselves from the machined narrative. Macdonald's California fire affects us less because of its damage to the ecology than because it brings characters into the open. It has no necessary relation to the plot and assumes a life of its own. The fire mocks the ambitions of this kind of novel: it seems to defy manipulation.

Crime fiction today seems to be trying to change its skin and transform itself (on the Chandler pattern) into picaresque American morality tales. But its second skin is like the first. It cannot get over its love-hate for the mechanical and the manipulative. Even mysteries that do not have a Frankensteinian monster or superintelligent criminal radiate a pretechnological chill. The form trusts too much in reason; its very success opens to us the glimpse of a mechanized world, whether controlled by God or Dr. No or the Angel of the Odd.

When we read a popular crimi we do not think of it as great art but rather as "interesting" art. And our interest, especially in the hard-boiled tale of American vintage, has to do more with its social, or sociological than with its realistic implications. I don't believe for a moment that Chandler and Macdonald tell it like it is, but perhaps they reveal in an important way why they can't tell it like it is. The American "realist in murder," says Chandler, has purged the guilty vicarage, exiled the amateurs, thrown out Lord Peter Wimsey *cum* chicken-wing-gnawing debutantes. We therefore go to the American tale expecting a naked realism. What do we find, however? A vision that remains a mixture of sophisticated and puerile elements.

The American hero-detective is not what Chandler claims he is, "a complete man." He starts with death, it is true; he seems to stand beyond desire and regret. Yet the one thing the hard-boiled detective fears, with a gamblerlike fascination, is being played for a *sucker.* In Hammett's *Maltese Falcon,* the murder of Miles, who trusted Miss Wonderly, begins the action: Spade's rejection of Brigid O'Shaugnessy completes it. To gamble on Brigid is like gambling that love exists, or that there is, somewhere, a genuine Falcon. Spade draws back: "I won't play the sap for you."

No wonder this type of story is full of tough baby-talk. So Archer in *The Chill:*

> "No more guns for you," I said.
> No more anything, Letitia.

Taking the gun from Letitia, at the end of *The Chill,* is like denying a baby its candy. It seems a "castration" of the woman, which turns her into a child once more.

In Ross Macdonald's novels the chief victim is usually a child who needs protection from the father or society and gets it from Momma as overprotection—which is equally fatal. Enter the dick who tries to save the child and purge the momma. Children are always shown as so imprisoned by the grown-up world that they can't deal with things as they are; and so the child remains a "sucker." There is often little difference between family and police in this respect. The psychiatrist is another overprotector. "They brought me to Dr. Smitheram," Nick says bitterly in *The Goodbye Look,* "and . . . I've been with him ever since. I wish I'd gone to the police in the first place." The detective alone is exempt from ties of blood or vested interest, and so can expose what must be exposed.

Both the arrested development of the detective story and its popularity seem to me related to its image of the way people live in "civilized" society—a just image on the whole. For we all know something is badly wrong with the way society or the family protects people. The world of the detective novel is full of vulnerable characters on the one hand, and of overprotected ones on the other. Macdonald complicates the issue by emphasizing the wrong done to children, and especially to their psyches. Dolly in *The Chill,* Nick Chalmers in *The Goodbye Look,* and Susan Crandall in *The Underground Man* are as much victims of what Freud calls family romance (that is, family nightmare) as of society. We don't know what to protest, and sympathize with the adolescents in *The Underground Man* who kidnap a young boy to prevent him from being sacrificed to the grown-up world.

Yet "protective custody" doesn't work. In *The Chill,* relations between Roy and Letitia Bradshaw are a classic and terrible instance of the man being forced to remain a man-boy as the price of making it. Roy, the social climber, married a rich woman who can send him to Harvard and free him from class bondage. But the woman is old enough to be his mother and they live together officially as mother and son while she kills off younger women to whom her "child" is attracted.

Protection, such novels seem to imply, is always bought; and much of the price one pays for it is hidden. Macdonald tends to give a psychological and Chandler a sociological interpretation of this. Chandler is strongly concerned with the need for a just system of protection and the inadequacy of modern institutions to provide it. He indulges, like so many other crime writers, in conventional woman-hating, but he suggests at the same time that women become bitches because they are overprotected. Helen Grayle, in *Farewell, My Lovely,* is the exemplary victim who (like the Sternwood sisters in *The Big Sleep*) is allowed to get some revenge on her "protectors" before she is caught. Yet Chandler often lets his women criminals escape, knowing sadly or bitterly that they'll be trapped by the system in the end.

To avoid being a sucker and to expose a crisis in the protective institutions of society are psychological and social themes that are not peculiar to the American detective novel. They have prevailed since chivalric Romance invented the distressed damsel and her wandering knight. But the precise kinds of family breakup, together with new and menacing groups (similar to crime syndicates) which the detective is pitted against, give crime novels a modern American tone. That the detective is a *private* sleuth defines, moreover, his character as well as his profession and makes him the heir to a popular American myth—he is the latest of the uncooptable heroes.

Yet detective stories remain schizophrenic. Their rhythm of surprising reversals—from casual to crucial or from laconic detail to essential clue—is a factor. The deepest reversals involve, of course, feelings about the blood tie. As in Greek tragedy pathos is strongest when there is death in the family. The thrill of a "thriller" is surely akin to the fear that the murderer will prove to be not an outsider but someone there all the time, someone we know only too well—perhaps a blood relation.[12]

In Macdonald's fiction human relations tend to polarize: they are either quasi-incestuous (Roy and Letitia Bradshaw in *The Chill*) or markedly exogamous, exhibiting that inclination toward strangers so characteristic of the hero-detective. It is as if our kinship system had suffered a crazy split. There seems to be no mean between the oppressive family ("I felt . . . as if everything in the room was still going on, using up space and air. I was struck by the thought that Chalmers, with family history breathing down his neck, may have felt smothered and cramped most of the time") and the freewheeling detective. Nothing lies between the family and the loner but a no man's land of dangerous communes: virile fraternities, like criminal mobs or the police, which are based literally on blood.

It is, then, an exceptional moment when we find Lew Archer lingering with Stanley Broadhurst's widow and her young son, at the end of *The Underground Man.* For one moment the family exists and the detective is the father. The woman touches him lightly, intimately. It ends there, on that caress, which already has distance and regret in it. We must soon return, like the detective, to a world of false fathers and disabled mothers, to children as exposed as Oedipus or Billy Budd, and to a continuing search for manifest justice. "O city, city!" (*Oedipus Rex*).

NOTES

1. S. H. Butcher, ed. and trans., *Aristotle's Theory of Poetry and Fine Art,* 4th ed., XI.6 (1452b 9–13). There is a second brief mention at XIV.4 (1453b 17–22).
2. See Gerald Else, *Aristotle's Poetics* (Cambridge, Mass., 1967), pp. 356–58.
3. See Jacques Barzun, "The Novel Turns Tale," *Mosaic* 4 (1971): 33–40.
4. The elliptical "cuts" of Eliot's *Wasteland* often produce a similar effect. Ellipsis joined to

the technical principle of montage (in Eisenstein's conception) consolidate the international style we are describing.

5. *Maidstone* is a blatantly eclectic script-tease: it flirts with crime, sexploitation, politics, and film about film. Its plot consists of a wager by Norman T. Kingsley that the actors in the film will invent that scene of passion which he, the director, cannot or will not invent—that they will kill the King, that is, the director, that is, Norman.
6. For a straight psychoanalytic interpretation, see Marie Bonaparte, "The Murder in the Rue Morgue," *Psychoanalytic Quarterly* 4 (1935): 259–93; G. Pederson-Krag, "Detective Stories and the Primal Scene," *Psychoanalytic Quarterly* 18 (1949): 207–14; and, especially, Charles Rycroft, "The Analysis of a Detective Story" (1957) reprinted in his *Imagination and Reality* (London, 1968). In what follows I emphasize the eye rather than the cry; but, as in Wordsworth's ballad, there is often something ejaculative or quasi-inarticulate (a "tongue-tie," to use Melville's phrase in *Billy Budd*) accompanying.
7. See Freud's piece "The 'Uncanny'" (1919). His analysis of repetition in relation to (ambivalent) reanimation may prove essential to any psychoesthetic theory of narrative. This may also be the point to introduce thematics, especially the thematics of the genius loci: animism, ghosts, ancestor consciousness, quasi-supernatural hauntings of particular places. Freud connects them either with memories of an intra-uterine (oceanic) state or with the later illusion of "omnipotence of consciousness." In Poe, one might speculate, the mystery story is intra-uterine gothic while the detective story is omnipotence-of-consciousness modern. See also note 8.
8. This almost inverts the sense of the gothic novel, which Poe transformed into a modern tale of detection by dividing its mystery part from its rationalizing part. The mystery story, as he develops it, deals mainly with *vestiges* that intimate someone's *life-in-death,* and he exploits the horror of that thought. His detective stories tend to sublimate this theme of the "living dead" by demystifying vestiges as clues: signs of (and for) a persistent or mad or "omni-potent" consciousness. Fredric Jameson's "On Raymond Chandler," *Southern Review* 6 (1970): 624–50, gives an interesting account of how the "formal distraction" of the detective quest leads into genuine revelations of death-in-life.
9. Sterne's *Tristram Shandy* may be the original of this comic anamnesis which cannot begin (find the true starting point) and so cannot end.
10. See my "Voice of the Shuttle" in this collection.
11. Andersch is a distinguished German journalist and man of letters who has written several novels and was one of the original members of the famous postwar association of writers called Group '47.
12. Charles Brockden Brown's *Wieland* (1797) remains the classic instance of a pattern which recalls Freud's understanding of family ambivalences.

Hitchcock's *North by Northwest*

We find certain things about seeing puzzling,
because we do not find the whole business of seeing puzzling enough.
—Wittgenstein

Cable television occasionally opens a twenty-four-hour movie channel free of charge, to tempt viewers like myself. I confess I succumb; not only because I quite enjoy an hour here, an hour there of mindless watching, but because I become fascinated with the fact that so many of the movies fall into a formulaic pattern that can be endlessly varied. A person fights his or her way through, against impossible odds: where the intelligent thing might be to give up or get away, the individual becomes the just one, the involved one, struggling without help against an organized mob, which may include the police itself. Moreover, about these films there often hovers a ballet-like aura; they orchestrate sights and sounds more than sights and words. Fights, chases, and pantomimic scenes of mute eyeing and sleuthing are relieved only as necessary by expository dialogue. In the Bruce Lee films only the ballet, really, counts—the marvelous gestures, grunts, crashes, sighs, and quasi-verbal phaticisms. We know perfectly well that almost everything is dubbed, that the sound track is superimposed on the action; yet our enjoyment resembles that of seeing dancers on stage and hearing the music to which they move. The difference is that in the realistic cinema, motion and sound seem to come from the same source, which allows us not to think about their relation.

In short, we are transported into a utopian sphere, a secular seventh heaven where what passes for love or justice is winged by pain as by music, and the film is at once a ritual ordeal and a dance of triumph celebrating the ecstatic end of an obsessional quest. From no higher perspective can I view Alfred Hitchcock's *North by Northwest.* Its gaunt luxuries are quasi-oriental; the face of Cary Grant is a vulnerable mask; the face of Eva Marie Saint blandly expressive; together they form a hendiadys, as stylized and slick as the smooth rock face over which they must finally climb to the upper bunk of marital happiness.

Not only, then, do words have to compete with images; they have to compete with a sequence of images that barely need words—with that absence of words; and, additionally, with sound itself in the form of a powerful score. The technique of film composition allows hundreds of shots of a particular scene, "pieces of film" as Hitchcock calls them, that can be spliced as the director wishes; but there are no "pieces of words" unless they become exotic or erotic syllables.

In *North by Northwest* words are generally specious, as in the bad-faith monologue of Cary Grant to his secretary (they don't make secretaries like that any more!) which opens the film; or they are entrapping lies; or jerky, cool banter, similar to motions in the silent movies; or deliciously inappropriate comments (Saint to Grant, after his harrowing escape from the deadly plane, an encounter which she, of course, had helped engineer: "How did it go today?"). Though there is no counterpoint or deliberate dissociation of image and sound, as in Resnais's *Last Year at Marienbad,* meaning is a sur-face at best. The face of those worded images remains smooth, slippery; they are pictures determined not to be words; they insist on a pictographic as well as semiotic content, a nonsensuous visual stenography. Especially, therefore, do we relish the sequences: long after other details of the film are forgotten, we still recall Cary Grant hunted by the plane with almost no cover, all the redcaps being twirled around, the angular face-off (one of many) of Grant and James Mason at their first meeting, or the final twilit getaway. A choreographic quality dominates image as well as word, effaces everything except surfaces and the precision of the orchestrated sequence.

I have some affection, even admiration, for Hitchcock. Yet many European pictures do more for me, however heavy their symbolism. How tediously searing the end of Werner Herzog's *Stroszek,* for instance—those conditioned fledglings performing their stupid dance. I resent that, too; but I am moved by the overt choreographic symbol, as by almost every major French, German, Italian, Polish, Spanish, or Czech film that deals with types that remain persons, and where you feel a more creative relation between the actor and the part, or a greater freedom in the actor who assumes the part, in distinction to a relation between actor and director. In Hitchcock everything is on a string, the director's umbilical cord; and the string is cut when and where he wants it.

No wonder mother keeps intruding. She is the watchful presence, mocked at the beginning of *North by Northwest,* and returning alarmingly as the bogus housekeeper at the end. And when I see Cary Grant in that eternal business suit (which he eventually sheds), I think of him as an overgrown dressed-up kid (remember those sailor suits?) or expect him to change at any moment like Clark Kent into . . . *Superman.* Wouldn't mother be surprised if she saw him now! Well, mother is always there, and sometimes she *is* in for a surprise. But no one, of course, could be more watchful than the director, more designing and controlling than Mother Hitchcock.

Hitchcock's precision is legendary. Nothing is left to chance in plots filled with chance encounters. The theme of control or of mastering the uncontrollable is everywhere. At the beginning of *North by Northwest* Grant has everything firmly in hand, yet things immediately get out of hand. The first casual indication concerns his mother; he has asked his secretary to phone her but then realizes she cannot be reached by phone. Anxious to correct his mistake, Grant, as Roger Thornhill, unwittingly enables the error that precipitates him into the plot: the bellboy pages a Mr. Kaplan, and as Roger gets up to send his mother a telegram, he gives the abductors cause to think he is answering the boy—that *he* is Kaplan. From another angle, of course, this *hasard objectif* hardly matters; it merely motivates an irrational and absurd intrusion that throws the emphasis on how Roger will face a disorienting course of events. He is immediately divested of his identity, one that sits on him as easily as his suit. Only toward the end is he momentarily back in control, when he tricks the professor and rescues Eve, as played by Saint; but not even then, because the last saving shot—I mean the one before that by which the camera guarantees a happy ending—that shot comes from on high and is an *ex machina* ending keeping the director in charge.

Hitchcock's eye-in-the-sky shots are famous. In *North by Northwest* there is also the glimpse of Roger as fugitive, taken from the top of the United Nations building; a more notorious example comes in *Psycho,* when the camera swoops down, screeching and killing, as the detective reaches the top of the stairs. "This matter is best disposed of from a great height," Mason (Van Damm) says ominously, planning Eve's death. The improbably ending is a high-angle shot that saves as it kills; yet that it saves is not sure. The penultimate image of Roger and Eve bedding down may be a fantasy flash.

There is generally an oblique angle of this kind within the right angle of the picture frame. For though things coincide—that is, meet at the angle—are not all meetings *trucage?* The angle becomes a slope, a slippery slope: from the strangely tilted credits, turning into the reflecting plane of skyscraper windows, to Roger climbing the steel beams of Van Damm's hideout and the airplane that has to calculate its angle of descent; from Roger in the death car spinning on top of the cliff, to the lovers' hanging on to the edge of Mount Rushmore. Cars and trains, in Hitchcock, are mere vehicles to remove the ground from under you; to put someone else's skids on you; in the scene on Mount Rushmore the rock face becomes treacherous terrain and creates a comic cliff-hanger.

If understanding means finding something firm to stand on, then understanding is often removed from both character and audience. We have to take pleasure in the illusion of control *and* in seeing that illusion evaporate. Remember Roger's expression when he thinks he has outwitted another eye-in-the-sky, that plane? Exhilarated cunning, and then a funny abject perplexity. An equally sustained sequence is Roger's roller coaster ride, his drunk bravado in handling the car as he pretends he is in control. In *Strangers on a Train,* where the sinister-angle theme is symbolized by Bruno's psychotic design, his *crisscross,* everything that can go out of control does. Think of the carousel at the climactic finish, with its vertiginous turmoil of hands and feet, of hands against feet; hands and feet, they haunt us throughout this film too.

Where there is the desire for control, there is the fear of things not in control, of going out of control; yet what is the nature of those things? Are they the images themselves as fantasies? Do these images have a "nature," a knowable "substance," or are they surfaces in essence: as smooth or tough as faces that have no certain relation either to privacy of thought or to the words issuing from mouth instead of from eyes?

In literary criticism the question of substance often coincides with that of high seriousness: but "high" in Hitchcock is an angle from which to shoot. The question of substance or seriousness frustrates many viewers: they enjoy Hitchcock's movies, as I do, in an inconclusive and famished way. What is there to understand? There is fascination rather than understanding. The characters have little depth: they are flat, they simply fall for, or toward, each other. They are "blanks," decoys often: persons that need to become real, or be saved from their own role-playing. The heavy psychoanalytic stuff, even in *Psycho,* points to a crypt or a vacuity, like the middle initial in the R. O. T. that appears on Roger Thornhill's monogrammed matchbook, signifying a central blank or zero.

One might argue that in "pure cinema," as it has been called, the framing of every detail replaces questions of substance: that all things empty, as it were, into a cinematic, primarily imagistic, field. The medium itself constitutes a denial of the "myth of depth." Yet is not the world viewed, to echo Stanley Cavell, a world view? Is there something to know or not? To say there is a "language of images" is to substitute metaphor for analysis.

Some progress can be made by returning to our first concern: the relation of images to words in Hitchcock's films. To diminish the space given to words raises the question of the importance of images. Yet it is hard to claim that a Hitchcock movie makes us trust images rather than words. To some extent, in fact, because the words have a screwball charm—especially so in *North by Northwest*—they are lighter on the mind; the images, however, as silent as they are striking, gain their haunting significance mainly by repetition and juxtaposition. They do not have an "inside" more verifiable than the words. Those who claim there is a language of images must mean there is a nonlanguage of images: that the edited sequence has a logic all its own. Things are not helped by the fact that from a certain perspective, that of the written script, the images dub the words—*dumb* them, sometimes. Understanding the editing process, moreover, adds to the problem, since editing involves decisions on what in a potentially infinite series should be shot or selected. It brings back the question of the control exerted by a director, especially one who prefers the authority of the commonplace to iconoclastic experimental techniques, and elides himself into a presence as conspicuously inconspicuous as his fleeting appearances. No other auteurs have Hitchcock's *concept* of style, though they all have a style that singles them out.

Can we define Hitchcock's style in conceptual terms? Might it not be better to talk about his technique or speculate on themes that recur as if they were obsessions? I will argue, however, that we can understand our fascination with him, even if that fascination resists the analysis it provokes.

The principal compositional feature of movies after the silent era is that montage now affects sound as well, so that editing is not only deciding what to shoot, cut, splice, but how to place sound itself, how to accommodate it to the spatial form, or, better, the spatial rhythm, of the images. Moreover, since in the history of the medium the silent image came first, the sounded image—the synchronization of sound and image—is not an automatic gain. It is something to justify, like the third character in Greek tragedy or the third dimension of pictorial perspective. Each new technique, even when intended to be in the service of mimesis, of lifelikeness, alters our consciousness of what life is like. It has a critical as well as an illusionistic dimension: in Hitchcock's case, it makes us aware of the power and impotence of words by comparison with images. As Stanley Cavell has remarked (in *The World Viewed*): "It is the talkie itself that is now exploring the silence of movies. . . . With talkies we got back the clumsiness of speech, the dumbness and duplicities and concealments of assertion."

Assertion is one thing, art another; they stand in a relationship of opposition. By assertion Cavell means, at this point, the aggressive summing up of a person or a truth in words, a summing up that is meant to impose or deceive. Assertion, in the plot of *North by Northwest,* begins with the bland, imposing stream of Roger's dictation, and continues along a more intense, explicit plane when Roger is denied his own identity, and so is forced to reaffirm it. Like the moving camera, or the network of rails itself, we track from this opening toward a now converging, now diverging pattern and never stop being amazed that the "subject" carried down those tracks, as the plot gains momentum, is not derailed, that the switching, splicing, matching, crosscutting leads to closure instead of an indefinite parallelism or *frayage.*

The problem, then, could be stated as the relation of art to assertion in this vertiginous context. Art finds what can be ranged *against* assertion without being *for* weakness—that is, without allowing the vertigo of indecisiveness or nonidentity to foster by reaction even more dangerous—psychotic or Cold War—assertions. The issue of weakness is central in the detective story. You can't afford to be a sucker. You can't even afford to seem to be one. How can anything except the aspiration to invulnerability and total control survive? In the political sphere this aspiration is coupled with a doctrine of righteousness. Yet art, we know, has always been considered a weak sister, a feminization of culture. It is worse than religion, which, being self-righteous, retains some political clout. Hitchcock takes *the* macho genre, the detective story, and gives it a nonassertive strength, the peculiar strength of art. He creates a music of images, films that could be characterized as urban ballet. Yet they are utterly different from the American musical as it produces its form of urban ballet: *West Side Story* and such descendants as *Hair, Fame,* and *All That Jazz.*

No doubt, as in that other tradition, there is in Hitchcock a movement toward marriage or communion, toward a renewed pastoral oneness with woman, city, or cosmos. In *West Side Story* the mean streets are transformed: gang warfare leads to a larger mythical atonement through the spirit of carnival music. But Hitchcock mocks his mock communions and will not touch massively operatic devices. I don't recall a moment as blatantly communal as the scene in Frank Capra's *It Happened One Night* when the people on the bus are drawn into singing "The Daring Young Man on the Flying Trapeze."

Though Hitchcock too leads us back to a transcended or obsolete form, in particular the silent movie and its rural vestiges, what he wishes to carry over is their economy of means, which is the opposite of a carnivalistic catharsis. His films keep to a *pas de deux* and come often nearer to ballad than ballet: they are elliptical narratives, as grim as folktales in their plot. I sense the "Twa Corbies" behind *Psycho;* and many Hitchcock characters could have come out of Hardy or the *Spoon River Anthology* or the "novel turned tale" (Jacques Barzun), as in O. Henry.

It all hinges, in any case, on Hitchcock's sense of economy. In *North by Northwest* we move from city to country, or to a silent milieu, a treacherously empty milieu. In that emptiness the slightest trace becomes charged: you neglect it at your risk. We barely notice that as the bus opens in the cornfield scene it discloses the warning (first glimpsed in the open door of the Chicago train): "Please watch your step." The spectacular develops out of a mere dot on the horizon, as with the crop-dusting, man-hunting plane and the inferno of its crash.

It is with time as with place: every shot counts. Other contemporary thrillers are crowded by comparison. Their suspense is created by multiplying an action, by expense. But Hitchcock is a penny-pincher. A particularly thrilling scene occurs in *Strangers on a Train,* when the variable length of a tennis match is juxtaposed with the time it takes the killer to get to the fair and darkness to fall. A similar deadline effect is created when Roger has to catch Eve's attention before she is taken onto the arriving plane and so to her death.

Another kind of reserve also pressures time. Hitchcock's protagonists may be placed in a situation where they cannot know what the stakes are, so that a childlike game of bluff ensues. Roger acts blindly throughout the first two-thirds of *North by Northwest.* The film, it is true, has no word-scene as charged and implicating as the opening conversation between Guy and Bruno in *Strangers on a Train,* or as casual and scary as that between Marion and Bates in *Psycho.* Yet words are not wasted in *North by Northwest.* The banter can turn dangerously precise, paid out like hard cash in the Depression. That clerk at the ticket window, wondering why Roger is wearing dark glasses indoors: "Is something wrong with your eyes?" Roger: "They're sensitive to questions." Roger to Van Damm: "I don't deduce, I observe." Or, my favorite, Van Damm to Roger: "Games—must we?"

This *must* involved in what should be a *game* leads back to the film as art. We go to films to pass the time, to play. We expect a representation, not an assertion; a timed magic that confines us to our seats, that glues eyes and ears to the screen. Yet on that screen we see people who cannot tolerate time except by controlling it. Time is there to scheme with, to lick one's fantasies with, before striking like a clock, or as neatly as Bruno's "Are you Miriam?" "Yes," and the mute strangling that follows at once.

"Games—must we?" From what I have said it is tempting to conclude that an economy of scarcity mingles uneasily, in Hitchcock, not only with Hollywood largesse (its expense of spirit) but with a compensatory game compulsion involving the director as *magister ludi.* His fabled neatness means little if we do not see through it as well as by means of it. As viewers, we are kept off balance between so much and so little; a paunchy Hitchcock pares his medium and disappears from sight. We see as in a very bright glass darkly.

To insist, however: Do Hitchcock's images reach some sort of inwardness, at least an "echo of thought in sight"?

Consider Roger's ignorance, which obliges him to use his bare eyes. They repeat the dumb focus of the camera eye. The compulsive viewing by a person who knows next to nothing makes him teeter on the verge of finding out too much. Through Roger's eyes we approach a deferred moment of revelation. That moment becomes inseparable from his quest, because it should deliver him not only from ignorance but also from the necessity of testing and role-playing: it should convert *role* into *identity,* something that is what it is, knowable through and through. "Now I know in part; then I shall understand fully, even as I have been fully understood" (I Corinthians 13:12). Yet this transparency is the predicament rather than the resolution of desire. For against it, against such "exposure" of the self, can there be a cover? The blanket Bates asks for at the end of *Psycho* is as useless as Roger's dark glasses, or the name he chooses, or the starved corn that gives him momentary shelter.

Indeed, the tension I have described has its gothic culmination in *Psycho* where the eye avenges itself on the eye, because it is so knowing. Bates kills in order not to be watched, not to be seen. Escape is sought from that eye-in-the-sky, or wherever it zooms from at the beginning of the movie as it enters birdlike an anonymous window in—of all towns—Phoenix. The human predicament here is the impossibility of protecting one's inwardness from an intruding, alienating, tricky eye. Bates flees from this eye by washing all ocular proof down a sinkhole (cellar, swamp) as dark as the pupil or the sexual cavity.

Let me recall that sequence from *Psycho,* so brilliant in its obsessional detail that it reflects on Hitchcock himself, and suggests that not words alone but also images are subject to his cinematic hygiene. We are shown Marion in the shower, letting it make love to her with its lustrously spending overhead eye; then, after the stabbing, which we scarcely believe, sinking as though satisfied, not dead; then a still of her still eye and the final lustration, the housewifely care with which Bates's mop and bucket perform the erasure, leaving nothing behind—a no-thing, rather, a place that is cursedly clean, that should have no claim on sight. "Pure cinema"? What is evoked is an *ultimate* purification or "inoculation." To see, oneself unseen, as at the movies, is only less than the ecstasy of an unseeing seeing: of going beyond the non-language of images to the non-language of non-images, or a glance that is not guilty, that is both knowing and pure. "I am nothing. I see all" (Emerson).

Why are we willing to go to such lengths to indulge the fantasy of guiltless viewing? In *Dressed to Kill,* for example, Brian de Palma's remake of *Psycho,* the violent plot is but a device to let us enjoy a number of erotic scenes. In order to ogle a woman in a shower (who plays at "being seen without being seen") we are obliged to endure the emetic of several bloodlettings. There is only one fine portrayal that escapes the camera's heavy visual breathing. It takes place in the Metropolitan Museum and shows Angie Dickinson absorbed in art. She gazes with a steady glance, a Mona Lisa kind of smile, at the pictures, and the stray viewers viewing the pictures; and we *almost* recapture the innocence of inwardness or self-effacement, of vanishing into the act of viewing.

What of inwardness in *North by Northwest?* That film is almost too healthy. Roger learns vigilance without being traumatized. The psyche is not involved, or not as a perverse emptiness, always escaping from being watched and therefore ever wary. It is there only potentially, in the ingenious plot idea of the dummy agent who does not exist, who is inferred exactly like the "fingered" psyche by purely external indices (suits, room numbers, etc.). His visibility is a trick function of his invisibility. Roger, however, who barely thinks, who is hardly given time to think—he is portrayed as a silly, yet at best courageous and instinctive, creature—turns up again and again, as apparitional as a ghost. In fact, after disliking him, we become his accomplice, because his heroism does not have the support either of extreme intelligence or any other expensive or ingenious equipment: he throws the enemy off balance by simply reappearing, sporting no weapon other than his own eyes, hands, and feet. *North by Northwest,* glossier than most of Hitchcock's films, uses the overenlarged optics of cinema and the mechanically rousing formulas of detective fiction to honor a purely human economy. Grant is not granite; Eva is no statue. Hitchcock humanizes, even tenderizes, the triumph of the will, exhibiting it in its simple, relentless, unenlarged, unmechanized form.

Despite those huge, unmovable faces of the presidential range, and despite the fact that every spot within the reach of "camera reality" is either monumental or ominous, we adventure toward a very simple place, that is our own—purged, ideally, of fear and guilt. It should be free of those strange vanishing points that disrupt ordinary life and make the most familiar acts—seeing, talking, eating—overconscious. I have called *North by Northwest* utopian because it cannot give up the fiction that there exists a good place of this kind, and a good marriage in that good place.

A last comment, however, must focus on Hitchcock's own morality as filmmaker. What is his attitude toward the inbuilt giantism of his medium, toward the machine of a camera that penetrates the field of sensibility and creates "panoramic sleights" (Hart Crane) so powerfully illusionistic that even when we remind ourselves of their fictive nature, they may enervate our capacity to respond to less massive stimuli? "No one can intensely and wholeheartedly enjoy and enter into experience whose fabric is as crude as that of the average superfilm without a disorganization which has its effects in everyday life. The extent to which second-hand experience of a crass and inchoate type is replacing ordinary life offers a threat which has not yet been realized" (I. A. Richards).

Of course film is not the first medium to raise the problem. It exacerbates the "application of gross and violent stimulants" Wordsworth noted toward the beginning of the Industrial Revolution. For Wordsworth, frantic novels and news-mongering generally expressed a mortal danger inherent in industrialization, as it crowded people into cities and blunted their senses by replacing natural rhythms with a machine-made environment. This intrusion of the machine, or any such artificial enlargement of the senses, into all aspects of ordinary life has been analyzed by many sociological thinkers aware of Hollywood and Madison Avenue as well as of totalitarian modes of propaganda.

Hitchcock recognizes machination as a problem that existed before the machine gave it an uncanny extension. He tries to bring it under his control by various means; yet to control it may encourage a "mastery" that may have spawned the monster in the first place. As a director Hitchcock alternates between tricking us into a self-conscious, impotent complicity with visual fascination, and parodying his own magical enterprise through the camera's (and the story's) cat-and-mouse game, one that makes viewers realize how endlessly exposed they are to the manipulation of appearances. The viewer is the ultimate "darling decoy" (Eva's fond description, toward the end, of Roger).

"Pure cinema" is moral only in the sense that though the camera is invisibly guided, we cannot throw off our complicity with it. It expresses our own automatism: viewing as an act of baffling and intricate perversity that would like to, yet cannot, come to rest. Through Hitchcock the uncanny eye becomes a canny mechanism, but still a mechanism. Filming is the good use of bad omens.

EPILOGUE

The spectatorial attitude of moviegoers is that of most persons in our culture as well. Through Hitchcock's manipulation we become Romans at the circus, enjoying the gladiators or Christians facing the lions. By deciding who should live or die—that is, when and for how long we should identify with the characters on stage—he makes us understand the inbuilt callousness, the cultural sangfroid of our situation as visual consumers. Through his films we realize how difficult it is to be moral without taking the camera into our own hands, or initiating a program to educate the eyes—perhaps through the ears, or by becoming aware of a necessary interaction of visual and aural. It is a fact, I think, that the visual arts in this country are not a serious part of the curriculum except in special schools. We rarely use our eyes creatively, and we are certainly not encouraged to *think* about them.

But an educational system that condemns the visual media to marginality is bound to render its students all the more passive and susceptible. This is not to argue that we should replace reading with visual education; on the contrary, reading should be intensified—that is, associated with the study of film, television, and the arts generally. They too are texts. We have not caught up with the fact that, as Henri Lefebvre puts it, "the sense of hearing has acquired a greater aptitude for interpreting visual perceptions and the sense of sight for interpreting auditive ones, so that they signify each other reciprocally." The senses, he adds, "are becoming 'theoreticians'; by discarding immediacy they introduce mediation, and abstraction combines with immediacy to become 'concrete.' Thus objects, in practice, become signs, and signs objects; and a 'second nature' takes the place of the first, the initial layer of perceptible reality" (*Everyday Life in the Modern World*).

Lefebvre tries to account for this development and then to criticize it. His account rests on an attractive yet simplified historical speculation, of the kind introduced by Spengler and continued by McLuhan. He posits a "decline of referentials" and attributes it to technological advances that climaxed around 1910 in the "reign of electricity." However thin his thesis may be, it does connect city life, the media, and detective fiction. We are now faced with a new, quasi-religious duplicity of the quotidian, an authentic inauthenticity that produces "intolerable loneliness" within the very heart of modern society's unceasing stream of communication and information. We have learned, in short, to depersonalize images and words, to merchandise them like any other goods. "Of all the referentials," claims Lefebvre (this was written circa 1968), "only two are still left standing; one, philosophy in the highest sphere of culture; the other, in the most trivial and commonplace sphere, everyday life." But to have everyday life as the sole reference point is unendurable. So, in fact, "we are left with one referential and that the prerogative of higher culture." "One might as well say," he concludes, that "all referentials have vanished and that what remains is the memory and the demand for a system of reference."

The decline of referentials, or the "uncoupling," as Lefebvre also says, of signified and signifier, has lately been *the* preoccupation of both philosophy and theory of art. Today, the energies of everyday life cannot be opposed any more to the idle or mystified energies of the upper classes and their ideologues. Everyday life seems now as uncreative as any other. The detective novel, particularly its cinematic embodiment, suggests at once the desire and the difficulty of giving to daily existence that "seriousness" which Erich Auerbach saw emerging in the great realistic novels of the nineteenth century. For the hopeful and productive aspects of industrialization are being replaced by a purely semiotic and indifferent urbanization. "We are surrounded by emptiness," Lefebvre sighs, "but it is an emptiness filled with signs! Meta-language replaces the missing city."

Hence the ghostly sensationalism of detective film, in which every detail, however small, is potentially a telltale sign of human purposes, even if it disappoints an imagination that it excites into voyeurism. Hence also the new ghostliness that invades our notions of privacy or inwardness, which retreat once more into the nonquotidian, "a make-believe privacy, embellished and sheltered from the outside world, from view, from the sun, by partitions . . . curtains, draperies." Hitchcock conveys to us this lack of authentic privacy or inwardness; he strikes, like a dagger, through those draperies; but the draperies are still those of everyday reality. As Lefebvre sadly insists, "self-realization [now] is a life without history,—total quotidianness, but unseen and evaded as soon as possible."

Can we recover the romance of the quotidian? Or is the very notion of "reality" so technologized, semioticized, mediated, and therefore demystified that it cannot be disalienated any more? I leave this as a question; a question intensified for me by Hitchcock's movies; but once the senses have become theoreticians, once theory is part of the concrete and environing world, it would be fatal to ignore it and rely on some natural and instinctive balm to restore pristine perception. We can educate the senses, that is all: educate them to resist the media by an active rather than passive understanding, and so take back from the media what is our own.

Walter Benjamin in Hope

The dramatic—and nomadic—circumstances of Walter Benjamin's life are such that it is difficult not to be justly distracted by them: the political foreground competes with the enormous erudition, the sheer bookishness, of the background. Yet the attention of Benjamin the critic to what he reads or analyses, that attention called by Malebranche the natural prayer of the soul, is so strong that he comes through with revisionary perspectives and startling trains of thought that make one stop and wonder at the physiological and mental mechanisms he reveals.

That wonder, at the same time, does not dissolve into either specialized knowledge or philosophy, although the pressure of conceptualization is always there, and philosophy is acknowledged to be a sibling of the work of art, useful in questioning art's strangeness, its combination of intimacy and discretion. Yet though art remains cen-

This essay was first presented as a paper at a conference on Benjamin held at Yale University, 26–27 September 1997. It was published in slightly different form in *Critical Inquiry* (Winter 1999) just before this book went to press.

tral as a structure of feeling, Benjamin sees it as changing according to contemporary social and economic conditions. Art is no longer quite the cultural value it was: he is not tempted to say to it, in its singularity, charm or in situ monumentality: "Verweile doch, du bist so schön."

With film, especially, distractedness (*Zerstreuung*) and concentration (*Sammlung*) enter into a new relationship, quite different from what used to characterize the plastic or verbal arts. Indeed, film helps us become used to a new form of awareness, or rather unconsciousness, which goes beyond the optic of intense individual contemplation that marks art criticism at its empathic best. The older contemplative attitude, or the capacity for attention I have just praised with words taken from Malebranche, may not be able to resolve dilemmas imposed on our receptive faculties by a fast-changing era. Intimacy and distance are being replaced by shock and diversion; and Benjamin refuses to value them negatively. Signaling an increase in the proletariat and the formation of the masses, the shock and diversion promise a collective achievement, a structure of feeling beyond the concept of experience based on the perceptions of the privileged individual. At the same time, fascism and imperialism exploit the mass spectacle. In different ways, they force mankind to enjoy the prospect of war and large-scale destruction by filtering them through the lens of the older contemplative aesthetics. At this crucial point, Benjamin breaks off the essay on art and technology I have been summarizing, and cites without comment communism's answer to fascism: Don't aestheticize politics; instead, politicize art.[1] At the end, then, nothing is clear except that the merging of art and technology has produced an apparatus that penetrates perception more deeply or subliminally, so that art graduates from being a cultural object, an objet d'art, to a matter of life and death.

I admire the speculative vigor of the later Benjamin. I have suggested that for him art is not transcended; indeed, it may still be overestimated by him. His worried engagement with the status of art, as exploited by politics and altered by technology, could be a desperate gesture of hope, a defense against his own dispersion. In this brief comment I want to understand his perspective on the past, a perspective which not only persists but counterpoints the future shock he anticipates so uncannily.

Benjamin's emphasis after 1936 is history as much as art, and his paradoxes become more startling. He talks of the historian as "kindling a spark of hope in

1. See Walter Benjamin, "Das Kunstwerk im Zeitalter seiner technischen Reproduzierbarkeit" [The work of art in the era of its technical reproduction] (1936), *Gesammelte Schriften,* ed. Rolf Tiedemann and Hermann Schweppenhäuser, 7 vols. in 14 (Frankfurt, 1972–89), 1:2:431–69.

the past," a sentiment directed against cheap versions of progress.[2] He refuses to place hope exclusively in the future, or to proceed as if the past were transcended—nothing but inert, ruined choirs. He talks less of faith or love than of that more revolutionary virtue, hope, which refuses to leave even the dead undisturbed. Like Scholem, who restored the neglected Kabbalah to high profile, the true historical thinker addresses the past—or has the past address us, like the dead at Thermopylae from whom Demosthenes kindles an eloquent adjuration. Yet is there not something spooky in resurrecting the dead this way; or, conversely, suggesting that they could be undone a second time: "even the dead will not be secure, if the enemy wins" ("UBG," 695).

Hope, though envious and all too human, is the cardinal virtue for Benjamin; but it is not eudaemonic. The hope for others competes with the hope for oneself. Missed opportunities for happiness ("women who could have given themselves to us") seem to have an intimate relation to past generations, *their* missed opportunities, *their* abortive desires or claims ("UBG," 693). It is as if the quantity of hope allotted us had already been preempted by this demanding link to the past and the dead. Benjamin praises Goethe's recognition in *Elective Affinities* that hope (*Elpis*), the last of the *Urworte*, can be dramatized only in the form of symbols (such as the rising of the stars): it cannot be explicitly transmitted as doctrine or message.[3] His concluding sentence on Goethe's novel reverses a saying of Kafka's: "Only for the cause of those who have no hope is hope given us."[4] But as if his own message had not gone through, he fails to give that hope to himself.

One would certainly like to know what news the famous angel brought to him: Klee's *Angelus Novus*, chosen by the conference held at Yale University as its logo. How could Benjamin express historical materialism through this childlike and uncertain signifier? It is true that the astonishing ecphrasis describing the angel of history in the "Geschichtsphilosophische Thesen" tries to incarnate his message that hope is the revolutionary virtue, however ruinous it may be. But is anyone who compares Klee's picture and Benjamin's reading of it convinced? It only adds the enigma of the messenger to that of the message.

2. Walter Benjamin, "Über den Begriff der Geschichte," *Gesammelte Schriften*, 1:2:695, hereafter "UBG").

3. Perhaps Benjamin is thinking that this symbol is really an allegory, as he exposited the concept in his *Trauerspiel* book.

4. Benjamin, "Goethes Wahlverwandtschaften," *Illuminationen: Ausgewählte Schriften*, ed. Sigfried Unseld (Frankfurt, 1961), 147.

What kind of *novum,* then, does this evangelist bring, with his thick candelabra fingers and heady excrescences, curlers which it is tempting to see as unfolding scrolls, possibly Torah scrolls? I cannot make out extended wings and staring eyes. I see a grotesque being, dissymmetric, demon rather than angel, helplessly reading itself, and becoming in this way a symbol after all, a sacred papier mâché. The image has more expressionless than expressive force, to borrow a Benjaminian category. The apparent angel is, to adapt Stanley Cavell, a European "hobo of thought," or rather, the caricature of a priest pretending to be a hobo.[5]

In Benjamin, truth seems to stand in the way of truth, or more exactly, truth and its transmission get in each other's way. He explicitly ascribes that dilemma to Kafka, but he could have pointed to Klee's forests of signs pretending to be correspondences. Truth is always too deadly, and transmission deceptively accommodating. Benjamin, as is well known, would have liked to circumvent this dilemma: he dreamed of writing a book made up solely of quotations, as if there were still, within speech, pristine fragments, moments of impersonal directness. No leakage of attention, no distraction, nothing but concentration absorbing the shock of words. The sounds of proper names, he suggests, which we try to make meaningful through etymology, are residues of an original God-given language.

But in a postprophetic age, proclamation and revelation are dangerous simulacra. In one way or another, Benjamin refuses to confine the identity of the literary work to a message or reader-directed intention, one that could reach its destination. A counterpropagandistic reticence always intervenes—a reticence that is not particularly cryptic but rather aesthetic, a shade or veil (*Hülle; Verhülltes*) which still allows us to recognize heart or body in hiding, but asks us to forgo imagining that from which we are excluded.

In the older aesthetics, this nonmessaging, this extreme discretion, is how the beautiful veils the sublime, because (or so I understand it) naked truth is on the side of excessive hope and can be attained only by not being attained. The angel of history moves on, but from ruin to ruin. Though he has passed beyond

5. I am told that a study of Klee's notebooks at the time the picture was composed reveals that it may have rendered his impression of Hitler, who often passed through Klee's district. But pictures, like books, have their own fate. The New Angel motif, as Scholem knew and communicated to Benjamin, plays a peculiar role in midrash Genesis Rabba, where a commentator suggests that God creates each dawn a new host of angels to sing his praise, who are then dissolved. The dawn song is their swan song.

hedonism, he remains messianic: he would like to pause, to wake the dead and make whole the maimed and mangled. A rival pleasure principle, however, a storm called progress, blows in from Paradise; revolutionaries are children of Paradise who do not rest content, any more than Faust, with "a green thought in a green shade."

Benjamin does not give up completely on the beautiful. He sets the beautiful appearance against its illusory promise of happiness and harmony. Erotic passion in Goethe's *Elective Affinities* is touched by that promise. What lovers in Goethe actually discover is something in stillness that is beyond words, in the sense of being not transcendent, but convergent on a mythic or mute substratum, and so representable only by a music of the ordinary. Goethe blends the motif of music with the most prosaic nature descriptions, as prose and poetry, working together, anticipate a sort of reconciliation: that of the lovers with each other, or rather with their pain, "l'imperfection incurable dans l'essence même du présent," as Proust said.[6]

Benjamin, in fact, darkens the possibility of reconciliation. The "redoubled happiness [enjoyment] of sound," Goethe's "Doppelglück der Töne," which, orgasmic or not, raises prosaic words to the power of music, is no crowning of earthly pleasure, according to Benjamin, but "the first weak intimation" of a dissolution, a perverse kind of aubade, "a still almost hopeless glinting of day which dawns for the tormented lovers."[7]

There is also, of course, an aggressive side to Benjamin's discretion. With the pressure of time, and as we enter the 1930s, he becomes assertive as well as gnomic. Yet he never abandons his own version of what the modernist tradition in France named impersonality. This topic raises the issue of whether Benjamin's methodical turn toward a socioeconomic interpretation of art and a materialistic philosophy of history displaces the spirituality that so often breaks through—not only in his refusal to abandon hope but also in such passing suggestions, which I have called spooky, that we have a "geheime Verabredung" with the dead, a secret appointment with previous generations ("UBG," 694).

Benjamin is always alert to what he names the saving correspondence, using

6. Quoted in Walter Benjamin, "Zum Bilde Prousts," *Illuminationen: Ausgewählte Schriften* (Frankfurt: Suhrkamp, 1961), 357.

7. Benjamin, "Goethe's Wahlverwandtschaften," 137.

"correspondence" in its Baudelairean sense: some link that keeps us attached to this world, vesting in it what sacredness—redemptive possibilities—there might be. More than ideology prompts the thought that we are unconsciously in contact with a buried energy, suppressed by positivistic history-writing or the fear of a bad-news revelation. The cultural critic takes responsibility for the anonymous victims of historical progress, victims of the unlived life, revenants expecting their due. In 1985, forty years after the war and the Holocaust, Jürgen Habermas develops Benjamin's hint about that "geheime Verabredung" by joining it to an adjacent phrase in the second of the "Geschichtsphilosophische Thesen": the phrase that each new generation is endowed with a "*weak* messianic power" ("UBG," 694) on which the past has a claim. Habermas suggests that young Germans can still identify with the Jewish victims, but only through cultivating memory's "weak power of solidarity."[8]

There are forces, however, that move us away from memory and the Baudelairean intuition of correspondences. They purge a mythic and literary language and seek relief in a transparent society—freed from the bondage of the past and given over to an economy of commodification or, alternatively, to a demystification that is so sure of itself that it sees nothing but one and the same thing. What is at risk is not only human variety or noncomformity, as they are indeed endangered by the reduction of human relationships to things, but also a certain quality of perception. For the thinker's *Wahrnehmungsapparat* is in danger of seeing everything in the same light, tainted by a "heroic melancholy" (an expression borrowed by Benjamin from Melanchthon) which cannot escape the ennui emanating from the massive, interchangeable conformity it is always uncovering. One of Benjamin's most chilling aphorisms from "Central Park" is "The stars represent in Baudelaire the enigma [*Vexierbild*] of the commodity. They are en masse that-which-is-always-the-same." More sinister still, if it alludes to the novum of the New Angel, is the following: "For humanity, as it is today, there exists only one radical piece of news—and that is always the same: death."[9] Even the concept of *correspondance* does not escape Benjamin's radical reduction of everything to an allegory of commodification, as if the scientist had succumbed to the infection he sought to cure.

8. Jürgen Habermas, *Eine Art Schadensabwicklung* (Frankfurt: Suhrkamp, 1987), 141: "Diese Toten haben erst recht ein Anspruch auf die schwache anamnetische Kraft einer Solidarität, die Nachgeborene nur noch im Medium der immer wieder erneuerten, oft verzweifelten, jedenfalls umtreibenden Erinnerung üben können."

9. Walter Benjamin, "Zentralpark," *Gesammelte Schriften,* 1:2:660, 668.

It is this ad absurdum and melancholy clarity which inspires Benjamin's Counter-Enlightenment. It cannot be gainsaid except by Levinas's intuition that to see the other as other and not as an assimilable commodity requires more than bodies arranged in a lighted space. "The interval of space opened up by light is instantaneously absorbed by light."[10] Except for this deadly, totalizing clarity without a breach (against which he launches the mystical dart of a *Jetztzeit* illumination), I see no superstition in Benjamin, any more than in Baudelaire or the great Romantics. His turning to the past, to that *underground* of stars, is a utopian form of hope—the dead must be saved from the enemy by flashing into the present with a different light, by escaping their equivalence as the dead and so the indifference of memory. Benjamin's materialistic commentary (anticipated in the opening remarks to his essay on Goethe's *Elective Affinities*) reactivates the inertial mythic dimension. The triumph of the latest gods is resisted by remembering their victims, those who have no temple, or who lie waiting for the Messiah in mass graves.

We now understand better Benjamin's concern for the human Wahrnehmungsapparat. The day of the media begins to appear like the day, that is the night, of the locusts; and from Marshall McLuhan to Debray, mediology has played a fatal role in the attempt to achieve the full exposure of the paparazzi: always exciting, of course, as in "whom the Gods wish to destroy they make mad." The videosphere, to use Debray's word, yields no cover; to be is to be seen. All of history returns not as farce but as film, and the antitheatrical prejudice finally gives up its ghost. Zappers, we can now be as protean and forgetful as we like.

Given a society which is a perpetual scene of transformation (as Valéry, already, said), and media that have conquered ubiquity, telluric virtues called character or ethos are undermined by the very intensity of our nostalgia for them, so that we shuttle between, on the one hand, a desperate, credulous search for the one good man or woman and, on the other, the suspicion that everything is hypocrisy or *trucage.* The plastic demon of mutability, fed by the media, is no longer typified by the eternally maligned Semite, by comparison with the solidly rooted burgher-patriot: everyone now is tarred with the same brush.

Yet some thinkers hold out the possibility of finding a new grounding, without relapsing into mystification. Vattimo is one of them, who seeks to revive hermeneutics, who refuses to give up the verbal and historical sedimenta-

10. Emmanuel Levinas, *Le temps et l'autre* (Paris: Presses Universitaires de France, 1983), 47.

tion—call it a weak semantic power—that grounds the interpretive enterprise.[11] Benjamin is another; and he perseveres by the density, sometimes the severity, of his phrasing, by moral and often contrarian reflections in which abstract thought is almost obscured by the most homely imagery. "The destructive character," he writes for example, "is the enemy of the etui-man": reading this we suddenly see how important—almost as important as for the Japanese—packaging is for us, even though the etui, of course, is a more permanent and less discardable frame for the precious or comforting object.

The etui with its velvet lining is what we would like to fit into; though uncomfortably close to a casket, its miniaturizing of our desire to collect ourselves condones the small hope for integrity we have left. The etui is to be homely, not *unheimlich;* a negation of the jack-in-the-box, or exploding parcel. It allows us to hide out, as in childhood, not hide in. But when we read, again in Benjamin, that "the destructive character stands in the front line of the traditionalists," we are discomfited; and Benjamin's paradox leads by an insidious demarche to an impasse. "The destructive character stands in the front line of the traditionalists. Some pass things down to posterity, by making them untouchable and thus conserving them; others pass on situations by making them practicable and thus liquidating them. The latter are called the destructive."[12]

Whose liberal pride does not suffer a shock on reading this? The traditionalist and the progressive are both brought into question by the impossible choice Benjamin offers. Either you conserve tradition by giving it sacred and untouchable status and so remove it from circulation, or you make it more practicable, fungible, that is, modernize it—but that is to play a game which could gamble away what you wish to transmit.

In his famous essay on technology and art—and I want to end by returning to it—Benjamin realized that art was itself at risk in this game. An era of mechanical reproduction, of printing and photography, facilitates translatability from place to place and culture to culture; so that art suffers the same fate as the sacred, losing its aura in the very process of transmission. Benjamin meant by aura primarily the prestige and testimonial power that come from originating in a particular time and place, even if that localization seems accidental. Perhaps the only way we can preserve the idea of the unique, or the

11. Gianni Vattimo, *The Transparence of Society* (Baltimore: Johns Hopkins University Press, 1992).

12. Walter Benjamin, "The Destructive Character," *Reflections: Essays, Aphorisms, Autobiographical Writings,* trans. Edmund Jephcott; ed. Peter Demetz (New York: Harcourt Brace Jovanovich, 1978), 301–303.

truly local and material, is by recognizing the peculiar fact of religion, which, though urbi et orbe, claims to start in a particular place ("terribilis est locus iste") and is committed to an idiom that resists translation. The accident of origin is viewed not as an accident but as a revelation; and to accommodate or discount the event's proper names, wild images, and other erratic details would be to disembody an appearance lodged firmly in the familiar, phenomenal world and kept there as "holy." The material conditions, in short, become part of the sacred event and are counterconceptual to the quest for transparence.

I have taken too long—perhaps because commentary today has no rhetorical form like the proem of ancient midrash. The darshan or preacher had his home plate; he knew the verse with which each portion of Scripture recited on a specific Shabbat began; and the aim of his sermon was to choose a verse as far away from home as possible, so that only he knew how he would get back. My problem is that I have no home base, that a diasporic and disseminative fling is all I can offer. But it is not unfitting to leave Benjamin the last word, which I translate from his essay on Goethe. "Neither the veiling form [*Hülle*] nor the veiled object is the beautiful, but the object in its veiled containment. Unveiled, it would prove to be infinitely withdrawn from appearance (*unendlich unscheinbar*). . . . Thus, in the face of everything beautiful, the idea of unveiling turns into the impossibility of unveiling. This impossibility is the idea inspiring criticism of art. Its task is not to remove or elevate the veiled form, but rather through the most precise knowledge [*Erkenntnis*] of that form to raise itself to a true perception [*Anschauung*] of what is beautiful."[13]

13. Benjamin, "Goethe's Wahlverwandtschaften," 141. My translation. See also Stanley Corngold's translation of this passage in *Walter Benjamin: Selected Writings*, 1913–1926, ed. Marcus Bullock and Michael W. Jennings (Cambridge: Harvard University Press, 1996), 351.

Speculations

The Interpreter's Freud

Freud alone proves Emerson's observation that a significant institution is the shadow of a great thinker. We cannot understand Freud without understanding the peculiar quality of his greatness: that quality which made him, which still makes him, a scandal, a shadow we negotiate with. He has imposed on us with the force of a religion. "One must have a very strong and keen and persistent criticism," Wittgenstein remarked about Freud, "to see through the mythology that is offered or imposed on one. There is an inducement to say, 'Yes, of course, it must be like that!' A powerful mythology."

Freud, however, wished to found a science of mind and not a mythology. His first major book, *The Interpretation of Dreams,* planted the banner of rational and methodical inquiry in the very swamp of unreason, where few had ventured and, of those, very few had come back, their sanity intact. Yet these rationalist aspirations of psycho-

Given as the 1984 Freud Lecture at Yale, an annual event sponsored by the Kanzer Seminar for Psychoanalysis in the Humanities, the Western New England Psychoanalytic Society, and the Whitney Humanities Center.

analysis by no means disprove its redemptive and communitarian nature. Though psychoanalysis is not a religion, it still exhibits many features of past religions, including reasoning about unreason, about the irrational forces we live with and cannot entirely control. Where is language in this field of forces? Especially the language of the interpreter as it takes for its subject other language constructs, presenting themselves as textual, like literary artifacts, or presenting themselves as a mysterious code belonging also to another medium, like hysterical symptoms or dream images. It is not necessary to overemphasize what we have learned about language since Freud and again since Lacan. The discourse of the analyst remains within the affective sphere of the discourse it interprets; it is as much a supplement as a clarification; and instead of an asceptic and methodological purism, which isolates the interpreter's language from the so-called object-language, creating in effect two monologues, we have to risk a dialogue in which our own often unconscious assumptions are challenged. "The analysand's discourse," André Green has written, "is a stream of words that . . . the analyst cannot shut up in a box. The analyst runs after the analysand's words."

In psychoanalysis especially, because it involves transference and countertransference, because it puts the interpreter, not only the text or person interpreted, at risk, this exchange of words does not always lead to an urbane dialogue. The word *dialogue,* in fact, is deceptive, for there may be, in this situation, more imposition and resistance, more "crisscross" or crazy connections, than when Dostoyevsky or, for that matter, Hitchcock, gets strangers together on a train. The Romance of the Railroad penetrates the interpreter's discourse, which hurtles toward its uncertain destination along a branching track of words with exotic expectations, mysterious switches, and—it is to be hoped—good brakes.

To understand Freud's power as an interpreter (whether or not we agree with his findings or their claim to be scientific), it is necessary to read him with an attention solicited by his own immense culture, in which a sensitivity to language stimulated by literature played its part. I begin, therefore, by taking a sample from *The Interpretation of Dreams* to give it a close, literary reading. It is equally important, however, to gauge the transferability of Freud's interpretative method. The second half of my essay, then, will take up a nonanalytic text, a poem of Wordsworth's, and do two things: see it in a Freudian context, but also see Freud in its context.

It is a striking truth that literary analysis, like Freud's dream analysis, does no more and no less than disclose a life in images or words that has its own momentum. Ambiguities, overdetermined meanings, and strange linkages are more obvious than the coherent design they seem to flee from. "My thoughts crowd each other to death," Coleridge wrote. He finds himself in the grip of what he named "the streamy nature of association"; in his Notebooks, especially, not only the dreams he puts down but also his speculative etymologies and related word chains accelerate into a futile "science of the grotesque" (a phrase I take from Kenneth Burke's fine essay on Freud, in *The Philosophy of Literary Form*). But many writers acknowledge explicitly an experience similar to that of racing thoughts. "I often felt the onset of madness," Flaubert confesses. "There was a whirl of ideas and images in my poor mind, and my consciousness, my ego, seemed to be foundering like a ship in a storm. . . . I played with fantasy and madness, as Mithridates did with his poisons." Or Keats, in a lighthearted vein: "I must be quaint and free of Tropes and figures—I must play my draughts as I please. . . . Have you not seen a Gull, an orc, a Sea Mew, or any thing to bring this Line to a proper length, and also fill up this clear part; that like the Gull I may *dip*—I hope, not out of sight—and also, like a Gull I hope to be lucky in a good sized fish—This crossing a letter is not without its associations—for chequer work leads us naturally to a Milkmaid, a Milkmaid to Hogarth Hogarth to Shakespeare Shakespeare to Hazlitt—Hazlitt to Shakespeare and thus by merely pulling an apron string we set a pretty peal of Chimes at work."

"A pretty peal of Chimes—" Keats's insouciance puts us at an equal distance from the purely formal character of rhyme, as it suggests a flirtatious harmony, and the tongue-tying phenomenon of clang associations. When Freud encouraged "free" association in himself and his patients, he simply took the burden of self-judgment away, so that this inner speech, to which Flaubert and Keats allude, might be fully disclosed. *The Interpretation of Dreams* remains a disconcerting work because of this: Freud's interpretive method is not as separate as one might expect from the dream which is its object. Both dream and dream analysis are streamy, associative structures. The only difference between reported dream and analytic commentary is that the dream is more elliptical in the way it passes from sentence to sentence or image to image. Freud's interpretation fills up these ellipses or "absences" in the dream; as Keats too is aware of having to fill in spaces by moving figures across a chequer board without being checked.

Quite often too, like Keats, Freud introduces explanatory material that branches off with a digressive life of its own—especially when that material is a name. An example will be helpful here. In trying to understand a dream about three women, one of them making dumplings (*Knödel*), Freud recalls the ending of the first novel he has ever read, in which the hero goes mad and keeps calling out the names of the three women who has brought him the greatest happiness—and sorrow. One was called *Pélagie;* and by a path at least as eccentric as that of Keats, the three women become the three Fates; *Pélagie* becomes a bridge to the word "plagiarize," which then also throws light on *Knödel* as a name (the name of a person) rather than a common noun. Suddenly everything alliterates or "chimes." Here is a portion of Freud's analysis from the section on "Infantile Material as a Source of Dreams" in chapter 5.

> In connection with the three women I thought of the Fates who spin the destiny of man, and I knew that one of the three women—the inn-hostess in the dream—was the mother who gives life, and furthermore (as in my own case) gives the living creature its first nourishment. Love and hunger, I reflected, meet at a woman's breast. . . . So they really were Fates that I found in the kitchen when I went into it—as I had so often done in my childhood when I was hungry, while my mother, standing by the fire, had admonished me that I must wail till dinner was ready.—And now for the dumplings—the *Knödel!* One at least of my teachers at the University—and precisely the one to whom I owe my historical knowledge . . . would infallibly be reminded by *Knödel* of a person against whom he had been obliged to take legal action for *plagiarizing* his writing. The idea of plagiarizing . . . clearly led me to the second part of the dream, in which I was treated as though I were the thief who had for some time carried on his business of stealing overcoats in the lecture-rooms. I had written down the word 'plagiarizing' without thinking about it, because it just occured to me; but now I noticed that it could form a bridge [*Brücke*] between different pieces of the dream's manifest content. A chain of associations (*Pélagie—plagiarizing–plagiostomes* or sharks . . . —a *fish's swimming-bladder*), connected the old novel with the case of *Knödel* and with the overcoats, which clearly referred to implements used in sexual technique.

This is not the end: a further train of thoughts immediately takes off from the "honored name of Brücke," leading ("as though the need to set up forced connections regarded *nothing* as sacred") to the memory of Fleischl (*Fleisch:* meat), a second respected teacher, linked to Freud's experiments with cocaine in what he calls the Latin Kitchen (the dispensary or pharmacy).

In literary studies we often ask what the genre of a work may be. It is a question raised when the reader confronts a new or puzzling form; and it certainly arises when we read *The Interpretation of Dreams.* It is hard to call the book a work of science and leave it at that. Often the fugal connections and especially the word chains are not furnished by the manifest content of the dream: though they may belong to the dream thoughts, they do only by virtue of an analysis which is interpolative and similar to an elaborate joke. One is reminded of Freud's own aphorism: "The realm of jokes knows no limits." What, then, is the genre of this book?

My quotation from the Knödel dream suggests that Freud finds a strange and original way to write a *confession.* I mean an autobiography that lays bear whatever it may be—certainly sexual wishes, guilt feelings, and social envy, as well as the infantile emotions that spur the quest for scientific fame. *The Double Helix* cannot compare with Freud for disclosing the *libido* of science. "Freud's frankness," Kenneth Burke wrote, "is no less remarkable by reason of the fact that he had perfected a method for being frank. . . . What for him could fall within the benign category of observation could for [others] fall only within its malign counterpart, spying."

It is the reversal of malign into benign *and vice versa,* which risked, as Burke saw, a "drastic self-ostracizing act—the charting of the relations between ecclesia and cloaca." Freud's confession, entitled *The Interpretation of Dreams,* even transcends Augustine's and Rousseau's, because in addition to a very moving if oblique narrative of self-justification, it launches an extraordinary mode of reading, one that is both wilder and more daring in its very rage for order than either rabbinic exegesis or the figural and typological method of the Church Fathers. Freud's way of interpreting dreams becomes a powerful hermeneutics, rivaling that of the great Western religions. Though his dreambook is an unlikely candidate for a scripture—being, I have suggested, more like a Confession—it fashions a secular key out of phenomena that this same civilization repressed by calling them sacred, then irrational, then trivial. Freud not only redeems this excluded mass from insignificance; he also introduces strange new *texts* for our consideration: texts neither literary nor scriptural but whose discovery throws doubt on the transcription of all previous inner experience. Freud reveals much more than a code for the decipherment of dreams: he invents a new textuality by transcribing dreams in his own way. It is not just the dream that is important, but also the dream text. After Freud we all have Freudian dreams; that is, we report them that way—except for those chosen few who are Jungians.

Psychoanalysis, then, creates new texts as well as transforming our understanding of those already received. Yet because the religious systems of the past also disseminated methods of interpretation that were radically revisionary, it is important to emphasize two features that distinguish psychoanalytic interpretation from those influential modes.

The first difference concerns the transactive relation of text and commentary. The dream text is not an object with scriptural fixity. Scripture itself, of course, or the many books (*biblia*) we now call the Bible, had to be edited and fixed by a succession of interpretive communities. But Freud allows us to see the commentary entering the text, incorporating itself with the dream: what he called his self-analysis, working on dreams he had, so invests and supplements an original version that it becomes less an object and more a series of linguistic relays that could lead anywhere—depending on the system of rails and who is doing the switching. The dream is like a sentence that cannot find closure. Freud keeps coming up with fragments of something already recounted, as well as adding meaning to meaning. This extreme indeterminacy, even if it was there in what we now call Scripture, is no longer available to us, despite suggestive residues of freedom in the early rabbis whose midrashim exposed every inconsistency or gap in the sacred text, or who elicited new interpretations by changing speculatively the received voweling, the *nekudoth*.

A second feature that distinguishes psychoanalytic interpretation is its *kakangelic* rather than *evangelic* nature. I admit to coining this discordant word. The New Testament claims to bring good news, and reinterprets the Old Testament—that is, the Hebrew Bible—in the light of its faith. If the Gospels emphasize mankind's guilt, they also counter it by the possibility of salvation. But Freud brings bad (*kaka*) news about the psyche, and offers no cure except through the very activity—analysis—which reveals this news. "A single Screw of Flesh / Is all that pins the Soul" Emily Dickinson wrote; and her homely metaphor keeps the hope open that on the other side of the "Vail" or "Gauze" of the body, her soul could enter into its freedom and see God or the loved one in full presence. Yet in Freud the "Screw of Flesh" or *la chose genitale* (Charcot) cannot be totally sublimated, not even through the noncarnal conversation which psychoanalysis institutes. For its precisely through this conversation that the patient becomes more aware of the "mailed [maled] Nerve" as something—pin, penis, pen—without which there is no soul, no signification, good or bad.

The dream analysis I have previously cited reflects this kakangelic vision, this "inverse Freudian piety toward the sinister" (to quote Philip Rieff). Knödl, Fleischl, and Brücke do not appear as proper names in the dream, yet Freud's interpolative commentary dwells on the dream's misuse of such names. He calls it "a kind of childish naughtiness" and an act of retribution for witticisms made about his own name. He also mentions a mock-heroic verse written by Herder about Goethe. "Der du von Göttern abstammst, von Gothen oder vom Kote" ("Thou who art the descendant of Gods or Goths or dung"), and he answers it in the name of Goethe by quoting from the latter's *Iphigenia:* "So you too, divine figures, have turned to dust!" That Freud takes it on himself to answer Herder's quibble with a line of such pathos (it alludes to the death of many heroes during the siege of Troy) indicates something more than a regressive sensitivity about one's name. The dialogue of those two verses makes a little drama whose subject is the ambivalence that surrounds great men who have become ego ideals; and the ease with which their names can be profaned, dragged in the dust, causes Freud to balance Herder's childish punning with a compensatory impersonation. In *Totem and Taboo* the avoidance of the name of the dead in primitive societies, though more elaborately explained, still hinges on the same kind of envy or ambivalence. Freud has realized, in short, the profaning power of dreams; yet not of dreams only, but of language as it allows that chiming to mock and madden anything sacred. He has to decide whether *Götter* or *Kot,* ecclesia or cloaca, evangelism or kakangelism is to be the dominant trend of his commentary. It happens that two members of that strange trinity, Knödl, Fleischl, and Brücke, are sacred to Freud; yet the dream degrades them from proper to ordinary nouns. As ordinary nouns, however, they can become quiet conduits for the dream-work; though the plot thickens when we ask what the dream-work is seeking to reveal.

For the teaching of two of these men nourished Freud's scientific ambitions: they were among his male Fates. We do not learn particulars of what they taught him, since the dream is after something more universal. If we suppose that the dream conspired with Freud's wish that dream analysis be recognized as a science, then a hieratic form of discourse must appear, analogous to the hieroglyphs the dream itself presents. Yet the dream's mode of expression remains distinctly vernacular rather than hieratic—that is, without terms from the Latin Kitchen. While the language of the dream, then, forged in the real kitchen of women and dumplings, reaches for a mysterious vernacular, or mother tongue, the chain of associations characterizing the language of the interpreter fails to transform the dream text into the "purer" discourse or sacred instrument of the scientist: his white overcoat or sublime condom.

Freud is brought back to his childlike if ambivalent veneration for Brücke, Fleischl, etc. He also experiences a related anxiety, that he may be a plagiarist like Knödl and so must clear his name. The dream discloses what infantile jealousies still prop the scientific project; but part of that project—not analyzed by Freud—is the ideal of a flawless discourse, a Latin of the intellect, a dream-redeeming sacred commentary. *Not the dream is holy but the power of the interpretation as it methodizes and universalizes itself.*

"Behold, the dreamer cometh." That is said mockingly of Joseph in the

Pentateuch; yet Joseph gains fame not as a dreamer but as a dream interpreter. We glimpse in Freud the dreamer rising to fame not through vainglorious dreams but through the art or science of dream interpretation, which he called the royal road.

The name Sigmund Freud is indeed a misnomer. For in wrestling with the angel of the unconscious, with the evasive dream thoughts, Freud strips away so many layers of idealization, so many euphemistic formulas, that only wounded names are left. But through his unconsciousness-raising we learn what we are up against: profanation, defamation, self-slander, equivocation, distortion, ambivalence, displacement, repression, censorship. Freud neither curses nor blesses that hard-won knowledge; and so his greatness, finally, may be his moral style, that he neither palliates nor inculpates human nature.

From Freud I turn to Wordsworth, respecting his own statement that "The poets were there before me." My text is from the Lucy poems, a group of short lyrics on the death of a young girl, which is a motif that goes back to the Greek Anthology and evokes three highly charged themes: incompleteness, mourning, and memory.

A slumber did my spirit seal;
  I had no human fears:
She seemed a thing that could not feel
  The touch of earthly years.

No motion has she now, no force;
  She neither hears nor sees;
Rolled round in earth's diurnal course,
  With rocks, and stones, and trees.

"A slumber did my spirit seal." After that line one would expect a dream vision. The formula is, I fell asleep, and behold! Yet there is no vision, or not in the expected sense. The boundary between slumber and vision is elided. That the poet had no human fears, that he experienced a curious anesthesia vis-à-vis the girls' mortality or his own, may be what he names a slumber. As out of Adam's first sleep an Eve arose, so out of this sealed but not unconscious spirit a womanly image arises with the same idolatrous charm. Wordsworth's image seems to come from within; it is a delusive daydream, yet still a revision of that original vision.

There is, however, no sense of an eruption from the unconscious: brevity and condensation do not lead, as they do in dreams, to remarkable puns, striking figures, or deviant forms of speech. Nor is it necessary to be psychoanalytic to recognize that the trance is linked to an overidealization of the loved person. The second stanza, which reports that she has died, should, in that case, express disillusionment. Yet remarkably, this does not occur: the poet does not exclaim or cry out. Both transitions, the passage from slumber to dream, and the breaking of the dream, are described without surprise or shock.

Is there nothing that betrays how deeply disturbing the fantasy may have been? Perhaps, if the emotion was strong, it is natural enough that the words should seek to understate and to seal the impression. There is, however, an uncanny *displacement* on the structural level that is consonant with what Freud calls the omnipotence of thoughts and a general overestimation of psychical acts attributed by him to primitive cultures and, in contemporary civilization, to art.

This displacement is, rhetorically speaking, also a transference: in the initial stanza, the poet is sealed in slumber; in the second that slumber has passed over, as if intensified, to the girl. She falls asleep forever; and her death is specifically portrayed as a quasi immortality not unlike what his imagination has prematurely projected onto her. "Rolled round in earth's diurnal course," she indeed cannot "feel / The touch of earthly years." This subtle transfer, this metaphor as extended structure rather than punctual figure of speech, is anticipated by at least one local condensation. *Human* in "I had no human fears" (line 2) is a transferred epithet. The line should read: "I had no such fears as would have come to me had I considered her a human—that is, mortal—being." We do not know which way the transfer goes: from the girl to the poet or vice versa. And yet we *do* know: surely the illusion took rise in the poet and is an error of the imagination. Yet Wordsworth leaves that illusion its moment of truth as if it were natural, and not in any way out of the ordinary. He does not take pains to demystify it. Nature has its own supernatural gleam, however evanescent it is.

The supernatural illusion preserves the girl from a certain kind of touch, "of earthly years" in the first stanza, but in the second she is totally distanced. Coleridge surmised that the lyric was an imaginary epitaph for Wordsworth's sister, and F. W. Bateson seized on this to claim that "A slumber" (and the Lucy poems as a whole) arose from incestuous emotions and expressed a death wish by the brother against the sister. The poem removes an object of love by moving it beyond touch. In all but one important respect it confirms Freud's analysis about the way neurotics evade reality. Freud shows how the whole world is eventually embargoed, put beyond touch or contact by a widening fear of contagion. The only difference is that in Wordsworth the whole world enters in the second stanza as an image with resonances that are more positive than sinister.

Wordsworth's poem, moreover, practically offers itself for inclusion in a section of the dreambook that contains Freud's most famous literary interpretation. In "Dreams of the Death of Persons of Whom the Dreamer Is Fond" (chapter 5) he discusses the story of Oedipus. We readily respond to the death of Oedipus, says Freud, "because it might have been ours—because the oracle laid the same curse upon us before our birth as upon him." That curse is understood to be an unconsciously fulfilled wish, a pattern we also suspect is present in "A slumber." But the question for literary criticism, even as it engages with psychoanalysis, is why such a wish, at once idealizing and deadly, and as if fulfilled in the second stanza, does not disturb the poet's language more. Even if the death did not occur except in idea, one might expect the spirit to awake, and to wonder what kind of deception it had practiced on itself. Yet though the poem can be said to approach muteness—if we interpret the blank between the stanzas as another elision, a *lesion* in fact—Wordsworth keeps speech going without a trace of guilty knowledge. The eyes of the spirit may be open, but the diction remains unperturbed.

I want to suggest that Wordsworth's curious yet powerful complacency is related to euphemism: not of the artificial kind, the substitution of a good word for a bad one, or the strewing of flowers on a corpse, but an earthy euphemism, as it were, a balm deriving from common speech, from its unconscious obliquity and inbuilt commitment to avoid silence. To call it euphemism may be inadequate, but the quality I point to resists overconsciousness and demystification.

It is generally the task of the critic to uncover euphemism in any sphere: literary, psychological, political. When Freud told a patient the meaning of one of her flowery dreams, "she quite lost her liking for it." A kakangelic unmasking may be necessary, although not many would go as far as Kenneth Burke, who praised Freud's method as "an interpretive sculpting in excrement" and put praise in action by suggesting we read Keats's "Beauty is Truth, Truth Beauty" as "Body is Turd, Turd Body." What makes Wordsworth's poetry so difficult to psychoanalyze is its underlying and resistant euphemism, coterminous with ordinary language, and distinguished from the courtly and affected diction of the time.

Consider the word *slumber* as such a euphemism. Then consider the entire second stanza as a paraphrase for "she is dead." The negative aspect of these phrases can be heightened. The "slumber" may remind us of bewitchment or fascination, even of hypnosis. It could be a hypnoid state in which one hears voices without knowing it or performs actions on the basis of these voices. In another Lucy poem, "Strange fits of passion," such automatism is strongly suggested, and a voice does intrude at the end in the form of an incomplete sentence that expresses, in context, a premonition, but in itself is more ambiguous: "If Lucy should be dead!"

That we may be in the domain of voices is made more probable by the word *passion* in "Strange fits of passion": it meant an outcry under the impact of strong emotions. Yet to pursue this analysis would mean to go from the issue of euphemism to that of language as a synthesis not only of sounds but of speech acts, and especially—if we look to infancy—of threats, promises, admonitions, yesses, and noes that come to the child as ideas of reference in vocal form, even if (or because) not every word is understood. Such an analysis would also oblige us to explore the text of poetry as an undoing of that synthesis, or a partial recovery of the elements behind the deceptive neutrality of language. Ordinary speech, from this perspective, is a form of sleep-walking, the replication of internalized phrases or commands without conscious affect; poetic speech is an exposure of that condition, a return to a sense of language as virtually alive—in any case with enough feeling to delay our passage from words to things. Speech re-enters an original zone of stress and inhibition and becomes precarious.

That precariousness is both acknowledged and limited by Wordsworth's euphemism. The second stanza of "A slumber," unlike the end of "Strange fits," does not cry out: as a periphrasis for "she is dead" it amplifies and even embellishes that reluctant phrase. It is hard to think of the lyric as a stark epitaph skirting aphasia. And though the traumatic or mortifying event may occasion the euphemism, it cannot be its cause. We must find a "feeding source" (to use one of the poet's own metaphors) elsewhere; and we can find it only in the other threat to speech: the near-ecstasy depicted in the previous stanza. A common source of inarticulate or mute behavior, such ecstasy, whatever its nature, carries over into the second stanza's euphemia.

Epitaphs, of course, are conventionally associated with consoling and pleasant words. Here, however, not all the words are consoling. They approach a negative that could foreclose the poem: "No . . . No . . . Neither . . . Nor. . . ." Others even show Wordsworth's language penetrated by an inappropriate subliminal punning. So *diurnal* (line 7) divides into *die* and *urn,* and *course* may recall the older pronunciation of *corpse.* Yet these condensations are troublesome rather than expressive; the power of the second stanza resides predominantly in the euphemistic displacement of the word *grave* by an image of *gravitation* ("Rolled round in earth's diurnal course"). And though there is no agreement on the tone of this stanza, it is clear that a sub-vocal word is uttered without being written out. It is a word that rhymes with *fears* and *years* and *hears,* but which is closed off by the very last syllable of the poem: *trees.* Read *tears,* and the animating, cosmic metaphor comes alive, the poet's lament echoes through nature as in pastoral elegy. "Tears," however, must give way to what is written, to a dull yet definitive sound, the anagram *trees.*

Pastoral elegy, in which rocks, woods, and streams are called upon to mourn the death of a person, or to echo the complaint of a lover, seems too extravagant a genre for this chastely fashioned inscription. Yet the muted presence of the form reminds us what it means to be a nature poet. From childhood on, as the autobiographical *Prelude* tells us, Wordsworth was aware of "unknown modes of being" and of strange sympathies emanating from nature. He was haunted by an animistic universe that seemed to stimulate, share, and call upon his imagination. The Lucy poems evoked a nature spirit in human form, perhaps modeled after his sister, and the forerunner of Cathy Linton in *Wuthering Heights.* It makes no sense to suppose a death wish unless we link it to the ecstatic feelings in this poetry. Yet where do these feelings come from? Wordsworth does not actually say he projected his starry emotions upon the girl. It is, rather, *our* habit of giving priority to the psychological state of the writer, *our* inability to consider his euphoria as a contagious identification with the girl, that makes us assume it is a dream and a delusion. For to think otherwise would return us to the world of pastoral elegy or even to a magical universe, with currents of sympathy running along esoteric channels—the very world described as primitive in *Totem and Taboo.*

Reading Freud through Wordsworth now brings us closer to a critique of Freud. The discovery of the role played in mental illness by large-scale wishful thinking, by omnipotence of thought, is a proven achievement. Yet Freud's description of the thought process of primitives and their licensed contemporary relic the artist is for once not reflective or dialectical enough. Freud wants so badly to place psychotherapy on a firm, scientific foundation that he exempts himself from an overestimation of psychical acts. At the same time he has made it hard for *us* to value interpretations not based on the priority of a psychological factor. Animism is accepted as a functional belief only in fiction—in Jensen's *Gradiva* or Wordsworth's poems or *Wuthering Heights*—but is considered dysfunctional, unless demystified by psychoanalysis, when it comes to mental health. Perhaps the decisive matter here is not a compulsion to demystify (to be kakangelic) but a failure to draw a certain type of experience into that special dialogue established by psychoanalysis. For the problem with art as with nonclassical anthropological data is that interpretation cannot find enough associations for it. Psychoanalysis distrusts, with good reason, the appearance of autonomy in such artifacts even while recognizing their force, which is then labeled primitive.

Yet Freud could acknowledge, in passing, that his persistent, even obsessive, mode of interpretation might share the delusional character of superstitions it sought to analyze and dispel. He himself may have suffered from a fear of contagion that, as Jacques Lacan and other have claimed, placed too many protective barriers between his hermeneutics and religious hermeneutics. Those barriers are coming down, or do not seem as impenetrable as they once were. Indeed, in the first part of my talk, I suggested some analogies that made religion and psychoanalysis enemy brothers. But I can be somewhat more specific, in conclusion, about what Freud saw yet tried to close out.

His attitude toward eudemonic feelings, the kind that Wordsworth expressed in "A slumber," was always distrustful and demystifying. He considered them a "thalassal regression" (to use Ferenczi's phrase), an attempt to regain an inertial state, the nirvana of preoedipal or undifferentiated being. Wordsworth's attitude was very different. In all his most interesting work he describes a developmental impasse centering on eudemonic sensations experienced in early childhood and associated with nature. Whether beautiful or frightening, they sustain and nourish him as intimations of immortality; and though Wordsworth can be called the first ego psychologist, the first careful observer of the growth of a mind, he shows the strength and usurpation of those ecstatic memories as they threaten the maturing poet who must respect their drive. If there is a death wish in the Lucy poems, it is insinuated by nature itself and asks lover or growing child not to give up earlier yearnings—to die rather than become an ordinary mortal.

This developmental impasse is quite clear in the present poem. Divided into two parts, separated formally by a blank and existentially by a death, the epitaph does not record a disenchantment. The mythic girl dies, but that word seems to wrong her. Her starlike quality is maintained despite her death, for the poet's sense of her immutability deepens by reversal into an image of *participation mystique* in the planet earth. There is loss, but there is also a calculus of gain and loss which those two stanzas weigh like two sides of a balance. Their balancing point is the impasse I have mentioned: such a death could seem better than dying into the light of common day. Yet to think only *that* is to make immutability of such value that human life is eclipsed by it. Ideas of preexistence or afterlife arise. My analysis has tried to capture a complex state of affairs that may resemble religious experiences or pathological states but which Wordsworth sees as an imaginative constant, ordinary and incurable. For those who need more closure in interpretation, who wish to know exactly what the poet felt, I can only suggest a phrase from his famous "Ode: Intimations of Immortality from Recollections of Early Childhood." The meanest flower, he writes, can give him "thoughts that do often lie too deep for tears." The girl has become such a thought.

Yet even here we meet a euphemism once more. Naming something "a thought too deep for tears": Is that not a remarkable periphrasis for the inability to grieve? This inability seems to be a strength rather than a weakness if we take the figure literally. "Too deep for tears" suggests a place—a mental place—beyond fits of passion or feelings, as if Wordsworth desired that grave immunity. To call the words euphemistic is to acknowledge at the same time that they are so affecting that mourning is not absent but continued in a different mode. The work of writing seems to have replaced the work of mourning. Is there a link, then, between writing and grieving, such that writing can be shown to assist those Herculean psychic labors Freud described for us, whose aim is to detach us from the lost object and reattach us to the world?

My main concern has been to understand yet delimit Freud's kakangelic mode of interpretation. Wordsworth enabled me to do this by showing that euphemism can be an ordinary rather than artificial aspect of language, especially when the work of mourning is taking place, which is pretty much all the time. I have argued that this euphemism cannot be demystified because it is not simply a figure of speech covering up naked truth. Looking closely at a poem by Wordsworth reveals a far more complicated situation. The strongest euphemisms in Wordsworth are also the most naturalized; they seem to belong to language rather than being imposed on it. They are not in the service of evading reality or putting the best face on things. They have an energy, a force of their own, one that counters a double threat to speech: expectedly, that which comes from loss; but unexpectedly, that which comes from ecstasy, even if it is a remembered ecstasy, and so touched by loss. I have sometimes talked of euphemia rather than euphemism, both because we are dealing with a feature basic to language, and not simply to one poet's use of language, and also because the aphasia it circumscribes remains perceptible. Wordsworth's euphemia, in short, is nourished by sources in language or the psyche we have not adequately understood. They bring us back to an awareness of how much sustaining power language has, even if our individual will to speak and write is assaulted daily by the most trivial as well as by traumatic events.

This sustaining power of language is not easily placed, however, on the side of goodness or love (eros) rather than death. Writing has an impersonal, even impersonating, quality which brings the poet close to the dead "whose names are in our lips," to quote Keats. *Personare* meant, originally, to "speak through" another, usually by way of an ancestral mask, which made the speaker a medium or an actor in a drama in which the dead renewed their contact with the living.

It is not surprising, therefore, that there should be a hint of the involuntary or mechanical in stanza 2 of "A slumber": a hint of the indifference to which the girl's difference is reduced, and which, however tragic it may be, obeys a law that supports the stability a survivor's speech requires. "O blessed machine of language," Coleridge once exclaimed; this very phrase is symptomatic of the euphemia without which speech would soon cease to be, or turn into its feared opposite, an eruptive cursing or sputtering, as in Tourette's syndrome. Coleridge has to bless the machine *as* a machine; yet his blessing is doubly euphemistic, for he knew too well what the machine could do in its unblessed aspect, as an uncontrollable stream of associations which coursed through him by day and especially by night.

It is here we link up once more with Freud, who created a new hermeneutics by charting compulsive and forced connections which "regarded *nothing* as sacred." Someone said of a typical lecture by Emerson that "it had no connection, save in God." Freud's kakangelic method removes all vestiges of that final clause. The recovered dream thoughts have no connections save in the negative fact that their capacity for profanation is practically without limit. All other connections are the result of a secondary process extending from the dream-work's disguises and displacements to more conscious revisions. At times, therefore, the manifest dream content may appear saner than an interpretation that reverses the dream's relatively euphemistic bearing or disintegrates its discursive structure. Instead of completing dream texts, or by extension literary texts (or, like Jung, encouraging their synthesis), Freud makes them less complete, less fulfilling. The more interpretation, it seems, the less closure.

But did Freud himself regard nothing as sacred? I have already suggested that if the dream is unholy, and is shown to be so by the interpretation, the power of that interpretation as it methodizes and universalizes itself is something very near to holy. One wonders how else Freud could have continued his work without falling mute, without being overcome by the bad news he brought. The dream peculiar to Freud, as interpreter and scientist, a dream which survives all self-analysis, is of a purified language that remains uncontaminated by its materials, that neither fulfills nor represses an all-too-human truth. I hope Freud's shade will understand this parting remark as a blessing on the only scientist I have ever been able to read.

Words and Wounds

Let me suppose that words are always armed and capable of wounding: either because, expecting so much of them, looking to them as potentially definitive or clarifying, we are hurt by their equivocal nature or because the ear, as a *psychic* organ, is at least as vulnerable as the eye. What is unclear about the first hypothesis is why we should expect so much of words. This overestimation, which may turn of course into its opposite, into contempt of talk, can suggest that words themselves caused the hurt we still feel, as we look to them for restitution or comfort. (Where there is a word cure, there must be a word-wound.) I prefer, initially, the other way of stating our hypothesis, that within the economy of the psyche the ear is peculiarly vulnerable or passes through phases of vulnerability. The "cell of Hearing, dark and blind," Wordsworth writes in *On the Power of Sound,* is an "Intricate labyrinth, more dread for thought / To enter than oracular cave."

Every literary interpreter and some psychoanalysts enter that cave when they follow the allusive character of words, their intentional or unintentional resonance. "Strict passage," Wordsworth continues, describing the auditory labyrinth, "through which sighs are brought, /

And whispers for the heart, their slave." Othello's speech fills Desdemona's ear: "[She'd] with a greedy ear / Devour up my discourse." There exists a lust of the ears as strong and auspicious as the lust of the eyes about which so much has been written since Saint Augustine. The two are, doubtless, interactive: the Story of the Eye (as in George Bataille's pornosophic novella of that title) always turns out to be, also, the Story of the Ear. But whereas "the ineluctable modality of the visible" (Joyce) has been explored, especially by analysts interested in primal-scene imagery, the ineluctable ear, its ghostly, cavernous, echoic depth, has rarely been sounded with precision.

Wordsworth's phrase "strict passage" points to the "constricted" or narrowing, and therefore overdetermined, character of the sounds that make it through, but also to a moral dilemma. The ear must deal with sounds that not only cannot be refused entry, but penetrate and evoke something too powerful for any defense: Wordsworth depicts it as akin to sexual lust or the intoxication of a blood sport, "shrieks that revel in abuse / Of shivering flesh." The *percé-phonic* power of poetry, song, or music to undo this wounding, "warbled air, / Whose piercing sweetness can unloose / The chains of frenzy, or entice a smile / Into the ambush of despair," suggests a sweet piercing that counters or sublimates a bitter one.[1]

"Chains of frenzy" tells us how close we are to the theme of madness; "the ambush of despair," how close to depression. Moreover, to "entice a smile / Into the ambush of despair" is ambiguous, and "unloose / The chains of frenzy" has a double-negative effect that may undermine rather than reinforce the idea of a liberating cure. These phrases, like the ear itself, are constricted; and even should we attribute them to the highly condensed diction of the Pindaric ode Wordsworth is imitating, this merely rehearses the entire problem, and does not bring us a step forward. For while imitation can be therapeutic it can also be compulsive, or expressive of a word-wound that still binds the hearer. At this point, obviously, clinical material on the relation of word and wound should be adduced; not being a clinician, I shall fall back on literary examples.

NAMES AND WOUNDS

> No wound, which warlike hand of enemy
> Inflicts with dint of sword, so sore doth light
> As doth the poysnous sting, which infamy
> Infixeth in the name of noble wight.

So Spenser, in the sixth book of *The Faerie Queene,* alluding to the wound inflicted by the Blatant Beast, enemy to courtesy and an allegory for slander.

Psychology and anthropology agree on the importance of the motif of the *wounded name.* To achieve a good name, or to maintain it, has been a motivating force in both heroic and bourgeois society. Fiction corresponds to life in at least one respect, that slander and rumor—hearsay more than sightsay—determine the drama of errors that besets reputation. A peculiar and powerful theory of what it means to redress a wounded name is developed by Jean-Paul Sartre. He speculates that his contemporary Jean Genet, a convict turned writer, fashioned his identity out of a "dizzying word" addressed to him when he was a young boy.

The word was a vocative, an insult, a common malediction like "You thief!" flung at him by a foster parent. It is said to have made Genet aware of his radically disinherited state. Genet was an illegitimate child; his mother too was a thief, or of the insulted and despised. That word, therefore, became a call, a vocation, which not only helped to establish a negative identity for Genet but redeemed that of his mother through him. A chance remark becomes, in Kierkegaard's words, "the infernal machine which sets fire to the tinder which is in every soul" (*Journals* of 1837). Genet grows up a thief, a homosexual, a powerful writer with his own magnificat and gospel: John ("Jean") becomes Saint John. The connections are very complex, and it takes Sartre a voluminous and immensely dialectical book to account for what happened.[2]

I am interested more in the elements that go into the theory than in the exact truth-value of the theory itself. What in Sartre's view wakes the child to the problem of identity is not a sight, an ocular fixation as in the famous case of Augustine's friend Alypius, but an aural experience.[3] Moreover, in verbal structure what Genet hears is a vocative, and ritually it approaches an act of nomination or even annunciation. Identity is bestowed on Genet by a ghostly scene of naming, a curse that is taken to be an act of grace.

Genet, then, is word-wounded by the insult or curse, but he makes it into an identity badge through a psychic reflex, and then through a lifelong fixation. And the tinder, the inflammable material rendering him vulnerable, is the very absence of an authentic name—an absence that provokes endless fillers or substitutes.

"You thief!"—only one such filler—happens to suggest that Genet must *steal* a name if he is to own one. For Genet is a name that points to the absence of a proper name: it is the mother's surname and suggests moreover a figurative origin because it is a "flower of speech." Genet, that is, takes *genêt* ("broom flower," Leopardi's *ginestra*) and turns it via his ritualistic and flower-name-laden novels into a literal figure; into something truly his own.

"Flowers of speech" is a designation for the figures or metaphors that characterize literary discourse and distinguish it from apparently straighter or more scientific kinds of writing. Genet links figurative language, or flowers of speech, with the "language of flowers," or the principle of euphemistic and courtly diction. He depicts what are criminal events in the eyes of bourgeois society in a sublime and flowery style. No one is deceived, of course: the reader sees through to the sordid wound and understands this inverse magnificat.

Yet Genet steals back his name less to magnify himself than to magnify the absent mother, or rather mother tongue. His name, elaborated, founds an artificial diction that is his only source of healing and salvation.[4] This stealing back of a name is not as naïve or exceptional as it seems, for those who have a name may also seek a more authentic and defining one. The *other* name is usually kept secret precisely because it is sacred to the individual, or numinous (*nomen numen*): as if the concentrated soul of the person lodged in it. A perilous or taboo relation may arise between the given (baptismal) name and the truly "proper" name, and then a psychic search unfolds for this hidden word under all words, this spectral name.[5] It is a quest that often leads to the adoption of pseudonyms and nicknames, and even to anonymity. So Malcolm Little erases his family name by an X curiously like the mark of the illiterate slave yet which he endows with a redemptive meaning:

> The Muslim's "X" symbolized the true African family name that he never could know. For me, my "X" replaced the white slave-master name of "Little" which some blue-eyed devil named Little had imposed upon my paternal forebears. The receipt of my "X" meant that forever after in the nation of Islam, I would be known as Malcolm X. Mr. Muhammad taught that we would keep this "X" until God Himself returned and gave us a Holy Name from His own mouth.[6]

Twelve years later Malcolm gives himself that name, or a likeness of it from his own mouth, when he calls himself, having gone on a pilgrimage to Mecca, El-Hajj Malik El-Shabazz.

NAMES AGAINST WOUNDS

> I would to God thou and I knew where a
> commodity of good names were to be bought.
> —*William Shakespeare,* Henry IV, Pt. 1, I.ii.80–81

"Call me Ishmael." We don't know the original name of Melville's storyteller. Perhaps there is no original name; or it is extirpated, like Pierre's family name by the end of the novel *Pierre.* Only the act of self-naming is apparent. Yet the adopted name is not empty, of course: if not as grand as Malcolm's, it still points East, to the Orient or the Oriental tale, to a lost origin, or a compelled sympathy with exile and alien.

Ishmael, the ending of which rhymes (at least approximately) with the first syllable of Melville's name, may evoke the homophonic word *male.* The trouble with this kind of rhyming, this illness of the ear, as W. H. Auden once defined poetry itself, is its infectiousness. What if *Melville,* when heard with *Ishmael,* elicits further echoes? Male(v)ill, Male Will? Or should the ear pick the assonance of *el* as the deceptive key, in its Hebrew meaning of "God" and its Arabic force as definitive article: the *the?*

Though names, then, may be medicinal, they are never simples. Yet the class of proper nouns, or names, comes closest to having the magical force of certain herbs called *simples.* Why should that be?

An observation of Saussure's on the semiotic structure of names may be relevant. Whereas ordinary nouns, *table* and *chair,* not only point to a referent in the world of things but rely on a concept of table and chair in order to signify, names seem to be pure signifiers that have only a referent (the indicated person or place) but no concept or signified. We cannot conceptualize names unless we make them into trade names (like Kodak) or type names (as by calling a woman a Griselda).[7]

Naming does have a spectral dimension if we seek to perpetuate someone by calling a child after that person. (It makes the child a *revenant,* Freud said). A gap opens, nevertheless, between name and meaning; and this is clearest in etymological speculation, extending from Isidore of Seville or the *Legenda Aurea* (*Golden Legends of the Saints*) with their beautiful and fantastic elaboration of the meaning of saints' names, to Derrida's punning transformation of *Hegel* (the philosopher's name) into *aigle* (the bird's name).

This would suggest that words become magical the closer they move to the status of pure signifiers or name equivalents. Approaching the character of an "acoustical image" (Saussure), names accrue the mystery or magic of an *Open Sesame.* We can make believe that there exists a naming formula, anagram, or password to pierce the opacity of our ignorance and open the treasure house of meaning.

Perhaps the second-order discourse we call "metalanguage"—terms of art, explanatory or classifying schemes, words about words—aspires to the same magic, that of pure signification. Here Linnaeus, who established the Latin nomenclature for plants and animals in his *Systema Naturae* (1735; 10th ed., adding animals to plants, 1758), was crucial. The virtue of flowers (birds, etc.) joined with the virtue of Latin to produce a (re)naming of all creatures in a manner at once scientific and fantastic. The Latin appellation, in its very strangeness and strictness, merely succeeded in putting the vernacular name of the creatures in relief and so induced a more complex verbal consciousness, a doubling of signifying systems: the Latinate order (itself binominal in Linnaeus) as well as the common language designation. But the wound inflicted on language, through this propagation of names, analogous to the wound inflicted by Linnaeus's discovery of sexual characteristics in plants (on which his nomenclature was partially based, and which gave a shock to the "language of flowers")—this wound proved fortunate in some respects. The new, more complex name could be used as a stronger potion for the perturbed spirit. Take the liturgy of Christopher Smart, who, aware of Linnaeus, impresses the various names of the creatures as if to heal language itself after its fall from simplicity:

> Let Shallum rejoice with Mullein Tapsus barbatus good for the breast.
> For the liturgy will obtain in all languages.
>
> Let Johnson, house of Johnson rejoice with Omphalocarpa
> a kind of bur. God be gracious to Samuel Johnson.
>
> Let Adna rejoice with Gum Opopanax from the wounded root
> of a species of panace Heracleum a tall plant growing to be
> two or three yards high with many large wings of a yellowish
> green—good for old coughs and asthmas.[8]

I don't think we can know the "smart" that "Christopher" bore, except to say on the evidence of the text before us that it had to do with his sense of "existimation," a word that seems to conflate *exist, estimate,* and *esteem.* "For my existimation is good even among the slanderers and my memory shall arise for a sweet savor unto the Lord." The wound dressed or redressed is associated with naming, and this would not exclude, of course, the "smart" of love or the "smart" use of words to achieve or reestablish reputation.

So naming and the problem of identity cannot be dissociated. So literature and the problem of identity cannot be dissociated. Literature is at once onomatopoeic (name-making) and onomatoclastic (name-breaking). The true name of a writer is not given by his signature, but is spelled out by his entire work. The bad or empty name or nickname may be countered by the melodious or bardic magic of art:

> There is nothing in a name. The name Menschikoff, for instance, has nothing in it to my ears more human than a whisker, and it may belong to a rat. As the names of the

> Poles and Russians are to us, so are ours to them. It is as if they had been named by the child's rigmarole, *Iery wiery ichery van, tittle-tol-tam.* . . . At present our only true names are nicknames . . . We have a wild savage in us, and a savage name is perchance somewhere recorded as ours. . . . I seem to hear pronounced . . . [the] original wild name in some jaw-breaking or else melodious tongue. [Thoreau, *Walking,* 1862]

"LOOK WITH THINE EARS" (*KING LEAR*)

The motif of the wounded name, which at first seemed rather special, leads into the crucial problem of self-identity and its relation to art and writing. But let us also consider the issue from the reader's point of view.

It may prove hard to say anything definitive about the capacity of words to wound. Or about the obverse effect, their medicinal, defensive qualities. The whole theory of defenses, originated by Freud, is involved in metaphor, and becomes ever more elaborate. Moreover, we have to recognize that hearing—a receptive and, as overhearing, involuntary act—is already within the sphere of hurt. We are in bondage to our ears as to our eyes. We are all like Shakespeare's Emilia in *Othello* (V.ii) when it comes to the aggressing power of words. Emilia to Iago: "Thou hast not half that power to do me harm / As I have to be hurt." That statement is itself a converted threat and suggests how much depends on hearing what is said in what is being said.

Yet this is where the study of literature enters. Reading is, or can be, an active kind of hearing. We really do "look with ears" when we read a book of some complexity. A book has the capacity to put us on the defensive, or make us envious, or inflict some other narcissistic injury. When literary critics remark of literature, "There's magic in the web," they characterize not only what distinguishes the literary from the merely verbal, but what distinguishes critical from passive kinds of reading. Critical reading, then, which almost always leads to writing, allows us to estimate words as words, to use rather than abuse their effective powers, to determine as well as be determined by them. These things are obvious, and I feel preachy repeating them; but too often we conceive of reading as a scrutiny or content or form rather than more generally of the status of words in the psyche and the environing culture.

What active reading discloses is a structure of *words within words,* a structure so deeply mediated, ghostly, and echoic that we find it hard to locate the *res* in the *verba.* The *res,* or subject matter, seems to be already words. Even images, as Freud noticed in his analysis of dreams, turn out to have the form of a *rebus,* or words (parts of words) that appear in the disguise of things. These reified verbal entities must then be translated back into the original sounds, like a charade. But words themselves, of course, may reify, by being taken too literally or absolutely. Psychoanalysis, with its emphasis on the overdetermined or ambivalent symbol, and semiotics, with its disclosure of the radical obliquity of signification, undertake to correct that abuse.

Writing and reading of the active sort are certainly homeopathic vis-à-vis the "wound" left by literalism *and* the "wound" that that literalism seeks to cure: equivocation. The search for the absolute word, or minimally for the *mot juste,* is like that for the good name. There is bound to be a noncorrespondence of demand and response: an inadequacy or lack of mutuality that relates to our drive to make words into things. However precise words may seem, there is always understatement or overstatement, and each verbal action involves itself in redressing that imbalance.

NOTHING AS THE MOT JUSTE

Take Cordelia's famous "nothing," which initiates one of the bloodiest of Shakespeare's plays. It is only ponderable when we think about the status of words. Cordelia exercises, of course, her power of nonreceiver, of not responding to a "Speak" that would enjoin the very words to be spoken. But within this paralegal situation her "Nothing" raises a more basic issue. Lear wants to exchange power for love; initially, words of power for words of love. Cordelia's reply contains not only a judgment that the quality of love cannot be constrained but that there may be something disjunctive in language itself that makes such an exchange—or reversal, if Lear, who wants to "crawl unburdened toward death," desires a licensed regression to childhood—as unlikely as reconciling love and power in the real world. Lear's fiat, his quasi-divine command, remains naked of response, therefore; and since the original fiat in *Genesis* was answered not only by obedience ("Let there be. . . . And there was") but also by recognition and blessing ("And God saw it was good," "And God blessed. . . ."), Cordelia's "nothing" has, in its very flatness, the ring of a curse.

Lear gives all, Cordelia nothing. The disproportion is too great. In Lear's view, order itself is threatened, and his great rage is just. But order, here, is the order of words, the mutual bonding they establish. Lear is asking no more than his daughter's blessing; which is, moreover, his one guarantee in a situation where he is about to divest himself. And instead of word-issue Cordelia utters something that sounds as sterile to him (for "nothing will come of nothing") as a malediction. It is painful to recall how much of the ensuing drama is curse, rant, slander, and impotent fiat:

> Hear, Nature, hear: dear goddess, hear:
> Suspend thy purpose if thou didst intend
> To make this creature fruitful.
> Into her womb convey sterility,
> Dry up in her the organs of increase,
> And from her derogate body never spring
> A babe to honor her
>
> (I.iv.265–270)

> You nimble lightnings, dart your blinding flames
> Into her scornful eyes! Infect her beauty,
> You fensucked fogs drawn by the pow'rful sun
> To fall and blister
>
> (II.iv.160–163)

> Blow winds, and crack your cheeks! rage! blow!
>
> (III.ii.1)

Cordelia's "nothing" proves to be sadly prophetic. It exhibits the power of words in seeming to deny them.[9] As such it may be representative of all word-wounds, given or suffered, as they approach the status of *curse* or the incapacity to *bless.* Our speculations are becoming a shade more definitive.

CURSE AND BLESSING

> "I will not let thee go, except thou bless me." And he said unto him, "What is thy name?"
> —Gen. 1:32.27–28

> [He] in the porches of mine ears did pour
> The leperous distilment
> —*William Shakespeare,* Hamlet I.v.63–64

Curse and Blessing are among the oldest types of formalized speech. Like oaths and commandments, to which they are akin, they seek to bind the action of those to whom they are addressed, yet unlike oaths or commandments they are resorted to when legal instruments are not appropriate or have failed. Legal codes may contain curses as a reinforcement or obversely seek to limit a curse—but it is clear that curse and blessing have a psychological aspect, as well as a legal or ritual role.

Supposing the psyche demands to be cursed or blessed—that it cannot be satisfied, that it cannot even exist as a namable and conscious entity—as ego or self—except when defined by direct speech of that kind, then we have a situation where the absence of a blessing wounds, where the presence of a curse also wounds, but at least defines.

Perhaps direct speech itself is the problem here, the desire for a fiat, an absolute speech act. The evil eye, for instance, as in *The Rime of the Ancient Mariner*— the "glittering" eye or "stony eyes / That in the moon did glitter"—is surely a curious form of that direct speech which is so condensed that *sema* is *soma.* (Perhaps all "images" have a similar structure.) It "shoots" with as unerring an effect as the crossbow with which mariner killed albatross. Time is punctured in this poem of intolerable moments of stasis, which also features as its speaker a constricted persona. Curse is primary, blessing secondary; the one must be drawn out of the other, like story and story time out of a negative and arresting fiat. The very desire for a fiat is at the heart of this compulsive narrative, with its fitlike motion.

I have inferred a verbal cause, or placed the wound in the word. But it turns out that by *wounding* I mean principally the expectation that a self can be defined or constituted by words, if they are direct enough, and the traumatic consequences of that expectation.[10] To quote from *Othello* once more, "The bruised heart was pierced through the ear." Moreover, because the demand to be cursed or blessed stems from the same source, and life is as ambivalent in this regard as words are equivocal, the psyche may have to live in perpetual tension with its desire to be worded. It may turn against as well as toward words. The equivocations put into the mouth of Shakespeare's clowns or fools are, thus, a babble that breaks language down because it cannot draw a "just" or "definitive" statement out of the crying need to curse or bless or to do both at once.

> Do you *hear* how Fury sounds her blessings forth?
>
> (Aeschylus, *Eumenides*)[11]

Lear opens with something like a curse, a decreating as well as a deflating word. Ordinary language, influenced perhaps by literary stereotypes, teaches us to think of "a father's curse" and "a mother's blessing." It is as if the action of *Lear* strove toward "a mother's blessing" but could attain only "a father's curse."

Shakespeare, in fact, is so puissant because he is explicit, because everything becomes utterable as direct speech. There is an Aeschylean and cathartic quality in him that is absent from most other poets. The defining wound is always before us, in every brazen word. And the dramatic action is as direct as the words. When Edgar, disguised as Tom o' Bedlam, meets Gloucester, his blind and beggared father, he utters a foolish cry that manages to word a terrible wound: "Bless thy sweet eyes, they bleed" (*King Lear* IV.i.54).

This outrageous pun, one of several about eyes, suggests on the basis of a link between *blessing* and *bleed* (the etymological meaning of *blessing* is "to mark with blood in order to hallow") that *since* the eyes bleed, *therefore* are they blessed. Shakespeare moves repeatedly toward imagining the worst in the form of a divestment, a making naked, a making vulnerable, of which one symbol is this castration of the eyes. But when Shakespeare calls on that darkness, in his play's general *fiat nox,* the curse the action labors under can still generate a bearable blessing.

Blessing and curse, euphemism and slander, praise and blame undermine statement. However neutral or objective words seem to be, there is always a tilt of this kind produced by the very effort to speak. There are those who must curse in order to speak, and those who must bless in order to speak: some interlard their words with obscenities, some kill them with kindness expressions. These are the extreme cases that suggest how close we are to muteness: to not speaking at all unless we untangle these contrary modes. Their tension is, for the purpose of literature at least, more basic than any other; and it needs no witch doctor or psychiatrist to tell us that despite our will to bring forth unambiguous issue, words that point one way rather than the other, we remain in an atmosphere as equivocal as that of the witches' chorus in *Macbeth:* "Fair is foul and foul is fair / Hover through the fog and filthy air."

Let me also refer to Aeschylus's *Eumenides:* how, by a retrospective myth, it founds a city-state on a transfiguration of the cursing principle. The judicial process instituted by Athena is merely a breathing space or asylum in the play, like the navel stone or her idol. The real issue is the breathless rush of the Furies, unremitting, unrelenting.

> We are the everlasting children of the Night,
> Deep in the hall of Earth they call us Curses.

The final chorus, therefore, has to convert the Curses into an energy that is equal and contrary. It must honor the Furies in terms they understand, which affirms them in their onrush, their dark and eternal function:

> You great good Furies, bless the land with kindly hearts,
> You awesome Spirits, come—exult in the blazing torch,
> exultant in our fires, journey on.
> Cry, cry in triumph, carry on the dancing on and on!

FLOWERS OF SPEECH

How thoroughly the human condition is a verbal condition! The medicinal function of literature is to word a wound words have made. But if we have learned something about the limit of poet as medicine man, we have also learned something about the limit of all verbal expression. Objectivity in language is always a form of "You great good Furies": a neutralizing or musicalizing of badmouthing. The very production of speech may depend on a disentangling of blessing and curse, on the outwitting of that eternal complex. Everything we say has to bind the Furies in the fetters of benevolence. Flowers of speech, as Baudelaire made explicit (laying the ground for Genet), are also flowers of evil. These equivocal flowers or figures characterize the literary use of language.

I give two examples of how a great writer outwits the intolerable tension of curse and blessing and founds a language of his own that enables, and sometimes disables, ours.[12]

In *Finnegans Wake* James Joyce's (or Jeems Joker's, as he signed himself) hero is HCE. This acronym, though given various interpretations, may be a truncated reversal of E-C-H-O, reinforcing HCE's name of "Earwicker." The ear does become ineluctable in this book, which is the extended ballad of *Perce-Oreille.* Joyce methodically exposes the vulnerable ear by showing the unvirginal or contaminated state of language. In his "mamafesta" no phrase remains simple. Sexual innuendo subverts or thickens every sentence, as it often does in Shakespeare. Words *are* jokes: they betray their compound or compoundable nature; they are not from eternity but rather created and adulterated, of equivocal generation, beautiful in corruption. "In the name of Annah the Allmaziful, the Everliving, the Bringer of Plurabilities, haloed be her eve, her singtime sung, her rill be run, unhemmed as it is uneven!"

Yet here the wounded name is joyfully plural. Language has suffered a fortunate fall ("O fortunous casualitas"). Blasphemy is reconciled with good humor, and lust sings in obscene echoes that perpetually hollow and hallow this prose, as in the following "joycing" of the language of flowers:

> Bulbul, bulbulone! I will shally. Thou shalt willy. You wouldnt should as youd rememser. I hypnot. 'Tis golden sickle's hour. Holy moon priestess, we'd love our grappes of mistellose! Moths the matter? Pschtt! Tabarins comes. To fell our fairest. O gui, O gui! Salam, salms, salaum! Carolus! . . . I soared from the peach and Missmolly showed her pear too, onto three and away. Whet the bee as to deflowret greendy grassies yellowhorse. Kematitis, cele our erdours! Did you aye, did you eye, did you everysee suchaway, suchawhy, eeriewhigg airywhugger?

An ancient belief held that there was in nature a "general balm" (John Donne, "A Nocturnal upon St. Lucie's Day") with the virtue of sealing all wounds. A related group of superstitions considered excretions like sweat or blood or even excrement as therapeutic. Joyce releases into language a "Thinking of the Body" that would be unthinkable but for a language of flowers. Literature sweats balm, and heals the wound words help to produce.

My second example is an episode from *King Lear.* In act IV, scene vi, Lear enters "fantastically dressed with wild flowers." The scene is marked by ear-piercing puns as well as moments of terrible pathos. At one point Lear's rambling language, itself tricked out with wild figures, culminates in the dialogue:

> LEAR. . . . Give the word.
> EDGAR. Sweet marjoram.
> LEAR. Pass.

What is being reenacted by Lear in his traumatized and defenseless condition is a type-scene of defense: getting past sentinel or guard. Also being reenacted is the first scene of the tragedy, his command to Cordelia, the "speak" that led to "nothing." But Edgar plays along, and the password he gives is taken from a language of flowers close to the mother tongue: "sweet marjoram." Literature, as figurative language, extends that password.

THE LANGUAGE EXCHANGE

> The stutter is the plot.
> —*Charles Olson,* on Melville's *Billy Budd*

Edgar's word *recognizes* the game Lear plays; its meaning resides in this act of recognition rather than in its semantic appropriateness. It is not quite a nonsense word, but almost any word would have done. That it is drawn from the language of flowers converts the royal, now all-too-human, challenge into a childlike game, like riddle or charade. Infancy is close: the king still leads, but as "His Majesty, the child." That *marjoram* is a near-palindrome, related to vernacular feelings or beliefs, aids this sense of a redemptive word that has retained a link with childhood. To keep talking, in this situation, is to allow Lear not only to keep up appearances but to maintain a trust in words themselves. *La séance continue.*

Such speech acts remind us how much responsibility falls on the respondent, on the interpreter. Dialogue itself is at stake, and the medium becomes the meaning at this crucial point. Literary speech, quite obviously, is not eloquent for the sake of eloquence; if eloquence plays a part, it is because mutism, the failure to speak or to trust in speech, is never far from the deceptive flow of words. Every strong instance of verbal condensation is as much a stutterance as an utterance and skirts aphasia, like a riddle.

A word, then, on riddles. Do they provoke a response or silence? Riddles divide into a silent and pointed part (the presumed answer) and a periphrastic and expressed part. They have been called a simple form (A. Jolles), but they are rarely found except as components of developed and complex literary structures. Lear's "Give the word" is like the demand of the sphinx, and yet very unlike, since the implied riddle is so general (life as the mystery, Lear's fate as the mystery) that any word of recognition, or response, might do. We realize that even in less pathetic circumstances this contradiction between word as meaning and word as act of speech prevails. For do we not address many situations with words that are essentially passwords: signs of obeisance or identity or mutual recognition? When Lear tests Cordelia and her sisters, the word he demands, the giving of it, seems all too easy. A verbal satisfaction is necessary, as in a rite of passage; and the link between survival and readiness of speech is publicly affirmed.

Wit, the presence of mind in words, is the opposite of a failure to speak. Yet wit, pointed or periphrastic, is often felt as a wounding of language, of "natural" language. Wit is called for in moments when words might fail as meanings: when the code is unknown, or when it is in such danger of devaluation that it must be rescued by surcharge. Love produces such dangerous moments. It beggars words, as Cordelia knows, yet it continues to demand them. The language of love can become, therefore, a cliché, as in the periphrastic language of flowers; or it can fall pointedly silent.

Goethe's commentary on his own *West-East Divan* (imitations of Oriental poetry) includes a section entitled "Exchange of Flowers and Signs" ("*Blumen- und Zeichenwechsel*"). The flowery diction associated with Oriental style is shown to be a necessity rather than a luxury. It brings things and words into a single system of signs, and so facilitates the exchange of feelings. The diction, or lover's discourse, is established in the following way. The lover sends a gift to the beloved who must pronounce its name and figure out which among the rhymes of the word designating the received object completes the message and solves the riddle. "Amarante: Ich sah und brannte" (Amaranth: I saw and burned). "Jasmin: Nimm mich hin" (Jasmin: Take me with you). "Seide: Ich leide" (Silk: I suffer).

It is not possible—though Goethe refuses to say so openly—to guarantee this private code, for the code is always in the process of being established. It depends on a twofold gift: that of flower or precious object and of the responsive word ("Give the word"). Thus the skill or will of the interpreter is essential: the skill in playing, the will to find or else to impose a meaning. Goethe calls this literary game a "passionate divination." It brings ear and wit into play and may occasionally create a short novel by the establishing of a "correspondence"—Goethe means, probably, of word and thing, of word and rhyming word, as well as of the feelings of the lovers in a letterlike exchange.

There are analogies here to the interpretive situation generally. Emily Dickinson could call her poems "my letter to the world"; so the literary text or artifact is a gift for which the interpreter must find words, both to recognize the gift and, then, to allow it to create a reciprocating dialogue, one that might overcome the embarrassment inspired by art's riddling strength.

Goethe does not develop these analogies; nor does he explore an important contradiction. Each exchange of things and words involves a private language that at its limit is intuited; and each exchange involves the contrary, a public and highly stylized word system. He simply apposes these two aspects: In the next section of his commentary on the *Divan,* entitled "Codes" ("*Chiffer,*" literally "Ciphers"), he reports how in Germany around 1770 the Bible was so crammed into educated youth that many were able to use it wittily to "consume Holy Writ in conversation." It was possible, therefore, to make a date with a book (*ein Buch verabreden*), that is, by a ciphered system of allusions to make it the textual intermediary to a secret rather than open exchange of thoughts. This conversion of a public system of signs into a sort of *trobar clus* also enters Goethe's section on the exchange of flowers and words, for Goethe suggests there that the "passionate divination" he has described could return to the speechlessness in which it began: the silence not of embarrassment, concealment, or evasion, but of perfect divinatory understanding. "Lovers go on a pleasure trip of several miles and spend a happy day together; returning home they amuse themselves with charades. Not only will each guess immediately what is intended as soon as it is spoken, but finally even the word that the other has in mind, and intends to cast into the form of a verbal puzzle, will be anticipated and pronounced by immediate divination."

How much Goethe takes for granted! That love needs secrecy and a code, or a special system for exchanging tokens and thoughts, is not explicitly related by him to any psychic or social condition (to the danger of persecution, for example, or the sense of self-esteem). He describes what is, not the reason for it, since this Eastern phenomenon is understandable in the West, and has its own parallels there. Goethe is valuing established genres as archetypes or primal phenomena. He does not wish to repristinate or orientalize what is current in the West, because his understanding can divine the same pattern there without an explanatory or analytic scheme. He sees the genre in the idea of it.

Yet this intuitive procedure (Goethe sometimes called it *Anschauung*) papers over the problematic breach between private and public language, as between intuition and expression. It is necessary to reflect that the happiness associated with being intuitive, with the intimacy of understanding or being understood, may be the obverse of not being understood, or of having been understood and betrayed. Betrayal, breach of promise, breach of trust, misunderstanding, misinterpretation, persecution—these are equal realities. The more intimacy, the more potential misery. Goethe's "correspondence"—the exchange and the system of meaning built on it—cannot be guaranteed, intellectually or socially. It is always a dangerous liaison.

One should not talk of understanding, therefore, as if it were a matter of rules or techniques that become intuitive and quasi-silent. There is, of course, an internalization; but the life-situation of the interpreter has to deal with riddles as well as puzzles: what is sought is often the readiness to take and give words in trust, rather than the answer to a problem. "Language," Iris Murdoch writes, summarizing Sartre, "is that aspect of me which, in laying me open to interpretation, gives me away." Troth rather than truth: the ability to exchange thoughts in the form of words; to recognize words of the other; or to trust in the words to be exchanged. One breaks words with the other as one breaks bread. What is guaranteed by recognition, in the political sphere too, is the language exchange itself.

The art of divination Goethe describes can indeed be cultivated by parlor games whose purpose is to diminish shyness or strangeness. But this parleying aspires to recognition and not to absolute knowledge; and indeed, there is much to be said against being known by others. The other's words, which may be riddling—inherently so, if words are not subject to pure anticipated cognition—these words are allowed to create a value by means of our own reception, by our formal willingness to interpret them. Each transaction consists of exchanging words for words as well as sounding out the words in words.

Partial knowledge is the *normal* condition, then, of living in the context of words. Words themselves help us tolerate that state: recognition must precede as well as follow cognition. To put the entire emphasis on the cognitive function (*connaissance*) will damage the recognitive function (*reconnaissance*) and the language exchange as a whole. Values continue to be created that may seem purely ritual, or not entirely perspicuous. Even when art represents a movement from ignorance to knowledge, it is not for the sake of clearing up a simple misunderstanding or emending the human mind in an absolute manner. Tragedy, for instance, hinges on a mistake that questions the very possibility of language exchange: in the case of Oedipus, a human understanding mistakes the language of the gods. Oedipus is faced with an oracular statement that forces interpretation to go blind, to stumble along by means of tense, stichomythic exchanges, "epitaphic comments, conflictingly spoken or thought" (Melville, *The Confidence Man,* chap. 2). The oracular allows no development, no capacious response.

Or tragedy flows from a scene of nonrecognition, deliberate rather than resulting from ignorance or mischance. In Faulkner's *Absalom, Absalom!* Sutpen (unlike King David, who laments aloud over his estranged son, calling him by name) refuses to recognize a son of mixed blood, to accord him the honor of the family name. That nonrecognition may expose its victim to the elements, to a position outside the law. The very possibility of having one's words regarded may then be lost.

Simple misunderstandings are not the proper topic for comedy, either, and barely for jokes. Jokes based on mistaking the sense of words produce a forced laughter; to be effective, they must be deliberate and dangerous *jests,* and so they skirt tragedy again. Therefore, in *Love's Labour's Lost,* Berowne is sentenced by his lady Rosaline to a year's jesting in a hospital ("to move wild laughter in the throat of death"), so that his indiscriminate mockery, his "wounding flouts," may heal instead of hurt, or, proving impotent, will be self-cured. In a jest the laughter is ultimately on words: at the expense of language that can't and must be trusted.

Trusting and words: there is a scene of passionate divination in Tolstoy's *Anna Karenina* (part 4, chap. 13). Levin is together with Kitty, who had rejected him at the time when she was in love with Vronsky. Their conversation turns on the vanity of arguments and what causes them to end so suddenly. Levin explains his theory to Kitty, who "completely grasped and found the right expression for his badly expressed thought. Levin smiled joyfully: he was so struck by the change from the confused wordy dispute with his brother and Pestov to this laconic, clear and almost wordless communication of a very complex ideal." Kitty then goes to a table covered by a green cloth in preparation for a game of cards and begins drawing on it in chalk. Levin wants to propose to her a second time, and is afraid to do so in so many words; yet he must find the words. A private game follows in which he chalks on the same cloth the initials of the words he wishes to utter; she divines them and answers with initials of her own. He takes the lead, but Kitty overtakes him; and though the initials are a kind of stutter, because of Kitty's intuitiveness the potentially hurtful words are twice-born, and the language exchange is restored:

> He sat down and wrote out a long sentence [in the code]. She understood it all, and without asking if she was right, took the chalk and wrote the answer at once. For a long time he could not make out what she meant, and he often looked up in her eyes. He was dazed with happiness. He could not find the words she meant at all; but in her beautiful eyes, radiant with joy, he saw all that he wanted to know. And he wrote down three letters. But before he had finished writing she read it under his hand, finished the sentence herself, and wrote the answer: "Yes."[13]

INTERPRETATION

> Je m'immisce à de sa confuse intimité.
> —*Stephane Mallarmé*

What I have called, conscious of the metaphor, a word-wound has so far been discussed under two aspects. The word-wound may be real, in the sense of being a wounding word that is actually experienced or fantasied. Lacan launched the clinical myth of a mirror phase or specular image; and I have argued that there exists also the fantasy of a specular or spectral name, which is at once degraded and recalled by the wounding word, its "negative" force of characterization. But there is a second aspect of the word-wound that does not lend itself to empirical evidence, or to the creation of a clinical myth that seems to uncover that evidence. Language itself, in the extruded form of words, their equivocal, fallible, tricky nature, exposes us to continual psychic hurt. There is no pure intuition: the interpreted words remain to be interpreted. There is no complete internalization: words cannot be whited out by truth, because understanding cannot take place without trust or troth. But these are as fragile as the words that commit us to them.

Interpretation, in short, is not only intuitive; it is also counterintuitive. It is not difficult to appreciate this after the advent of psychoanalysis: the analyst may find the "wrong" word or meaning for the gift (dream or artifact) brought by the other.[14] In one contemporary theory, that of Harold Bloom, reading is therefore viewed as misreading and analyzed into a number of richly perverse conformations of text and reader. Interpretation has the same kind of "error" for its subject as tragedy or comedy: not a simple error that can be corrected (though this error also exists), but an inevitable error, whether deliberate or unconscious, arising from an ideal of communication that seeks absolute intimacy.

Kitty's reading of Levin is highly intuitive. Interpretation and intuition converge to produce an exceptional intimacy. But the result is that words become mere tokens. The lovers exchange glances as well as words, and the context points to something beyond speech. Here, as the language exchange is restituted, words are paradoxically left behind.

The reason may be that for Tolstoy there is a religious as well as an erotic intimacy, which bases capable understanding on a preunderstanding associated with benevolence; and between this benevolence and human love there is, ideally, no fissure. (That is why the relation between Anna and Vronsky is so disturbing, so obtrusive: *their* love cannot, does not, remain in the sphere of benevolence.) Levin is shown to be Kitty's scholar from the beginning of the chapter, when he joins the conversation in the drawing room by fulfilling "the promise he had made her, of thinking well of and always liking everybody." Or, to quote from 1 Corinthians 13, "Charity thinketh no evil."

That basic principle of Christian hermeneutics appears dramatically in the opening pages of Melville's *The Confidence-Man.* A mute stranger holds the Corinthian sentence up, chalking it on a slate in its various Pauline versions. He exhibits it adjacent to a placard "offering a reward for the capture of a mysterious impostor, supposed to have recently arrived from the East." A further contrast is furnished by "a gaudy sort of illuminated pasteboard sign" hung up by a barber and reading "NO TRUST."

The Pauline doctrine in 1 Corinthians 13 and 14 contrasts speaking in tongues with prophesying. The former makes use of unknown language, perhaps divine; the latter uses a language equally divine but addressed to the human understanding. Paul seeks to regulate the speaking in tongues rather than to repress it utterly. The problem is put as one of housekeeping or churchkeeping: order, decency, avoiding confusion, building the community are stressed. No tragic epistemic division is suggested between human and divine with regard to language; tongues are known or unknown, and the known is preferred to the unknown because it is "edifying" in its effect. The charity Paul considers more important than speaking in tongues—the charity that, indeed, makes Christian interpretation possible—is applied to the gift of tongues itself.

But in Melville a tragicomic question arises, because there are many tongues and no interpreter. The appearance of the mute stranger and potential interpreter takes place on April Fool's Day, and close to Pentecost. True, the tongues we hear in those opening pages are not tongues precisely in the Pauline sense, but that all speak in a known character is only a semblance, for within it a split has widened to become Babel. Having no interpreter means now the lack of a communitarian or edifying principle. Even the Pauline hermeneutic of charity or benevolence is but one tongue, idiolect, or sociolect. Melville mocks the interpretive and religious principle of charity by having a "gentleman" propose a Society, called the World's Charity, which might levy "one grand benevolence tax upon all mankind" in order to do away with the present system of promiscuous contribution. It sounds like a parody of Tolstoy before Tolstoy—though not before Emerson.

The opposition between Basic Trust (Charity, Benevolence) and No Trust is like that between Blessing and Curse, and it seems unresolvable in a world where imposture is rife. So ambiguity prevails, and all sorts of inscriptions or extruded words jostle each other. The author is no longer Prophet or Interpreter, but the place where this confusion of tongues becomes conscious.

In Tolstoy there is a greater, an almost musical feeling of Basic Trust, which suffers and absorbs contraries and does not worry excessively about the imposture at the very heart of things. It is no accident that the conversation Levin joins concerns itself with communal systems and the "choral principle." The dream of community and the dream of communication are closely linked, perhaps as closely as words and music; yet words are often more jarring, and so Levin remarks, moving toward Kitty and away from the controversy: "What I miss in the country [is] music." The recurrence of music as theme or metaphor (Levin will later find a deeper music in the country) reminds us that interpretation is not an argument that resolves arguments or dissolves words. It brings understanding without agreement, or charts the very space between understanding and agreement.

THE CONSCIOUS EAR

> Semel emissit volat irrevocabile verbum.
> —*Horace*

> I wake
> To caress propriety with odd words.
> —*Geoffrey Hill*

It would take me too far to discuss the different consequences for literature of intuitive and counterintuitive concepts of interpretation. The religious tradition would have to be brought in: both the contemporary developments in hermeneutics and such older issues as inspiration and accommodation. We seem to have no settled concept, at present, of interpreter or critic. The Interpreter was often defined as one who translated strange or unknown tongues into an edifying idiom, or one who could bring contradictory words and aspects of a text into harmony. The critic was often defined as one who distinguished the authentic text from the inauthentic, or authentic from inauthentic in a text. What has happened is that those who call themselves interpreters now claim an edifying or reconciling function even when the language of the text is well known, while the critics adopt a methodically suspicious or doubtful attitude toward the value of every text, secular or sacred. These functions, moreover, mingle confusingly within the same person. At best, as I have suggested, critical readers resist the intuitive and accommodating approach and chart the distance between understanding and agreement: they defer the identification of agreement with truth by disclosing how extensively understanding is indebted to preunderstanding.

If critical reading becomes self-reflective and explores this area of preunderstanding, an embarrassing question arises. Why can't we look into ourselves without the detour of a text? Why does pure self-analysis seem beyond our competence? Some philosophers, including the Heidegger of *Being and Time,* who contributed greatly to defining preunderstanding, actually think it is possible, that there is self-exegesis. But Heidegger saw that even without a text there would be a text, that is, our own reflections in written or writable form; and this suggests, then, that to look into ourselves is always to "look with ears."

To put it differently: critical reading is not only the reception (*Rezeption*) of a text but also its conception (*Empfängnis*) through the ear. No doubt the crossover from silent eye to reactivated ear is partly inspired, partly necessitated, by print culture: Andrew Marvell, celebrating (in imitation of Brebeuf and Lucan) the invention of writing, calls it the ingenious art of "lending an ear to eyes"; Rilke imagines "yeux sonores" in one of his French lyrics. The idea of a conception through the ear counterbalances that of the immediacy of the eye, suggesting an antiocular internalization or transformation: "O Orpheus singt! O hoher Baum im Ohr!" (O Orpheus sings! O tall tree in the ear! [Rilke, *Sonnets to Orpheus*]).

So we substitute one mode of intuition for another. Yet reading, especially in a print culture, is often used to blind the ear. In principle, the Gospel injunction "He that has ears to hear, let him hear" should be facilitated by reading as dissemination (a word I prefer to the evangelical notion of "proclamation" or

Verkündigung), but the sowing of words by means of the written page seems often to harden the ear, as if indeed "when they have heard, Satan comes immediately and takes away the word that was sown in their hearts" (Mark 4:3–20). And that is why poetry makes its curious alliance with critical reading, in order to reactivate the ear. Both are auscultations that have the capacity of putting us on the alert toward the silence in us: the wrongly silenced words as well as the noisy words that get in their way and prevent thoughtfulness. The words of a text, in their silence, are but divining rods to disclose other words, perhaps words of the other.

This movement of discovery is not for the sake of discovery alone, as if a source—a secret source—could magically satisfy the act of reading. There *is* a secret, but it amounts to the fact that words have interiority, that there is always a *sermo interior;* and critical reading allows us to describe that interiority, to estimate words as words, to see them as living in and off us.

Let me concentrate on this recovery of words in their silence. It is by no means a resolving or transcending of the word as wound. The hurtful element in words cannot be removed, because it is at once potential and potentiated: that is, intrinsically associated with an ear that cannot chose but hear, and with *some* actual experience of wounding words. It may be possible to discover the very words, but it is not necessary to do so; what *is* necessary is the assumption that the experience of a word-wound is inevitable and will affect our relation to words generally. Reading, from this point of view, is an activity full of suspense, seeking yet avoiding a penetrating word, a definitive *de te fabula narratur.* The suspense provided by a good plot satisfies that need openly: our wish to find that which is (not) to be heard.

That which is (not) to be heard is a secret. But this secret, in literature, is a formal assumption, even a device to be motivated. The secret as lost object (grail, primal scene, spectral and identifying name, seductive charm) becomes from the aspect of a literary reconstitution of language an *a priori* or intentional rather than imitated object. It has the status of an anticipation, something known, yet not as a direct object; something known as if always already forgotten, and therefore present only preconsciously, absentmindedly. In a psychologistic era, of course, it is tempting to suspect a compulsive or infantile element in the a prior secret. Formalization, moreover, does not help to remove so just a suspicion. For the insistent verbal play, the acrostic, alliterative, cipherlike hide-and-seek that intrigues us in literary texts (the gradation, for example, of O/Orpheus/O/hoher/Ohr in Rilke's verse) provokes an erection of the ear (Rilke's "Tempel im Gehör") by means of nonsensical or spectral sounds.

If like causes like, then words are caused by words, or by something "like" words. Yet a theory of literature cannot simply point to the multiplication and interelaboration of texts. The literary word is a language-sensitive word; and so the question arises what this language-sensitivity may be. Here I return to my initial hypothesis, that the ear is vulnerable, or passes through phases of vulnerability. Its vulnerability is linked—the actual causes being obscure—to real or fantasied words, to an ear-fear connected with overhearing; or to the word as inherently untrustworthy, equivocal, betraying its promise of immediacy or intimacy.

When these two types of vulnerability converge, the effect is especially traumatic, and the ear becomes intolerably conscious. This happens, for instance, when a solecism is thought to have occurred. A specific phrase becomes the focus, one that shocks or shames, and at the same time the very hope of acceptance and intimacy is compromised.

The fear of committing a solecism is probably worse than the fact, but it should not be dismissed because it is so trivial a cause for language-sensitivity. Walter Pater reports in his essay on Prosper Mérimée: "Gossiping friends, indeed, linked what was constitutional in him and in the age with an incident of his earliest years. Corrected for some childish fault, in passionate distress, he overhears a half-pitying laugh at his expense, and has determined, in a moment, never again to give credit—to be for ever on his guard" (*Miscellaneous Studies*). The collocation of gossip, overhearing, a (perhaps) imagined slight or embarrassment, is very distressing: the reaction seems so extreme, and one wonders why Pater gave credit to it. Was it really the solecism or a similar fault, a mere faux pas, that explains it?

Geoffrey Hill's *King Log* (1968) contains a cycle of poems attributed to an apocryphal Spanish poet, "Sebastian Arrurrúz: 1868–1922," who is said to have abandoned society after a solecism was discovered in his first publication. Well, if Pater can choose a French surrogate, Hill can choose a Spanish one; but it may be too easy a way out to characterize as an English disease this "anxiety about *faux pas,* the perpetration of 'howlers,' grammatical solecisms, mis-statements of fact, misquotations, improper attribution."[15] That a national identity is specified is the important fact: it may be a displaced identity, but it confirms that a particular language-centered culture rather than a general sense of honor is involved. The writer's sense for language is so exquisite, so care-ful, that we think he is dealing not with language but with a virginal or sacred object. Henry James had the very same sense of adjacency, in words, of faux pas and fatal step.

Style may be a *continued* solecism. The language-sensitive writer makes the transgression habitual. His cryptic or idiosyncratic manner is an expressive mask. Publication itself is a sort of public self-exposure, fraught with danger to oneself and others. "Infection in the sentence breeds." "Could mortal lip divine / The undeveloped Freight / Of a delivered syllable / 'Twould crumble with the weight" (Emily Dickinson). The casual phrase may contain a carnal blunder. Certain authors, such as Coleridge or Flaubert, exhibit a related or parallel anxiety: that of an uncontrollable stream of consciousness, as in the compulsion to confess or in a nervous seizure. "One feels images escaping like spurts of blood," Flaubert wrote in his letters. When this attack takes the form of words, does it resemble the phenomenon of speaking in tongues?

The word is only "like" a word in these situations: it is divinely stupid or a ghostly sound. It is, precisely, a word that does *not* contain other words, that therefore cannot be translated or interpreted and enter the language exchange. The structure of words within words, while complicating the process of understanding, also founds the possibility of interpretation or of exchanging word for word. To this process, however, there is no bottom, and so no truth in the ordinary sense. Writing goes on and on, and always at risk. "I write, write, write," said Mme Blavatsky, "as the Wandering Jew walks, walks, walks."

One tries to find ways, of course, to allay this infinitude; and these ways constitute what is called closure. But there is also a foreclosure, this glossolalia, that takes words away before they can be profaned by the language exchange. They are withdrawn from circulation as soon as uttered; they are at once elliptic and epileptic. They suggest an intransitive intimacy, or the wish to encrypt in oneself the womb—the maternal (paternal) source—of verbalization. If that is so, we understand better the importance of inner dialogue, of chatter and babble developing into verbal thought. But verbal thought remains a precarious self-probing, as in Gertrude Stein's prose, so close to a beginning that never ends, to an insistently euphemistic and cryptic style that is both a continued solecism and inviolably retiring: "Always then from the beginning there was in me always increasing a conscious feeling loving repeating being, learning to know repeating in every one, hearing the whole being of anyone always repeating in that one every minute of their living. There was then always in me as a bottom nature to me an earthy resisting slow understanding, loving repeating being" (*The Making of Americans*). In the beginning was the Word, and the Word was the loving repeating being, the ticking of the watchful heart, the soft namings of a maternal voice.

NOTES

1. Wordsworth's lines are themselves already allusive: they echo the ending of Milton's *L'Allegro,* the "Cheerful Man," which is paired with the poem *Il Penseroso,* the "Melancholy Man." On "*le nom tout à la fois floral et souterrain de Perséphone* [*percé-phone*]" (Michel Leiris), see Jacques Derrida's "Tympaniser—la philosophie," the overture to his *Marges de la philosophie.*
2. See Jean-Paul Sartre, *Saint Genet: Actor and Martyr,* trans. B. Frechtman (London: Heinemann, 1988). See also chap. 4 in my *Saving the Text.* The obverse theme, that of a "speaking wound," becomes therefore the literary conceit par excellence: it at once offers and negates the possibility of muteness. See Julia's address to Eusebio in Calderón's *Devoción de la Cruz,* or Northumberland's speech to Morton in *Henry IV,* Part 2 (I.iii).
3. Alypius succumbs to a spectacle in the Circus: "As soon as he saw that blood, he drank down savageness with it; he did not turn away but fixed his eye and drank in frenzy unawares, delighted with the guilty combat, intoxicated with the bloody sport" (*Confessions,* book 6, chap. 8). It is significant, however, that his eyes open when he hears the crowd shout. Augustine's own conversion was initiated by a voice, or the aural event *tolle, lege.* See also Hans Robert Jauss, *Aesthetische Erfahrung und literarische Hermeneutik* (Munich: Fink, 1977), pp. 136–60, which defines Alypius' experience as a perverted form of *compassio* (sympathetic identification) and connects it with the role of catharsis in aesthetic experience.
4. Cf. *Saving the Text,* chap. 4. A remarkable account (true or not) of the rejection and countercreation of a mother tongue is found in Louis Wolfson, *Le schizo et les langues.* Kenneth Burke's criticism abounds in speculations on the psycholiterary role of proper names: see, e.g., the remarks on "Thomas" Eliot, and on a character in one of his own stories, in *Attitudes Toward History* (Berkeley: University of California Press, 1959), 1: 109–11 and 2: 108–10.
5. I develop the idea of a spectral name more fully in *Saving the Text,* chap. 4. In applying the idea to Genet I owe a debt to Derrida's *Glas.* Concerning the relation of spectral to "absent" name, cf. Lacan: "The neurotic has been subjected to imaginary castration from the beginning; it is castration that sustains the strong ego, so strong, one might say, that its proper name is an inconvenience for it, since the neurotic is really Nameless" (*Ecrits,* p. 323).
6. From *The Autobiography of Malcolm X,* as told to Alex Haley (New York: Grove Press, 1965), chap. 12.
7. The point can be made in different ways, with different implications. Bertrand Russell says, "Only such proper names as are derived from concepts by means of *the* can be said to have meaning, and such words as *John* merely indicate without meaning." Leo Spitzer remarks in an essay on Villon that (I translate) "there is a poetry inherent in proper nouns . . . one can enjoy a name as *matière sonante,* as the material basis for reverie." Cf. Roland Barthes, "Proust et les noms," in *To Honor Roman Jakobson* (Paris: Mouton, 1967).
8. I excerpt from W. H. Bond's edition of *Jubilate Agno.* To go into the etiology of Smart's disturbance would mean to go beyond the boundary of what is empirical—as Freud did,

toward the end of *Totem and Taboo,* a book as deeply concerned as Smart's poem with the "primal deed" or "primal wound" from which culture may have sprung, and which may still echo in feelings of guilt and ambivalence.

9. Cf. Theodor Reik on psychoanalysis, which "reveals the power of the word and the power of withholding the word, of keeping silent" ("Die psychologische Bedeutung des Schweigens" [1926] in *Wie man Psychologe wird*). Reik's essay is a short yet remarkably comprehensive analysis of the emotional interdependence of *Sprechen* (speaking) and *Schweigen* (keeping silent), and raises the possibility that silence is always, to some degree, deathlike.
10. What is more effective with regard to self-definition—curse or blessing? *The Rime of the Ancient Mariner* shows a man still laboring under a curse, yet promulgating a message of blessing, a good spell. Set against the "merry din" of a marriage feast, the poem seems to affirm, almost as a blessing, our *manque à être:* the peculiarly human sense of incompleteness, of ontic lack and separation from "bird and beast," together with the desire for completion, or rejoining the community of creatures. Perhaps, as Freud surmised, too much of human development takes place outside the womb, so we feel intrinsically premature, untimely separated from sustaining nature.
11. All renderings of Aeschylus are from the Robert Fagles translation of *The Oresteia* (Harmondsworth: Penguin, 1977).
12. The cycle of words and wounds continues, because great writers so often reduce us to muteness, or else require us to echo them deviously. The creative way in which this "curse" of the precursor's greatness weighs on later poets is the subject of Harold Bloom's work on the "anxiety of influence." I should also pay tribute here to Kenneth Burke's concern throughout *The Philosophy of Literary Form* with the connection of art to homeopathic "medicine." The quotations from Joyce's *Finnegans Wake* that follow in the next paragraphs are taken from the definitive eighth edition (New York: Viking, 1958), pp. 44, 175, 104, 360.
13. In quoting Tolstoy I use the Louise and Aylmer Maude translation.
14. See, for example, Freud's sexual interpretation of a dream about flowers, with the result that "the dreamer quite lost her liking for this pretty dream after it had been interpreted." *The Interpretation of Dreams,* chap. 6D.
15. Geoffrey Hill, "Poetry as 'Menace' and 'Atonement,'" *University of Leeds Review* 21 (1978), 66–88—quotation on pp. 72–73. Cf. Christopher Ricks in *Keats and Embarrassment:* "Is embarrassment not only a nineteenth-century sentiment but a narrowly English one?" (Oxford: Clarendon, 1974). Ricks describes the poet's closeness to a heightened consciousness whose effects seem physiological but whose cause is not a specifically social "offense." How this "offense" should be defined involves the imagination as it reveals or risks itself in a conventional circle. See Thomas M. Greene, "*Il Cortegiano* and the Choice of a Game," *Castiglione: The Ideal and the Real in Renaissance Culture,* ed. Robert W. Hanning and David Rosand (New Haven: Yale University Press, 1983), pp. 1–15. The ideal, as Greene states it, is that "nothing will be said . . . which the resilience of this circle [the particular social group] will not contain." Other courtesy books, especially Gracian's *Il Discreto,* also contain hints that these trivia are not trivia: Gracian has a remarkable conversation on the good listener.

In "Manners, Morals, and the Novel" (*The Liberal Imagination*) Lionel Trilling does not deal directly with solecism and deals only in passing with social offense; however, he states the subject of the modern novel as the conflict between "solid" reality and "artificial" manners. In a symposium devoted to him moreover, the question of social offense surfaces in a way that causes Trilling to wonder: "Is the true self in some sense a product of your imaginative reflection on the offense you've given or the forgiveness you've received?" (*Salmagundi* 41 [Spring 1978], 92). Forgiveness, of course, as in Dostoevsky, can itself, when religiously public and fervent, act as a social offense, an insult thrown back at "manners."

Part of the attraction of adopting Basic English as a universal language, C. K. Ogden argues, is that it will reduce to a minimum the "'fear of committing the slightest breach of etiquette' (like the average Englishman when he stumbles over the eccentricities of French gender)." But the subject remains relatively unexplored, even in social history. An exception is J. M. Cuddihy's *Ordeal of Civility*, (New York: Basic Books, 1974), which proposes that a revisionist perspective on culture like Freud's is not only *received* as a solecism on a grand scale, but may have been *based* on Freud's own experience of social offense—on the situation of a Jew among Gentiles. Cf. also Ernst Leisi on code disturbances in *Paar und Sprache* (Heidelberg: Quelle & Mayer, 1978), pp. 119–32.

On the relation of the (family) name to "honor" and the social code, cf. Walter Benjamin, *The Origin of German Tragic Drama* (London: NLB, 1977), p. 87. In Ballanche's *L'homme sans nom* (1820), the regicide-executioner of Louis XIV seeks to expiate his guilt by withdrawing into a state of namelessness.

Cuddihy's view may bear some relation to Van Wyck Brooks's *Ordeal of Mark Twain*, a book that helped to rescue a "bitter" Twain for American studies. Brooks himself was so mortified by a sense of American cultural inferiority that he was relieved to discover that the name of Tolstoy's birthplace, Yasnaya Polyana, was but the equivalent of Plainfield, his own New Jersey hometown. Also of interest is Erving Goffman's *Stigma* (Englewood Cliffs, N.J.: Prentice Hall, 1963), which emphasizes *visual* or *public* traits, although the effect is the same as the one here discussed: "An individual who might have been received easily in ordinary social intercourse possesses a trait that can obtrude itself upon attention and turn those of whom he meets away from him, breaking the claim that his other attributes have on us. He possesses a stigma, an undesired differentness from what we had anticipated" (p. 5). His analysis of "passing" (pp. 73 ff.) suggests that the desire to be accepted, to go from marked to unmarked status, extends over a very large range of relatively normal experiences. This desire, moreover, often complicates life as if it were an intricate novel. So the stutterer dodges certain words, "substituting non-feared words in their places or hastily shifting . . . thought until the continuity of . . . speech becomes as involved as a plate of spaghetti" (cited, p. 89).

Friedrich Schlegel asks laconically, in one of the *Athenaeum* fragments (I translate): "Why is one thing always absent from all fashionable listings of basic moral principles: the Ridiculous [*das Ridicüle*]? Is it because this principle has general validity only in experience [*in der Praxis*]?" That Schlegel uses a Gallicism, "*das Ridicüle*," perhaps better rendered as "the Outlandish," indicates that we are dealing with social error: with false wit, malapropism, an unconscious or breach of decorum or affection. The tyranny of neoclassical ideals intensified the possibility of ridicule and embarrassment: in Heinrich von Kleist's "On the Marionette Theater" a vulgar art form is praised as exhibiting a type of physical grace that is infinitely beyond a beauty easily marred by embarrassment. A young man is said to have lost his "innocence" before the narrator's "very eyes" because of a remark that made him self-conscious, so that he could not recover the classical grace of posture he had sought to emulate. How hardy and healthy is Shakespearean comedy, which both releases wit from shame by allowing its outrage, its discountenancing of everyone, and makes it serviceable by the kind of labor Rosaline imposes on Berowne in *Love's Labour's Lost.* In this play, Don Adriano de Armado, called a "fantastical Spaniard," can be considered the extravagant obverse of Geoffrey Hill's Arrurrúz.

The Reinvention of Hate

Rimbaud said that love must be reinvented. But in our century hate is being reinvented.

It will not be a surprise that even hate has a "second nature" or constructed aspect. Yet it remains a scandal how far some regimes have gone to culture, as well as acculturate, hate. I refer to the deliberate growth and development, as in test-tube culturing, of an instinct whose origins remain obscure, though it seems closely linked to aggressive self-preservation. I refer also to a culture of hate that is the organized result of such a process.

Usually hate is something we hide; we feel ashamed of it. But this shame may also exacerbate a hate officially sanctioned by party or state. Hate then turns against shame; xenophobia becomes pitiless; the humiliated self scapegoats a group—gets rid of its own sense of shame by heaping it on someone else, who is treated as evil by nature, at once responsible and abjectly other. Not all personal shame can be removed, of course—there is too much around—but a specific taboo, such as anti-Semitism, when lifted can become a cultural imperative.

In that case, however, what was once dammed threatens to overflow and flood everything. Because repression and the guilt or shame that accompany it are common psychical facts in civilized society, the hate released is massive. But it feels like a renewal of virility, like breaking through a social lie. Clear identification of the enemy promises true conflict, the establishment of irreducible principles as politics turns fundamentalist. Politically acceptable hate, no longer just instinctive, becomes a rationalized passion supported by ideology. In Nazi Germany it was used as a weapon, even against civilians, both by the military and by a coordinated bureaucracy. Triumphant Nazi documents record a chilling disregard, a ferocious contempt, for the humanity of the victims. Thus civilization succeeds not in diminishing hate but in making it dirigible.

Hatred, linked to anger, is not always ignoble. It inspired the oldest epic in the canon, Homer's *Iliad*, and has a complex tie to revenge as an instrument of justice. Achilles' fury make him appear larger than life and comes close to being a prophetic attribute. Whether or not poetic furor shares in this attribute, everyone, I will assume, feels a thrill in reading or seeing—at a safe distance—expressive candor breaking through restraint.

Jonah's flight from the mission of prophecy, and the readiness of the Athenians to impose fines on playwrights who offended them, indicate the problematic nature of forceful speech, whatever its motivation or affect. Extreme humor, too—bawdy, or Mikhail Bakhtin's carnivalesque—puts itself as well as its subject at risk. Consider how William Blake plays with strange fire, though he is usually admired (shielded by his canonical status) rather than questioned in this regard.

Blake's "Proverbs of Hell," such sayings as "Prisons are built with stones of Law, Brothels with bricks of Religion," show him to be a "Tyger of wrath" rather than a "horse of instruction." Indignation as well as a particular rage—against hypocrisy—plays its part in his fierce social critique. (He would have cursed William Bennett for prescribing self-censorship based on "constructive hypocrisy.") Yet is Blake himself free of a *libido destruendi,* the aggression Freud described in *Civilization and Its Discontents*? His savage clairvoyance, cutting through euphemism and piety, could be motivated by a resentment of the instinctual sacrifices that civilized behavior demands. A libidinal anger certainly animates not only many of his proverbs ("He who desires but acts not, breeds pestilence"; "Sooner murder an infant in its cradle than nurse unacted desires") but also his over-long allegories of fiery, apocalyptic purgation. They are fueled by the sevenfold mayhem of *Revelations:* poetic and prophetic fury merge in repeated descriptions of the "human harvest" at the end of days. The poet intersperses pastoral songs of liberation, singing "Odors of life," as he calls them, with orgiastic portrayals of how the new human wine is extracted:

In the Wine Presses the Human grapes sing not nor dance,
They howl & writhe in shoals of torment, in fierce flames consuming,
In chains of iron & dungeons circled with ceaseless fires,
In pits & Dens & shades of death, in shapes of torment & woe;
The Plates, the Screws & Racks & cords & fires & floods,
The cruel joy of Luvah's daughters, lacerating with knives
And whips their Victims

(*The Four Zoas,* Night the Ninth)

The secret we would like to learn is what makes this fury creative rather than sadistic.

Blake, it must be stressed, attacks the system—priest, king, government, the ideology of natural religion—rather than a scapegoated group. And he claims that his poetic pyromania is really a depiction of "mental fires." Yet at what point, or under what circumstances, does figurative speech explode into literal belief and harmful performance?

Allow me a *passage à la limite* by way of an incongruous comparison—for Blake's cutting speech and a military commander's savagery seem worlds apart. In an official report it was disclosed that the Bosnian Serb commander General Mladic, had summoned U.N. peacekeepers and ordered a pig's throat slashed in front of them to show how he would evacuate the Muslims from the safe haven his forces had taken, if his conditions were not met. Is this symbolic speech or a form of terrorism? We know that the threat in this figure was fulfilled. A rictus followed rhetoric's open mouth.

Having found a sanctioned target, uncivil hatred relishes naked expression. It was hard for contemporaries to take literally the venomous rage of a Louis-Ferdinand Céline or the shameless, vituperative journalism that sprang up in Germany and occupied Europe under the influence of National Socialism. It is hard to believe even now that the language found in, say, the newspaper *Je Suis Partout* was meant, as well as meaningful, and that it intimidated and infected a mass of people. Leon Poliakov, in his *Bréviaire de la haine* (*Harvest of Hate*), recalls how a Wehrmacht guard reacted in 1940 when a prisoner (Poliakov himself) said he was a Jew: "But why do you tell me this? In your place I would rather die of shame than admit it." Such a reaction could not have come about without a relentless propaganda that segregated the Jews as unclean, shameless and irremediably evil in a Manichaean world strictly and comprehensively divided into sacred and profane.

Jews became not only legal outcasts but objects of scared horror. As Robert Kanters (quoted in Poliakov's *Harvest of Hate*) has pointed out, "From the simplest to the most important act, from entering a café to marrying, [a German] can do nothing without first taking care to recognize the barrier that separates the two worlds." Blacks in the United States and South Africa have been subjected to a similar apartheid, but in Germany the war against the Jews was all the more vicious because, almost indistinguishable in physical and cultural characteristics from other Germans, they had to be marked to prevent them from "passing." Yet nothing could mark the assimilated Jews adequately. Julius Streicher's caricatures were sadly, laughably crude and relied mainly on claiming to expose the Jews' two-facedness—their cunningly disguised Orientalism under the assimilated surface. The attempt to separate Jew from German escalated from defamation to isolation to Jews' being expelled from the professions and stigmatized by a special passport stamp, a tribal name (Israel, Sarah), and the yellow star. Eventually all were deported, imprisoned in ghettos and concentration camps, subjected to slave labor, torture, random murder, and, finally, systematic extermination.

I shall return to this fatal usurpation of all life by a political religion. My initial and more innocuous question is: Can we learn anything from literature about a social order based on hate and hate speech?

There is a telling moment in Milton's *Paradise Lost,* when Satan first sees Eden, the earthly paradise. The fallen angel addresses the sun in a powerful and peculiar monologue, culminating in a curse that contains a reluctant blessing:

> to thee I call,
> But with no friendly voice, and add thy name
> O sun, to tell thee how I hate thy beams
>
> (4.35–37)

Satan's naming, though not unlike Adamic naming, is also a parody of it and transforms acknowledgement into hate. Satan spits out the name. Outcast and spoiler, he recalls his former sunlike state and is afflicted beyond despair by a sort of protest against beauty and innocence, a protest close to jealousy. Involuntarily, therefore, he hails the creation.

Hate, as this depiction suggests, need not lack a connection to love. An equivocation of words or ambivalence of feeling may enter—but this is an undesired or unconscious complication that incites even more ferocity in the attempt to purge the emotion of anything except itself. Let me instance a dramatic gesture in Shakespeare's *Troilus and Cressida* (it should be compared to the Serb general's strategy and chilling warning). Achilles conceives a sinister desire to look at Hector before their fight. He summons the Trojan and gloats over him to locate exactly where he will inflict the fatal wound:

> Tell me, you heav'ns, in which part of his body
> Shall I destroy him? Whether there, or there, or there,
> That I may give the local wound a name;
> And make distinct the very breach whereout
> *Hector's* great spirit flew.
>
> (*Troilus and Cressida* 4.9)

In this symbolic aggression (a boast that seeks to weaken the enemy hero, to break his spirit) the virtual wound is on the way to becoming a real wound, whether through magic, psychological warfare, or imitation of the divine fiat. The directness, moreover, of Achilles' speech, its vicious, spearlike pointedness, mimics something that is intrinsic to hate as a passion. It has found its object; its aim is now unambiguous; the conversion seems complete of a powerful emotion that could have gone in the direction of love (here, homoerotic love) but is expressed as hate and contempt. I am not sure hate can be isolated, as in a chemical table of elements, from other destructive emotions, yet if we allow the similarity of anger and hate, we spot the obverse of its passionate simplification in Jakob Boehme's "Love is wrath quenched."

In any attempt to grasp the passion of hate, two aspects, then, must be recognized. First there is the simplification effected by hate and hate speech. They combine to find a very specific target. Naming is used as a fatal weapon to stigmatize the entire person or group. Naming and shaming merge. Then there is the link of hate with repressed jealousy, with the resentment of a creative power or glory (even an *election*) from which the hater feels excluded. But like a demiurge, the hater creates a counterdomain, in reality or fantasy. This domain is a hell rather than a chaos. The hater, that is, strives to solidify it as a counterworld with clear if bloody confines. It is not nothing, and not limbo; it is the hater's heterocosm, a sacred space that has definitively broken with pieties and substituted rigid rituals. The one thing this alternate reality cannot be is indirect—teeming with ambiguous situations, uncertainties, unintegrated elements—like the world in which we ordinarily live. Given this intolerance of the human condition, Theodor Adorno's hyperbole shocks but also makes sense. "Genocide," he wrote, "is absolute integration."

It is uncomfortable to recognize the frustrated creativity in hate, the idealism gone bad. But at least this insight saves us from another simplification, itself not devoid of resentment. Inspired by Marxism, it attempted to explain the hierarchical hell of the Nazi camps as an inverse, demystified image of capitalistic society, a stripping naked of its exploitative nature. This perspective was found, for instance, in David Rousset's remarkable *The Other Kingdom* (*L'univers concentrationnaire*), written immediately at the end of the war. Yet Rousset was right in calling the camps a universe and in describing how precise their rituals were. The amazing pseudolegality by which so many areas functioned in the Third Reich achieved its deadliest triumph in the camps. Hierarchy and regulation, however arbitrary, were all in all. Nothing, supposedly, was left to chance; every action was in principle dictated or bureaucratically automated. Yet even in the death camps accidents, or a sudden intervention, could save a life, or, rather, defer a death. Hate is reversible, in spite of the mental and emotional walls it deliberately constructs so that no ambivalence or "uncharted" desire can penetrate.

There is some truth, then, in popular fictional representations of the criminal world as a social order with its own rules—much more "clean-cut," on the whole, much less ambiguous, than rules in our own gray ambivalence-ridden life. Within that world, of course, something always breaks down and betrays it, because the dirt of love enters the machinery of hate, or something unanticipated and sentimental, perhaps a striving to get from the artificial to the real light, or a memory of the "outside," infiltrates disruptively. The criminal's totalizing fantasy, the illusion of creating a personal world, secure, heroic, invulnerable, is as improbable as the movies that exploit it and needs ever stronger fantasies to shore it up.

Varlam Chalamov, a survivor of Kolyma, protests literary depictions of the underworld by Victor Hugo and Fyodor Dostoyevsky, who had never known, as he had in Stalin's Gulag, the career criminal. He says they romanticize him and make him attractive by suggesting the survival of a core of charity within his coldness and ruthlessness. Although such "weakness" may exist, the underworld's attraction is quite different, according to Chalamov. He confirms that organized crime is a cosmos, even in prison: a highly structured order, and with a blood tie that is achieved not necessarily by having blood on one's hands but rather by a familylike submission to a veteran in-group.

The young, according to Chalamov, are particularly vulnerable to the world of crime. Its fascination goes beyond cloak and dagger and secret rites. More crucial is their recognition of a powerful group that has thrown off the scruples and cares that preoccupy their families at home; and they escape, in particular, the torment and queasiness of adolescence. By a real and bloody game, whose psychological tension is far more addictive and defining than disciplinary brotherhoods in the legitimate world—the police, the military, the Society of Jesus—they are forced, and wish to be forced, into premature manhood. Chalamov's picture of the young initiate is, I think, reliable testimony, and I wish to quote a small part of it:

> Penetrating with beating heart the underworld, the youngster associates with people who terrify his parents. He observes their pretended independence, their false liberty. He mistakes their bragging and bravado for cash. He considers them as men who have challenged the existing social order. . . . He does not think of the pain of the other, of the shed human blood which represents what his hero has stolen and which is present without accountability. . . . He dreams about the final touch, his definitive affiliation with the order: the prison, which he has been taught not to fear.

Hatred as a principle of order divides humanity coldly into friend *or* enemy, family member *or* alien, and builds this division, this split, into an easily recognized, all-encompassing mode of existence, one that has no room for equivocation or straying sympathies. We rediscover at this point the disconcerting fact that cultures often see themselves founded on a schizophrenic simplification: on a crime, like a war or a massacre, that is at best ambiguous or unintelligible, at worst morally unredeemable, yet must become an unchallenged foundation. We also pass here from a special development within nation or collectivity—namely, how a counterculture of hate takes hold—to a theory relevant to the formation of cultures generally.

In spite of recent efforts to envisage a multicultural nation with a wide tolerance for difference and dissent, political history shows rather that the greater the disunity or fear of civil war, the louder the call for a clear rededication to oneness through symbols of order that stigmatize opposition and even criticism as fatally subversive. The brave experiment of parliamentary democracy aims, of course, at overcoming this anxiety about pluralism. But our fearful imagination is not assuaged. It always senses behind what is firmly established the threat of a return of the repressed, of anarchic terror of some kind; and the ensuing tension requires—at least symbolically—an object of "sacred horror" to relieve it, to delimit the fear by giving it shape. Every unsolved murder also incites that fear, which may be related, in addition, to the sporadic outbreak of witch-hunts and scapegoating. To illustrate the role of sacred horror, I turn briefly to a poet's reaction to the civil war in seventeenth-century Britain.

Andrew Marvell, reflecting on Oliver Cromwell's career after the regicide, adduces a strange episode from the founding of Rome:

> So when they did design
> The capitol's first line
> A bleeding head where they begun
> Did fright the architects to run;
> And yet in that the state
> Foresaw its happy fate.

The king's beheading, Marvell suggests, provides that bleeding head for his own era. It is a happy omen in spite of the "fright" it elicits, and legitimates the new order. The decisive event is here shielded by a symbol, an augury whose sacred horror consecrates Cromwell's continued forceful actions. It sends a message that wounds of this kind are fortunate and necessary, that the integrity of the body politic is paradoxically secured by them. Yet Marvell's irony or equivocal poise, though its edge is keen, refuses to take sides, to speak for the future, to "cut" through the issue.

Terror—the terror of war, murder, bloodshed, and violence, but interpreted as a sacrificial necessity—is basic to national myths of birth or rebirth. Perhaps the emblem of Greater Serbia should be a pig's bleeding head. In much the same way the New Germany made the Jew into a desecrating horror to be removed from the *Volksgemeinschaft* by expulsion or, if necessary, bloody purification. Decisive foundational events often center on such a redemptive purge. Especially in terms of nation-building: the new or renewed culture wants to be absolutely clear—clearer than nature itself—about who is pure and who a contaminant. It pretends there is nothing in common between itself and the racial enemy.

Yet, as the proverb states, "Nature loves mixtures." Race purity, as a foundation of the new Reich, was doomed to fail, though not before exacting its sacrifice. There were many "Aryan" look-alikes; ironically, it was the assimilated Jews who at that time disproportionately supported Germany's high culture. A ridiculous bureaucracy developed, therefore, as well as blade-runners called the S.S., devoted entirely to the detection and liquidation of the Jew.

A fascinating moment in the film *Shoah* comes when Claude Lanzmann interviews Franz Grassler, second in command of the "Jewish District" (that is, ghetto) of Warsaw. Why were the Jews walled in? To control typhus and other epidemics, Grassler answers. But, Lanzmann retorts, quoting Adam Czerniakow, the Jewish head of the ghetto, hadn't the Germans always identified the Jews with typhus? "Yes, it is possible." A figure had become literal fact and metaphor murder. The Jews were disease itself; the entire state bureaucracy was based on racial hygiene. Such rage for order, incited by an ineradicable ambiguity, is merely an exaggeration of what Chalamov discerns as lust for "definitive affiliation" with "the order." Intellectuals, I must add, are as tempted by extreme political solutions as anyone else; perhaps even more, insofar as they suffer from hermeneutic perplexity and the endlessness of judgment.

Let me conclude by repeating an example I have written about before, which illustrates how a deliberate culture of hate is created. The plot of a typical Nazi-sponsored work, *Rabauken! Peter Mönkemann haut sich durch* (Rowdyism! Peter Mönkeman fights his way through, 1938), takes the form of a Bildungsroman. Peter, a young veteran of World War I and the Freikorps, copes with the disorder of the Weimar Republic and discovers that at all levels it is dominated and corrupted by Jews. To fight his way through and expose them demands that the true German modify his feelings and cultivate a murderous hate. But will this not produce a paralyzing self-disgust and spread over the human image in general? The novel suggests that only a diseased or noxious member is targeted, as in surgery. Yet there is no "safe hate." Given the explosive nature of anger and hate, to release those emotions is a tricky process. *Rabauken,* with its vulgarized Nietzschean message, is far from being stupid or irrational; it solves the difficulty by presenting the German character as innately sensitive and so *requiring* the suspension of that sensitivity where Jews are concerned. Nazi propaganda cultivated the image of a new stern breed of German who is asked to kill without mercy to "create [by genocide] a better and eternal Germany for our descendants."

Consider Mönkemann's outburst, when Dr. Singer, an influential Jew, mocks the notion that a small number of Jews (less than 1 percent of the population) could harm Germany:

> If someone notices the first sign of lice in his lodgings, and does not immediately fumigate—radically so, with poison gas and other substances—his pad will later be full of them and he won't be able to save himself from the vermin. Then the lice become masters in his own house. And this fumigation, [Mönkemann] adds, feeling the pressure and the hate, we have forgotten about. Unfortunately, it just didn't occur to us idiots.

The protagonist feels besieged or under pressure (*in Bedrängnis*) because he cannot entirely repress (*verdrängen*) an oversensitive conscience. This prevents the truth about Jews from getting through and has made the Germans forget their native virility. The lice-imagery and other bestial tropes, moreover, which dehumanize the Jews, are like an expression of peasant anger that remains ineffective as long as it is purely personal, without popular support and organizational backup. The anger must become policy: cold, calculated anti-Semitism.

At the same time, instinctive rage and outrage free the hero from repression and exalt him beyond enervating restraints. At one point he takes over the stage of a nightclub to denounce the Jewish danger to a startled audience: "A young warrior [*Recke*] stands there—who can divine the agony of his soul and the greatness of the hate goading his blood—a young churl, built like the son of a god, with flashing eyes of fire, ready to pounce like a panther, and as if he were already measuring the distance between himself and his deadly enemy." So this is the New Man—in embryo, of course, since he symbolizes a frustration and powerlessness that only organization (the party) will redeem.

However unpleasant it is, we have no choice but to study the structure of these demagogic ideas. Mönkemann's outburst touches on deep feelings: losing one's home, losing control, pollution, radical disgust. We are but a step away from the propaganda films of 1940 and 1941, which develop his analogy by depicting the Jews as a repulsive swarm of plague-bearing rats. Metaphor becomes murder when the dehumanization (*Menschenverachtung*) takes effect and poison gas is no longer a figure.

Why was this pornography of hate tolerated? How could such crude propaganda be effective? We do not know how many Germans actually believed what they were fed. Freedom of expression disappeared very quickly after 1933: passive collaboration, opportunism, and fear make it hard to judge the true state of conviction on this matter. Yet we can infer from anti-Semitic strata in France and Belgium what was effective as a *rationale,* and it had to do with the idea of a defense of culture. Where we detect a nearly fatal attack on culture, intellect, and civilized values, these strata, in their xenophobia and anti-Semitism—which was their only unifying bond, for many in France were anti-German—saw themselves as saviors of a degenerate society. French anti-Semites represented the exposure and expulsion of foreign elements as a Defense of the West, even though the Nazi ideal often presented itself as anti-French and anti-Western. (From the left, too, the cry arose that civilization had to be defended—against fascism.)

The rationale of anti-Semitism, then, was quite clear. It appealed to a widely shared anxiety about national decadence and even genetic degeneration. Novels like *Rabauken* insinuated what Nazi slogans disseminated stridently: the culture of the *Kulturvolk,* its potential as a *Herrenvolk,* is endangered, especially from within. The nation must be alerted to this danger, because in its very humanity the German character is reluctant to recognize the evil. Only if the Germans are instructed by ideology and the new racial science to look closely enough, only if they overcome liberal sentiments—about human equality, pity, and successful Jewish assimilation—will they penetrate beyond the mask, perceive irredeemable difference, and end equivocation. The Nazi *Kulturkampf,* in short, claimed to be a defense of culture, not its nemesis. Deliberate, organized hatred became a sanctioned principle of order, and we know with what result.

Public Memory and Modern Experience

What will public memory be like in the next century? Such memory is never entirely unified or clearly bounded; one could even doubt that the sum and structure of what is generally known can be determined. Still, a considerable amount of knowledge in the public domain consists of shared allusions, of references and norms that make for intelligibility. Books have been the main carriers of such memory, and nonverbal arts, like paintings and monuments, provide cultural reference points.

This shared knowledge, whether we talk of canon, cultural literacy or sociolect, though never static or uncontested, is an important yet often unconscious influence on personal identity. That influence begins with language acquisition; most sociologists, in fact, especially in the line that leads from Durkheim and Halbwachs to Pierre Nora, believe that what we remember always has a social context, and that words—or symbols that can be verbalized—both enable and sustain

Given at "The Future of Memory," the tenth anniversary conference of Yale University's Fortunoff Video Archive for Holocaust Testimonies.

memory. Language and memory converge, and this convergence is the site of contemporary confusions and battles, especially in literature. Is memory, in the form of tradition, a deadweight on individual talent, or its necessary and inevitable medium? Is there a more primary symbolism than language, or does the child's entry into language signal a decisive and irreversible step, on which all other forms of socialization depend? Could it be, given the new emphasis on memory's social context, that privacy and personal creativity are—saving—illusions?

Into this debate comes another factor: the massive effects of film and telecommunications. An "information sickness," caused by the speed and quantity of what impinges on us, and abetted by machines we have invented that generate endless arrays, threatens to overwhelm what personal space remains. The individual, we complain, cannot "process" all this information: public and personal experience are being moved not closer but farther apart.

Personal memory, then, may be ailing. Among the symptoms of its malady are endless discussions about the existence or nonexistence of a "posthumanist subject," a conference on "The Uses of Oblivion," and the fear that "our past will have no future in our future" (David Rieff). Even as we claim greater powers of retrieval and knowledge mastery, the machines on which that claim is based mock us:

> over and over the jolly cartoon
> armies of France go reeling towards Verdun.

Geoffrey Hill evokes the Chaplinesque character of early cinematography, the surreality of those small, speeded-up figures. But this effect is more than provisional; it signals not only an outmoded technique (which happens to catch the absurdity of war and a mechanical obedience that killed more than a million soldiers) but also our basically passive relation to sensory and information overload.

Technological progress—bigger and better images—has not fundamentally changed that passivity: we remain consumers dependent on a massive technical structure, including a state apparatus or bureaucracy. And when every movie aspires to be a version of *Apocalypse Now* or *Terminator II,* the gulf between screen and armchair, between media bombardment and the slower, more deliberate rhythms of the observer, widens. We cannot deal reflectively with all the incoming flak. The experiencing part of our being is affected by this, as well as the intellectual, with the result that stylization returns, and even the "jolly cartoon." We used to struggle *with* experience, and no doubt still do so; but now we also struggle *for* experience, for a more than abstract sense of the past, or virtual sense of the present.

The specific concern of my essay on signs of the times is the impact of the media. How can we focus memory, private or public, on traumatic experiences like War or Slavery or the Holocaust? Paradoxically, the very efficiency of modern information systems, their realism and representational scope, makes this a complicated task. Public memory, if it can still be called memory, is, as I have suggested, increasingly alienated from personal and active recall. When our senses are routinely assaulted, the imagination, defined as a power that can restore a kind of presence to absent things, has its work preempted and is in danger of imitating media sensationalism. There is reason to worry about a desensitizing trend, one that keeps raising the threshold at which we begin to respond.

The trend, which I will call derealization, or a general weakening of the sense of reality, was already noticed by Wordsworth near the beginning of the Industrial Revolution. He complained in 1800 of the mind's losing its ability to be stimulated by ordinary sights and events, by "common life" and "elementary feelings," because of "the great national events which are daily taking place, and the increasing accumulation of men in cities, where the uniformity of their occupations produces a craving for extraordinary incident which the rapid communication of intelligence hourly gratifies." He also lambasted, for good measure, "frantic novels, sickly and stupid German tragedies, and deluges of idle and extravagant stories in verse," which were driving out the good literature, the "invaluable work of our elder writers."

Since then derealization has made considerable strides. The contemporary problem is not Bovarysm or Quixotism—seeing the real world (defensively) with an imagination steeped in romance—but looking at whatever is on the screen as merely an interesting effect, a construct or simulation. Actuality is distanced by a larger-than-life violence and retreats behind all those special effects. One is not surprised that Robert Rosenblum, the art historian, should defend what he calls Warhol's deadpan by claiming that it reflects a "state of moral and emotional anaesthesia which, like it or not, probably tells us more truth about the realities of the modern world than do the rhetorical passions of *Guernica*."

Some reality loss, of course, is natural and inevitable: the passage of time, the disappearance of things into the past, cannot be reversed. There is always plenty of room, then, for fabrication in both the good and the bad sense: for scrupulous reconstruction or deliberate falsification, and, a matter more difficult to judge, for fictional representation. Public memory is influenced by these; also by historiographical debates, and trials like Klaus Barbie's that become media events. They set the stage for increased public and journalistic consumption, for what Habermas calls, more elegantly, the public use of history. Lest I be accused of being overly pessimistic or even of media-bashing, let me say at this point that increased public interest in the issues is a clear plus and would not be sustained without the media.

There exists, in fact, a continuous battle about what the public at large should believe. Because Barbie's trial, for example, took place so many years after the crime, and history does not stand still, new memories relativize or confuse older ones, political allegiances shift, and laws of justice, which claim a certain universality, must fight to maintain themselves against the very conditions of publicity that were to have made such a trial as Barbie's lesson in favor of memory, a nationwide pedagogical event. (The "future of memory" moves nearer when we learn that the videotapes of Barbie's trial will not be made available till 2007.) Ultimately, of course, it is not the legal or historiographical issues that make an impact on public memory, but themes of national honor, self-esteem, and legitimacy. A deep concern for the future integrity of an affected nation or group intervenes in the construction of reconstruction of historical events. As we try to survive, the main question always becomes what presence the past should have.

Yet if the present itself has now less of a hold, if the abstractness or derealization described has indeed infected us, can we remain sensitive to the past?

Consider, to begin with, the proliferation of museums that also serve as educational centers. This is a welcome development: it extends knowledge beyond the walls of the university. But do these museums resurrect the past, or do they give it a decent burial? Many of them authorize a more settled and safer notion of history, which then affects our reaction to present-day events and tempts us to "historicize" everything. Such historicizing is as much a mode of forgetting as of remembering. Works of art, in fact, are increasingly created for their museum or exhibition value: the conflict between historical and aesthetic disappears into a dignified art space, labeled avant-garde or modern. This type of derealization must lead us, in the special case of the Holocaust museum or similar memorial efforts, to think more carefully about that space: about the principle governing the arrangement of its contents. Is what we are shown merely an object of knowledge? The aim of the memorial museum is, on the one hand, to abolish distance, to disclose a past, however painful and shocking; on the other hand, the aim is to instruct rather than overpower, to encourage thoughtfulness and not emotional fixation.

Or consider what happens to history in the media. Given that our powers of mimesis or simulation have increased but that forgetfulness and mutability have not decreased—that the speed with which things fall into "the dark backward and abysm of time" has, if anything, accelerated—the greatest danger to public memory is the *official story.* Even the dead, as Walter Benjamin declared, are not safe from the victors, who do not hesitate to rewrite history. They consider public memory part of the spoils. Like Milan Kundera in the opening episode of *The Book of Laughter and Forgetting,* we look at their *dirigisme* with one laughing and one drooping eye. Kundera recalls how a discredited Communist leader was airbrushed out of a famous historical photo. So easily is history falsified and public memory deceived.

In a democracy, of course, investigative journalism prevents total management of the news. But though we are now able to see events almost as soon as they break, the pictures are rarely self-explanatory. Most of the time they simply reinforce the repeated and tendentious words of newscaster or commentator. A picture is worth a thousand words only because it endows those words with the illusion of immediacy and self-evidence. I do not mean that there is, necessarily, deliberate misrepresentation: it is our complicity with the medium that must be examined. If some responsibility rests with the viewer, then too little attention is paid to visual education in the schools. The power of live images joined to words cannot be overestimated, and the free speech that is one of the foundations of truth in a democratic "marketplace of ideas" also leads the media to a continual probing, testing, and even muckraking that has an unexpected effect on the integrity of the public life it was intended to assure.

For the more deceptions are intimated or actually exposed by media journalism, the more an insidious and queasy feeling of unreality grows in us. What are we to do with all the speculations about Kennedy's assassination that parade as docudrama or novel? It is as if the political realm, and possibly all of public life, were inauthentic—a mask, a Machiavellian web of continuous deception. This negative insight undermines the specific gravity, the uniqueness of lived events, and encourages a deep skepticism about the world—or a compensatory fundamentalism.

A tragic and nearly boundless untruth is the subject of Puenzo's film *The Official Story,* set in Argentina under the military dictatorship. It could also have taken place in Eastern Europe during the time of Soviet domination. Puenzo tells a tragic and typical narrative of public deceit and personal discovery. It is the story of a mother who suspects that her adopted child was stolen from a "disappeared" Argentinian woman. At first she does not suspect the truth, but a small doubt punctures the basic trust she has in the system: that doubt grows and grows, the search for the truth grows and grows, until—as also in *Oedipus the King*—a hidden past is revealed. But so much hinges on the social lie she sets out to expose and destroy that her family life, and the child herself, are put in jeopardy.

What I have described comes close to being a universal kind of plot, as old as the historical record itself. What is the difference, then, between past and present? The contemporary difference is summed up in Emerson's phrase: "We suspect our instruments." The very means that expose untruth, the verbal or photographic or filmic evidence, come under suspicion. Whatever evidence is produced is met with a demystifying discourse or charges of manipulation. The intelligent scrutiny to which we ordinarily submit appearances provokes a crisis of trust, a lack of confidence in what we are told or shown, *a fear that the world of appearances and the world of propaganda have merged through the power of the media.*

To undo this spell and gain true knowledge would then be as tricky as in gnosticism, which distrusted nature and tried to gain a knowledge of the true god behind the god of nature. But when we modern gnostics break through, or seem to, enlightenment does not bring relief. Now as before, "the tree of knowledge is not that of life." Byron's verse recalls Goethe as well as the Bible; yet Goethe's Faust challenged the devil to turn knowledge back into life, into joy. Our knowledge-sadness, however, has become too deep to be reversed by a Faustian wager.

One point of solace is that we may recover, in reaction to this will for disclosure or exposure, a sense of older, traditional, and often more indirect modes of statement. Hence our continued appreciation for a living and generational memory, passed down through canonical stories. Even though composed or transmitted by individual genius, they seem to have developed over time, respecting meter as well as meaning, or assimilating history to prevailing archetypes and paradigms.

The idea of such a "collective" memory has to be approached with caution. It can become a seductive political construct. But it responds to the situation I have described and should therefore be carefully critiqued rather than rejected.

When realism itself no longer has roots, when it turns into a formalistic imperative, we look for a link to family or place of origin as an authenticating birthmark. Indeed, the burden of modernity, of an abstractness augmented rather than relieved by media artifice, incites a strong nostalgia for "local romance," for stories that are, as it were, an emanation of particular places—places impressed on the collective memory. Such stories often crystallize around proper names, and especially place names (Beth-el; Guermantes; Winesburg, Ohio; Homewood), even though these names may sometimes be fictional, and the places imaginary. They outlive, in our imagination, referents they may never have had.

It is also this nominal genealogical bond which tempers the fear that the rapport between audience and singer of tales has frayed. "We have no institutions," Alasdair MacIntyre has remarked, "through which shared stories can be told dramatically or otherwise to the entire political community, assembled together as an audience, no dramatists or other story tellers able to address such an audience. . . . Our audiences are privatized and dispersed, watching television in homes or motel rooms." The storyless modern imagination is depicted as going from non-place to non-place, even enjoying, as Marc Augé points out, the anonymity bestowed by highways, airports, large hotels, and shopping malls. In this way the *lieu de mémoire* is lost, displaced by a *non-lieu.*[1]

Against that emptiness, which evokes a public memory that has become nothing but a public space, occupied by shifting and impersonal networks of information, a different, more responsible, but also burdened recollection asserts itself. Every time that we retrieve an oral history, even when, tragically, it tells of an ultimate *non-lieu* like the dehumanized landscape of Treblinka or Auschwitz, we are creating a line of resistance to this effacement of an earlier kind of memory, linked to place, and through place to identity.

Monuments too are *lieux de mémoire,* involving like stories real or legendary places. The German filmmaker Alexander Kluge comes to terms with the pressure of the past by incorporating images of ruined or deserted Nazi architecture. These negative *lieux de mémoire,* once glorified in Nazi films, serve as a reminder of the "eternity of yesterday." Symptoms of a fatal collective dream that has not really passed away, they play on in the "cinema animal" we have become. Yet stories are the perennials of time, and outlast—so the poets tell us—steel, brass and marble.

Marshall McLuhan realized that an electronic culture was replacing these canonical or twice-told tales. But he thought of this as potentially a creative advance, a restoration of "village" gifts by specifically modern means. The facts have proved to be somewhat less friendly, and McLuhan's Mechanical Bride (his utopian hope for a fruitful wedding of humanism and technology) has simply made the groom mechanical too. Human memory harnessed to the machine is amazing, but it rarely contributes to a collective tradition of storytelling.

We have to acknowledge, then, a difficulty. If audio and video resources are not used to preserve those stories, we lose too much. If they *are* used, their content—whether Holocaust testimony or other forms of witness—offers no assurance that there won't be some loss of reality. The Mechanical Bride exacts a price: in an era of easy reproducibility, the testimonies too may suffer an experiential "fading," just as magnetic tapes show a loss of visual definition over time and must be recopied onto a more permanent medium.

Yet oral history, captured on tape, can make a difference to public memory. By recording an experience collectively endured and allowing anyone in the community a voice—that is, by not focusing on an elite—a vernacular and multivocal dimension is caught. The collective—"collected" would be a better word—memory produced this way is too diverse and specific to be become institutionalized or sacralized. Though we cannot foresee what qualities of these witness accounts will prove affecting or important in another hundred or thousand years, it is a good guess that then, as a thousand or two thousand years ago, storytelling will matter. Even if we have entered a postmodern world, where master or meta-narrative (what Jean-François Lyotard has aptly named the *grand récit*) has lost credibility and legitimating power, the personal story, as in the splintered testimonial narratives of the Yale Video Archive, or as glimpsed through the windows (a doubling of the camera's aperture) of *The Shop on Main Street,* will continue to make its presence felt.

The future of memory depends, in Shelley's words, on "arts, though unimagined, yet to be." These arts are foreshadowed by remarkable writers and scholars who make the archives come alive—who honor memories unrelated to their personal history. True history or true fiction has always required an extraordinary act of the sympathetic imagination: an identification with experiences or stories not our own.

Shortly after David Boder recorded the first testimonies in Displaced Person camps, John Hersey was at the YIVO Institute for Jewish Research, attempting to absorb a mass of documentary materials about the Warsaw Ghetto revolt. Using, like Boder, the newly invented wire recorder, Hersey's assistants, who included the historian Lucy Dawidowicz, translated the Yiddish and Polish manuscripts. But they themselves—the translators—became primary sources. Having some personal knowledge of the events, "as they translated they could interpolate, explain, underline, and clarify." This oral history, in its complexity and polyphony, was the basis of Hersey's book *The Wall.*[2]

Hersey goes on to mention something even more crucial than his collaboration as novelist with an extended oral history. To encompass as much material as possible, he at first adopted the fictional perspective of the omniscient narrator. It did not work, however, because there was, as he expressed it, "a fatal falsity in the universal point of view." The story, he decided, must be told by a person who had been there, by someone who would become a survivor. "Imagination would not serve; only memory could serve. To salvage anything that would be worthy of the subject, I had to invent a memory"—and so his central character Noach Levinson was born. Is what Hersey achieved, this creative solution to the pressure of fact on imagination, as possible today?

Not only is the chain of testimonies, at present, stretched to the breaking point as we move further from the event, but the media themselves become an event in that chain, substituting for an original and originating complexity. The television movie based on Hersey's novel gives the ghetto uprising renewed life and pathos yet also weakens its human and historical specificity. We are left with a simplified and overcollectivized memory-image. Some will say this has always been the case; history is a chaos that can be ordered for transmission only by being regularized through a "fatal falsity," through a dubious omniscience created by official myth, historiographical paradigm, or even fictional exploitation.

Today, therefore, even Hersey's eloquent phrase "to invent a memory" makes us uneasy; we remind ourselves that he means a memory based on memories, on retrievable and convergent witness accounts. For there is another kind of invested memory, one that has proved to be deadly: it feeds on heroic images and underwrites political opportunism, or fundamentalist notions of national destiny and ethnic purity. This unreal memory is the enemy. It can be countered, but only if survivors like Levinson give testimony, and novelists like Hersey, or younger bystanders, whether artists or scholars, agree to be part of the chain of transmission and continue to bring these stories, these modern and often terrible ballads, before our eyes.

NOTES

1. Marc Augé, *Non-lieux: Introduction à une anthropologie de la surmodernité* (Paris: Seuil, 1992). *Non-lieu* in French can also refer to the legal dismissal of a case.
2. David P. Boder, *I Did Not Interview the Dead* (Urbana: University of Illinois Press, 1949). For Hersey, see his lecture at the Baltimore Hebrew University, "To Invent a Memory," given in 1983 and published by the university in 1989. The novel itself, published in 1950, has an "Editor's Prologue" that is already part of the fiction. It describes uncovering a buried archive and gives the imaginary names of two translators. On the novel's copyright page, however, the following statement suggests the tension in Hersey between history and what will later be called "faction." "This is a work of fiction. Broadly it deals with history, but in detail it is invented. Its 'archive' is a hoax." John Hersey, *The Wall* (New York: Knopf, 1950). A selection from Emmanuel Ringelblum's archive had been published in *Bleter far Geszichte,* Warsaw, 1948.

Art, Consensus, and Progressive Politics

Could it be that taste belongs among the political faculties?
—Hannah Arendt

Art criticism has a function considerably larger than reportage or the articulation of opinion. It is not limited to statements that describe, explicate, illuminate, compare, or moralize the work of art. All these are, it is true, modalities of commentary. But what turns commentary into criticism, what gives it critical edge and focus, is, above all, its concern for the quality of public agreement about works of art.

Kant's analysis of the aesthetic judgment raised the issue of how a critical act is possible that relies on subjective response and on the fallible and changeable standard of taste. Do we want to disqualify the rationality of criticism by holding that art it not worth quarreling over, or that opinions about it are intractably private, requiring the tolerance we reserve for personal foibles? What a life, if all we could fight about in conversation were politics! The danger, in fact, is that once we disqualify reason in matters of art, a case might be made for disqualifying political disputes as also blindly personal. Art could be a test case. Minute or judicial criticism, which separates the beauties from the defects of particular works of art, was displaced though not disabled by the larger Kantian perspective. We have a need which is more than a need, and which in public matters becomes a necessity: that of striving for consensus.

It is not, however, consensus as an end product that is important in and of itself, but the mutual and moral factors that come into play as we move toward agreement. Here progress resides in process—a due process whose rules are not all conceptualizable or prescriptive. (Habermas has called that process a "communicative action" leading to a free rather than enforced convergence.) In this court there are, of course, rules of evidence, methods of distinguishing between fact and opinion, ways of authenticating texts, and so forth; but there are also endless appeals on almost any ground. We aim less at consensus than at *quality of consent.* We want to hear the individual voice within the collective judgment and do not insist on erecting a scientific or completely stable epistemology. Nor is the critical act a matter of finding the most persuasive rhetoric. Persuasion without coercion remains the ideal of every "aesthetic" endeavor, but when rhetoric is merely a craft that panders to opinion or plays on human anxieties, it should be the target rather than the aim of criticism.

We need to explore how criticism, in this enlarged sense of a communicative action motivated by an ideal of noncoercive persuasion, gets linked to criticism as close reading—all the more so because reading had first to loosen its ties to the casuistry or "exegetical bonding" (so David Apter has named it) of sacred hermeneutics. I can only speculate that to counter renewed authoritarian modes of instruction centering on Marx, Lenin, Hitler, Mao, and others, as well as the commercial manipulation of culture, an independent pedagogy developed to save art from such appropriation or distortion. Close reading becomes, then, a form of exegetical bonding that does not deprive us of quality of consent. So the New Criticism may be seen as partially inspired by an effort to teach the distinction between propaganda and art.

We have seen the terrible cost in lives, communities, and moral probity exacted by the staged unanimity of fascism and the ideology-machine of communism. Even during its time of domination, Václav Havel criticized communism for creating "the illusion of an identity, of dignity, and of morality, while making it easier for [people] to *part with them.* . . . [It is] a veil behind which human beings can hide their own 'fallen existence,' their trivialization, and their adaptation to the status quo." The recent collapse of communism as a monolithic force shows again how deceptive (but no less dangerous for that) a social ethos can be that substitutes slogans and propaganda for freshness of perception and a critical prose that won't accept what the French philosopher François Lyotard calls a regime of phrases.

If I stress quality of consent rather than liberty of interpretation, it is because art, too, demands *some* bonding, if only in the form of a temporary suspension of disbelief. Works of art issue a very strong challenge to the reader, viewer, or listener; our imagination is under siege. Responsiveness here is responsibility. In short, as critics we try to make our response an active reception; we scrutinize the feelings, thoughts, and language that art awakes in us. We allow art to "govern" us in areas we felt were beyond dispute or challenge. The drama of individual *assent*—art's demand on each of us and our response or resistance to it—should carry over and influence, so we at least hope, the quality of our *consent* in public and political matters.

By sharing this hope, am I confusing art criticism and political philosophy? Though art criticism may be political philosophy by other means, those means remain important. They have to do with the attempt in imaginative writing to understand different perspectives and to draw upon a precarious reservoir of empathy that is always in great demand. That there is an intersection of the two activities is clear. As Hannah Arendt has written, in reference to Kant: "The art of critical thinking always has political implications" because it takes place through, and even is dependent on, social intercourse. "Critical thinking is possible only where the standpoints of all others are open to inspection. Hence, critical thinking, while still a solitary business, does not cut itself off, but by the force of imagination it makes the others present and thus moves in a space that is potentially public, open to all sides. . . . To think with an enlarged mentality means that one trains one's imagination to go visiting."

While attracted to this comment, I am not fully at ease with its colloquial turn. I recall Kant's or Heidegger's intense writing and indeed Arendt's own heavier philosophizing elsewhere. This conflict of styles—between technical and journalistic prose—expresses an unresolved issue basic to literary and philosophical criticism. It is not a matter of separate and unreconcilable vocabularies, for there is a measure of translatability from one style to the other. The conflict turns on claims about whose speech will be more effective in moving us toward a just society. That society is generally described as democratic—the hope being that politics, in a democracy, would not deform but rather consolidate such virtues of civil society as freedom of association and expression. A highly technical mode of writing might send too academic or cultist a signal, as if thinking took place only within the confines of a field called philosophy. Here

Heidegger's antiphilosophical philosophical jargon does not attract Arendt. She seems to have fallen momentarily under the spell of the notion that the style of philosophy may be freed up or converted into a conversation, which is precisely where her argument is tending when she affirms the intersection of critical thinking and politics in a "space that is potentially public." Whatever the *res* (the subject matter) of critical inquiry, its words move toward a *res publica.*

Yet "potentially" in Arendt's sentence is troublesome. It betrays the abstract and always unrealized vision of a "republic of letters"—"that uniform and peaceful empire of letters, extending itself over a diversity of peoples and . . . stronger than the empire of arms," as Rivarol wrote in 1783. With one word she evades the gravamen of Schiller's twenty-seven letters arguing for the existence of a transitional "aesthetic state." The problem that Schiller posed in his *Letters on Aesthetic Education* (1795) remains open: How is a free society to be envisaged as more than a utopian hope or sentimental abstraction? (In *The Art of Being Ruled,* Wyndham Lewis mocks "the *abstract man* of democracy, the great European make-believe.") Can the politics of transition to a final, as yet unknown civic structure be influenced by "aesthetic education"?

Utopian or not, the motivating ideal is a res publica linked to a broad mental space, "open to all sides." Arendt's style anticipates a move that has become overt with "conversationalists" like the pragmatic Richard Rorty, who wants to emancipate his discipline from the heavy breathing of priestly ambition and masterful systems. "The human self which philosophy has been avoiding," he writes, "is the one described in all the vocabularies which are of no use for predicting and controlling people—the vocabularies which are useless for science, and for philosophy when it is conceived as a quasi-science."

Schiller, Arendt, and Rorty may not confess the same politics but they stand squarely in the same tradition. It expresses a central insight joining Kant's *Critique of Judgment* to European Romanticism; and it continues to be, in one way or another, the muse of our endeavors. In the fine arts, Wordsworth wrote, the only infallible sign of genius is "widening the sphere of human sensibility, for the delight, honor and benefit of human nature." Expanding our sensibility through art becomes from that time on an explicit motive. "To train one's imagination to go visiting" is Hannah Arendt's version.

Today, then, we are hardly at the forefront of a movement; we are still trying to make it a reality rather than a frustrating political debate. Herder's exemplary anthology, *Voices of the Nations,* was published more than two centuries ago. It set the pattern for Romantic historicism and its effort to value forgotten or foreign traditions as a contribution to an expansive sense of the human family. "Everywhere," Emerson later complained in "Self-Reliance," "I am hindered of meeting God in my brother, because he has shut his own temple doors and recites fables merely of his brother's God. Every new mind is a new classification." Presumably, what we learn from neglected "voices"—whether in Judeo-Arabic poetry or slave narratives—will stretch our minds and contribute, however modestly, to intercultural understanding. It delivers us from the darkness of parochial and nationalist prejudice.

Why write criticism? We can't help it: we are moved not only by the work of art itself but also by the vision of art's attachment to the cause of liberty and democracy.

Yet even as I acknowledge this ideal, a certain weariness sets in, and the demon of doubt rises up. Have the national prejudices and ethnic rivalries really subsided? Where is this fabled republic of letters? When you see a great play by Shakespeare, Kleist, Strindberg, or Chekhov, does it really free your feelings for others, or does it sadden you with a sense of the limits of human sympathy? If pity helps us to identify with the protagonist, what about the terror that cuts down the tragic hero or ordinary victim, the resentment that poisons the damaged characters portrayed by the modern novel, and comedy's rictus at mad or stunted or fumbling-and-stumbling types. Can we afford to suffer with those whom we see suffer? Modern shipwreck is more extreme than what Miranda conjectures, thanks to Prospero's art, in Shakespeare's *Tempest.* Will anything prepare us for the inhumanity of certain recent events? Are you ready to perjure yourself by claiming that you can take into and upon yourself what happened in the Holocaust? Medusa still turns us to stone.

Why write criticism? We might now give a very different answer. Democracy as a political and social faith has developed its own orthodoxy. Like any faith, it relies on the evidence of things not seen and requires a sobering opposition—from the political Right, if need be, but preferably from within. The new orthodoxy has taken the form of a stubbornly optimistic story, a grand narrative of humanity's self-emancipation. The heady call for liberation and empowerment by the democratic Enlightenment is the perfect message for the advertising age, although liberation and empowerment often take the form of a choice of cars or hair-styles. Now the message, as McLuhan observed, is a massage: a caressing, ubiquitous, seductive propaganda can effectively bypass questions of consent.

In such an atmosphere, criticism has no choice but to function as a disintoxicant. It questions the quality of our thinking about the possibility of consensus. One understands better Marcuse's fear that the combination of liberal democracy and the culture industry may be strong enough to commodify even the work of art or weaken its contestatory dimension. "The alien and alienating oeuvres of intellectual culture," according to Marcuse, "become familiar goods and services."

Marcuse suggests that a crucial difference exists between the reception of art in a society that is pluralistic in theory but repressive in fact (he invents the term "repressive desublimation" to characterize that state of affairs) and art's true reception, which is more like a resistance. "The absorbent power of society," he writes, "depletes the artistic dimension by assimilating its antagonistic contents. In the realm of culture, the new totalitarianism manifests itself precisely in a harmonizing pluralism, where the most contradictory works and truths peacefully coexist in indifference."

After all we have said about the motivating power of the idea of consensus, it may be that actual consensus is never more than a conformity brought about by social pressure, or a false unanimity that is the product of political artifice and manipulation. Kant's Third Critique might be less relevant here than Rousseau's First Discourse and the cold eye it casts on society.

Yet Kant rejects the position that we agree on art only because it is in the interest of sociability to do so. The Third Critique, while interested in polite society as an end product, does not see politeness itself as a force strong enough to achieve that political result. The *consensus omnium,* or universal assent, that enables aesthetic judgment points to a "production though freedom," to a social contract that stands equally beyond conformity and coercion. "A regard to universal communicability is a thing everyone expects and requires from everyone else, just as if it were part of an original compact dictated by humanity itself."

Whether or not Kant has deduced the exact status of the ideal consensus we aspire to as critics, it is clear he wishes to focus on its quality and therefore invokes aesthetic experience. "The intelligible that taste has in view" (and identified by him with beauty as the morally good elsewhere in the *Critique of Judgment*) cannot be produced by a set of rules or precepts. Any attunement between imagination and the conceptual is "exemplary" rather than dogmatic. The conceptualizing of art and the dogmatic formation of rules of art do not simply convert the implicit into the explicit: they violate an important constraint and unbalance the faculties. It is like wrenching a statement out of context and seeing it as propositional and universal. Such didactic interventions tend to be politically motivated and jeopardize the very consensus Kant has in mind. So the difference between construing Schiller's famous "All men shall be brothers" ("Ode to Joy") as a command rather than a wish may seem trivial, yet by not respecting the context, by adopting the phrase as a slogan with imperative moral force, the wish can become a threat.

My example is not chosen lightly. That a joyful expectation would become a tyrannous demand, that "brotherhood" would be the *mot d'ordre* of totalitarian regimes enforcing absolute consent and the semblance of unanimity, is the experience we have passed through since the French Revolution and the heyday of the Enlightenment. Any insistence, therefore, on universal sympathy—including that of the left-liberal consensus—must be carefully examined. Marc Shell has shown how kinship and especially sibling metaphors can rationalize a deadly political machinery of exclusion. His emphasis falls on the sinister side of Christian universalism. I want to limit myself to the era of progressive politics and its attractive doctrine of the sympathetic imagination, one that romanticism put into circulation.

Three issues require attention. The first is: how long and truly can we sympathize with others? John Keats's honesty gives us pause. Just after his oft-quoted statement, "If a Sparrow come before my Window I take part in its existence and pick about the Gravel," he admits to a coldness that is rarely cited. "I beg now my dear Bailey that hereafter should you observe any thing cold in me not to put it to the account of heartlessness but abstraction—for I assure you I sometimes feel not the influence of a Passion or affection during a whole week—and so long this sometimes continues I begin to suspect myself and the genuineness of my feelings at other times—thinking them a few barren Tragedy-tears."

A second issue turns on what happens when we use our humanitarian feelings to understand alien or even criminal modes of behavior, including those opposed to the very capacity for sympathy by which we seek to understand. Hannah Arendt trained her imagination to go visiting—and in *Eichmann in Jerusalem: A Report on the Banality of Evil,* she wrote about her antihero with such understanding that many were offended. The effort to understand or merely to *present* becomes suspect, and the required point of view is one that excludes the consideration of abhorrent beliefs or practices.

The issue of how to present abhorrent subject matter is a special if extreme case that helps us to understand why premodern poetics set representational limits. So Lessing held that Laocoön's agony, in the famous sculpture, had to be softened if a law of beauty were not to be transgressed. But poetry, a temporal art not dependent on single, fixed moments of visual representation, might safely depict such agony. Rules like this are ultimately based, I would suggest, on an economic view of human feelings. They hold not only that there is a limit to our feelings but also that it is dangerous to allow them to be engrossed by certain sights and scenes. During the seventeenth and eighteenth centuries, the conflict in art between Christianity (especially that of the Counter-Reformation) and classicism turned on the question of how much imaginative and emotional life should be devoted to the "passionate" aspects—the blood and tears, the death-agony—of Christian story. The same issue surfaces today as we recall scenes more bloody and cruel by far: those of revolutionary terror and genocide.

This line of thought would have to pursue two related historical matters: the rise of a posttheological hermeneutics that still promulgates Christianity, but now in the form of a secular and sociopolitical doctrine of sympathy, and the counterindicative knowledge that Christianity, while claiming to be a religion of love that opened a restricted covenant, showed in its subsequent history not only traits of intolerance more acute than those of the religion it denounced but also a willingness to suppress difference through forced conversion.

Seen in this light, the modern historicist or multiculturalist conviction that by imaginatively reproducing the significantly other we will come to respect it, or at least augment rather than exhaust our sympathetic powers, may be as questionable as the claim of a previous and more specifically religious doctrine of charity. The difficulty elided by all these doctrines is that the history of sensibility points away from such hopes. This history, like *Candide,* mocks the optimism of liberal thought. Freud's findings do not change the picture; for him, fantasy leads as much to fixation and dissociative behavior as to a growth in fellow feeling. To invoke imaginative literature as evidence that a self-transcendent empathy is possible proves neither that there has been a collective improvement in sensibility nor that, if there has, works of art have had a decisive impact on it. The gap between expectation and reality was never so painful as when a *Kulturvolk* committed the greatest of genocides.

A third and final concern appears at this point: does the demand of progressive politics for human rights, when extended to cultural, ethnic, and sexual difference, express a widening of sympathy? Or is it, again, something utopian and abstract, a fallacious language of hope rather than an enlightened estimate of what is possible? The insistence on rights tests the limits of a politics which seeks to alter not only social structures but the economy of human feelings.

We may wish to decide that a language of hope, however fallacious, is better than no such language, and that a politics based upon it is better than the old xenophobic strictures. But the utopian premise, in that case, should not be allowed to cover up the difficult history we have passed through and are passing through. There are indeed "surprising effects of sympathy," but there are also surprising failures.

The truth before which thinking about aesthetics has stalled is similar to the truth before which, according to Michael Ignatieff, thinking about progressive politics has stalled. "The more evident our common needs as a species become," he writes in *The Needs of Strangers,* "the more brutal becomes the human insistence on the claims of difference." The very forces that could unite us—religion, nationality, gender, culture—also pull us apart. The sympathetic imagination cannot keep up with demand; it burns out or falls prey to illusory promises and redemptive schemes. Language itself shows a sad incompetence. Ignatieff challenges an inherited "language of political allegiance which no longer speaks for the needs we have," and this may affect the entire discourse of civic humanism that intersects, as I have suggested, with a belief in aesthetic education. "It is a waste of breath," Ignatieff concludes, "to press the claims of common human identity on men and women prepared to die in defence of their claims of difference. There will be no end to the dying."

Such a world has made classical political economy (the discipline inspired by Adam Smith) obsolete, because "the order which [it] is now called upon to understand is an order of strangers extending to the ends of the earth." And in such a world it is doubtful that the "need for belonging in all its murderous intensity" can be assuaged or that the liberal and humanitarian basis of the idea of consensus can prevail. The stranger at the gate, whether seen as a number of persons seeking admission to the state or as a demand for the recognition of different and often mutually antagonistic beliefs, will provoke intensely self-protective acts on the part of those who are home free. Once we enter a global market that escapes the ethos of colonialism, a new situation assails our conscience. Ignatieff describes it as "an order in which so innocent an act of consumption here in London as the making of a cup of tea implicates us in the oppression of tea workers in the British plantations in Bangladesh and Sri Lanka."

It seems to me, however, that the perception of such an "order"—the word seems ironic in this context—can only have two results. Either we return to ascetic practices, limiting consumption to avoid a guilt incurred by living off others, or we find a countervision that is equally all-encompassing but free of religious excesses and desperado politics.

Since we are in a global economy, to limit consumption may not help the tea workers in Bangladesh. It may produce a symbolic protest and clear our conscience, but unless we posit the political effectiveness of symbolic acts—taking Gandhi, for example, as a model—nothing will change radically at the global level. We can hardly guarantee that self-denial will effect any political or economic improvement. Indeed, the impulse toward ascetic purification (so powerfully expressed in Rousseau's First Discourse) may increase religious fundamentalism and give rise to a new politics of righteousness. Even if this does not happen, the conscientious, reasoning individual will find countless other occasions for abstinence, until the very basis of human life, its right to exist under predatory or impure circumstances, is put in doubt.

The alternative is a countervision which also cannot escape all religious overtones but which seems, on balance, less suicidal. This countervision is, according to Adorno, a task of philosophy, and he describes it as the "attempt to contemplate all things as they would present themselves from the standpoint of redemption. Such knowledge has no light but what is shed on the world by redemption; all else consumes itself as mere reconstruction, an instance of technical skill. Perspectives must be fashioned that dislocate and defamiliarize the world, reveal it to be, with its rifts and crevices, as needy and transfigured as it will appear one day in the messianic light."

But this returns us to art, as well—something more than technique or even philosophical insight. Where else should we look in order to find the missing language of needs, both at the primal and at this comprehensive and visionary level? Vision itself is a need, not just the sublimation of a need. Whether sympathy is progressive or merely chancy and chastening, every time there is a "state of emergency" in Benjamin's sense, every time the observer cannot normalize injustice, oppression, suffering—when, in short, justification fails—an opening is made for a redemptive act, one whose understanding is within the reach of art.

If I have cited a text in which "redemption" appears as a word that, like an intimate look or gesture, transgresses normative academic prose, it is to make this point about human needs. Adorno's use of the word guards against the degeneration of vision into technique. Art and especially film can lend themselves, in this era of photography and mechanical reproduction, to massive effects, to a penetration of the entire acoustic and visual culture. They can manipulate audiences and create pseudo-consensus. From the First World War through the Holocaust, technology in the service of a fanatic political faith engineered mass mania and mass death; this disastrously negative side of technique, together with its potential for outright falsification, for manufacturing history, placed an even greater burden on art to exercise what Malraux called a "lucid horror of seduction."

To understand Adorno within an English range of allusions the artistry of *King Lear* or *The Tempest* may be invoked. Shakespeare is able to induce a redemptive perspective without losing sight of the "rifts and crevices" in a world that is disastrously human. The "great thing by us forgot" at present, and unlikely to be remembered in the future except as a belated secular magic, is art's countervision. Yet Prospero breaks his staff and renounces his magic at the end of *The Tempest,* perhaps to signal that vision should not turn into technique or that the restoration we have witnessed is only an effect of art. Given the passionate return of fundamentalism today, in religion or the political religions, how effective can even a Shakespeare be? There is some comfort, however, in knowing that his work has survived, and that it is still creating a shared public space—in which, though opinions clash forcefully, consent is courted, as Kant once said, rather than coerced.

Higher Education at the Millennium

I want to describe an important if obvious tension in the university today. The pressure to modify the openness of American society, coming from those who say that an unthinking or unrestricted cultural relativism will damage education and so jeopardize, if not the state directly then the quality of citizenship we bring to it, is countered by those who claim that this openness is either inadequate or a sham, and that racial, cultural, and gender-based exclusions continue to keep a sizable proportion of citizens from their rightful place in the social order.

Despite this conflict, we enjoy, on the level of theory, a relative consensus about the ends of higher education and its contribution of civil society. What Robert Hutchins said about the University of Utopia, in a clear and courageous little book published in the midst of the McCarthy era, is as useful today as then: his remarks on a fearless "philosophical diversity" within a single theory of education

The author was a participant in the 1992 Commonwealth Center seminar "Educational Forces Outside the Academy."

(derived from principles of academic freedom) can still be pertinent, even if the pressure on the universities comes at this time more from within than from state agencies. It is exerted mainly by teachers, or a changing student body that speaks for those excluded from the social covenant and sometimes, in effect, from equality before the law. Hutchins's emphasis on discussion and conversation, and his rejection of advocacy teaching ("indoctrination"), are close to absolute:

> In Utopia a professor is a citizen and as a citizen may engage in any activity, public or private, in which any other citizen may legally engage. The reason why the law sets the limits of a citizen's conduct is that the Utopians are determined that those limits shall not be set by the shifting prejudices of the times. They see no alternative but the law. The real academic crime is indoctrination, which is only slightly worse in Utopia than the crime of refusing to discuss. For these crimes a Utopian professor can be removed after a hearing by the academic body. I am told that the sentence of removal, followed by the ceremony of disgowning, is often visited upon a Utopian professor for trying to indoctrinate his students with the principles upon which the Utopian Constitution is genuinely based in the common opinion and for failing to cooperate with his colleagues in bringing other interpretations of the Constitution and of the common opinion to the student's attention. The Utopian professor is supposed to have convictions, the deeper the better. He is not supposed to pump and pound them into his students, even though his opinions are shared by the overwhelming majority of the population.[1]

There are problems, however, with this visionary blueprint. First, the unrestricted conversation propounded by Hutchins here and in similar books, while it helped to create a body of liberal opinion about the democratic process and its ideal of "communicative action" (Habermas), did not sufficiently move that process or communication itself toward a largely disenfranchised group, which has grown since then because of increased immigration. Ethnic movements, and also the new feminism, have made their claims and gains after, rather than because of, Hutchins.

The second problem is that, as Hutchins indicates, the "civil religion" (a later term) embedded in the constitution of Utopia forbids itself—unlike other religions—to inculcate a conviction it takes for granted. Doubt about itself is tolerated, even methodically practiced; the disbelief of others toward its position is tolerated; all to keep faith in free discussion alive. But cultural relativism (including a dramatic increase in historical knowledge and images communicated directly through modern media) has raised the issue of whether any society can be just, and whether ours, then, is really preferable. Justification moves from the religious to the social sphere. In a society that is increasingly a juvenocracy, moreover, the battle for a democratic faith has to be won already in the universities; it is the universities that are under the greatest pressure to transform an ethos of inquiry into one of advocacy or affirmation. How can America's "public philosophy" (Walter Lippman's term) maintain its hold without indoctrination, or without abandoning that task to nonuniversity agencies whose agenda may be suspect?[2]

The conflict over the canon, or what gets taught in university curricula, should be seen in this context. This call for reinstituting Common Studies, based largely on great books, recognizes that our "attestive gaze" (Yaron Ezrahi)—that is, what we see and credit—is formed by which kinds of experience are thought to be objective, or which testimonies count. Both sides in the controversy (of whether the canon should privilege Western civilization or whether it should favor works that are critical of and even antagonistic to the dominant culture) appreciate the instrumental and determinative force of sociocultural choices.

Both sides are equally uncomfortable, therefore, with such movements as deconstruction, that seek to de-instrumentalize reason or culture. They view this attempt as an evasion of political realities or as a recipe for nihilistic doubt. Even those who argue for an open canon (a contradiction in terms, but expressive of a concern stated early by the Romantics, with Novalis asking, "Who declared the Bible closed?") are instrumentalists. They advocate the inclusion of minority writers as a step toward the inclusion of the minority as a whole.

Yet the argument for great books is not primarily an instrumentalist one: we may read them for self-improvement or urge that they be read for either acculturation or a progressive and even revolutionary end, but there is no certainty that their impact on the individual mind will fall into a niche of that kind. These are books that have provided instruction *and* enjoyment for reasons that are difficult to pin down and that very fact seems to be part of our pleasure in them. Whatever their ethnic provenance or original commitment, they have accrued a fascinating variorum of meanings. These classics, then, are not representative so much as hermeneutic, and their aesthetic or historical distance from how concern states itself today could stimulate a less constrained debate. The most didactic thing that can be said of them is that as survivor-books they express values that do not (or not without significant traces) repress adversative or adversarial elements. A great novel is distinguished by what Bakhtin called heteroglossia, even as it illustrates the limits of sympathy in the fictional characters it depicts.

The restitutive aim, moreover, of instrumentalists who wish to open the canon entails more than a plea for inclusion. To find the classics of their own speech, to search the past for these or oblige the present to create them, is complicated by a perception that the dominant culture seems to be preemptive, inhabited by an alien muse. Vernacular artists must therefore win recognition by defining themselves in someone else's terms, even in the language tradition of an alien culture. This is a psychological bind yet also the condition of an achievement whose pattern was set when the European vernaculars sought classical dignity in the Renaissance and began to enrich the dialect of the tribe.

On the contemporary effort to create, for example, a black speech literature, John Edgar Wideman's "Black Fiction and Black Speech" is relevant.[3] That the restitutive aim is more than a demand for inclusion, that it challenges the dominant culture, is seen in Wideman's claim: "Black speech is not simply faulty English but a witness to a much deeper fault, a crack running below the surface, a fatal flaw in the forms and pretensions of so-called civilized language." No parallel exists for this critique of civilized language in the Renaissance, where the act of composing vernacular classics was in harmony with the aim of recovering the classics themselves as models to be emulated. There was, at most, a critique of the school learning and intolerance that had suppressed—to the point of losing—a tradition that now appeared more "civilized" than heavily Christian and scholastic works of learning. *This* critique has its contemporary parallel in Pierre Bourdieu's major point that cultural transmission is—with the growth and centralization of the school system—acculturated transmission. Bourdieu discloses an unacknowledged limit to Hutchins's claim that the university as a pedagogical institution can foster an unrestricted "conversation."

A third problem with Hutchins's blueprint is the change signaled by the label "modern," a change he treated only under the heading of "industrialization." To be an educated citizen should not mean, he thought, being preoccupied with technological progress, even in an industrialized society. He did not mention, however, what writers long before the 1950s were already struggling with: the media and information explosion, or the valuing of "noise." Previously noise had to be removed to let the signal through; now our technological skills are such that we can let an astonishing and deafening number of signals through. Whatever technology will be developed to offset this technology, the individual citizen, the one whose spark or independent thinking we rely on, may be worse off than before. We are burdened by a *surnomie* that can become an *anomie,* a bewildering or paralyzing surplus of norms, values, demands that prompts many to talk of a postmodern condition and to seek refuge from it in the "one thing necessary" to salvation.

The situation is especially confusing in the schools. Students are told that education is memory training, a progressive historical anamnesis in which they participate. Then they are told they must remember to forget, if they are to remain sane. Then that they must never forget that their just society is based on a history of unjust actions, and that they should establish a juster society by bringing to consciousness what has been left out in the official histories. Then that culture and reason are themselves suspect, having led to, or not prevented, two world wars and the Holocaust. They may also be told to do something about oppression worldwide, to prevent a new genocide, to save the ecology and harness scientific knowledge to a productivity that would benefit everyone instead of concentrating on weapons for a nuclear holocaust.

"O," as Dorothy says plaintively in *The Wizard of Oz,* "I fear we are no longer in Kansas." Nor at the University of Utopia in Chicago in the late 1940s. But how to proceed from there to here is another matter, which I do not wish to avoid entirely.

Today the consensus for multiculturalism in the American university, especially in its literature and cultural studies departments, is so strong that advocacy teaching has become a normal complement to affirmative action. The complaint is heard that a coercive atmosphere prevails, jeopardizing academic freedom and making it unsafe for scholars to be politically incorrect. Horror stories are circulated about the repressive effects of the new orthodoxy in many universities.

If you give someone a bad conscience, he will turn around and stick you with one. The conservatives complain that the liberal consensus leaves them out. They strike back at the self-righteousness of the left-liberal coalition, and it returns the favor by charging that the conservatives, who still dominate national policy through the inertia of existing attitudes and institutions, are hypocrites. The plea of those in power and who feel endangered is always that they are powerless. The conservatives mock the reply of the liberals and argue that it is time for those who really determine opinion in the universities to give up the pretense that they are powerless. The debate is not very edifying or productive, and both sides are guilty of slander—quite enjoyable at times, given our habitual jargon of civility. But one point made against us "fellow teachers" cannot be passed by. I will reformulate it in terms that do not simply assert, in the conservative manner, a dereliction of duty, but which suggest the depth of an issue centering on the question of consensus.

While some conflict between university studies and the world of community standards or civic authority is to be expected, the present situation is particularly troubling. For though academics keep talking to academics, the gap widens in the meantime between those who pursue an ideal of justice within the university and those who actually influence society through the full spectrum of political activities. It is less the right-wing journals that should bother us than the evidence they bring that the work of university intellectuals is once again seen as self-regarding and abstract—out of touch with the very realities these intellectuals would like to change.

Precisely the university may have failed to achieve a consensus based on quality of consent. Political action there takes place in a protective milieu or through street theater: it no longer respects the implicit contract between society and academy which says that, dedicating yourself to a certain political faith, either you work *extra muros,* on a pragmatic and worldly basis, or you engage in the intellectual equivalent of work by creating a university "space," a forum open to all opinions and tolerating debate.

The idea of such a forum is realized in a place like the university campus as well as in the moratorium interposed between adolescence and full civic responsibilities. In matters of this complexity, of course, there are no absolutes, only balances: on the one hand, being a student cannot mean renouncing all protest, even on campus; and on the other, debate in the university is not a free-for-all—the English Hyde Park approach would merely inflame or reconfirm every possible prejudice. The purpose of that forum space, of extensive discussion in the at once competitive and nonadversarial frame of university study, is to make sure the facts, texts, arguments, and rules of evidence are adequately known and that participants learn to live with complexities and ambiguities that never go away, whatever decision must be made. We are asked to experience as fully as possible what Hegel called, with a pathos I like, "the suffering and labor of the negative."

The complaint against the politically correct curriculum comes down to this: the present multicultural consensus is a pseudoconsensus, for the *omnes* in this *consensus omnium* share mainly a certain rhetoric but act in an exclusionary or counterexclusionary way. For it is not enough to assert that the integrationist or assimilationist ethos has broken down. The crucial issue remains precisely the same in both the newer and the older political cultures: *there is a grave discrepancy between theory and practice, between words and actions.*[4] In the new political culture a rhetoric of sympathy for otherness is still accompanied by an intolerance of dissent and the creation rather than elimination of yet another "hegemonic discourse."

What is to be done? We cannot, it is clear, return to the status quo. Yet a fruitless debate over the canon goes on and on because, in an increasingly populist educational structure, pressure groups are always forming, so that we face a constant demand to include this or exclude that, to prescribe or proscribe courses or books. We find ourselves in a "parliamentary" situation in which one required reading list replaces another. The result tends to be confusion rather than diversity. The notion of a core curriculum (sometimes called Common Studies) has such appeal because its sanction comes from a longer-lived consensus and prevents newer and hence even more restricted canons from being imposed.

It is possible, however, that we have exaggerated the static nature of our literary past. Its status may have been more agitated than many would like to believe. It is true that when the Bible, Aristotle, and some classics constituted the beginning and often the end of education and it was dangerous to reject them, opportunities for disagreement were generally restricted to specific matters of interpretation rather than to the specific choice of books. But as long as precise information on the consensus that formed the canon remained scarce, it was possible—though risky—to reenvision the original community of consensus or to claim that one still participated in it by direct inspiration. So the Reformers who rebelled against the Catholic Church created, by martyrdom if necessary, their own community of "saints." Authority breeds visionary counterclaims when based on a compact sealed in the distant past: the situation today continues to inspire historical fables such as the Black Jesus or Black Moses movements.

Yet another recourse, more subtle than myths of origin, of original community, was available against an imposed consensus. This recourse can still help today. Historically, the canon would have become a dead letter if a principle had not entered derived from the canonical imperative of preserving the letter of the text. *This secondary principle was interpretation itself,* which does not seek to change those letters but to reinforce their meaningfulness and so to carry them into the future, to maintain the text against historical change and messianic impatience. Saving the text by reinterpreting it produced astonishing creative and intellectual feats that must be classified as commentary as well as art: think of Dante's *Commedia* or Bernard of Clairvaux's sermons or the Jewish Kabbalah.

Today that secondary principle has become primary[5] and sustains literary work in the university. The desanctification of texts means that the authority of every book hangs in the balance. Interpretation tips the scale and bestows or takes away authority. But the reason canonical books hang on is not only the aesthetic prowess of clever interpreters. Acrobats, clowns, jongleurs entertain, but they don't alter the law they seem to defy. The classic work of art is so hard to discredit because we learn interpretation not from a separate set of rules but primarily from a number of great books set in a commentary tradition which has become their integral rather than adventitious frame. The struggle of commentary upon commentary, Bourdieu writes not without irony, lifts the work "from the state of a dead letter, a mere thing subject to the ordinary laws of ageing, [and thus] the struggle at least ensures it has the sad eternity of academic debate."[6]

Consider Milton's reputation. Leavis tried to dislodge Milton in the 1930s, and some feminists are still dislodging him. Milton survives, not because he is endlessly open to interpretation but because he has become exemplary for interpretation. He teaches the future reader as well as the future poet. *Lycidas* saved the pastoral tradition when a new reality had made an older type of poetic speech seem obsolete. The special case of pastoral became linked to something general: the case of poetry. Not the fate of pastoral alone but the fate of poetry was in the balance: a strange, older speech showed its life through Milton's erudite intervention.

There is a parallel between Milton's effort to maintain poetry and the strain of theory in critics like Cleanth Brooks who opened the canon to modern verse. Learned improvisation, whether by poet or critic, is a crucial technique for saving texts. Yet there are those who make genius into a mystery, a force of nature that subverts the intellectual reclamation I have been describing. Despite the fact that popular art absorbs, or even steals, a lot of traditional material, there is an ideological temptation to link genius to a mysterious and liberating energy; this dangerous move leads me to a further historical and cautionary observation.

I want art to survive as more than an advertisement for a particular product, even the product called democracy. I therefore support art's claim to a certain independence, call it authenticity or autonomy or creative mystery. This claim, nevertheless, makes me anxious, because reinforced by notions of sublimity or the genius-idea, it was appropriated rather easily by fascism. The sublime experience allows the mind to rebound after a moment of ravage or depression and feel potentiated and freer than before; in cultural politics, however, this sense of exaltation and power can be used against the freedom of the individual. The genius-idea, mixing with identity politics, can underwrite, as in fascism, a virulent and delusive theory of national culture.

To understand the bind of politically progressive criticism, it is useful to return to the Romantic period, which linked the sublimity of art—*le sacré du poète*—to the greatness of particular national cultures. Before that time, the notion of sublimity had served as a safety valve for neoclassical decorum. This decorum held that feelings had their own restricted economy and should not be burdened beyond measure. Cultural pluralism would have seemed utterly unrealistic, because human sympathy, though not the imagination, was thought to have clear limits. The rationale behind the decorum was very different from the bravado of Blake's famous proverb of hell: "If the doors of perception were cleansed every thing would appear to man as it is, infinite."

Yet neoclassicism's limitary attitude existed side by side with a vivid sense of the sublime that obliged writers like Edmund Burke to distinguish it from the beautiful, and other *social* virtues. Though embarrassed by the felt power of the sublime, as by the originality and unruliness of genius, they acknowledged its presence. A description had to be found for the impact of this force on human affairs. The pressure of the sublime (or what Goethe named the daemonic) on the sociable, like that of power on freedom, culminated in the poetry of the Romantics. Hölderlin in his difficult odes, Blake in his Prophetic Books, Shelley in "Mont Blanc" and Wordsworth, in the "Visitings of imaginative power" he described, created an art that could not be fully socialized, even when artists like Wordsworth wished its isolating and radicalizing aura to be redeemed that way.

As late Romantics—and progressive critics—we are attempting the impossible: instead of acknowledging a tension between art and social forms, we pretend we can normalize or instrumentalize art's charisma, transgression, wildness, innovation; we bestow an a priori acceptance on these qualities and insist on a focus so broadly empathic, so open on principle, that the sublime becomes an abstract and spasmodic technique, a routinized ecstasy, a mere flicker of itself like the photographically distorted grimacings of MTV's perpetual *danse macabre.*

It can be argued that this sustained death rattle of the sublime, these fantastic gothic formulas that cannibalize so much contemporary art, are a specifically American form of the sublime rather than its terminal contortion. American cultural practice, according to this view, has outstripped that of the Old World, which is still struggling to "waste" the sublime from above—that is, by way of theory. Charles Olson leads the way with his unparalleled description of European high culture as "a great shitting from the sky"; and Camille Paglia, playing Madonna to the academic establishment, celebrates the absence, the energetic bypass in American popular culture, of anxiety-ridden sclerotic distinctions between high and low. Our "rude, vital, brassy" phase, which reached its apogee in the 1960s, does not, according to Paglia, need the faddish academic radicalism of Lacan, Foucault, and Derrida. Deconstruction does something quite unnecessary in America when it "systematically trashes high culture by reducing everything to language and then making language destroy itself."[7]

Yet Paglia's hyperbolic self-identification with a generation that "put the myth of Dionysus into action" simply acts out what she herself described as "our problem": "not repression but regression . . . the constant eruption of primitivism, of anarchic individualism" (33). Seeking by her prose to compete with the beat of rock and rap (somewhat like Henry Miller in his jazzy expectorations of what she underplays as a "defunct modernism" [29]), Paglia falls for a progressive-regressive paradigm without understanding its ghoulishly devouring demand on even the most capable and liberated sensibilities.

My point is not the degeneracy of art and literary theory or their loss of function in the society in which they must exist. It is the continuing necessity of criticism as a disintoxicant as well as a creative player. Even Alvin Kernan's *Death of Literature* and Allan Bloom's *Closing of the American Mind* are useful: a countertradition comes into view whose focus is the limit upon which democratic ideals have bruised themselves. The scholarly equivalent of satirical novels about academia, they remind us of that countertradition. Not our potentially infinite humanity is assumed but . . . human finitude.

I have tried to suggest the complex cultural and political pressures on the university of what is called, variously, historicism, relativism, perspectivism, pluralism, multiculturalism. Yet my effort has something of a contemplative smell to it; it is not a brief supporting a case, or an opinion rationalizing a decision. I would defend that contemplative procedure: by reviewing the past, by reading precedential works, we do not distance ourselves from the urgency of the moment but rather define where we are in relation to issues and positions that recur. I take it that one of the urgent questions for the university in the 1990s and beyond must be: when does the insistence on ethnicity become productive, and when counterproductive?

The question, you may think, is an impossible one, because it would be answered differently, even divisively, depending on whether one belonged to a community still seeking to present its ethnic credentials or to an established group. Yet if a general agreement exists on what is productive, a conversation can take place. I think there is such an agreement and want to state it as follows. The insistence on ethnic factors is intended to further *autonomy* in both the psychological and cultural sense of the word: the fullest development of each person or family within the community, and of the community within a multicultural state. I assume, at the same time, that we are not in a Balkan situation, where ethnic groups are striving for political independence through secession.

Even though this definition of a common aim is not conceptually precise—it does not pause to ask who a person is, what is meant by a community, what autonomy is—if you respond to the definition, something is gained. Instead of the word "autonomy," which I use here in the Kantian sense of an ideal situation, in which individuals feel that the laws of the state or the rules of society are *their* laws and rules, in *their* interest rather than somebody else's—instead of "autonomy," then, you could use words from the Declaration of Independence citing the right of every citizen to life, liberty, and the pursuit of happiness.

Let me start with what is counterproductive. Counterproductive, in my view, is the pressure within each group for ideological conformity or an outright profession of loyalty. This would make the group a cult rather than a culture-bearer. It is important that the group tolerate bystanders who are neutral or still in a reflective stage, that it not force acts of witness from its members. The tendency toward the compulsory profession of loyalty was a factor that eventually drove Nazi Germany into a warlike mentality; in wartime, loyalty must be close to unconditional. Coming to power, the National Socialists introduced a *Bekenntnis* mystique that politicized scholarship and discouraged free inquiry. *Bekenntnis* (confession of loyalty) determined *Erkenntnis* (cognition and knowledge acquired through scholarship). Relativity theory was despised because a Jew, Einstein, had formulated it. Everything Jewish was denounced as abstract rather than vital, an injurious to the day-to-day concerns of the New German ethnic community, the *Volksgemeinschaft.*

Counterproductive also is a confusion between ethnic and racial. Nazi Germany is again the extreme and cautionary, though far from exclusive, instance. (I have no wish to identify the present with the past.) The Germans knew perfectly well that they were genetically and culturally a mixed bag. But instead of simply urging a restitutive inward turn, or an anticosmopolitan stance (suasions dangerous enough), Nazi philosophy, through no less than two ministries, promulgated a deliberate fiction. It claimed that there was an Aryan character type, and that the Aryan was exclusively the creative force among all ethnic strains.[8]

Mere assertion, however, can only do so much, even when the future rather than the past is appealed to. Aryan purity was presented as a project, a political fiction that had reconstructive power, not only for Germany but for the world. "Today Germany, tomorrow the world." This appeal to the future erased a mixed and humiliating past or explained it away by race pollution and the conspiracy of nations lower in the racial scale against the dominance of Germany. This so-called *Weltanschauung* had nevertheless to find philosophical backing. It did so by resorting to the idea of genius: genius, the argument held, could not be reduced to rule, because it acted in harmony with an unknown law of nature. It was not imitative but foundational and nomothetic. (This was an important Romantic idea, supporting art's inarticulate reason, its *différend* as Lyotard names it.) Transferred to the corporate and mystical base of the *Volksgemeinschaft,* genius was then identified exclusively with the Aryan character type, becoming thus not only ethnocentric but also racist. The boast that the Germans were a *Kulturvolk* of *Denker und Dichter* (thinkers and creators), which contributed to one of the greatest massacres of modern times, found its support in this nationalization of creativity.

Turning more directly to what is productive, it would seem that just as general culture must be acquired or reacquired through university study, so must the particular culture of ethnic groups. We are not in a traditional society where ethnicity is everywhere handed down through the family and its close link to social practices. The university is essential as a place of learning to recover a heritage that was interrupted or marginalized, as well as to study the history and literature of other cultures, and ethnology generally.

Here we encounter, at the same time, campus activism. How productive of autonomy is it to spend time at college this way? Many students and teachers feel that the extension of ethnic consciousness to every sphere of life, to every aspect of the university, is called for. With my question I do not look for a yes or no but want to stimulate an analysis of the university as a social structure somewhat offside to society, or to the achievement of specific social reforms. The situation is complicated by the fact that the university is itself not of one type. European universities are different from each other as well as from the American academy; in the United States, moreover, we have a variety of institutes of higher education: community, city, state, and private colleges.

In all of these, however, a contradiction is present which may be anthropologically founded rather than peculiarly American. University study is liminal in Van Gennep's sense: according to this great ethnographer, the candidate who is tested by initiatory "rites of passage" must be provisionally separated from his social group before being accepted in (aggregated) once more. So the academy, I suggest, inserts a second latency period at the very juncture when adolescent and social identity pressures reach a flash point. It is a latency period vis-à-vis social obligations yet an arousal period vis-à-vis the intellectual development of the candidate. This approach sends a mixed signal. Anthropologically it is a time for separating from family and group, a time to go into the wilderness or through a deliberately induced danger period. But the academy converts this time into a "moratorium," to allow a protected and structured stage of development away from home. The contradiction that besets university life as an institutionalized rite of passage lies in that rituals of initiation in traditional societies expose the young person to powerful demons in the absence of social mediations, whereas in a university setting the danger of direct exposure is modified by a protective system. This protection guarantees (and often helps to pay for) an "academic freedom" in which unorthodox as well as traditional knowledge can be pursued. There is bound to be confusion, then, when the threshold separating society and university is crossed by campus reformers who protest against the society affording them protection and tolerating their liminal status. It is unclear, in short, whether universities, as presently organized, are in fact the ideal places to learn about either (intellectual) freedom or (social) obligation.[9]

Yet they remain for the time being the best chance we have for promoting independence of mind while training the young for specific social roles. The change since the late 1960s is that it has become harder to separate university study as a learning opportunity, in which particular ethnic cultures become an important field, from a protest movement affirming descent cultures within an institution seen as predominantly hostile—as a stepmother rather than an *alma mater.* And when learning fails to separate itself from activism, the result is omnipolitics. Everything is then subjected to a political test, including the curriculum.

As long as the general culture is not neglected or falsified, these intensities are for the good. They enact collectively a hermeneutics of suspicion directed toward the general culture, its covert assumptions or universalized standards, its smugness or ingrained xenophobia. But if the culture is perceived only as hostile, the motive for learning about it is pretty well destroyed. Activism will then increase that learning disincentive and substitute a negative conviction for scholarship. A situation is created in which there is no call for a temporary suspension of judgment or for comparative study that would restrain such dispiriting labels as "repressive," "racist," "patriarchal," "colonialist," and so on. The activism coming from the right wing is equally unhelpful: blindly affirmative of the status quo, it also encourages labeling rather than thoughtful criticism. It confuses the questioning of common beliefs with subversion, forgetting Emerson's "We suspect our instruments. We have learned that we do not see directly, but mediately" (*Experience*). One could also quote these eloquent words from Karl Mannheim's *Ideology and Utopia:* "To see more clearly the confusion into which our social and intellectual life has fallen represents an enrichment rather than a loss. That reason can penetrate more profoundly into its own structure is not a sign of intellectual bankruptcy. Nor is it to be regarded as intellectual incompetence on our part when an extraordinary broadening of perspective necessitates a thoroughgoing revision of our fundamental conceptions."

Most of the time it is not the general culture that is being criticized, for what students know of it is too sparse or disheartening: they see injustice around them, and they react accordingly. The general culture in its complexity and historical variety may even escape being explored for a usable past. Wishing to hold reality and justice in one thought, and having limited time, in the university, to do so, we are in danger of turning both reality and justice into very partial concepts.

NOTES

1. Robert Hutchins, *The University of Utopia* (Chicago, 1953), p. 95–96.
2. So the Christian Broadcasting Network and the National Legal Foundation (Pat Robertson is founder and director of both) distribute copies of the Constitution "to effect a common legal philosophy designed to reclaim the rule of law in the U.S."
3. John Edgar Wideman, "Black Fiction and Black Speech," in *Writers Speak: America and the Ethnic Experience,* ed. Jules Chametzky (Amherst, Mass., 1984), pp. 24–39.
4. The issue of "performativity," in regard especially to academic theory or discourse, has been raised cogently by Eve Kosofsky Sedgwick in such articles as "Socratic Raptures, Socratic Ruptures: Notes Toward Queer Performativity," in *English Inside and Out: The Places of Literary Criticism,* ed. Susan Gubar and Jonathan Kamholtz (New York, 1939), pp. 122–36. My argument concerning the character of university "space" is very different from hers: she argues that there is a utopian element in the deconstruction of that space, in challenging students to break it down or to become aware of how it encourages mere (nonperformative) discourse, whereas I suggest that utopia has already entered into the construction and maintenance of that space, which must perforce remain precarious, at

risk vis-à-vis conformist social pressures but also internal tensions, exemplified by Sedgwick's own position and agenda.

5. In some influential cases, however, both principles are active. When Harold Bloom recreates the Biblical documentary source called J in his *Book of J* (New York, 1990), he speculates on its historical origin in addition to reinterpreting it in the light of certain modern writers like Kafka.
6. Pierre Bourdieu, *The Field of Cultural Production: Essays on Art and Literature* (Cambridge, 1993), p. 111.
7. Camille Paglia, "Ninnies, Pedants, Tyrants and Other Academics," *New York Times Book Review,* 5 May 1991, p. 29; hereafter cited in text.
8. Hitler's declarations in *Mein Kampf,* though based on nothing but declarative whim, became dogma. "What we today see before us of human culture, events in art, scholarship, or technology, is almost exclusively the creative project of the Aryan." Göring, in justifying the Nuremberg racial laws, adds a religious twist. "God created the races. He did not intend equality. . . . There is no such thing as equality. We . . . must fundamentally reject it in our laws and pledge [*bekennen*] ourselves to the purity of the race as established by Providence and nature." See *Das Dritte Reich und seine Denker: Dokumente,* ed. Leon Paliakov and Josef Wulf (Berlin-Grünewald, 1959), pp. 5, 7.
9. The young in the inner city have less home protection, but the relative security of university life is therefore all the more crucial for them. In their case, too, the protective structure is exposed to stress. A sense of having achieved maturity against terrible odds can make it more difficult to accept without challenge a protected status based on a second or extended latency. Those whose childhood has been curtailed by social circumstances may not only require more catch-up time; they may also fight this need in order to maintain self-reliance and a degree of separation from the general culture.